Diasporic Homecomings

Diasporic Homecomings

Ethnic Return Migration in Comparative Perspective

Edited by Takeyuki Tsuda

Stanford University Press
Stanford, California

Stanford University Press
Stanford, California

Library of Congress Cataloging-in-Publication Data
Diasporic homecomings : ethnic return migration in comparative perspective / edited by Takeyuki Tsuda.
     p. cm.
  Includes bibliographical references and index.
  ISBN 978-0-8047-6274-8 (cloth : alk. paper) — ISBN 978-0-8047-6276-2 (pbk. : alk. paper)
  1. Return migration—Cross-cultural studies. 2. Emigration and immigration—Cross-cultural studies. I. Tsuda, Takeyuki.
  JV6217.5.D53 2009
  304.8—dc22
                              2009010150

Typeset by Bruce Lundquist in 10/14 Minion

Contents

Introduction

Diasporic Return and Migration Studies

Takeyuki Tsuda

Ethnic Return Migration: A Global Phenomenon

Immigration scholars have recently become increasingly interested in dias-poras—ethnic groups that have been territorially dispersed across different na-tions because of ethnopolitical persecution or for economic reasons and are united by a sense of attachment to and longing for their country of ethnic ori-gin (the ethnic homeland) (e.g., see Cohen 1997; Safran 1991; Tölölyan 1996; Van Hear 1998). A number of scholars have examined how diasporas have con-tinued to evolve through further migratory scattering, but relatively few have studied how certain diasporic peoples have also been returning to their ethnic homelands (Stefansson 2004: 6). In general, there are two types of diasporic return. The first is the return migration of first-generation diasporic peoples who move back to their homeland (country of birth) (see Gmelch 1980; Long and Oxfeld 2004; Markowitz and Stefansson 2004). The second is *ethnic* return migration, which refers to later-generation descendants of diasporic peoples who "return" to their countries of ancestral origin after living outside their eth-nic homelands for generations.[1]

The contributors to this book provide a comparative ethnographic overview of most of the world's major ethnic return migrant groups. In recent decades, the total volume of ethnic return migration has increased significantly. The most prominent example is the millions of Jews in the Diaspora who have migrated to Israel since World War II. The largest group of Jewish ethnic return migrants has been from the former Soviet Union; more than 770,000 Russian Jews entered Israel between 1990 and 1999. In Western Europe, 4 million ethnic German

Table I.1 Origin states, diasporas, and ethnic return migration

Diasporic origin states	Geographic location of diasporic peoples	Ethnic return migrants
Israel	Middle East, Eastern Europe (mainly Russia), Western Europe, North America, South America (fewer)	Most from Eastern Europe, but also from other parts of the world
Germany	Eastern Europe, North America, South America	Eastern European ethnic German descendants (*Aussiedler*); a few from South America
Spain and Italy	Mainly North and South America	Predominantly Argentines of Spanish and Italian ancestry
Ireland, Sweden	United States, Western Europe	Small numbers of Irish Americans and Finland Swedes
Greece	United States, Western and Eastern Europe, Asia Minor	Ethnic Greeks from former Soviet Union, Albania, and Asia Minor; small numbers of Greek Americans
Hungary	Neighboring Eastern European countries, United States, Western Europe	Mainly ethnic Hungarian descendants from Romania
Poland, Slovakia, Slovenia, Romania, Ukraine, Latvia	Neighboring states in Eastern Europe, United States, Western Europe	Co-ethnic descendants from neighboring Eastern European countries
Russia	Surrounding countries in Eastern Europe, Central Asia, and the Caucasus; North America, Western Europe	Ethnic Russian descendants from Soviet successor states in Eastern Europe, Central Asia, and the Caucasus
Japan	Mainly North and South America	Predominantly Japanese Brazilians and Peruvians (*nikkeijin*); a few Japanese Americans
South Korea	North America, East and Central Asia, Russia, Middle East, South America (relatively few)	Mainly Korean Chinese (*chosŏnjok*); some ethnic Korean descendants from Russia, Central Asia, and the Middle East; a few Korean Americans and Korean Japanese
China	East and Southeast Asia, North America, Western Europe, Latin America (relatively few)	Mainly highly skilled ethnic Chinese descendants from Southeast Asia; a few Chinese Americans
Taiwan	China, North America	Highly skilled overseas/diasporic Chinese
Philippines, Malaysia, Vietnam, Cambodia, Laos	East and Southeast Asia, North America, Western Europe (relatively few)	Smaller numbers of highly skilled diasporic descendants from various countries

descendants from Eastern Europe return-migrated to their ethnic homeland between 1950 and 1999.[2] Other European countries, such as Spain, Italy, Greece, Poland, and Hungary, have received much smaller populations of ethnic return migrants from Latin American and Eastern Europe. After the collapse of the Soviet Union, 2.8 million ethnic Russians living outside Russia in Eastern Europe, Central Asia, and the Caucasus returned to their ethnic homeland between 1990 and 1998.[3] In East Asia, close to 1 million second- and third-generation Japanese and Korean descendants scattered across Latin America, Eastern Europe, and China have return-migrated to Japan and Korea since the late 1980s. China and Taiwan have also been receiving ethnic Chinese descendants from various Southeast Asian countries. There has even been limited ethnic return migration to various Southeast Asian countries. Table I.1 shows the various countries that have produced diasporas, the geographic location of these diasporic peoples, and the groups that have returned to their ethnic homelands.

Most ethnic return migration has been primarily a response to economic pressures (i.e., diasporic descendants moving from developing countries to richer ethnic homelands in the developed world). Other important factors that influence the migration are ethnic ties to ancestral homelands, a nostalgic desire to rediscover ethnic roots, and the efforts of homeland governments to actively encourage their diasporic descendants living abroad to return "home" through preferential immigration and nationality policies. The total volume of ethnic return migration is not only substantial but also generally permanent in nature. Diasporic returnees in the Middle East and Europe often migrate in order to settle permanently in their countries of ethnic origin. Although some ethnic return migrants (especially in East Asia) are sojourners who intend to remain only a few years in their ancestral homelands (as labor migrants and target earners), a number of them are prolonging their stays and settling, often with family members.

After analyzing the causes of diasporic return in Part 1, the contributors to this book focus on the ethnic and sociocultural experiences of ethnic return migrants in their ancestral homelands (Parts 2 and 3). Although many return migrants feel a nostalgic ethnic affiliation to their countries of ancestral origin, because they have been living outside their ethnic homeland for generations, they are essentially returning to a foreign country from which their ancestors came. As a result, diasporic homecomings are often ambivalent, if not negative experiences for many ethnic return migrants. Despite initial expectations that their presumed ethnic affinity with the host society (as "co-ethnics") would facilitate their social integration, they are often ethnically excluded as foreigners in their ancestral homelands because of the alien cultural differences they have acquired while living abroad for generations (cf. Capo Zmegac 2005: 199). They are also often socioeconomically marginalized as unskilled immigrant workers and perform low-status jobs that are shunned by the host populace.

Why do the ethnic ties between diasporic return migrants and the homeland population not improve the migrants' ethnic reception or socioeconomic position in their country of ancestral origin? When migrants and hosts are ethnically related through common descent, does it produce unrealistic cultural and social expectations that are bound to be disappointed? To what extent are the negative diasporic homecomings of ethnic return migrants a product of their cultural differences and/or their low social class position as immigrant workers? How does their unexpected ethnic and socioeconomic marginalization in their ethnic homelands force them to reconsider their ethnonational identities and loyalties as well as their previous notions of home and homeland? How do we account for variations in their ethnic experiences and their levels of social integration as immigrants?

This book's comparative approach will help answer some of these fundamental questions because it examines a wide variety of ethnic return migrant groups in different countries. Some groups have been living outside their ethnic homelands for many generations (such as Jews and ethnic Germans), whereas others, such as Japanese Brazilians and Korean Chinese and Korean Americans, are only a couple of generations old. Some have retained their cultural heritage to a considerable extent, such as ethnic Hungarians in Romania and Finland Swedes in Finland, whereas others, such as Russian Jews and ethnic Germans, are quite assimilated and have lost much of their ancestral culture, despite retaining distinct ethnic identities. Although most diasporic returnees are labor migrants from poorer countries, the contributors to this book also consider the ethnic return migration of professionals and students from developed countries, because their different global positioning and higher socioeconomic status in their ethnic homelands seem to produce more positive ethnic outcomes.

The comparative framework of this book therefore allows the contributors to analyze how the differing sociocultural characteristics and national origins of ethnic return migrants influence their levels of social integration or marginalization in their ethnic homelands and subsequent transformations in their ethnonational identities. The contributors also assess how differing migration patterns, homeland immigration and nationality policies, and host society receptions affect the ethnic return migration experience.

An international and interdisciplinary group of the best scholars studying various ethnic return migrant groups from around the world was assembled for this edited volume. A highly successful two-day conference was held at the Center for Comparative Immigration Studies at the University of California at San Diego to present and discuss the submitted papers, which led to fruitful discussion, commentary, and exchange of ideas and feedback. I subsequently selected the best papers from the conference and provided extensive comments for revision to all authors. Because of the considerable amount of intellectual exchange between the chapter contributors and me (as well as among the contributors themselves), I hope that this edited volume has much greater conceptual unity than most others.

With the exception of the two chapters in Part 1 that analyze ethnic return migration policy, all contributors have conducted in-depth fieldwork among ethnic return migrants (interviews and participant observation), often in both the migrant-sending and migrant-receiving countries. Therefore, in contrast to previously published work on the topic, which has mainly relied on survey questionnaires, media reports, and statistical, governmental, and archival sources (e.g., see Münz and Ohliger 2003; Pilkington 1998; Rock and Wolff 2002), the contributors to this book examine ethnic return migrants in much greater depth through ethnographic accounts and analyses of their actual ethnic experiences. Such detailed ethnographic field data are supported by the use of these other sources in order to document broader trends and provide policy and historical context.

Contributions to Migration Studies

Ethnic return migration shares some similarities with the return migration of first-generation emigrants to their country of birth, because both groups are returning to their homeland (a place of origin to which an individual feels personally and emotionally attached). However, return migrants are going back to their *natal* homeland (i.e., place of birth), whereas ethnic return migrants are later-generation diasporic descendants returning to their *ethnic* (or *ancestral*) homeland, where their ethnic group originated. As Markowitz and Stefansson's (2004) edited volume on return migration demonstrates, the homecomings of even first-generation return migrants are fraught with problems, and these migrants are rarely reintegrated smoothly into their natal homelands (see also Long and Oxfeld 2004). Such difficulties are compounded for ethnic return migrants, because they were born and raised abroad and are essentially strangers in an ethnic homeland that has become a foreign country for them. In fact, their relatively poor social integration in the host society resembles that of other labor migrants because they have become immigrant minorities in their countries of ancestral origin.

Despite the relatively large number of ethnic return migrants around the world, the topic has not received much attention in migration studies. Usually referred to in the literature as ethnic affinity migration, most research has dealt with Jewish and ethnic German diasporic return (e.g., see Münz and Ohliger 2003; Remennick 2007; Rock and Wolff 2002). Although a few books have been published recently on other groups of ethnic return migrants (Louie 2004; Pilkington 1998; Roth 2002; Tsuda 2003), no general comparative analyses of this phenomenon as a distinctive type of migration have been conducted.[4] The study of ethnic return migration can therefore make a number of important contributions to the field of migration studies.

Ethnicity and Migration

Because ethnicity plays a greater role in structuring migration patterns and experiences in ethnic return migration, it provides immigration researchers with the opportunity to further explore the relationship between ethnicity and migration. Ethnicity is based on a collective consciousness of both shared racial descent and commonalities in cultural heritage that differentiate a particular social group from others. In other words, ethnicity has both a racial and a cultural component. Although some researchers consider racial identity separately from ethnic (cultural) identity (e.g., see Smith 1986), I view a consciousness of common descent and racial origins to be a part of ethnic identity (even if not all ethnic minority groups are seen as racially or phenotypically distinct from the dominant majority). This is consistent with Weber's classic definition of ethnicity as a subjective belief in common descent shared by a social group because of similarities in both cultural customs and physical appearance (Weber 1961). So what exactly is ethnic about ethnic return migration, and how is it different in this respect from other types of migration? This is a fundamental question that the contributors to this book attempt to address.

Despite its name, most ethnic return migration is not driven by the search for ethnic roots and ancestral heritage but by global economic disparities, which have caused diasporic descendants from poorer countries to return to their richer ethnic homelands. Although ethnicity by itself does not cause or initiate ethnic return migration, it channels and directs the migratory flow to specific countries (see Chapter 1). In response to economic pressures, many diasporic descendants decide to return-migrate because of their presumed ethnic ties to their ancestral homelands and because homeland governments have generally welcomed them back through preferential immigration and nationality policies as "ethnic brethren" (see Chapters 1, 2, and 3).

Despite its mainly economic motivations, diasporic return also has serious ethnic consequences, especially in terms of the relative salience of race and culture. The transnational ethnic affiliation of diasporic descendants with their ethnic homelands is based primarily on shared *racial* descent and ancestry. However, when they return-migrate, many of them become marginalized in their ancestral homelands as ethnic minorities because of their alien *culture*, a product of their foreign upbringing. As a result, the definition of ethnicity shifts from race to culture during the migratory process, as initial ethnic inclusion on the basis of race leads to ethnic exclusion on the basis of culture. In this manner, ethnicity is highly situational in practice, and perceptions of racial and cultural commonality and difference are constantly subject to redefinition depending on particular social contexts.

Therefore, although ethnicity is not the primary motive of ethnic return migrants, nor does it improve their immigrant reception in the ancestral homeland, it remains important in structuring diasporic return migration patterns, homeland governments' immigration and nationality policies, host society perceptions, and the ethnonational identity outcomes of the migrants themselves, as shown by the various contributors to this book. In fact, the presumed ethnic affinity between migrants and their hosts may actually magnify the ethnic impact of immigration because interaction with a similar ethnic group can have a more profound effect on ethnic consciousness than contact with a completely foreign group whose characteristics have no ethnic relevance. Because both migrants and hosts anticipate that the diasporic return of co-ethnics will be less problematic than other types of immigration, the mutual ethnic and social alienation that results is all the more disorienting, forcing both migrants and hosts to fundamentally reconsider their ethnic identities. This is the "problem with similarity" that Cook-Martín and Viladrich refer to in this volume (Chapter 5).

Immigration, Transnationalism, and Ethnic Return

In addition to its ethnic aspects, the return of diasporic descendants to their ethnic homelands is different from the migratory patterns that have dominated immigration studies.[5] Because they are returning to the country from which their ancestors came, the reverse directionality of the migrant flow introduces interesting new dynamics to previous studies of immigration.

Traditionally, immigration scholars have tended to analyze population flows as unidirectional: Migrants leave the sending society, immigrate and settle in the host society, and eventually assimilate. This perspective is also unipolar because it focuses almost exclusively on the host society by examining its reception of different immigrant groups, their social integration and socioeconomic success, and their eventual assimilation (or segmented assimilation) into the dominant host society (e.g., see Alba and Nee 1997; Gordon 1964; Portes and Rumbaut 1996; Reitz 2003). The impact of emigration on sending communities is usually neglected.

In recent decades a number of anthropologists and sociologists have argued that migration is not merely a unipolar one-way process of immigration, settlement, and assimilation confined to the receiving nation-state. Instead, they have emphasized the transnational aspects of migratory flows by focusing on their circular and ongoing nature as part of the constant global movement of peoples, commodities, and information across national borders. Instead of simply assimilating and being absorbed into singular national communities, migrants (and their descendants) retain economic, social, and political ties to their homelands, live in transnational communities that simultaneously span two or more nation-states, and develop multiple and diffuse transnational identifications that challenge nationalist loyalties and agendas (e.g., see Basch et al. 1994; Glick Schiller 1997; Pessar and Waters 2002; Portes et al. 1999; Rouse 1991; Smith and Guarnizo 1998). The analysis is bipolar, encompassing both the migrant-receiving and the migrant-sending societies, and technically requires multisite fieldwork.

Ethnic return migration points to a third migratory pattern. Not only can migrants become permanent settlers in the host society or circular transmigrants, but they (and their descendants) can also return to the homeland and stay. Although this pattern is relevant to issues raised by the previous two migration paradigms, the study of diasporic return also provides a new perspective to them. Most ethnic return migrants are marginalized as minorities in their ethnic homelands, but this has not discouraged them from settling long term in their countries of ancestral origin, where economic opportunities and living standards are better. Thus issues related to immigrant settlement and social integration and assimilation have become important not only for immigrant-receiving countries but also for the original migrant-sending country, which has now come full circle and become the host society, as the descendants of emigrants who left generations ago have now returned. Although the immigration-assimilation paradigm assumes that the social integration of co-ethnic descendants will be relatively smooth, it is often just as difficult and complicated as the social incorporation of immigrants who are complete foreigners. Because of initial presumptions of ethnic similarity, the sociocultural differences that emerge between migrants and their hosts in their ethnic encounter are unexpected and unsettling. Again, this is the "problem with similarity."

The study of diasporic return also contributes to the transnational perspective by emphasizing that migration is not a unidirectional phenomenon that eventually comes to an end but rather an unpredictable, ongoing process not only among first-generation migrants but also for their second- (and later-) generation descendants, who can uproot themselves and become trans-migrants all over again, long after immigrant settlement and assimilation have taken place. Ethnic return migrants also live in transnational communities that link both immigrant-receiving and migrant-sending countries,[6] but unlike ordinary migrants, their cross-border ties are constructed between two homelands (the ethnic and natal homelands). Although they may therefore be seen as prime candidates for developing transnational identities based on an affiliation to multiple nation-states (homelands), diasporic return often weakens previous attachments to ethnic homelands and can strengthen parochial nationalist sentiments (see Chapters 6, 7, 9, 11, and 12).

Diasporic Studies

The concept of diaspora has been increasingly invoked to capture the qualities of migratory dispersal and dislocation and the transborder nature of migrant communities and identities. The diasporic perspective is technically multipolar (i.e., involving several nation-states), because it includes the ethnic homeland and the scattered communities of diasporic descendants in various countries.

Because of the diversity of diasporas from which ethnic return migrants originate, the contributors to this book have adopted a broad definition of diaspora that encompasses not only the migratory dispersal of ethnic groups to various countries because of ethnopolitical persecution (victim diasporas), but also dispersals resulting from economic opportunity (economic diasporas) and past colonization and imperial expansion (colonial diasporas).[7] Ironically, among all the diasporas considered in this book, only Jews, who scattered across the globe for centuries mainly in response to ethnopolitical persecution, fit the classic definition of a victim diaspora. Other ethnic return migrants are from primarily economic diasporas (such as the Korean and Japanese diasporas). Some are also from previous colonial diasporas, such as the ethnic Germans who settled in Eastern Europe as a result of conquest and colonization since the 1000s and the ethnic Russians who migrated to surrounding countries during earlier Russian imperialist expansion and more recent Soviet expansion during the cold war. Other ethnic return migrants are from what can be called nonmigratory diasporas, which are not the product of migratory dispersal at all but of changing territorial borders. This is especially the case in Eastern Europe, where national borders were contested and shifted for centuries. When nation-states lost territory as a result of political conflicts and treaties, their peoples formerly living on their territorial fringes became a part of the "diaspora" of co-ethnics in neighboring countries (without emigration). Parts of the Hungarian, Russian, Polish, and German diasporas are examples of such nonmigratory diasporas.

In addition to this diversity in diasporic types, the age of diasporas that have produced ethnic return migration is equally varied. Few are as ancient as that of the Jews, but some are hundreds of years old, such as parts of the German and Russian diasporas. Others are of much more recent origin and are less than a few generations old, such as the Korean and Japanese diasporas. Still others are somewhere in between, such as the Spanish, Italian, Greek, and some Eastern European diasporas.

As noted at the beginning of this introduction, most studies of diasporas tend to focus on the continual dispersal of peoples from the ethnic homeland to various countries around the world. Although diasporic peoples often retain strong ties to their countries of origin, certain definitions of diaspora are based on notions of exile: a fundamental separation between diasporic peoples and their homeland, which remains a distant place of nostalgic longing to which they cannot return (Safran 1991: 91; Tölölyan 1996: 14–15; see Clifford 1994: 304). This is especially the case for victim diasporas, where the cause of territorial dispersion is ethnopolitical persecution, making a return to the homeland difficult, if not sometimes impossible. Diasporic return also seems increasingly unlikely among later-generation diasporic descendants (see Sheffer 2003: 23). In contrast to many first-generation diasporic migrants, who remain marginalized and excluded in their host countries (Levy and Weingrod 2005: 17; Tölölyan 1996: 14), their descendants have been born and raised outside the ethnic homeland and have become socioculturally integrated into the majority society to a considerable extent. In fact, some scholars simply refer to them as ethnic groups (or ethnic minorities) and differentiate them from diasporic groups because they have become detached from their ancestral homelands (McKeown 2001: 94–97; Tölölyan 1996: 16–19).

The study of ethnic return migration serves as a corrective to this conceptualization by emphasizing not only that diasporic peoples *do* return to the homeland but also that such returns are not just limited to first-generation emigrants and exiles (see also Markowitz and Stefansson 2004). Expanding globalization not only has allowed diasporic descendants (ethnic minority groups) to reconnect with their ancestral homelands from afar but also has increased the volume of ethnic return migration, a form of diasporic "in-gathering" or the "unmaking of diasporas" (Münz and Ohliger 2003; Van Hear 1998: 6, 47–48; cf. Clifford 1994: 304). In fact, certain diasporas are now characterized by a tension between centrifugal and centripetal migratory forces. For instance, the German, Japanese, and Korean (as well as some Eastern European–based) diasporas simultaneously consist of people leaving the homeland permanently for foreign countries *and* diasporic descendants returning from abroad to settle in the ethnic homeland.

Some scholars have described diasporic returns as ethnic unmixing because an ethnic group that initially scattered to different countries to become ethnic minorities is being regrouped and reconsolidated in the ethnic homeland (see Brubaker 1998). Although most diasporic descendants are culturally assimilated in their countries of birth to a considerable extent, they continue to be seen as ethnic minorities because of their foreign ethnic origins (cf. Clifford 1994: 310–311; Safran 1991: 92–93).[8] However, when they return to their ethnic homeland, they are rarely reincorporated into the majority ethnic and ancestral populace but again find themselves becoming ethnic minorities because of their cultural differences.[9] Therefore, instead of unmixing ethnic groups, diasporic return migration is creating new ethnic minorities based on the cultural differences that have emerged among peoples previously united by shared descent but who have been living apart for generations. Ethnic return migration, therefore, does not imply a decline in either the number or the diversity of ethnic minorities around the world.

Overview of the Chapters

Part 1 of this book examines the economic, ethnic, and political causes of ethnic return migration. In Chapter 1, I discuss the causes of diasporic return by assessing the relative importance of economic push-pull forces, homeland governments' ethnic return migration and jus sanguinis nationality policies, and the nostalgic transnational affinity that many ethnic return migrants feel for their ancestral homelands.

Chapters 2 and 3 provide a comparative analysis of the preferential immigration and nationality policies of homeland governments that have enabled their ethnic descendants to return from abroad. In Chapter 2, John Skrentny, Stephanie Chan, Jon E. Fox, and Denis Kim argue that, whereas ethnic return migration policies remain strong in Asia, they have weakened in Western Europe. In Asia such policies are used for instrumental economic purposes, but in Europe they are justified on the basis of ethnic affinity or the protection of historically persecuted co-ethnics abroad, even if they are sometimes economically quite costly.

Chapter 3, by Christian Joppke and Zeev Rosenhek, is a case study comparing ethnic return migration policies in Israel and Germany. Israeli policy, which enables the return migration of all Jews in the Diaspora, has remained resilient in the face of emerging domestic political opposition because the return migration has been critical to the development of the nation-state. In contrast, German ethnic return migration policy was restricted to ethnic Germans in Eastern Europe vulnerable to persecution after World War II and has now lost much of its original historical rationale. It has been peripheral to the country's nation-state building and is now in decline. In this manner, the current geopolitical position of these two countries and the historical rationales for their ethnic return migration policies account for their divergent outcomes.

Part 2 of this book focuses on ethnic return migration in Europe. In Chapter 4 Amanda Klekowski von Koppenfels examines the changing status of *Aussiedler* (ethnic German descent returnees from Eastern Europe) in Germany. Although *Aussiedler* were once openly welcomed as ethnic brethren, the German government now restricts their immigration because the decline of ethnic German persecution in Eastern Europe has undermined the raison d'être of their return migration and they have experienced serious social integration problems as unwelcome outsiders in Germany. This has caused *Aussiedler* to be seen as and treated like ordinary immigrants instead of returning German ethnics.

Chapter 5, by David Cook-Martín and Anahí Viladrich, deals with the recent ethnic return migration of Argentines of Spanish descent to Spain. Despite the numerous benefits of their presumed ethnic affinity with the host society, they are disadvantaged on the labor market because as dual nationals with Spanish citizenship, they share native Spanish work orientations and expectations and are less willing than other immigrants to perform the unskilled, low-wage jobs they are offered. In turn, their local Spanish hosts (and employers) are disillusioned by the Argentines' apparently poor work ethic and come to see them as ill-suited for immigrant jobs. Cook-Martín and Viladrich conclude that ethnic return migrants who are granted citizenship expect the same rights and privileges as native workers, ironically hindering their labor market integration despite their cultural affinity with the host populace.

In Chapter 6 Charlotta Hedberg analyzes the ethnic return migration of the Swedish-speaking minority (Finland Swedes) from Finland to Sweden. Although they are a relatively privileged minority in Finland, they still experience some segregation and intolerance. They return-migrate to Sweden because of the cultural and linguistic affinity they feel for an accessible, neighboring ethnic homeland, not for purely economic reasons. Despite the ease of their social integration in Sweden, Finland Swedes are culturally distinguishable because of their Swedish dialect and feel somewhat socially excluded, causing their ethnic affinity with Sweden to initially decline and producing a greater national attachment to Finland. Over time, however, they tend to assimilate into Swedish society and retain their Finland Swede identities mainly in private.

In Chapter 7 Jon E. Fox examines the return migration of ethnic Hungarian descendants from Romania to Hungary. Over the past 15 years, Hungary has promoted a discourse of a broader, deterritorialized ethnic nation that includes Hungarian descendants in neighboring countries and has attempted to develop transborder political, cultural, and economic links with its co-ethnics abroad. However, ethnic Hungarians from Romania who have return-migrated to Hungary are economically marginalized and socially denigrated as unskilled "Romanian" labor migrants, despite their shared ethnicity with the host society. Instead of reunifying Hungarian descendants across national borders, as imagined by Hungarian political elites, ethnic return migration has reproduced national disunity and difference between ethnic Hungarians from Romania and those in Hungary.

Israel is included in this section despite its geographic location in the Middle East because it represents the largest and most important case of ethnic return migration.[10] According to Larissa Remennick (Chapter 8), because Jewish diasporic returnees are critical to Israel's ongoing nation building, they face greater expectations of national loyalty and assimilation than other ethnic return migrants. Although Russian Jews from the former Soviet Union return-migrate with considerable human capital, they have lost their Jewish linguistic and cultural background and have suffered a decline in occupational status in Israel. As a result, most experience significant social and economic marginalization and their cultural consumption remains mainly Russian. In general, there is more social integration in public and more separatism in their private lives, indicating that the immigrant community simultaneously manifests both tendencies.

Part 3 moves to East Asia, which has received both large numbers of ethnic return migrants from developing countries and also smaller populations from developed nations. In Chapter 9, I argue that the divergent ethnic homecomings of Japanese Americans and Japanese Brazilians in Japan are mainly a product of the different positions that Brazil and the United States occupy in the global hierarchy of nations. Because of the lower position of Brazil in the international economic and political order, Japanese Brazilians have negative ethnic experiences as they toil as unskilled migrant laborers in Japan and develop defensive, nationalist identities in response to ethnic degradation in their ancestral homeland. Meanwhile, many of their Japanese American counterparts from the United States migrate to their ethnic homeland as part of the global educational and professional elite, are accorded the appropriate respect of nationals at the top of the international order, and emerge from their migratory experiences with a stronger transnational and cosmopolitan connection to their ethnic homeland.

Chapter 10 is about Japanese Peruvians in Japan. Ayumi Takenaka notes that, although Japanese Brazilians strengthened their Brazilian nationalist identities in response to their ethnic marginalization in Japan, many Japanese Peruvians in Japan have been more ambivalent about their nationalist Peruvian identities and instead have strengthened their ethnic identities as *nikkei* (peoples of Japanese descent from abroad). Because of their greater cultural and racial differences, Peruvian immigrants are lower in the Japanese ethnic hierarchy than Brazilian immigrants and have fewer employment opportunities. In addition, Japanese Peruvians distance themselves from illegal non-Japanese-descent Peruvians as more privileged Japanese-descent *nikkei*. Therefore internal divisions within the Peruvian immigrant community are another reason they remain reluctant to identify nationally as Peruvians.

In Chapter 11, Changzoo Song discusses the causes of the ethnic return migration of Korean Chinese (*chosŏnjok*, also spelled *joseonjok*) to South Korea. Because of the nostalgic images of their ethnic homeland they had developed in China, Korean Chinese are disappointed by their ethnic and socioeconomic marginalization in South Korea; they face legal and employment discrimination and are forced to perform harsh, degrading immigrant jobs. On the host society side, South Korean elites, who view Korean Chinese as people who

have maintained Korean cultural traditions, are disillusioned that their ethnic brethren from China have an insufficient work ethnic, have become too
culturally Chinese, and are no longer loyal to South Korea. The alienation of
Korean Chinese in their ethnic homeland causes them to recognize that they
are more Chinese than Korean and to redefine China and not Korea as their
homeland.

In Chapter 12, Nadia Y. Kim looks at Korean Americans in South Korea.
Because Korean Americans continue to be racialized as nonwhite foreigners
in the United States, they have developed a romanticized view of South Korea
as the ethnic homeland where they truly belong as racial insiders. However,
when they return-migrate to Korea, they are not ethnically accepted as authentic Koreans, despite their shared racial descent, because they are seen
and treated as overly Americanized cultural foreigners. Because of such dis-
illusioning experiences, Korean Americans develop some negative attitudes
about South Korea and lose their previous emotional affiliation with their
ethnic homeland, which no longer feels like a "home." This causes them to
strengthen their identities as Americans and to redefine themselves as more at
home in the United States.

In the Conclusion, I draw from the case study chapters to address some
of the main concerns of the book. These include the reasons for the ethnic
and socioeconomic marginalization of ethnic return migrants in their ancestral homelands and how the difficulties inherent in diasporic homecomings
have forced homeland governments to reconsider their ethnic return migration
policies and their conceptions of citizenship and national belonging based on
shared bloodline. Finally, I discuss how the negative homecomings of ethnic
return migrants have transformed their ethnonational consciousness and their
understandings of home and homeland.

Notes

1. Although ethnic return migration is often referred to as ethnic affinity migration or ethnic migration in the literature, these terms will generally not be used in this
book because of their greater ambiguity.

2. In addition, between 1945 and 1949, 12 million ethnic Germans were expelled
from Eastern Europe after World War II and resettled in West and East Germany (and
Austria).

3. A number of these returnees are first-generation Russians who emigrated during Soviet expansion during the cold war. The proportion that are later-generation
ethnic Russian descendants is not clear.

4. Christian Joppke's book, *Selecting by Origin: Ethnic Migration in the Liberal State* (2005), is broader in geographic scope but focuses exclusively on the impact of ethnic preferences on immigration policy and is thus not specifically about ethnic return migrants.

5. This section was inspired by the comments of an anonymous reviewer.

6. Because ethnic return migration is also transnational, research on the topic should ideally involve the type of multisite fieldwork that most contributors to this volume have conducted.

7. This basic typology is used by Robin Cohen (1997: ch. 2).

8. In rare cases, diasporic descendants are part of the "majority" ethnic group (e.g., Argentines of Spanish and Italian descent who were considered part of the European-descent "white" majority in Argentina).

9. The only exception is ethnic return migrants who have maintained their cultural heritage and language for generations and are not ethnically and socioeconomically marginalized in the homeland. The only examples in this book are the Finland Swedes who return to Sweden and possibly a limited number of Spanish Argentines in Spain. Ethnic Russian descent return migrants in Russia may also have similar experiences.

10. Initially, a chapter on Palestinian ethnic return migration was to be included as part of a section on the Middle East.

References Cited

Alba, Richard, and Victor Nee. 1997. "Rethinking Assimilation Theory for a New Era of Immigration." *International Migration Review* 31:826–874.

Basch, Linda, Nina Glick Schiller, and Cristina Szanton Blanc. 1994. *Nations Unbound: Transnational Projects, Postcolonial Predicaments, and Deterritorialized Nation-States.* Amsterdam: Gordon and Breach.

Brubaker, Rogers. 1998. "Migrations of Ethnic Unmixing in the 'New Europe.'" *International Migration Review* 32(4):1047–1065.

Capo Zmegac, Jasna. 2005. "Ethnically Privileged Migrants in Their New Homeland." *Journal of Refugee Studies* 18(2):199–215.

Clifford, James. 1994. "Diasporas." *Cultural Anthropology* 9(3):302–338.

Cohen, Robin. 1997. *Global Diasporas: An Introduction.* Seattle: University of Washington Press.

Glick Schiller, Nina. 1997. "The Situation of Transnational Studies." *Identities: Global Studies in Culture and Power* 4(2):155–166.

Gmelch, George. 1980. "Return Migration." *Annual Review of Anthropology* 9:135–159.

Gordon, Milton. 1964. *Assimilation in American Life.* New York: Oxford University Press.

Joppke, Christian. 2005. *Selecting by Origin: Ethnic Migration in the Liberal State.* Cambridge, MA: Harvard University Press.

Levy, André, and Alex Weingrod. 2005. *Homelands and Diasporas: Holy Lands and Other Places.* Stanford, CA: Stanford University Press.

Long, Lynellyn D., and Ellen Oxfeld, eds. 2004. *Coming Home? Refugees, Migrants, and Those Who Stayed Behind.* Philadelphia: University of Pennsylvania Press.

Louie, Andrea. 2004. *Chineseness Across Borders: Renegotiating Chinese Identities in China and the United States.* Durham, NC: Duke University Press.

Markowitz, Fran, and Anders Stefansson, eds. 2004. *Homecomings: Unsettling Paths of Return.* Lanham, MD: Lexington Books.

McKeown, Adam. 2001. *Chinese Migrant Networks and Cultural Change: Peru, Chicago, Hawaii, 1900–1936.* Chicago: University of Chicago Press.

Münz, Rainer, and Rainer Ohliger, eds. 2003. *Diasporas and Ethnic Migrants: Germany, Israel, and Post-Soviet Successor States in Comparative Perspective.* London: Frank Cass.

Pilkington, Hilary. 1998. *Migration, Displacement, and Identity in Post-Soviet Russia.* London: Routledge.

Portes, Alejandro, Luis Guarnizo, and Patricia Landolt. 1999. "Introduction: Pitfalls and Promise of an Emergent Research Field." *Ethnic and Racial Studies* 22(2):217–237.

Portes, Alejandro, and Rubén G. Rumbaut. 1996. *Immigrant America: A Portrait.* Berkeley: University of California Press.

Reitz, Jeffrey, ed. 2003. *Host Societies and the Reception of Immigrants.* Center for Comparative Immigration Studies Anthology Series. La Jolla: University of California at San Diego.

Remennick, Larissa. 2007. *Russian Jews on Three Continents: Identity, Integration, and Conflict.* New Brunswick, NJ: Transaction.

Rock, David, and Stefan Wolff, eds. 2002. *Coming Home to Germany? The Integration of Ethnic Germans from Central and Eastern Europe in the Federal Republic.* New York: Berghahn Books.

Roth, Joshua. 2002. *Brokered Homeland: Japanese Brazilian Migrants in Japan.* Ithaca, NY: Cornell University Press.

Rouse, Roger. 1991. "Mexican Migration and the Social Space of Postmodernism." *Diaspora: A Journal of Transnational Studies* 1(1):8–23.

Safran, William. 1991. "Diasporas in Modern Societies: Myths of Homeland and Return." *Diaspora: A Journal of Transnational Studies* 1(1):83–99.

Sheffer, Gabriel. 2003. "From Diasporas to Migrants, from Migrants to Diasporas." In *Diasporas and Ethnic Migrants: Germany, Israel, and Post-Soviet Successor States in Comparative Perspective*, Rainer Münz and Rainer Ohliger, eds. London: Frank Cass, 21–55.

Smith, M. G. 1986. "Pluralism, Race, and Ethnicity in Selected African Countries." In *Theories of Race and Ethnic Relations*, John Rex and David Mason, eds. Cambridge, UK: Cambridge University Press, 187–225.

Smith, Michael Peter, and Luis Eduardo Guarnizo, eds. 1998. *Transnationalism from Below*. New Brunswick, NJ: Transaction.

Stefansson, Anders H. 2004. "Homecomings to the Future: From Diasporic Mythographies to Social Projects of Return." In *Homecomings: Unsettling Paths of Return*, Fran Markowitz and Anders Stefansson, eds. Lanham, MD: Lexington Books, 2–20.

Tölölyan, Khachig. 1996. "Rethinking Diaspora(s): Stateless Power in the Transnational Moment." *Diaspora: A Journal of Transnational Studies* 5(1):3–36.

Tsuda, Takeyuki. 2003. *Strangers in the Ethnic Homeland: Japanese Brazilian Return Migration in Transnational Perspective*. New York: Columbia University Press.

Van Hear, Nicholas. 1998. *New Diasporas: The Mass Exodus, Dispersal, and Regrouping of Migrant Communities*. Seattle: University of Washington Press.

Weber, Max. 1961. "Ethnic Groups." In *Theories of Society*, Talcott Parsons, Edward Shils, Kaspar Naegele, and Jesse Pitts, eds. New York: Free Press, 305–309.

The Causes of Diasporic Return

Why Does the Diaspora Return Home?

The Causes of Ethnic Return Migration

Takeyuki Tsuda

MOST OF THE DIASPORIC DESCENDANTS considered in this book are culturally as-similated and socially well-established in their countries of birth. So what has caused millions of them to return to their ethnic homelands in recent decades after living outside their countries of ancestral origin for generations? To what extent are both economic and ethnic factors involved? The primary cause of most diasporic returns is economic pressures and not a desire to return to one's ethnic roots and ancestry per se. However, economics alone does not sufficiently explain why so many people have returned to their ethnic home-lands. Although economic motives initiate migration, ethnic ties and affini-ties ultimately *channel* the migrant flow to the ethnic homeland. Therefore any complete explanation of ethnic return migration must consider the dynamic interaction between economic and ethnic factors. Despite its fundamentally instrumental economic basis, diasporic return continues to be more ethnically driven and emotionally charged than other types of labor migration. It is, after all, an ethnic homecoming.

The Economics of Ethnic Return Migration

Most diasporic descendants are not returning to their ethnic homelands sim-ply to reconnect with their ancestral roots or to explore their ethnic heritage. Instead, in general, they are migrating from less developed countries to more economically prosperous ancestral homelands (often in the developed world) in search of jobs, higher incomes, and a better standard of living. Although the desire to eventually return to the ancestral homeland is often invoked in definitions of diasporic peoples (Safran 1991: 83–84; Tölölyan 1996: 14), most of their descendants, who are quite rooted in their countries of birth, would not do so without sufficient economic incentives. Ethnic return migrants are generally in search of better economic opportunities, not ethnic roots. In this sense, diasporic return from the developing world initially appears to be another form of international labor migration caused by widening economic disparities between rich and poor countries.

This is especially true with Russian Jews and ethnic Germans who live in poorer Eastern European countries, ethnic Korean descendants in China and the former Soviet Union, and Latin Americans of European and Japanese descent, who started returning to their ethnic homelands when faced with economic crises in South America in the late 1980s. Even when economic disparities between sending and receiving countries are not large, the primary motive remains economic.[1] In these cases, ethnic return is to easily accessible neighboring countries with whom diasporic descendants have maintained relatively strong linguistic and cultural ties, lowering the economic threshold for migration.[2]

Although ethnicity is generally not a "pull" factor that draws diasporic descendants to the ancestral homeland in search of ancestral heritage, it can be a "push" factor that forces them out of their country of birth. In the past, large ethnic return migration flows were instigated by ethnopolitical persecution caused by major geopolitical disruptions, such as the dissolution of empires, colonial regimes, and multiethnic states, and not by direct economic pressure per se (see Brubaker 1995, 1998; Capo Zmegac 2005). For instance, the collapse of the Austro-Hungarian and Ottoman empires led to the mass repatriation of ethnic Hungarians and ethnic Turks from Eastern Europe and the Middle East, and the defeat of Germany after World War II caused the expulsion of 12 million ethnic Germans from Eastern Europe, most of whom resettled in West and East Germany. The end of European colonial empires caused large numbers of European descendants living in colonized territories to return to their ethnic homelands (especially in the case of Britain and France). In these cases, ethnic return migration was mainly caused by ethnic discrimination and persecution, as diasporic peoples from the conquering homeland were left behind as their empires receded, becoming "enemy" ethnic minorities and former colonizers who lost their privileged sociopolitical status and were pressured, if not forced, to migrate back to their countries of ethnic origin.

In recent decades, ethnopolitical persecution has not caused any large-scale ethnic return migrations, which have become primarily economic in nature. For instance, although Jewish diasporic return to Israel began after World War II in the wake of the Holocaust, most Jews in the Diaspora today migrate from less developed countries to Israel for economic reasons. Even diasporic returns caused by the dissolution of multiethnic states and empires have had a notable economic component in recent decades. The collapse of the Soviet Union was the most recent geopolitical event that enabled a number of ethnic minorities within its territories to return-migrate to more economically developed ethnic homelands. Most notable of these are the diasporic return of Russian Jews to Israel and a second wave of ethnic German return migration from Eastern Europe after the cold war (the two largest recent ethnic return migration flows). Perhaps the only example of large-scale ethnic return migration caused by ethnopolitical persecution in recent decades was during the dissolution of the former Yugoslavia, which forced ethnic minorities such as Croats and Albanians living outside their homeland territories to return-migrate under threat of ethnic persecution and genocide.

Nonetheless, ethnic discrimination can play a role even in cases of economically motivated return migration. For instance, continuing ethnic insecurity and discrimination in Eastern Europe has sometimes worsened the socioeconomic situation of ethnic minorities in these countries, causing them to leave for their ancestral homelands. After the collapse of the Soviet Union, the millions of ethnic Russians and their descendants who were left outside their Russian homeland in Soviet successor states suddenly became ethnic minorities of diminished socioeconomic and political status and were subject to deteriorating ethnopolitical relations, discrimination, and an uncertain economic and ethnic future, causing Russia to allow their repatriation (Brubaker 1995: 208–209; Brubaker 1998: 1059–1061; Pilkington 1998: 123–138; Vishnevsky 2003: 162).[3] Likewise, the diasporic return of Russian Jews to Israel was caused by a combination of economic crisis, political instability, and increasing Russian nationalism, anti-Semitism, and discrimination (Remennick 1998: 247; Remennick 2007: 36–37, 42–43). The migration of ethnic Hungarian descendants from Romania to Hungary was a response to their comparatively dismal economic future in Romania, exacerbated by the perception of ethnic discrimination (Fox 2003: 452). In these cases, diasporic return migration is still motivated by underlying economic causes, but ethnic discrimination and persecution serve as an additional impetus that helps push diasporic descendants out of their countries of birth.

Ethnicity seems to play a greater role for ethnic return migrants from developed countries. Coming from rich countries, such individuals have much less economic incentive to migrate to their ethnic homelands (which are sometimes poorer countries), and therefore their numbers are limited. Although many are seeking professional, educational, or business investment opportunities in their countries of ancestral origin, the desire to reconnect with their ethnic roots and explore their cultural heritage seems to be a stronger motive compared to ethnic return migrants from poorer, developing countries. This is especially the case with student ethnic return migrants, who usually have a desire to study their ancestral language and learn about the homeland culture.[4] Asian Americans in East Asia cite the desire to explore their ethnic ancestry as a reason for return migration (see Chapters 9 and 12), as do Korean Japanese who return to South Korea (Kweon 2006).[5] Some later-generation Asian Americans also feel that they have become too assimilated in the United States and have lost their cultural heritage, thus motivating them to return to their homelands to recover their ethnic ancestry as a source of cultural authenticity. For the Finland Swedes who return to Sweden, cultural and linguistic affinity with their ethnic homeland and concerns about their weakening minority culture in Finland are primary motives for return migration in addition to educational and professional opportunities (Hedberg and Kepsu 2003; Chapter 6). A limited number of individuals from developed countries travel to their ancestral homelands as cultural heritage tourists to explore their ethnic roots; sometimes organized tours are sponsored by ethnic organizations and homeland governments that wish to recover ties to wealthy diasporic descendants abroad and promote their economic investment in the ethnic homeland (e.g., see Kibria 2002b; Louie 2001, 2002, 2003). The most notable examples of such organized ethnic tourism are to Israel, China, and South Korea.[6]

Transnational Ethnic Ties and Diasporic Return

Although diasporic returns have been caused more by economic pressures than by persisting ancestral ties across borders, such transnational ethnic affinities determine the direction of these migrant flows. In response to economic pressures, diasporic descendants have chosen to migrate to their ethnic homelands instead of to other advanced industrialized countries because of their nostalgic affiliation to their country of ethnic origin and because of the ethnically preferential immigration policies of homeland governments, which have enabled them to return-migrate.

Imagining the Ethnic Homeland from Afar

Most ordinary labor migration flows are structured by preexisting social net-works and institutional connections between sending and receiving countries, which provide transnational linkages that enable migrants to move across bor-ders and relocate to foreign countries. In ethnic return migration, however, most diasporic descendants have lost any substantial transnational social con-nections or cultural contacts with their countries of ethnic origin,[7] except in a few cases in which the ethnic homeland is located in a neighboring country. Despite literature that suggests that transnational social connections with the ethnic homeland persist after the first immigrant generation (e.g., see Levitt and Waters 2002; Smith 2006), most second-generation diasporic descen-dants considered in this book do not have substantial contact with their par-ents' country of origin. Therefore the transnational ethnic ties that channel diasporic return migrants to their ethnic homelands are based on an imagined, nostalgic ethnic affinity to an ancestral country that most have never visited. In this sense, their ethnic return migration is a type of "forged transnationality" (Schein 1998)—the creation of new transnational connections instead of the continuation of preexisting linkages.

Although most diasporic descendants have developed a nostalgic identi-fication with their ethnic homelands (cf. Ali and Koser 2002), the strength of such sentimental ethnic attachments varies. For instance, Russian Jews do not have a strong transnational ethnic affiliation to Israel because of their cultural assimilation and suppression of nationalist sentiment among ethnic minorities in the former Soviet Union (see Remennick 2003). Others, like the Argentines of Spanish and Italian descent, do not have a strong awareness of their ethnic heritage but develop an appreciation for it while recovering their homeland nationality (Cook-Martín 2005).

Immigrant ethnic minorities sometimes develop strong transnational iden-tifications with their countries of ethnic origin in response to the discrimina-tory exclusion and marginalization they experience in their country of birth (e.g., see Espiritu 2003: 86–88; Levitt 2001: 19–20; Parreñas 2001: 55–59; Portes 1999; cf. Kibria 2002b), which makes them feel that they do not fully belong there. For instance, ethnic Hungarian descendants in Romania feel solidarity with the greater Hungarian nation partly in response to their adversarial rela-tions with majority Romanians. Ethnic Germans in Eastern Europe seem to have had analogous experiences in the past when faced with discrimination. Some ethnic minorities (such as Asian Americans and Japanese-descent *nikkeijin* in

Latin America) are forever racialized as foreigners with essentialized cultural attachments to their native countries of origin because of their phenotypic differences from the mainstream populace, which can cause them to construct a romanticized view of their ethnic homeland as the country where they racially belong (Chapter 12; Louie 2002: 313–314; Tsuda 2003: ch. 2).[8]

However, ethnic minorities can also develop relatively strong homeland attachments because their ethnic ancestry and countries of origin are constructed and portrayed in a favorable manner. Indeed, most diasporic descendants imagine their ancestral homelands from afar in rather idealized, romantic, if not mythical ways (cf. Cohen 1997: 184–185). Many of these positive images come from their parents and grandparents, whose nostalgic romanticization of their homeland is a product of their prolonged separation from their countries of origin (see Grossutti, n.d.; von Koppenfels 2003: 316; Tsuda 2003: ch. 2; Viladrich, n.d.; Chapters 4 and 12). Other images come from the globalized mass media and popular culture, which have become the primary means of imagining homelands from afar (Appadurai 1996: 38, 49; Gupta and Ferguson 1992: 11). At times, such nostalgic longings for their country of ethnic origin can cause diasporic descendants to cling to archaic ancestral traditions that are no longer actively practiced in their ethnic homelands.

Positive identifications with ancestral homelands seem to be especially prominent among "positive minorities," who enjoy a relatively higher socioeconomic status than the majority society and are ethnically respected, such as Japanese Brazilians, Finland Swedes, certain Asian Americans, and even ethnic Hungarians in Romania (see Fox 2003: 459; Hedberg and Kepsu 2003: 72; Tsuda 2003: ch. 2; Chapter 6). Some of these ethnic minorities can be positively stereotyped by mainstream society because of sociocultural qualities associated with their ethnic homelands, especially for those in developing countries whose ancestors came from more developed countries. Of course, images of the ancestral homeland can vary over time, depending on historical circumstances, and ambivalent, conflicting perceptions often coexist (see Louie 2003; Tsuda 2001).

Attachments to homelands are especially strong for diasporic peoples located in neighboring countries where ethnocultural links exist across national borders, as with Hungarian Romanians and Finland Swedes (Hedberg and Kepsu 2008).[9] In addition, both of these groups are generally raised and educated in cohesive ethnic communities and have retained their ancestral languages to a certain extent. Unlike other diasporic descendants, such peoples never left their ethnic homelands to migrate to faraway countries and assimilate to foreign cultures. Instead, the ethnic homeland technically left them (in neighboring countries) when it lost territory and national borders shifted or were consolidated.[10]

Therefore, when diasporic descendants are faced with economic pressures to emigrate, many naturally have turned to their ethnic homelands instead of migrating to other advanced industrialized nations because of their sentimental ethnic attachments to their countries of ancestral origin. These countries seemed more ethnically accessible, and it was presumed that their co-ethnic status would facilitate their immigrant social integration. In addition, such transnational ethnic affiliations have been substantiated by homeland governments, which have adopted immigration and nationality policies that reach out to their diasporic descendants abroad and allow them to return to their ethnic homelands. These governments have granted the right of ethnic return because of their own sense of ethnocultural affinity and historical connection to their diasporic peoples. To fully understand the factors that have enabled diasporic return, therefore, we must analyze the rationales behind the ethnic return migration policies of homeland states.

Ethnic Return Migration Policy: Encouraging the Diaspora to Return "Home"

Although most liberal democratic states have abandoned the ethnically discriminatory, racist immigration policies of the past, which excluded certain immigrants by race or national origins, a number of states continue to have ethnic preference policies that privilege ethnically desirable immigrants (see Joppke 2005), usually drawing from the country's pool of diasporic descendants abroad. The shift has therefore simply been from negative discrimination to positive discrimination in ethnic selectivity (cf. Joppke 2005: 19). Not only have governments reached out across territorial borders to their first-generation emigrants to ensure their continuing national loyalty and engagement in their home countries (Glick Schiller 1997: 160–161; Guarnizo 1997: 305, 309; Smith 2003), they have also attempted to incorporate second- and third-generation diasporic descendants into their "deterritorialized nation-states" by encouraging them to return to their ethnic homeland.

The ethnic preference policies of homeland governments are based on the essentialized assumption that ethnic descendants, despite being born and raised abroad, would be culturally similar to the host populace because of their shared bloodline. Diasporic descendants have been imagined as an integral part of a broader deterritorialized cultural nation of "co-ethnics" living in other countries but united by common descent (cf. Joppke 2005: 159), thus invoking a natural ethnic affinity between the nation-state and its diaspora. However, the specific reasons that homeland governments decided to welcome back their ethnic descendants from abroad vary according to geographic region.

Ethnic return migration policies in Europe (and Israel) are generally based on an ethnic protection or ethnic affinity rationale that emphasises the historical connection of these countries to their diasporic peoples abroad (cf. Chapter 2; see also Joppke 2005: 23–24). In Israel and Germany, these policies were initially implemented to protect their diasporic peoples from ethnic persecution. When the state of Israel was established after the Holocaust, all Jews were granted the right to return to their ancestral homeland, partly to provide them with a safe haven from future persecution and partly to build up and strengthen the Jewish state (see Chapter 3). Likewise, in Germany, ethnic German descendants expelled from Eastern Europe after World War II and those living in Communist countries during the cold war were allowed to return as *Aussiedler* under the presumption of ethnic persecution.

In contrast, ethnic preferences in immigration policy and nationality law in other European countries (Spain, Italy, Greece, Hungary, Poland, and Russia) are based almost exclusively on an ethnic affinity rationale with diasporic descendants born abroad as part of a greater ethnic nation beyond state borders (Joppke 2005: 116–117, 245–246). Because of historical and racial ties to the diaspora, ethnic descendants are seen by their respective homeland governments as "our people," who therefore have a right to return to their ancestral homeland. Although some type of ethnic protection rationale can be invoked,[11] the underlying justification is based on a sense of state responsibility for or obligation to their diasporic descendants abroad (Cook-Martín 2005; de Tinguy 2003: 116–119; Joppke 2005: 246; Chapter 2).[12]

Unlike their European counterparts, East Asian and some Southeast Asian countries have invited back their diasporic descendants mainly for economic purposes (see Chapter 2; see also Joppke 2005: 158–159). Japan and South Korea have imported large numbers of ethnic return migrants in response to acute unskilled labor shortages caused by decades of economic prosperity coupled with low fertility rates. South Korea and China (and to some extent Taiwan, the Philippines, Malaysia, Vietnam, Cambodia, and Laos) have encouraged wealthy and highly skilled ethnic descendants in the diaspora to return-migrate in order to promote economic investment from abroad and to tap their professional skills (see Cheng 2002: 91–92; Chapter 2). However, these countries generally decided to allow diasporic return because they assumed that ethnic return migrants of shared descent and presumed cultural affinity would be easier to assimilate and socially integrate than other immigrants and would therefore not disrupt the country's ethnoracial balance.

Because of the different justifications that European and East Asian countries have used to welcome co-ethnic descendants from abroad, it is not surprising that the legal status they enjoy in their ethnic homelands is quite different. European countries (and Israel), which have accepted ethnic return migrants as people who deserve to be included in and protected by the nation-state, either grant them citizenship upon ethnic return (as is the case in Israel, Germany, Poland, and Greece to some extent) or allow them to recover their ethnic homeland nationality and become dual nationals, which gives them the right to return-migrate (as is the case in Spain, Italy, Ireland, Poland, and Russia) (Grossutti, n.d.: 2–5; Iglicka 1998: 1008; Joppke 2005: 245–247; Chapters 2 and 5). Unlike most of the other countries, Spain and Italy do not have preferential ethnic immigration policies that specifically target co-ethnic descendants abroad and actively encourage them to return-migrate.[13] Instead, ethnic return migration is enabled through their jus sanguinis (descent-based) dual nationality laws, which their ethnic descendants (mainly in Argentina) have used to migrate to their ethnic homelands in response to economic crises at home.[14] The main exception to such policy trends in Europe is Hungary, which does not confer nationality to its co-ethnics abroad; Hungary does not even have a stable guest worker program for them, forcing most ethnic return migrants to work illegally.[15] Hungary is also not interested in actively recruiting ethnic return migrants (Brubaker 1998: 1055; Chapters 2 and 7) because its economy is less prosperous and cannot support a large number of immigrant workers and because its ethnic descendants are mainly in surrounding countries, which creates certain policy constraints.[16] Likewise, although Russia remains committed in principle to accepting all ethnic Russians who return from Soviet successor states, it does not actively encourage repatriation because of the limited ability of its fragile economy to accommodate and integrate them (Brubaker 1998: 1061; Pilkington 1998).

In contrast to most European countries, ethnic return migrants in East Asia are generally given only preferential visas (and not citizenship) because they are being imported primarily as immigrant workers.[17] The Japanese government issues indefinitely renewable visas to ethnic return migrants, and China has even offered permanent residence to its highly skilled diasporic returnees (see Chapter 2). In South Korea, ethnic Koreans from China and the former Soviet Union have been offered only a limited number of work visas (industrial trainee visas in the past and now five-year visas under the new "Visit and Work Program"). Because most of its diasporic descendants are located in neighboring and poorer China, the Korean government has been concerned about a flood of Korean Chinese labor migrants and has therefore not adopted a more open policy toward them. This has caused many of them to immigrate illegally— but with the tacit consent of the Korean government, which has conveniently looked the other way (Lim 2006: 241).

Such open ethnic immigration policies have been an important factor in facilitating diasporic return by enabling co-ethnic descendants abroad secure access to their ancestral homelands by virtue of their ethnic heritage and descent (Van Hear 1998: 48). Although these policies have not been a direct cause of ethnic return migration, they have certainly channeled these migration flows by determining their destination. Many diasporic descendants have chosen to return-migrate to their ethnic homelands for economic reasons because of the much greater ease of entry compared to other countries of immigration (cf. Tsuda 1999). If homeland governments had not openly admitted their diasporic descendants, most ethnic return migration flows would have remained quite small and many of the migrants would have headed to other advanced industrialized nations. In this sense, the transnational ethnic connections that enabled ethnic return migration were forged both from below by diasporic descendants, who imagined their ancestral ties to the ethnic homeland, and from above by the policies of these homeland governments, which have reached out to their ethnic descendants abroad and encouraged them to return "home" (see Guarnizo and Smith 1998).[18]

Case Study:
The Ethnic Return Migration of Japanese Brazilians

To illustrate the dynamic nexus of economic and ethnic factors that cause diasporic return, I briefly examine the migration of second- and third-generation Japanese Brazilians from Brazil to their ethnic homeland of Japan as unskilled foreign workers. Japanese Brazilians are the largest group of Japanese descendants (*nikkeijin*) in South America, and close to 300,000 of them have return-migrated to Japan.

Economic Motives

Although the Brazilian *nikkeijin* are solidly middle class in Brazil, they still earn five to ten times their Brazilian incomes as unskilled factory workers in Japan. Many of them are aware that the money they can earn in Japan in just a few years may take decades to earn in Brazil. However, such wage differentials alone, which have always existed between the two countries, usually do not cause migration. It was the simultaneous conjunction of an economic crisis in Brazil and a labor shortage in Japan in the 1980s that instigated the return migration of Japanese Brazilians.

Throughout much of the 1980s, Brazil's economy suffered from massive hyperinflation, stagnant or declining growth, and increasing unemployment and underemployment. Because of their relatively high middle-class status, the Brazilian *nikkeijin* were able to weather the economic crisis better than many other Brazilians and did not experience severe unemployment. However, they were suddenly unable to maintain their middle-class lifestyle because of a decline in income and an inability to find jobs commensurate with their educational levels and aspirations. Because they had become accustomed to their privileged socioeconomic status, they were less willing to accept a deterioration in their standard of living than many of their poorer compatriots. This made them more likely to emigrate (in an effort to maintain their middle-class lifestyles) than lower-class Brazilians, who were more willing to accept worsening economic conditions and remain behind. Therefore it was relative, not absolute, economic deprivation that caused Brazilian *nikkeijin* to return-migrate to Japan. When reflecting on their reasons for emigrating, remarks such as the following from a Japanese Brazilian woman were typical in my interviews:[19]

> We never suffered from a lack of money or had serious economic problems back home. There was always enough to live on, to put food on the table, to buy basic necessities. The problem was that because of the economic crisis and Brazilian inflation, we couldn't do anything more than this with our salaries— couldn't buy a house, buy a car, or plan for our futures.

Such macroeconomic pressures were the push factor that caused the Brazilian *nikkeijin* to leave Brazil.

Meanwhile, Japan was faced with an economic crisis of its own, albeit of a different sort. Because of decades of economic prosperity coupled with declining fertility, an aging population, and socially mobile youth unwilling to perform unskilled jobs, the country was suffering from a crippling shortage of unskilled labor by the late 1980s, which was especially acute among small and medium-size businesses in the manufacturing and construction sectors. In addition, alternative sources of labor were increasingly being depleted as the flow of internal migrants from rural areas dried up, further large increases in the employment of women and elderly became unfeasible, and labor-saving mechanisms such as automation and rationalization of production had begun to show serious limitations. As a result, labor-deficient firms turned to foreign workers as the only realistic and cost-efficient source of labor power. This rising economic demand for migrant labor was the economic incentive that pulled Japanese Brazilians to Japan.

However, although such macroeconomic conditions often initiate migration, the simultaneous conjunction of economic push forces in one country and pull forces in the other does not by itself specify the destination of the migrant flow. To understand why the Brazilian *nikkeijin* migrated specifically to Japan instead of to other advanced industrialized countries in need of migrant labor, we must consider their transnational affiliations with their ethnic homeland.

Transnational Ethnic Affinities:
Imaging the Japanese Homeland from Brazil

Japanese Brazilians are Brazil's largest and oldest Asian minority and have become socioculturally well-integrated into mainstream Brazilian society. Most live in the country's most economically developed urban areas as part of Brazil's middle class and are culturally assimilated to a considerable degree. Nonetheless, they continue to maintain a rather strong transnational affiliation with their ethnic homeland of Japan, which has come to be imagined from a distance in a positive and nostalgic manner.

Undoubtedly, some of the idealized perceptions that Japanese Brazilians have of Japan are constructed from images of Japan passed down from their parents and grandparents. Most of the original Japanese immigrants did not intend to settle permanently in Brazil and continued to dream of returning to Japan for decades. As a result, many speak with nostalgic fondness of their lost homeland and sometimes even glorify Japan in response to negative perceptions they may have of Brazilian society. A number of Brazilian *nikkeijin* also participate in local ethnic community associations and clubs, in which Japanese cultural traditions and activities are re-created. These cultural activities range from festivals, large dinners, and performances featuring Japanese karaoke, theater, traditional music, and dance to various sporting events and Miss Nikkei beauty pageants.

In addition, many of the positive perceptions that Japanese Brazilians have of their ethnic homeland are based on globalized images of Japan disseminated by the media. Reports and stories in Brazilian newspapers, magazines, television programs, and commercials have saturated the country with favorable images and impressions of highly respected "first world" Japan. In addition to current news, plenty of stories feature Japan's industrial development and economic prosperity and highlight new Japanese products and technological innovations. The effectiveness of these images about Japan is further enhanced by the limited but increasing availability of high-quality Japanese products in Brazil (e.g., video and electronic equipment, automobiles), which are admired for their reliability and technological superiority. Such images of Japanese modernity are accompanied by favorable portrayals of Japanese culture based on hard work, intelligence, discipline, and perseverance. In addition, nostalgic images of Japanese tradition, epitomized by ancient Japanese shrines, samurai, and kabuki, which are based on Japanese films and videos, books and vacation guides, and even Brazilian television, are widely available. In fact, non-*nikkeijin* Brazilians are now very interested in Japanese culture and language, which has lately come to be seen as refined, fashionable, chic, and exotic (Maeyama 1996: 491; Moreira da Rocha 1999: 289, 295; Reichl 1995: 45).

This global dissemination of positive impressions of Japanese modernity, culture, and tradition has enabled Japanese Brazilians to imagine their ethnic homeland in an idealized manner as a place of nostalgic longing and desire. In this manner, the development of global communications and mass media has enhanced the possibilities of the collective imagination (cf. Appadurai 1996: 8, 21–22, 53–54), allowing diasporic peoples scattered across various nations to maintain their identification with their countries of ethnic origin. Although most Japanese Brazilians do not personally affiliate themselves with Japan because they were born and raised in Brazil, they are constantly racialized as Japanese and directly associated with that country in the eyes of many majority Brazilians, some of whom do not clearly distinguish between the Japanese in Japan and the Japanese Brazilians in Brazil. However, because of the favorable manner in which their ethnic homeland has been constructed, few Brazilian *nikkeijin* have contested their essentialized connection with Japan, and some of them have actively asserted and promoted their Japaneseness and ethnic heritage.

Because of the strong consciousness among Japanese Brazilians of their transnational affinity to their ethnic homeland, when the economic crisis of the 1980s began to threaten their middle-class status in Brazil and created considerable pressure to emigrate, they naturally turned to Japan, in contrast to other middle-class Brazilians who emigrated to the United States (see Margolis 1994). As their country of ancestral origin, Japan seemed familiar and culturally accessible to Japanese Brazilians. The first migrants were also able to obtain sponsorship for visas and find jobs through their relatives in Japan.

Reaching Out to the Diaspora:
Japanese Ethnic Immigration Policies

However, what caused so many Japanese Brazilians to emigrate in such large numbers for economic reasons was not only their ancestral affiliation to Japan but also the Japanese government's strong awareness of their transnational ethnic ties with their *nikkeijin* descendants in Brazil. As a result, when faced with a crippling shortage of unskilled labor, Japan decided to welcome the Brazilian *nikkeijin* back to their ancestral homeland, despite its official ban on the importation of unskilled immigrant workers.

Japanese immigration policymakers were able to make the admission of *nikkeijin* migrant workers legally possible by appealing to an ideology of common descent and ethnic affinity with their Japanese descendants abroad. This allowed the government to obtain a much needed immigrant labor force, without contradicting, at least on the level of official appearances, the fundamental principle of Japanese immigration policy that no unskilled foreign workers will be accepted. Although it was evident that the *nikkeijin* would be working in Japan's factories to alleviate the labor shortage, officials from various ministries claimed that this was not the true intent of the policy and did not officially recognize the *nikkeijin* as unskilled foreign workers. Instead, the policy was ideologically justified as an opportunity provided by the benevolence of the Japanese government for those of Japanese descent born abroad to explore their ethnic heritage and visit their ancestral homeland. Of course, Japanese ministry bureaucrats admit that the *nikkeijin* are in fact working in Japan, but it is repeatedly stressed that the purpose of such labor is supposed to be for experiencing their ethnic homeland by visiting relatives, traveling, and learning the Japanese language and culture.

"We have allowed the *nikkeijin* to come to Japan to learn Japanese culture and the language and visit their relatives," one Ministry of Justice immigration policymaker claimed in an interview with a straight face. "Of course, if they decide to work in factories while they are here, there is nothing we can do about that. But that was not the intent of the policy." Likewise, a Ministry of Labor bureaucrat remarked:

> Previously, the *nikkeijin* didn't have opportunities to come to Japan. Now a lot of them come to Japan as *dekasegi* [migrant workers]. But I don't want people to forget that they are thus able to get to know the country of Japan and to visit their relatives. They are ancestral migrants—those that return to their ancestral homeland. Of course, they can do what they want in Japan—this is a right we respect. But it wasn't just for *dekasegi*. . . . For the *nikkeijin*, it is hard to go back and forth between Japan and Brazil with the money they earn in Brazil. So now, they can work in Japan and pay for their expenses during their stay. It simply makes Japan closer for them.

In addition, because of an essentialized racial ideology in which those of Japanese descent are expected to be culturally Japanese to a certain extent even if they were born and raised abroad, government policymakers assumed that the Brazilian *nikkeijin* would be culturally similar and assimilate smoothly to Japanese society in contrast to racially and culturally different foreigners. As a result, immigration policymakers also viewed Japanese Brazilian migrants as an effective way to deal with the labor shortage without disrupting Japan's cherished ethnic homogeneity. For instance, according to the chairman of the Liberal Democratic Party policy committee on foreign workers:

> One big argument for those who oppose opening the country to immigrant labor is that if we accept Asians with different cultures and customs, conflicts such as racial discrimination are likely to occur. . . . It would destroy the ethnic composition of Japan, which is close to an ethnically homogeneous nation-state. However, if it is our *nikkeijin* brethren, even if they can't speak Japanese adequately, we are not as concerned. . . . Even those who oppose the acceptance of foreign workers will probably not have many complaints with the special treatment of the *nikkeijin*, who have properly internalized Japanese customs. (Nojima 1989: 98)

By claiming that the *nikkeijin* were not immigrant workers per se but co-ethnic brethren who would therefore not be ethnically disruptive, immigration policymakers were able to import unskilled foreign labor without encountering any notable political or public opposition, in contrast to the intense debates that were being waged in the late 1980s among government bodies, interest groups, academics, and the mass media about whether Japan should open its doors to unskilled immigrants of other nationalities. As a result, the proposed *nikkeijin* policy was generally supported by immigration policymakers and did not cause any controversy among the involved government ministries. According to a Ministry of Justice bureaucrat:

> We didn't have any big conflicts [about *nikkeijin*] with other Ministries at the time like we did with other immigration issues. The *nikkeijin* issue was not consciously debated because everyone thought only a few would enter and no one expected so many would come. Also, we figured they were culturally close to the Japanese, so things would be easier with them.

Only the Ministry of Labor raised a short-lived quibble that the new policy would be inconsistent with Japan's immigration laws because the *nikkeijin* were de facto unskilled foreign laborers. As a result, the preferential ethnic admission of the *nikkeijin* was agreed on by the ministries and implemented quietly behind the scenes without Diet approval or public notification. This opened the floodgates, enabling the large-scale ethnic return migration of Japanese Brazilians.

Conclusion: Diasporic Return as a Migration System

Immigration specialists over the years have offered various theories for why people migrate, some based on simple economic explanations and others emphasizing transnational social networks, immigration policies, and even cultural and behavioral norms (for reviews see Castles and Miller 2003: ch. 2, and Massey et al. 1998). It is evident that any comprehensive understanding of population movements must adopt a dynamic and multicausal migration systems approach that examines various transnational economic and sociopolitical connections between groups of sending and receiving countries. These connections serve as bridges and links that channel and direct migrants to specific countries (see Fawcett 1989; Kritz and Zlotnik 1992). Although ethnic return migration is initiated by economic forces that are similar to other forms of labor migration, it is also structured by transnational ethnic ties between sending and receiving countries. These ties include both sentiments of nostalgic affinity among diasporic descendants with their ethnic homelands and homeland governments' ethnically preferential immigration and nationality policies, which are based on imaginings of a greater ethnic nation encompassing its diasporic descendants abroad.

Ultimately, ethnic return migration is a product of a complex dynamic between economics and ethnicity, with neither variable by itself sufficiently explaining the causes of diasporic return. Global economic disparities and pressures explain why ethnic return migrants leave (emigration) but not where they go (immigration). Transnational ethnic ties between homelands and their ethnic descendants abroad explain where they go but not why they leave. A full understanding of the migratory process, therefore, must simultaneously involve both economic pressures, which initiate migration, and transnational ethnic connections, which determine its destination.

The study of diasporic return migration therefore provides a new perspective to immigration studies by examining how migration can be structured by transborder ethnic ties between countries. Most other types of population movements (e.g., labor migrants, high-skilled and professional migration) are not ethnically motivated. For refugees, ethnicity (in the form of political persecution) may be a cause of migration, but it simply pushes them out of the sending country and is not a transnational variable that pulls them to the receiving country, as is the case with ethnic return migration. By illustrating how ethnic dynamics can influence the migration process, the study of diasporic return also highlights how migration can be the product of not only instrumental economic or political motives but also expressive and affective ties of ethnoracial group belonging that are constructed (and even imagined) across national borders. Even in the absence of actual transnational social or institutional connections between sending and receiving countries, migration can still occur because of primordial and sentimental ethnic attachments that people have to distant ancestral lands.

Notes

1. This is the case for ethnic Hungarian descendants from Romania returning to Hungary or for ethnic Russians from Soviet successor states returning to Russia, although economic causes for return migration are stronger for ethnic Hungarians than they are for ethnic Russians (Brubaker 1998: 1059–1060).

2. This is also the case for Finland Swedes who return to Sweden. Not only do they share strong cultural affinities with their neighboring ethnic homeland, but some also see their move to Sweden as internal migration because of the free movement across borders that is permitted in the European Union. As a result, many are moving without strong economic pressure (Hedberg and Kepsu 2003; Chapter 6).

3. In fact, ethnic Russian repatriates are classified as "forced migrants" by the Russian government, even though they resemble economic migrants more than refugees.

Another example of diasporic return that was partly motivated by worsening ethnic conditions is Estonian descendants in the former Soviet Union who migrated to Estonia (see Kulu 1998).

4. Of course, there are also students who migrate to their ethnic homelands from developing countries. For instance, a number of Korean Chinese in South Korea seem to be students (see Choi 2006; Yang 2006).

5. Second-generation Greek Americans have similar motivations for migration (Christou 2006: 1050–1051).

6. Some white Americans of European descent have also returned to their ethnic homelands (as tourists or otherwise) in search of their ancestral roots.

7. There are, of course, cases in which ethnic return migrants have maintained social connections to relatives in their homelands and have used these social networks to migrate.

8. This is sometimes reinforced by first-generation immigrant parents who tell their assimilation-minded offspring that they cannot deny their ethnic heritage because of their distinctive racial appearance and bloodline (Kibria 2002a: ch. 3).

9. In the case of Hungary, the government has actively reached out to its nearby diasporic communities and has granted them various legal and social privileges in order to promote a greater Hungarian ethnic nation across borders (Fox 2003; Joppke 2005: 247–250; Chapter 7).

10. In other cases, such as ethnic Germans in Eastern Europe and Korean Chinese, diasporic descendants reside in nearby countries but actively emigrated abroad and were historically isolated from their homelands by Communist regimes.

11. Joppke notes that the original purpose of the dual nationality law in Spain, which enables ethnic return migration, was to protect Spanish immigrants in Latin America, who were being forced to naturalize in their countries of residence in the late nineteenth and early twentieth centuries (Joppke 2005: 115–117). A protection rationale for ethnic preference immigration or dual nationality policies is also invoked by Greece.

12. Israel's policy also grants the right of ethnic return to all Jews as members of a deterritorialized diasporic community (regardless of whether they have been persecuted) and is therefore based on both an ethnic affinity and a protection rationale.

13. Spain does have preferential immigration policies toward Latin Americans and Filipinos based on linguistic and cultural affinities to people from its former colonies (Cornelius 2004: 410; Joppke 2005: 114–129; Chapter 2).

14. The Spanish and Italian governments allow Spanish and Italian Argentines to retain dual nationality by descent, and those (especially of the later generations) who have lost their ethnic homeland nationality are allowed to recover it. Many of them have done so in order to return-migrate for the economic opportunities, especially during periods of Argentine economic crisis in recent decades.

15. Although Hungary granted restrictive three-month guest worker visas to ethnic Hungarians in neighboring Romania as part of the 2001 Status Law, many of its provisions have since been weakened or revoked. A referendum granting dual nationality to co-ethnics abroad was also defeated because of insufficient voter turnout. Skrentny and colleagues (Chapter 2) claim that other Eastern European countries grant only preferential visas to co-ethnic returnees.

16. Hungary's ethnic descendants are in neighboring states because of the country's loss of territory after World War I. As a result, if Hungary actively encouraged them to "return" to Hungary, it would cause political tensions, raising fears of territorial "revisionism" among its neighbors. This is especially true in Romania, whose relations with Hungary have been especially tense because of the contested territory of Transylvania. Romania has in fact objected to Hungary's attempts to reach out to ethnic Hungarian descendants across its borders (Fox 2003: 455; Joppke 2005: 249–250; Kovrig 1994).

17. The exception seems to be Taiwan, which has recruited highly skilled diasporic Chinese through European-style dual nationality laws (Cheng 2002: 91–92).

18. Although "transnationalism from above" usually refers to global processes (such as transnational capital, media, and supranational organizations) that are above the nation-state, Guarnizo and Smith (1998: 29) warn us against equating it exclusively with global processes and note that transnationalism from above and below are relational and contextual terms.

19. Unless otherwise noted, all quotes are from interviews conducted in Japan by the author.

References Cited

Ali, Nadje al-, and Khalid Koser. 2002. "Transnationalism, International Migration, and Home." In *New Approaches to Migration? Transnational Communities and the Transformation of Home*, Nadje Al-Ali and Khalid Koser, eds. London: Routledge, 1–14.

Appadurai, Arjun. 1996. *Modernity at Large: Cultural Dimensions of Globalization*. Minneapolis: University of Minnesota Press.

Brubaker, Rogers. 1995. "Aftermaths of Empire and the Unmixing of Peoples: Historical and Comparative Perspectives." *Ethnic and Racial Studies* 18(2):189–218.

———. 1998. "Migrations of Ethnic Unmixing in the 'New Europe.'" *International Migration Review* 32(4):1047–1065.

Capo Zmegac, Jasna. 2005. "Ethnically Privileged Migrants in Their New Homeland." *Journal of Refugee Studies* 18(2):199–215.

Castles, Stephen, and Mark J. Miller. 2003. *The Age of Migration: International Population Movements in the Modern World*, 3rd ed. New York: Guilford Press.

Cheng, Lucie. 2002. "Transnational Labor, Citizenship, and the Taiwan State." In *East Asian Law: Universal Norms and Local Cultures*, Arthur Rosett, Lucie Cheng, and Margaret Y. K. Woo, eds. New York: Routledge Curzon, 85–105.

Choi, Woogill. 2006. "Ethnic Koreans from China: Korean Dreams, Adaptation, and New Identities." Paper presented at a conference on Korean ethnic return migration, University of Auckland, New Zealand, November 27–28.

Christou, Anastasia. 2006. "Deciphering Diaspora: Translating Transnationalism—Family Dynamics, Identity Constructions, and the Legacy of 'Home' in Second-Generation Greek-American Return Migration." *Ethnic and Racial Studies* 29(6):1040–1056.

Cohen, Robin. 1997. *Global Diasporas: An Introduction.* Seattle: University of Washington Press.

Cook-Martín, David. 2005. "The Long Way Home or Back Door to the EU? Argentine Claims of Ancestral Nationalities." Paper presented at the conference "Diasporic Homecomings: Ethnic Return Migrants in Comparative Perspective," Center for Comparative Immigration Studies, University of California at San Diego, May 20–21.

Cornelius, Wayne A. 2004. "Spain: The Uneasy Transition from Labor Exporter to Labor Importer." In *Controlling Immigration: A Global Perspective*, 2nd ed., Wayne Cornelius, Takeyuki Tsuda, Philip Martin, and James Hollifield, eds. Stanford, CA: Stanford University Press, 387–429.

de Tinguy, Anne. 2003. "Ethnic Migrations of the 1990s from and to the Successor States of the Former Soviet Union: 'Repatriation' or Privileged Migration?" In *Diasporas and Ethnic Migrants: Germany, Israel, and Post-Soviet Successor States in Comparative Perspective*, Rainer Münz and Rainer Ohliger, eds. London: Frank Cass, 112–127.

Espiritu, Yen Le. 2003. *Home Bound: Filipino American Lives Across Cultures, Communities, and Countries.* Berkeley: University of California Press.

Fawcett, James T. 1989. "Networks, Linkages, and Migration Systems." *International Migration Review* 23(3):672–680.

Fox, Jon E. 2003. "National Identities on the Move: Transylvanian Hungarian Labor Migrants in Hungary." *Journal of Ethnic and Migration Studies* 29(3):449–466.

Glick Schiller, Nina. 1997. "The Situation of Transnational Studies." *Identities: Global Studies in Culture and Power* 4(2):155–166.

Grossutti, Javier. n.d. "From Argentina to Friuli (1989–1994): A Case of Return Migration?" Unpublished English translation of "De Argentina al Friuli, Italia (1989–1994): Un caso de migración de retorno?" *Estudios Migratorios Latinoamericanos* 19(56):97–122 (2005).

Guarnizo, Luis Eduardo. 1997. "The Emergence of a Transnational Social Formation and the Mirage of Return Migration Among Dominican Transmigrants." *Identities: Global Studies in Culture and Power* 4(2):281–322.

Guarnizo, Luis Eduardo, and Michael Peter Smith. 1998. "The Locations of Transnationalism." In *Transnationalism from Below*, Michael Peter Smith and Luis Eduardo Guarnizo, eds. New Brunswick, NJ: Transaction, 3–34.

Gupta, Akhil, and James Ferguson. 1992. "Beyond 'Culture': Space, Identity, and the Politics of Difference." *Cultural Anthropology* 7(1):6–23.

Hedberg, Charlotta, and Kaisa Kepsu. 2003. "Migration as a Cultural Expression? The Case of the Finland-Swedish Minority's Migration to Sweden." *Geography Annals* 85B(2):67–84.

———. 2008. "Identity in Motion: The Process of Finland-Swedish Migration to Sweden." *National Identities* 10(1):95–118.

Iglicka, Krystyna. 1998. "Are They Fellow Countrymen or Not? The Migration of Ethnic Poles from Kazakhstan to Poland." *International Migration Review* 32(4):995–1014.

Joppke, Christian. 2005. *Selecting by Origin: Ethnic Migration in the Liberal State.* Cambridge, MA: Harvard University Press.

Kibria, Nazli. 2002a. *Becoming Asian American: Second-Generation Chinese and Korean American Identities.* Baltimore: Johns Hopkins University Press.

———. 2002b. "Of Blood, Belonging, and Homeland Trips: Transnationalism and Identity Among Second-Generation Chinese and Korean Americans." In *The Changing Face of Home: The Transnational Lives of the Second Generation,* Peggy Levitt and Mary C. Waters, eds. New York: Russell Sage, 295–311.

Kovrig, Bennett. 1994. "Hungarian Minorities in East-Central Europe: To Create Harmony in an Ethnic Mosaic." *Bulletin of the Atlantic Council of the United States* 5(4):3.

Kritz, Mary, and Hania Zlotnik. 1992. "Global Interactions: Migration Systems, Processes, and Policies." In *International Migration Systems: A Global Approach,* Mary M. Kritz, Lin Lean Lim, and Hania Zlotnik, eds. New York: Oxford University Press, 1–16.

Kulu, Hill. 1998. "Ethnic Return Migration: An Estonian Case." *International Migration* 36(3):313–336.

Kweon, Sug-In. 2006. "Returning Ethnic Koreans from Japan in Korea: Experiences and Identities." Paper presented at a conference on Korean ethnic return migration, University of Auckland, New Zealand, November 27–28.

Levitt, Peggy. 2001. *The Transnational Villagers.* Berkeley: University of California Press.

Levitt, Peggy, and Mary C. Waters, eds. 2002. *The Changing Face of Home: The Transnational Lives of the Second Generation.* New York: Russell Sage.

Lim, Timothy. 2006. "NGOs, Transnational Migrants, and the Promotion of Rights in South Korea." In *Local Citizenship in Recent Countries of Immigration: Japan in Comparative Perspective,* Takeyuki Tsuda, ed. Lanham, MD: Lexington Books, 235–269.

Louie, Andrea. 2001. "Crafting Places Through Mobility: Chinese American 'Roots-Searching' in China." *Identities* 8(3):343–379.

———. 2002. "Creating Histories for the Present: Second-Generation (Re)definitions of Chinese American Culture." In *The Changing Face of Home: The Transnational Lives of the Second Generation,* Peggy Levitt and Mary C. Waters, eds. New York: Russell Sage, 312–340.

————. 2003. "When You Are Related to the 'Other': (Re)locating the Chinese Home-land in Asian American Politics Through Cultural Tourism." *Positions: East Asia Cultures Critique* 11(3):735–763.

Maeyama, Takashi. 1996. *Esunishitei to Burajiru Nikkeijin* [Ethnicity and Brazilian *nik-keijin*]. Tokyo: Ochanomizu Shobo.

Margolis, Maxine L. 1994. *Little Brazil: An Ethnography of Brazilian Immigrants in New York City.* Princeton, NJ: Princeton University Press.

Massey, Douglas S., Joaquín Arango, Graeme Hugo, Ali Kouaouci, Adela Pellegrino, and J. Edward Taylor. 1998. *Worlds in Motion: Understanding International Migration at the End of the Millennium.* Oxford: Clarendon Press.

Moreira da Rocha, Cristina. 1999. "Identity and Tea Ceremony in Brazil." *Japanese Stud-ies* 19(3):287–295.

Nojima, Toshihiko. 1989. "Susumetai Nikkeijin no Tokubetsu Ukeire" [Proposal for the special admission of the *nikkeijin*]. *Gekkan Jiyu Minsu* (November):92–99.

Parreñas, Rhacel Salazar. 2001. *Servants of Globalization: Women, Migration, and Domes-tic Work.* Stanford, CA: Stanford University Press.

Pilkington, Hilary. 1998. *Migration, Displacement, and Identity in Post-Soviet Russia.* London: Routledge.

Portes, Alejandro. 1999. "Conclusion: Toward a New World—The Origins and Effects of Transnational Activities." *Ethnic and Racial Studies* 22(2):463–477.

Reichl, Christopher A. 1995. "Stages in the Historical Process of Ethnicity: The Japanese in Brazil, 1908–1988." *Ethnohistory* 42(1):31–62.

Remennick, Larissa I. 1998. "Identity Quest Among Russian Jews of the 1990s: Before and After Emigration." In *Jewish Survival: The Identity Problem at the Close of the Twentieth Century,* Ernest Krausz and Gitta Tulea, eds. New Brunswick, NJ: Trans-action, 241–258.

————. 2003. "A Case Study in Transnationalism: Russian Jewish Immigrants in Isra-el of the 1990s." In *Diasporas and Ethnic Migrants: Germany, Israel, and Post-Soviet Successor States in Comparative Perspective,* Rainer Münz and Rainer Ohliger, eds. London: Frank Cass, 370–384.

————. 2007. *Russian Jews on Three Continents: Identity, Integration, and Conflict.* New Brunswick, NJ: Transaction.

Safran, William. 1991. "Diasporas in Modern Societies: Myths of Homeland and Re-turn." *Diaspora: A Journal of Transnational Studies* 1(1):83–99.

Schein, Louisa. 1998. "Forged Transnationality and Oppositional Cosmopolitanism." In *Transnationalism from Below,* Michael P. Smith and Luis Guarnizo, eds. New Bruns-wick, NJ: Transaction, 291–313.

Smith, Robert C. 2003. "Diasporic Memberships in Historical Perspective: Compara-tive Insights from the Mexican, Italian, and Polish Cases." *International Migration Review* 37(3):724–759.

———. 2006. *Mexican New York: Transnational Lives of New Immigrants*. Berkeley: University of California Press.

Tölölyan, Khachig. 1996. "Rethinking Diaspora(s): Stateless Power in the Transnational Moment." *Diaspora: A Journal of Transnational Studies* 5(1):3–36.

Tsuda, Takeyuki. 1999. "The Motivation to Migrate: The Ethnic and Sociocultural Constitution of the Japanese Brazilian Return Migration System." *Economic Development and Cultural Change* 48(1):1–31.

———. 2001. "When Identities Become Modern: Japanese Immigrants in Brazil and the Global Contextualization of Identity." *Ethnic and Racial Studies* 24(3):412–432.

———. 2003. *Strangers in the Ethnic Homeland: Japanese Brazilian Return Migration in Transnational Perspective*. New York: Columbia University Press.

Van Hear, Nicholas. 1998. *New Diasporas: The Mass Exodus, Dispersal, and Regrouping of Migrant Communities*. Seattle: University of Washington Press.

Viladrich, Anahí. n.d. "Going Back Home? Argentine Return Migrants in Transnational Perspective." Paper presented at the conference "Diasporic Homecomings: Ethnic Return Migrants in Comparative Perspective," Center for Comparative Immigration Studies, University of California, San Diego, May 20–21, 2005.

Vishnevsky, Anatoly. 2003. "The Dissolution of the Soviet Union and Post-Soviet Ethnic Migration: The Return of Diasporas?" In *Diasporas and Ethnic Migrants: Germany, Israel, and Post-Soviet Successor States in Comparative Perspective*, Rainer Münz and Rainer Ohliger, eds. London: Frank Cass, 155–172.

von Koppenfels, Amanda Klekowski. 2003. "Who Organizes? The Political Opportunity Structure of Co-Ethnic Migrant Mobilization." In *Diasporas and Ethnic Migrants: Germany, Israel, and Post-Soviet Successor States in Comparative Perspective*, Rainer Münz and Rainer Ohliger, eds. London: Frank Cass, 305–323.

Yang, Young-Kyun. 2006. "The Return Migration of Korean Chinese (*Joseonjok*) from a Comparative Perspective." Paper presented at a conference on Korean ethnic return migration, University of Auckland, New Zealand, November 27–28.

Defining Nations in Asia and Europe

A Comparative Analysis of Ethnic Return Migration Policy

John Skrentny, Stephanie Chan, Jon E. Fox, and Denis Kim

IN RECENT YEARS research on immigration and citizenship policy in Europe and Asia has proliferated. Scholars rarely analyze both regions together, although there are exceptions (e.g., Massey et al. 1998; Skeldon 1997). We argue that comparative analyses of East Asia and Europe can shed new light on both regions. Our focus here is on an important aspect of immigration and citizenship policy: whether or not states discriminate between foreigners on the basis of ancestry or ethnicity. More specifically, we examine whether and how state policies in the two regions give preference to co-ethnics who are citizens of other states, including preferences in ethnic return migration and naturalization. Comparing these two regions shows that we must consider other ethnic preferences that are linked to ethnic return migration, such as preferences for co-ethnic investors, in order to fully understand state relationships with co-ethnics abroad.

Studying ethnic preference policy in Asia and Europe can yield significant contributions. First, the comparison can yield insights into the global status of the right to nondiscrimination, a human right enshrined in the Universal Declaration of Human Rights (1948) and the International Convention on the Elimination of All Forms of Racial Discrimination (1965). Although preferences for co-ethnics may be less reprehensible than exclusion of specific groups (Joppke 2005), they nevertheless treat group ethnic belonging or blood ties as real and important and violate the universalism and equal opportunity that are hallmarks of classical liberalism and human rights. The trend away from discrimination is especially apparent in the United States. The U.S. state, facing international criticism, moved away from a thoroughly discriminatory policy regime in immigration and other policies in the latter half of the twentieth century (Skrentny 2002). Have Asia and Europe followed suit?

Second, a regionally comparative approach can reveal whether policy designs and rationales are globally prevalent or whether states exhibit regional patterns. Third, the topic is important for studies of comparative nationalism. In deciding how to treat co-ethnic nonnationals, states are in effect defining the boundaries of the nation. The making of immigration and other policy regarding foreigners forces policymakers to consider billions of people and to decide whether all foreigners are essentially the same or whether their blood or ancestry matters. Policymakers are defining the boundaries of "us" and "them." Following Brubaker (1994), we argue that examining foreign ethnic preference policy is examining a category of practice of nationhood. Fourth, the explicit East-West regional comparison can yield insights for studies of globalization, regionalism, and conflict. If ethnic preference policies are globally prevalent, are there global standards for structure or method? Does East Asia represent an alternative to the West, an alternative vision of modernity (Tu 2000), and if there are regional variations, do they suggest possible conflict in the future (Huntington 1996)?

In this chapter we argue that comparative analysis shows both significant similarities and differences between the two regions. Specifically, both Western and Eastern European and East Asian states practice policies of preference for co-ethnic foreigners, although these policies are less common and waning in Western Europe, and various policy practices are found in both regions. At the same time, the two regions exhibit significant differences. Most important, the rationale for the policies varies across regions, and because of this, the policies look quite different, retaining a more instrumental cast in Asia and a more expressive cast in Europe (Lee 2004). Joppke, in his important 2005 study, describes policies in Europe and argues that there are three main justifications for ethnic preference: the easier assimilation of co-ethnics, protection for them against foreign persecution, and the expression of historical-cultural community. The first of these rationales is prominent in Asia, but the others are not, and in Asia we find a different justification. In Asia ethnic return policy is geared toward economic development. Korea and Japan rely on co-ethnics for the so-called 3D jobs (dirty, dangerous, and difficult), and Taiwan, Korea, and China have enacted policies to encourage investment from overseas co-ethnics, a policy pursued nowhere in Europe. Taiwan and Korea have special policies to encourage return migration of highly skilled co-ethnics, and Taiwan has a naturalization preference for highly skilled co-ethnics. Several Southeast Asian states also target skilled co-ethnics for return. No European states target their preferences in this way. In short, the direction of obligation is almost reversed in Asia. Rather than the state existing to help co-ethnics abroad, the co-ethnics abroad have a role to play to strengthen the state.

Case Selection and the Comparability of East Asian and European Immigration Policies

Our Asian cases center on Japan, South Korea, Taiwan, and China. These are the four largest economies in East Asia, and the first three are recent immigrant-receiving states. We include China because of its growing economic and political significance in the region and the world, its massive impact on global migration, and the large population of ethnic Chinese who have lived overseas for generations. Although Taiwan's status as an independent state remains in dispute, we include a brief discussion of Taiwan because it has experienced growth similar to Korea's, is now an immigrant-receiving state, and retains a complex relationship with China.

For Europe we focus our attention on several states, beginning with Germany, which is perhaps the best-known case of state preference for ethnic return migrants. We examine states that, like our Asian cases, have become immigrant receivers in the past few decades and are known to have large populations of co-ethnics abroad: Spain and Italy. Finally, we devote attention to states in Eastern Europe in which co-ethnic considerations in immigration or citizenship law are especially prominent.[1]

There are, of course, some considerations that justify exclusive focus on one region, but East Asian and European immigration policies are otherwise socially and politically comparable. First, both regions are home to large numbers of immigrants. It is true that foreigners make up considerably smaller percentages of the populations of Japan, Taiwan, Korea, and China than most states in Europe. It is not the case, however, that they are not significant migrant-receiving states. Japan, for example, was home to almost 2 million foreigners in 2005.[2] It is also the case that large numbers of migrants are not necessary for a state to have or for researchers to study immigration *policy*. Indeed, states may use ethnic preference to increase migration. As we will show, the China case is revealing even if the country does not receive large numbers of migrants.

Second, East Asia and Europe are comparable politically. The "liberal states" that have preoccupied scholars of immigration in Europe (e.g., Hollifield 1992; Joppke 1998) have their counterparts in Asia. By the definitions used in these works (Hollifield emphasizes legally protected rights and Joppke emphasizes independent courts in their respective definitions of a liberal state), three of our Asian states qualify as liberal states. Asian democracies now provide regular free elections, universal suffrage, free expression, and protection against arbitrary state actions, although some still show problematic characteristics, such as the tendency toward one-party rule (Pempel 1999). Japan, South Korea, and Taiwan have constitutional courts that have acted to overturn legislation, and they have done so at times on the basis of individual rights (Ginsburg 2003). Another distinction might be the workings of democratic politics, especially the client politics that may drive immigration policy (Freeman 1995). Yet South Korea has a dynamic democracy, notable for electing a former dissident to the presidency, and Japan's democracy is comparable to that in Western states (Richardson 1997). These states along with Taiwan (Hsiao 1992) have plentiful interest-group activity. We argue that it is also the case that understanding policy in nondemocratic states such as China can yield insights into possible regional patterns in Asian democracies.

The Asian Cases

Japan

Japan has a large number of emigrants living across the globe, but the most significant to contemporary Japan are those in South America. Japanese emigration to Brazil began in 1908 and continued, interrupted by the world wars, until the 1950s. Japan began to receive large numbers of ethnically Japanese return migrants from this region in 1989. In Japanese they are called *nikkeijin*. Their numbers increased rapidly from 8,450 in 1988 to 76,150 in 1990 (Shimada 1994). By 1993 there were about 200,000 return migrants in Japan. Data from the Japanese government show that of the 2 million legal foreigners living in Japan, 360,000 are from Brazil and Peru.[3] The vast majority of these are *nikkeijin* (for a discussion, see Tsuda and Cornelius 2004). Most are second and third generation and are consequently culturally Latin American, with limited Japanese speaking ability (Tsuda 2003). Although in Latin America the *nikkeijin* were usually educated white-collar workers, in Japan they almost all do blue-collar work, especially in manufacturing, which remains attractive because of wage differentials with their home countries (Tsuda and Cornelius 2004).

Preferential policy regarding *nikkeijin* began in 1990. Before then, Japan ex-cluded all unskilled immigrant labor, including *nikkeijin*, who were allowed into the country on a "visiting visa." It was assumed that they would be visit-ing relatives, although many in fact worked illegally (Mori 1997). The 1990 Revised Immigration Law stated that anyone with Japanese ancestry, with no geographic distinctions but up to the third generation, had unrestricted access to the Japanese labor market. Japanese ancestry was determined through links to a family registry system common in Asia. The Justice Ministry began to issue three-year visas that were renewable (Yamanaka 1993). As suggested, the law led to an immediate influx of *nikkeijin*, and employers began replacing other migrant workers with these ethnic Japanese (Yamanaka 2004). There are no preferential avenues to citizenship. There are no language or cultural compe-tence tests. Neither are there any national social integration policies designed to ease adjustment or help to settle *nikkeijin*.

The rationale for the policy is somewhat obscure, but clearly it is serving economic interests. Official statements maintain a thin illusion that other goals are at stake. Officially, the policy is designed to provide *nikkeijin* with opportu-nities to travel, meet relatives, and learn Japanese language and culture (Tsuda and Cornelius 2004). Elsewhere, however, Yamanaka (1993) reports that the policy's purpose is to supply cheap labor to small and medium-size companies in Japan and that official documents from 1989 emphasize concerns with the maintenance of ethnic homogeneity. Policymakers desired *nikkeijin* to alleviate the labor shortage without disrupting Japan's cherished ethnic homogeneity. They assumed, according to documents, that *nikkeijin* "would be able to assimi-late into Japanese society regardless of nationality" (quoted in Yamanaka 1993: 9). Another scholar called the policy "a stopgap attempt to preserve ethnic ho-mogeneity by substituting legal ethnic Japanese for illegal non-Japanese Asians" (Oka 1994: 42). Through co-ethnic guest workers, then, Japan could continue economic development with minimal social disruption. Policymakers ignored the fact that *nikkeijin* were in fact different culturally (Tsuzuki 2000). In this, the policy continued a Japanese tendency to conflate Japanese ethnicity or race with Japanese culture and a preference for those with Japanese blood, regardless of origins, over other foreigners (Lie 2001). Although the Ministry of Labor has attempted to prevent exploitation of *nikkeijin* (such as wage deductions and trafficking; Herbert 1996), no national social integration policies have been set to aid or settle this population. Any government accommodation is organized at the local level (Tsuda and Cornelius 2004).

Korea

Korea's ethnic preference policy is more complex than Japan's, although it similarly recognizes blood bonds and gives preferences to ethnic Koreans unavailable to other foreigners. The primary overseas Korean communities include the approximately 2 million *Joseonjok*, or ethnic Koreans living in China, and a smaller group, the *Goryeoin*, who number about 800,000 and are more scattered throughout Russia, Kazakhstan, and Uzbekistan.

Ethnic Koreans, especially *Joseonjok*, began to return to South Korea in the late 1980s; by 1991 there were more than 18,000 *Joseonjok* out of a total foreign population of 45,000. In 2006, Korea's foreign population was about 537,000, of which 170,000 were *Joseonjok*. The number of *Goryeoin* is far smaller. In addition, in 2005 there were 18,000 Korean Americans living and working in South Korea, mostly as professionals.[4]

The Korean government has always treated *Joseonjok* differently from other foreigners. After an initial period of indecision, Korea avoided giving *Joseonjok* free access to the labor market, comparable to what the *nikkeijin* enjoy in Japan. In addition, Korea separated *Joseonjok* from ethnic Koreans in the West. As described by Seol and Skrentny (2004), in 1991 policymakers created provisions for *Joseonjok* to participate in the new Industrial Technical Training Program, which was designed (despite its name) to provide cheap foreign labor to small and medium-size businesses. The main difference between Korea and Japan for purposes of this study is that Japan imported *nikkeijin* through a special visa program only for that group, whereas Korea imported *Joseonjok* within the confines of a larger labor importation program. Policymakers gave *Joseonjok* the largest quota in the program, separate from other Chinese workers, and *Joseonjok* were originally paid higher wages. They remain the largest group of foreigners in the program and the largest group among undocumented workers (Seol and Skrentny 2004).

In 2002 policymakers created another program for importing *Joseonjok* labor. In the Employment Management Program for Overseas Ethnic Koreans (*Chuieop Gwanri Jedo*), overseas Koreans older than 40 and with family (cousins or closer relatives) in Korea would receive special two-year visas to work in the labor-starved service industry, especially restaurants, cleaning companies, and nursing facilities (not as nurses but as "caregivers"); construction was added later. Employers can now hire up to 10 overseas Koreans, provided that they show they cannot find workers domestically.[5] Although nominally open to any overseas ethnic Korean, the program was clearly targeted to the relatively disadvantaged *Joseonjok* and *Goryeoin*.

Another policy giving preference to foreign co-ethnics is the 1999 Law of Entry and Status of *Chaeoe dongpo* (or co-ethnic or overseas brethren), or the Overseas Koreans Act. The law entitles *Chaeoe dongpo* to register as "domestic residents" when they want to stay longer than 30 days. This status gives rights almost equal to those of Korean citizens in areas such as banking, ownership of estate properties, medical insurance, and pensions.[6]

The law defines *Chaeoe dongpo* as "Korean citizens who live abroad in order to get the citizenship of the resident country and overseas Koreans who had South Korean citizenship in the past and their descendants." This definition means that among overseas Koreans only those who left Korea after the establishment of the South Korean government in 1948 were eligible to become *Chaeoe dongpo*. It therefore includes primarily Korean Americans and Korean Canadians and excludes *Joseonjok* and *Goryeoin* as well as Koreans in Japan. The law requires only citizenship documents to prove links to the Korean state; there are no cultural or language tests. However, the law prohibits *Chaeoe dongpo* from unskilled manual work, creating another barrier to an influx of *Joseonjok*.

In fact, the Ministry of Justice originally intended the category of *Chaeoe dongpo* to apply to all overseas Koreans, but this plan faced opposition from outside and inside the Korean state. First, both Chinese and Russian governments expressed their concerns that *Joseonjok* and *Goryeoin* are their citizens and subject to their sovereignty. Second, some policymakers feared economic and social problems that a mass influx of unskilled *Joseonjok* would cause. Third, there was a national security concern that North Korea might use the allowance "as a route for infiltration, thereby causing immediate security threats."[7] The *Chaeoe dongpo* law thus excluded the *Joseonjok*. Legal challenges have since officially opened the law to *Joseonjok*, *Goryeoin*, and Koreans in Japan, but because the law retains its prohibitions on unskilled labor, it offers few opportunities for ethnic Koreans in East Asia to come to Korea.

A final Korean policy regarding co-ethnics abroad deals with North Koreans. In fact, the South Korean constitution defines North Koreans as part of its own polity; technically, they are not foreigners at all (Lee 2003). Indeed, the only refugees that Korea accepts are those from North Korea, and because of their lack of familiarity with a capitalist economy, they are a burden on the state, requiring extensive settlement packages and adjustment. However, although their number is growing, it is still very small (only about 10,000), and South Korea does not encourage their movement (Seol and Skrentny 2004).

The rationale for co-ethnic preference in Korean policy is similar to that of Japan: providing needed labor or skills for economic development with minimal disruption of Korean society and the Korean labor market. To be sure, as in Japan, there is a thin veil of a helping or protection rationale to these policies, but it is important to note that, as in Japan, these policies all bring economic benefits and almost no cost. Thus the trainee program is ostensibly for transferring skills to foreign workers, but that rarely happens. A key difference with Japan is that the *Joseonjok* supply not only an ethnically identical workforce, but thanks to China's policy of granting Koreans their own semi-autonomous region, *Joseonjok* all speak Korean and to a great extent share Korean culture (Min 1992). According to Timothy Lim, South Korea officials preferred *Joseonjok* trainees because they would "pose less of a threat to South Korea's tight-knit, homogenous society" (Lim 2002: 19). The service job visa for *Joseonjok* also is justified as a form of economic aid to this group (allowing them opportunities to work in a relatively high-wage economy), but Korea obviously benefits economically at no cost. In addition, the Overseas Koreans Act states a nominal "helping" goal by explaining that one of the purposes of the act is to aid ethnic Koreans' adjustment to their countries of residence, and in fact Korean Americans lobbied for it (Park and Chang 2004).[8] However, this law, conceived during the economic crisis of 1997–1998, is obviously geared toward boosting Korea's economic development, and this is stated explicitly in several places in the law itself. In the opinion striking down the act's exclusion of *Joseonjok*, the Korean Constitutional Court stated that the law's purpose was "to promote globalization of the Korean society by encouraging more active participation of ethnic Koreans living abroad in all spheres of the Korean society" and that "the Act aims to encourage investment in Korea by simplifying regulations" on business dealings.[9] The limitation of the law to skilled workers indicates its economic rationale.

China

Including China at first may seem odd because it is not a liberal state and not normally understood as a country of immigration. China *does* have a substantial number of foreigners, though. The foreign population in China was 595,658 in 2005, but this figure is minute compared to the overall population size of 1.316 billion.[10] China's official figure of 30 million "returned overseas Chinese" is much larger, but this number includes a range of ethnic Chinese, including those of interest here (ethnic Chinese of foreign nationality) and any

Chinese nationals who lived for a time abroad, including students. In 2000, the China State Statistics Bureau counted an additional 34 million ethnic Chinese who remain abroad.[11] About 5 percent of overseas Chinese are Chinese citizens (Choe 2003). This figure includes millions of people of the Chinese diaspora who left to labor or set up shop in the West, other parts of Asia, and elsewhere decades or centuries ago and who later became successful entrepreneurs in a variety of businesses (Wang 1994). It is these skilled and/or wealthy Chinese abroad who entice China's policymakers.

The story here is one of ambiguity, specifically regarding the targets of policy. Many of China's policies on overseas Chinese technically seek to gain the return and investments of ethnic Chinese who are still nationals. At the same time, official pronouncements (and newspaper articles, which amount to official pronouncements because the news media are state controlled) typically include nonnationals in their calls to build China. The situation in China is also complex because, unlike the norm in most of the world, foreigners often have *more* privileges than Chinese citizens do. For that reason, a policy that treats a foreigner, ethnic Chinese or not, as a citizen in some circumstances might be more limiting than a policy that treats the foreigner as foreign.

China has a long history and a more complex patchwork of ethnic preference laws than other states in this study. Chinese leaders have long considered Chinese abroad to be sojourners who retain ties and loyalty to China, part of a belief that "once a Chinese always a Chinese" (Cheng 2003; Cheng and Katz 1998). The Chinese state's efforts to facilitate remittances from overseas Chinese led to the establishment of the Overseas Chinese Affairs Commission (OCAC) under the State Council in October 1949 (Thuno 2001). The Cultural Revolution in 1966 brought a drastic change, as the state turned antagonistic and suspicious toward this population and their family members who remained in China, subjecting them to persecution for their capitalist ties (Cheng and Katz 1998). The period was repressive but short-lived, and policymakers have been building new institutions and policies to take advantage of overseas Chinese ever since.

By 1974, the state reestablished the OCAC. In 1977, Deng Xiaoping proclaimed that "overseas Chinese affairs" needed to be incorporated into the government agenda and that the persecution policies were officially abolished. That year also saw the creation of a nongovernmental bureaucracy parallel to the OCAC, technically a reestablishment of a preexisting body called the All China Federation of Returned Overseas Chinese (Thuno 2001). In 1983, China created the Overseas Chinese Affairs Committee in the National People's Congress to keep this issue in play (Cheng and Katz 1998). All these offices were designed to encourage overseas Chinese to aid China's development (Bolt 2000).

In 1990 China passed the Law of the People's Republic of China on the Protection of the Rights and Interests of the Returned Overseas Chinese and the Relatives of Overseas Chinese Who Remain in the Homeland (referred to hereafter as the Protection Law), its first major law aimed at enticing those abroad to return. This law was primarily geared to reconciling with those who were formerly persecuted in China during the Cultural Revolution and to assuring overseas Chinese nationals who returned that they would be treated equally. The law's provisions include recognition of their full Chinese citizenship, protection from the types of injustices they experienced during the Cultural Revolution, and some preferential investment and educational opportunities. The Protection Law represented both the culmination of more piecemeal efforts to reconcile relationships with *all* Chinese migrants and a growing effort to appeal specifically to the highly skilled and wealthy migrants. In 1989, as evidenced by internal documents from State Council meetings, the Chinese government decided to begin focusing on highly skilled, professional, and wealthy overseas Chinese, including the new wave of migrants who left after 1978, when the strict controls on emigration under Mao were lifted. In its original and revised form, the Protection Law appeared on paper to apply only to Chinese nationals, part of an increasingly common struggle of developing nations to entice the return of their most skilled brethren (DeVoretz and Zhang 2004). But internal documents reveal increasing attention to noncitizen ethnic Chinese, and noncitizens have been able to take advantage (Bolt 2000; Thuno 2001).

Policymakers, especially in provinces and other subnational units, have increasingly appealed to both Chinese nationals and ethnic Chinese noncitizens since the 1980s. Preferences for co-ethnic foreign Chinese are most apparent in policies regarding regional economic development. As early as 1981, an official of the Fujian Provincial Chinese Communist Party explained to *Wenweipo*, a Hong Kong newspaper, that

> we will offer favorable terms to all foreign investors in Fujian and the terms for overseas Chinese investors will be even more favorable. . . . Foreign investors might not be willing to invest in some projects and we will not invite them to either. But no such restriction will be placed upon overseas Chinese investors, because we treat them as the people of the mainland and regard them as our compatriots. They may put forth any investment plan they wish. (Bolt 2000:60)

In 1984 the Provisional Measures of Guangzhou Municipality on Preferential Treatment for Overseas Chinese and Hong Kong and Macao Investors
stated that, among other benefits, "land use fees for enterprises invested in by
an Overseas Chinese, Hong Kong and Macao compatriot in Guangzhou Municipality shall be levied at the discounted rate of 80%" and a maximum of
two investor's friends or relatives could change their household registration
status (a system limiting geographic movement in China) from rural to urban
or township status.[12] In 1990, the same year that the Protection Law was enacted, the national state pursued regional development with the Provisions of the
State Council Concerning the Encouragement of Investments by Overseas Chinese and Compatriots from Hong Kong and Macao (or the "Overseas Chinese
Investment Provisions"). It promoted the economic development of inland
areas to catch up with coastal areas, previously opened up to foreign investment. The law created a national framework for inland governments to devise
plans to give preferential treatment to overseas Chinese investors. Competition
for foreign investment has even spurred the creation of city-level preferential
policies (Gang 2002). The encouragement of overseas Chinese to return—or to
invest—is so entrenched at the local level that nearly every level of government,
down to the township level, now has an Overseas Chinese Affairs Office.

Like Japan and Korea, China does not use citizenship as a prize to encourage return or investment and similarly uses an in-between status of privileged
foreigners. In 2004, to attract highly skilled foreigners, China initiated a "green
card" program to give the benefits of citizenship. In the press overseas Chinese
are specifically mentioned as potential beneficiaries of this program, which
would ease entry and exit and provide residence options, medical insurance,
and tax breaks.[13]

In official propaganda from the mid-1980s, there was encouragement for
mainland Chinese citizens to view foreign Chinese as part of the same nation or community and for all to loyally support China (Tu 1994). Overseas
Chinese would be a bridge to the mainland's prosperity (Ong 1999). Since
this time, government statements and events have promoted the dragon as
a primal ancestor and symbol of all Chinese and have used a song about the
dragon at government events. The government has also promoted Huang Di,
or the Yellow Emperor, as a first ancestor for all Chinese, continuing a long
history of the use of this image for nationalist purposes. Deng Xiaoping would
appeal to the Yellow Emperor when pressing for unity with Taiwan, and Chinese publications in 1986 described a Chinese American astronaut as "the first

descendant of the Yellow Emperor to travel in space." This view posits a global population of Chinese, linked by blood to the Yellow Emperor and the Chinese state (Sautman 1997: 84).

Thus, although the "green card" program and other policies are officially open to any skilled foreigner, the state encourages (and likely gives special preferences not written into the policy to) ethnic Chinese (Choe 2003). And these efforts appear to have had an impact. China's official news agency reported that for 1989 overseas Chinese (especially in Malaysia, the Philippines, Singapore, and Thailand) and Chinese in Hong Kong, Macao, and Taiwan invested $30 billion, about 70 percent of total foreign investment. The percentage was about the same 10 years later (Bolt 2000).

The rationale for these ethnic preference policies, as should be clear, is the economic development of China. Although China's 1990 Protection Law was officially aimed at any Chinese and thus promised equal (or better) treatment to any returning Chinese, most of its provisions and later amendments were meant for skilled and wealthy Chinese. The Chinese state even sought to manage this economic development, directing it to the poorest regions in the country. There is some evidence that overseas Chinese have pushed for these policies, and no doubt some of them, especially in Indonesia, see opportunities in the mainland as a kind of protection from persecution abroad. China also instituted some programs to resettle Chinese refugees from persecution in Southeast Asia (Cheng and Katz 1998). But it is also the case that China's permanent and most extensive policies are in its direct economic interest and offer mainly economic pluses with little in the way of costs, unlike some ethnic preference policies in Europe (see later discussion).

There are two political or potential economic minuses of China's policies. First, some non-Chinese foreigners have complained that the ethnic preferences are discriminatory and violate international nondiscrimination conventions. These complaints have had increasing power since China joined the World Trade Organization; international law and norms have relevance in China that they lacked previously. State officials and the news media regularly comment to this effect (Bolt 2000; Choe 2003).

Second, as in some European cases, China has incurred some expense in establishing educational programs for foreign or overseas co-ethnics. These efforts included 20 sets of teaching materials for use in 78 countries, 150 teachers sent to teach in 20 countries, the training of several thousand other teachers, and Chinese language summer camps for hundreds of thousands of second-

and third-generation ethnic Chinese (Thuno 2001). The Chinese state has also organized summer youth festivals designed to encourage attachment of overseas Chinese descendants, understood in racial and not political terms, and to further Chinese nationalism within the diaspora and economic development of China (Louie 2001). Arguably, however, these efforts are not seen as a good thing in their own right but are instrumental and geared to encouraging an attitude of loyalty and devotion to China's development but with a longer timeframe (Choe 2003).

Taiwan

The case of the Republic of China, or Taiwan, reinforces points and patterns made for the other Asian cases. As with the others, Taiwan's ethnic preferences are designed for economic development and come at little or no cost to the state.

Like Korea and Germany (see later discussion), Taiwan has a citizenship law that defines as nationals those living under the competing state (in this case, China). According to Taiwan's constitution, the Chinese are not foreign. But unlike Korea and Germany, Taiwan does not allow their co-ethnic and constitutionally co-national mainland Chinese to come to Taiwan as unskilled workers, with the Executive Yuan citing "population pressure, national security and social stability" as reasons (Cheng 2003: 92). This is the case even though Taiwan *does* accept low-skilled workers for the 3D jobs as part of a work permit program. In 2004 Taiwan had about 280,000 immigrant low-skilled workers in a population of 23 million (Seol 2005). The largest sending states are Thailand, the Philippines, and Indonesia, but Taiwan also has official agreements with other states, including Vietnam, Malaysia, and Mongolia. Policymakers selected these states with an interest in minimizing social problems, using as criteria the quality of the workers, crime rate, health and hygiene, and the state's interest (Seol et al. 2004).

However, Taiwan has ethnic policy preferences for highly skilled immigrant Chinese. Taiwan competes with China to attract the most skilled overseas Chinese. Unlike the other Asian states (and similar to a number of European countries), its policy to do this is a nationality law that allows dual citizenship. To avoid costly social problems and to target these efforts to the economic sectors most in need, however, the law allows dual nationality only for certain *skilled* occupations (Cheng 2003).

Nonetheless, Taiwan mostly fits the pattern of the other Asian states. It practices preferences for co-ethnics abroad, even if noncitizens, and does so for economic gain. Its exclusion of ethnic Chinese low-skilled workers, even while it imports unskilled workers from other countries, would seem to break the pattern. However, it is noteworthy that Taiwan excludes co-ethnic workers in the 3D jobs for the same reason that Japan and Korea prefer them: concerns for social order. What is different about Taiwan appears to be less its political culture and policy repertoire and more its special circumstances. That is, only Taiwan has a population base of co-ethnics abroad that dwarfs its own population. Indeed, there are more unskilled workers—unemployed and seeking work—in China than there are Taiwanese in Taiwan. Simply put, a policy of visas for mainland Chinese similar to what Japan offers *nikkeijin* would overwhelm the island.

Preference for Co-Ethnic Foreigners in Europe

The practice of co-ethnic preference in Europe is both similar to and different from that in Asia. For many of the policies and practices that we see in Asia, some state in Europe does the same thing or nearly so. A regional difference is that European ethnic preference is decoupled from skills considerations and there are no investment preferences. In addition, our European cases sometimes show concerns for cultural authenticity, unlike Asian states, and preferential paths to citizenship are more common in Europe than Asia.

Germany

The story of Germany's policies for co-ethnic immigrants is well known and so we will trace only its outlines here. The salient points are that ethnic preference policies were firmly entrenched in Germany for decades (and thus these types of policy are anything but specific to Asia) and that the rationale for the policies was not economic.

Despite denials that it is a country of immigration, since World War II Germany has accepted a large number of foreigners, and many have been ethnic Germans. Levy (2002) breaks the movement of ethnic Germans into Germany into three stages. The first occurred without the input of the German state. The Allies' Potsdam Agreement approved movement of about 12 million ethnic Germans, often called expellees (*Vertriebene*), from Eastern Europe to Germany, with about 8 million settling in what would become West Germany. The situation was a humanitarian disaster, with another 2 million dying during transit. The second stage was the movement between 1950 and 1987, which began with West German state policy. It involved about 2 million *Aussiedler*, or resettlers, mostly from Poland and Romania. A larger wave of *Aussiedler* then came in a third stage, beginning with the fall of the iron curtain in 1988. About 2.3 million settled in West Germany between 1988 and 1996, with about two-thirds coming from the former Soviet Union (Levy 2002: 19–21; also see Joppke 2005).

The policy that brought these millions of co-ethnics to Germany was Article 116(1) of Germany's Basic Law, or constitution, enacted in 1949, when the possibility of great numbers of ethnic Germans return-migrating was fading behind the hardening iron curtain. The Article 116 provision was for citizenship for ethnic Germans and seemed to follow from Germany's jus sanguinis model of citizenship. However, as Joppke (2005) has pointed out, the policy's major provision had no precedent: automatic citizenship for ethnic Germans who were citizens of other states and who may have never set foot in German territory. Moreover, the law applied only to ethnic Germans in Eastern Europe and the USSR; like Korea and Taiwan, Germany distinguishes among co-ethnics based on where they reside. Finally, the law applied to these areas because there was a presumption that ethnic Germans there faced persecution and needed help. Indeed, a 1953 follow-up law (which specified that Germans facing persecution in the West could take part if they could prove persecution and bizarrely added to the list whatever ethnic Germans might be in China) labeled the target population expellees, even if they left their host country voluntarily, and referred to those accepted as resettlers (and thus called *Aussiedler*), even if they had never lived in the German territory (Joppke 2005).

Besides the similar emphasis on co-ethnicity, the German policy and the policies in Asia have several differences. First, the prize was more grand: No Asian states offered automatic citizenship, and only Taiwan offered citizenship preference to co-ethnics (although requiring skills). Second, after a trickle of immigrants (an average of 38,000 resettlers a year; Levy 2002: 20) during the most repressive years of state socialism in the Soviet bloc, the German state had literally millions of takers for its offer, unlike the much smaller numbers that went to Japan and Korea, the most relevant cases for comparison with Germany. Third, unlike in Asia, Germany instituted measures of cultural authenticity in the program (Joppke 2005). After 1992, when the number of resettlers from Russia was skyrocketing, policymakers demanded that applicants demonstrate knowledge and familiarity with German culture, education, and especially language. They instituted a lengthy questionnaire along with a German language test. These criteria reduced the number of applicants, many of whom did not appear to be German at all, and between 30 percent and 40 percent failed the tests (Martin 2004). Other restrictions included the removal of the assumption of persecution for applicants from Eastern Europe (but not Russia) and exclusion of applicants born after 1993, thereby bringing about an eventual end to the program.

The most significant difference for our purposes is the rationale for the preference: protection from persecution abroad. Although states everywhere routinely express concern for the well-being of citizens and compatriots abroad, in Germany we find a protection and remedial rationale for ethnic preference that we do not find in Asia, save for a short-lived refugee policy in China. To be sure, ethnic Germans, especially the early immigrants, have played an important role in Germany's economic recovery (Kindleberger 1967). But this was not the rationale for opening the borders, and officials initially expected the immigrants to be a burden (Kindleberger 1967: 32). Although driven in part by historical responsibility for the postwar situation—as well as cold war ideological goals (von Koppenfels 2002)—in Joppke's (2005) analysis of the policy, we find again and again the stated rationales revolving around the perception of ethnic Germans as victims of some kind of ill-treatment that requires—as obligation—the German state's remedial efforts with little regard to the economic cost of such a policy. These costs, part of the overall integration package, which included housing and other adjustments, were considerable. Helmut Kohl stated that the reception of the co-ethnics was "a national task for all" and that if Germans turned their backs on their "compatriots," they would be a "morally deprived people" (Joppke 2005: 206). Early state provisions centered on culture, including establishment of archives, libraries, and research institutes to maintain a memory of the expellees' experiences (Levy 2002). Aid quickly grew and required new taxes. The German state committed itself to payments, education programs, business assistance, housing allowances, and pensions that inflamed a right-wing opposition (von Koppenfels 2002). It was in fact the cost of accepting ethnic Germans that led to efforts to restrict their numbers and to reductions in their benefits in Germany and efforts to aid them in their host countries (Joppke 2005).

New Immigrant-Receiving States in Europe

Other European states that stand out as most comparable to Asian states are those that are recently developed, recently began receiving immigrants, and have large diaspora populations, such as Spain and Italy. Spain is an especially comparable state to the Asian cases, in particular Korea and Taiwan, because of its recent economic development, its wealth being comparable to that of Korea (Guillen 2001), its similarly recent transition from an authoritarian regime to a democracy, its recent move to become an immigrant-receiving state, and its large pool of co-ethnics in low-wage countries (in Spain's case, Latin America). But Spain is also different. Most notably, it has offered preferences for some foreigners based on national origin, but these have not targeted co-ethnics.

Spain's migrant population is exploding. In 2005 the United Nations estimated that there were 4.8 million international migrants in this country of 43 million.[14] OECD data from 2004 show that Spain had 2 million legal foreign residents. About 560,000 were from Latin America (OECD 2006; for a discussion see Cornelius 2004).

For many years Spain has given special attention and preference to individuals from Latin America and the Philippines. However, with the exception of a provision in the 1978 Spanish constitution stating that the protection of emigrants abroad is the responsibility of the state (Fuentes 2001), Spanish immigration preferences are not "ethnic" preferences. They are based on the idea of a common culture uniting Spain with Latin America and the former colony of the Philippines, without an effort to identify people of any particular blood or ancestry. In 1951 Spain passed a law to allow dual nationality agreements with Latin American states. In 1969 it passed a law that exempted immigrants from Latin America and the Philippines from the requirement for a work permit and granted them access to social rights enjoyed by Spanish citizens. It also entered into bilateral reciprocal agreements with these states to waive the normal requirement for visas. Moreover, diplomas and professional titles from these states were recognized, allowing free movement back and forth. However, Spain put new restrictions in place in a 1985 law, and since 1992 Spain has required visas of several Latin American states, including Peru, Dominican Republic, Cuba, Colombia, and Ecuador. However, informal or administrative preferences remain; Latin American illegal immigrants are regularized during periodic amnesties at higher rates (Cornelius 2004; Joppke 2005). There are also preferences in naturalization. Most foreigners need ten years of residence in Spain, but citizens of Ibero-American states, the Philippines, Andorra, and Equatorial Guinea, as well as Sephardic Jews, have needed only two years' residency since the nationality code was reformed in 1982 (Fuentes 2001).

Yet these preferences are different from Asian preferences. As Joppke (2005) has shown, not only are these preferences not based on ancestry, ethnicity, or race (and thus are less offensive to liberal sensibilities), they are also not linked to work programs or other economic development goals, as are preferences in Asia. Instead, they are linked to a romantic recognition of *hispanidad*, or the cultural community that presumably links Spain to its former colonies in the Americas and Asia. Franco pushed the importance of these linkages, partly to compensate for Spain's isolation in Europe as a result of his repressive practices; *hispanidad* would allow Franco (and presumably other Spaniards) to feel important. Whether or not there were real cultural compatibilities was never seriously investigated. Instead, state officials assumed that Spain had (as a 1951 law stated) a "spiritual mission" to make these linkages and preferences (Díez Medrano 2003; Joppke 2005).

To be sure, the informal preferences exhibited in policy implementation or in the attitudes of the Spanish public have similarities with the patterns we see in Asia. Specifically, Spaniards see Latin Americans as more culturally similar and skilled and thus less disruptive to social order than other immigrants, especially those from Islamic countries (Izuierdo Escribano 2003). In addition, some mayors in the Aragón region of Spain are making local efforts to recruit ethnic Spaniards in Argentina to work in Spain (Cook 2005). But the fact remains that the Spanish state does not choose immigrants on the basis of ancestry, does not put co-ethnics in special work programs, and does not have any formal or obvious economic rationale for their preferences.

The same might be said for Italy, which similarly has made a transition to an immigrant-receiving state. The United Nations reported that in 2005, Italy had 2.5 million international migrants in a population of 58 million.[15] OECD data from 2003 that classify legal migrants to Italy by nationality do not reveal Italian ethnicity, but there is little indication that ethnic Italians are returning in large numbers to Italy. The top sending states are Romania, Albania, Morocco, Ukraine, China, and the Philippines (OECD 2006; for a discussion see Calavita 2004).

Despite a large population of co-ethnics in Latin America dating from the 1880–1914 period (Klein 1983) (the same period as Japanese immigration to Latin America) and a need for immigrants for 3D jobs, Italy has not made prominent policy efforts comparable to Japan and Korea to encourage ethnic return migration, nor does it prefer co-ethnics over others for work. Indeed, in Calavita's two in-depth case studies of the Italian immigration scene, preferences for Italian immigration are not mentioned at all (Calavita 2004).

There are some minor preferences for ethnic Italians, mostly from Latin America, especially Argentina, Brazil, Uruguay, and Venezuela, in the form of visa waiver agreements, but they are not for work. Italians from Argentina, for example, can come to Italy as tourists and stay for three months. Ethnic Italians also receive preference in naturalization; they have to live in Italy for only three years, as opposed to the normal ten-year residency (Pastore 2001). As in Spain, some subnational governments are making efforts to preferentially encourage return (Cook 2005). However, despite the demographic possibilities for Italy to create a program for importing co-ethnic workers, along the lines of Japan and Korea, the Italian state has not done so. Moreover, although the Italian state has historically benefited from remittances, its language in promoting preferences suggests romantic linkages rather than economic development, and it attaches no requirements for skills in its preferences. In 1992, Italy enacted a dual nationality law not for its own benefit but in response to requests to show "concern for loud demands expressed by the Italian community abroad" (Pastore 2001: 101).

Eastern Europe

In Eastern Europe, including Hungary, Slovakia, Slovenia, Romania, and Poland, policies are creating "fuzzy citizenship"—a status in between alien and citizen, designed specifically for co-ethnics abroad (Fowler 2004). Of course, this is similar to the statuses created for *nikkeijin* in Japan and skilled Korean Americans who go to Korea to work. But there are important differences.

All the Eastern European states mentioned have large co-ethnic populations in neighboring states, which are usually less developed (e.g., Hungarians in Romania and Romanians in Moldova). Although wealthier than their neighbors, Hungary and the other four countries are not wealthy states relative to the rest of Europe and in fact are seen as low-cost labor destinations for outsourcing manufacturing from the West (e.g., the car manufacturer Audi makes cars in Hungary). These states are not in need of low-skilled workers. More similar to China and Southeast Asian states, they would seem to need, if anything, skilled co-ethnics and investments.

But unlike many Asian states, they seem to make no serious efforts to encourage co-ethnic investment or skilled migration. These Eastern European states mostly follow the European model in their preferences for co-ethnics. Ethnic links are important and should be recognized for their own sake; in some instances they have a moral, obligatory, protective, or remedial rationale, and they are worth pursuing even if they have costs. As Fowler (2004) describes them, they are part of a process of the state's redefinition in the postcommunist period. With borders drawn and redrawn by foreign powers and with co-ethnic bonds suppressed by the Communists for decades, the new states are asserting themselves as representatives of cultural nations that span borders. Although these states may have benefited from economic activities of diasporic populations in the West, the policies usually are directed more toward the poorer co-ethnics to the south or east; they have a "reparative or compensatory" tone or suggest notions of at least symbolic care. In constitutions these obligations are mentioned as goods in their own right. For example, Poland "shall provide assistance to Poles living abroad to maintain their links with the national cultural heritage"; Romania "shall support the strengthening of links with the Romanians living abroad and shall act accordingly for the preservation, development and expression of their ethnic, cultural, linguistic and religious identity"; and Hungary "bears a sense of responsibility for the fate of Hungarians living outside its borders and promotes the fostering of their relations with Hungary" (Fowler 2004: 196).

Hungary has perhaps gone further than its East European neighbors in elaborating and institutionalizing a relationship with its transborder co-ethnics. In 2001 Hungary passed its controversial Status Law, a package of entitlements for transborder Hungarians that included educational allowances for parents sending their children to Hungarian schools (in the neighboring countries), a limited selection of health care and travel benefits, and, most significant, a guest worker program that allowed ethnic Hungarians to work in Hungary three months out of every calendar year (Kántor et al. 2004). Certain provisions of the Status Law were later watered down to bring Hungary's laws into alignment with EU strictures against ethnic discrimination (or favoritism). But in December 2004 Hungarians considered a national referendum on dual citizenship for transborder Hungarians. Although the referendum failed, it would have gone further than any other initiative in extending quasi-citizenship rights to all ethnic Hungarians in neighboring countries.

One finds in the Asian cases some of this same language, but the economic rationales are clear from the policies, which link migration to specific occupations (most obviously in Korea and Taiwan), allow only short-term if unrestrictive visas (Japan), or provide investment and property incentives (Korea, China, and several Southeast Asian states) and generally do not provide much if anything in the way of settlement, integration, and social rights. Indeed, in Korea, ethnic Koreans from China have had to struggle to have workplace injuries compensated. All the Asian countries actively encourage ethnic return migration because of its economic benefits, in contrast to Eastern Europe. In contrast, only Slovakia in Eastern Europe reduces barriers for co-ethnics to enter the labor force. Hungary's guest worker program (as part of the Status

Law) curtailed co-ethnic labor migration more than it facilitated it. The large number of ethnic Hungarians (mostly from Romania) who had worked illegally in Hungary over the past 15 years were now restricted to three months of work per calendar year. This is because Hungary does not wish to encourage the return migration of ethnic Hungarians to Hungary. Hungary would like its co-ethnics to consider themselves part of a larger cultural nation of Hungarians, but it would prefer them to do it from the safety of their own homes (Fox 2003). As such, most of Hungary's policies are aimed at improving the economic, political, and cultural well-being of Hungarians *in* the neighboring countries. Indeed, it is not the aim of kin-state politics more generally in Eastern Europe to bring co-ethnics home (Fowler 2004). These are not receiving countries; to the contrary, most of them are sending their own citizens to points farther west in search of work and the good life (Wallace and Stola 2001). Instead, kin-state politics in Eastern Europe are intended to give politically palatable expression to nationalist aspirations for national reunification. Co-ethnics need not return to their homelands; their homelands are coming to them.

Discussion and Conclusion

Cornelius and Tsuda (2004) argue that there are no regional variations in the common inability of industrialized states to control immigration because all states have converged on the same failed policy responses (such as employer sanctions for hiring undocumented workers) and the same gap between policy objectives (control) and outcomes (unwanted immigration). We investigate here a more specific type of immigration control: the ability of states to shape the ethnicity of their immigration flows. We do not assess the success or failure of these attempts but instead show states in different regions of the world similarly in apparent violation of global norms against discrimination yet using preference in different ways for different objectives.

The comparison of Asian states to European states shows some commonalities and differences. One key point is that co-ethnic preferences are found in both regions. Despite the ostensibly strong world norm of nondiscrimination, discrimination in immigration policy is common, especially so in Asia and Eastern Europe. This means that in different parts of the world, states are drawing boundaries of the nation in ways that do not fully respect territorial boundaries. States define nations through policy that gives special visas to co-ethnic foreign workers, special visas to highly skilled co-ethnic foreigners, special investment privileges to co-ethnic foreigners, or preferential access to citizenship.

For policymakers in both Europe and East Asia, "us" can include nationals of other states who have never stepped foot in their ancestral homeland.

But there are also some distinct regional patterns. Most important, Asian ethnic preferences are more instrumentally integrated into larger policy objectives than those practices in Western Europe, and specifically they are geared toward economic development, using skills and investment preferences. In contrast, the European policies, especially the strong moves toward ethnic preference in Eastern Europe, have been mostly expressions of ties or efforts at protection (see Table 2.1). Although Asian preferences are for economic development, European preferences are a kind of protective or expressive nationalism.

This interregional comparison thus suggests that the justifications noted by Joppke (2005) may be unique to or more pronounced in Europe. In addition, the comparison makes the European policies appear especially romantic or even irrational, as economic justifications are absent or muted and the policies do not clearly link the co-ethnics into the economy. Although European states enjoy economic benefits from ethnic return migration, they also sometimes absorb at least short-term losses or costs and leave it up to chance whether benefits will occur. At the same time, Asian states match their focus on economic development with a relative lack of interest in the kind of cultural authenticity tests found in European preferences. States in both regions appeal to blood-based kinship and the emotions that go with it, but they have different approaches and purposes. In Asia it is a means to an end, and in Europe it appears more as an end in itself.

It is beyond the scope of this chapter to explain the reasons that the European choice has been mostly to express ethnic ties as a good in their own right, but it may be due to factors unique to Europe. In other words, the lack of explicit focus on short-term economic development or gain may be the special feature that needs explaining, rather than Asia's economic focus. Mexico, for example, has policies on return migration geared strongly to economic development (Goldring 1998). Future research on regional comparisons may find European policy patterns elsewhere or may identify causes that make the European approach unique to Europe. One area of focus should be the role of emigrants themselves, never passive players in the process, and their ability to pressure kin states to enact policies enabling their return, either for the kin state's ethnic development or simply to maintain an affective tie.

The regional variations identified here suggest that there are no global standards for how states make links to co-ethnic citizens of other states. In fact,

Table 2.1 Commonalities and variations in ethnic return migration policy

Country or region	Immigration/visa ethnic preference	Citizenship ethnic preference	Investor ethnic preference	Cultural authenticity test	Skill requirement for preference	State or local government co-ethnic preference	Primary rationale
China	In official statements (not law)	No	Yes	No	No	Yes	Economic development
Japan	Yes	No	No	No	No	No	Economic development
Korea	Yes	Yes	Yes	No	Yes	No	Economic development
Taiwan	Yes	Yes	Yes	No	Yes	No	Economic development
Europe	Yes: Germany, Italy, Hungary, Slovakia, Poland	Yes: Germany, Ireland, Italy, Greece	No	Yes: Germany, Ireland, Greece, Slovakia	No	Yes: Italy, Spain	Protection, expressive nationalism

those links can be maintained and national boundaries drawn in a wide variety of ways, and the justifications for those links are equally variable. The prevalence of policies suggests that conflict is not likely, and there is no evidence of interregional conflict. Finally, although scholars have traditionally treated East Asia as somehow different and even representing an alternative modernity (Tu 2000), it is just as likely that Europe may be the unique region. Future research may fruitfully discern patterns of practice in Latin America and Africa regarding politics toward co-ethnic foreigners and the drawing of national boundaries across territorial borders.

Notes

An earlier version of this chapter was published in *International Migration Review* 41(4):793–825 (2007).

1. Although Britain and France are large economies and are immigrant-receiving states, we leave aside these former colonial states for several reasons. First, the most prominent ties between these states and their colonies have been between the states and colonial subjects, and because these ties are not based explicitly on ethnicity, they are outside our purview here. Second, although these states have indeed established preferences for the return of emigrants to colonies, most notorious being Britain's consideration of "patrial" status in immigration policy, this type of emigration is different from the other emigration types examined here. It went to territories politically controlled by the sending state, and one might expect special state consideration or obligation to return migrants from these territories. Our main purpose is to compare Asia with Europe, and these cases are different enough from the Asian cases that they will not likely yield insights from comparison (Japan's colonies in Asia were short-lived compared to most European colonies). Third, the numbers of colonial settlers are typically small. Finally, these cases do not contradict our arguments. They fit the pattern of preference typically found in Europe but not in Asia; that is, preferences for return migrants from colonies are not linked to economic goals and are based on a protective or expressive nationalism (for an extensive analysis, see Joppke 2005).

2. Population Division of the Department of Economic and Social Affairs of the United Nations Secretariat, "World Migrant Stock: The 2005 Revision Population Database," http://esa.un.org/migration, accessed November 19, 2006.

3. Data from the Japanese Ministry of Justice Web site, http://www.moj.go.jp/ PRESS/060530-1/060530-1.html, accessed November 19, 2006 (in Japanese).

4. Data available from the Korean Ministry of Justice and Ministry of Government Administration and Home Affairs, http://www.moj.go.kr/HP/COM/bbs_03/Board List.do; http://www.mogaha.go.kr (accessed November 26, 2006; no longer available).

5. *Joongang Ilbo*, July 18, 2002; *Chosun Ilbo*, July 18, 2002.

6. Originally, in the enactment process, allowing dual citizenship was considered, but it was excluded because of concerns regarding military conscription, taxation, and social sentiments.

7. *Act on the Immigration and Legal Status of Overseas Koreans* (Case 13-2 KCCR 714, 99 Hung-Ma 494, November 29, 2001).

8. The Korean Supreme Court also referred to the demands of Korean Americans as an impetus to the Act on the Immigration and Legal Status of Overseas Koreans.

9. *Act on the Immigration and Legal Status of Overseas Koreans* (Case 13-2 KCCR 714, 99 Hung-Ma 494, November 29, 2001, p. 724 [Korean version]).

10. Population Division, "World Migrant Stock," accessed November 24, 2006.

11. *China Daily*, October 26, 2000.

12. Guangzhou Municipal People's Government, 1984, "Provisional Measures of Guanzhou Municipality on Preferential Treatment for Overseas Chinese and Hong Kong and Macao Investors," http://www.novexcn.com/guanghou_hk_macao_invest .html.

13. *China Daily*, August 20, 2004.

14. Population Division, "World Migrant Stock," accessed November 19, 2006.

15. Ibid.

References Cited

Bolt, P. J. 2000. *China and South East Asia's Ethnic Chinese: State and Diaspora in Contemporary Asia.* Westport, CT: Praeger.

Brubaker, R. 1994. "Nation as Institutionalized Form, Practical Category, Contingent Event." *Contention* 4(1):3–14.

Calavita, K. 2004. "Italy: Economic Realities, Political Fictions, and Policy Failures." In *Controlling Immigration,* Cornelius et al., eds., 345–380.

Cheng, L. 2003. "Transnational Labor, Citizenship, and the Taiwan State." In *East Asian Law: Universal Norms and Local Cultures,* A. Rosett, L. Cheng, and M. Y. K. Woo, eds. New York: Routledge Curzon, 85–105.

Cheng, L., and M. Katz. 1998. "Migration and the Diaspora Communities." In *Culture and Society in the Asia-Pacific,* R. Maidment and C. Mackerras, eds. New York: Routledge, 65–88.

Choe, H. 2003. "National Identity and Citizenship in China and Korea." Ph.D. dissertation, Department of Sociology, University of California, Irvine.

Cook, D. 2005. "The Long Way Home or Back Door to the EU? Argentines' Claims of Ancestral Nationalities." Unpublished manuscript.

Cornelius, W. A. 2004. "Spain: The Uneasy Transition from Labor Exporter to Labor Importer." In *Controlling Immigration,* Cornelius et al., eds., 387–429.

Cornelius, W. A., and T. Tsuda. 2004. "Controlling Immigration: The Limits of Government Intervention." In *Controlling Immigration,* Cornelius et al., eds., 3–50.

Cornelius, W. A., T. Tsuda, P. L. Martin, and J. F. Hollifield, eds. *Controlling Immigration: A Global Perspective*, Stanford, CA: Stanford University Press.

DeVoretz, D. J., and K. Zhang. 2004. "Citizenship, Passports, and the Brain Exchange Triangle." *Journal of Comparative Policy Analysis* 6(2):199–212.

Díez Medrano, J. 2003. *Framing Europe: Attitudes to European Integration in Germany, Spain, and the United Kingdom*. Princeton, NJ: Princeton University Press.

Fowler, B. 2004. "Fuzzing Citizenship, Nationalising Political Space: A Framework for Interpreting the Hungarian 'Status Law' as a New Form of Kin-State Policy in Central and Eastern Europe." In *The Hungarian Status Law: Nation Building and/or Minority Protection*, Z. Kántor, B. Majtényi, O. Ieda, B. Vizi, and I. Halász, eds. Sapporo, Japan: Slavic Research Council, 177–238.

Fox, J. E. 2003. "National Identities on the Move: Transylvanian Hungarian Labor Migrants in Hungary." *Journal of Ethnic and Migration Studies* 29(3):449–466.

Freeman, G. P. 1995. "Modes of Immigration Politics in Liberal Democratic States." *International Migration Review* 24(4):881–913.

Fuentes, F. J. M. 2001. "Migration and Spanish Nationality Law." In *Towards a European Nationality: Citizenship, Immigration, and Nationality Law in the EU*, R. Hansen and P. Weil, eds. Houndsmills, UK: Palgrave, 118–142.

Gang, J. 2002. "Jiangsu Capital Lures Foreign Businesses." *China Daily* (Hong Kong edition), May 30.

Ginsburg, T. 2003. *Judicial Review in New Democracies: Constitutional Courts in Asian Cases*. New York: Cambridge University Press.

Goldring, L. 1998. "The Power of Status in Transnational Social Fields." In *Transnationalism from Below*, L. E. Guarnizo and M. P. Smith, eds. New Brunswick, NJ: Transaction, v. 6, 165–195.

Guillen, M. F. 2001. *The Limits of Convergence: Globalization and Organizational Change in Argentina, South Korea, and Spain*. Princeton, NJ: Princeton University Press.

Herbert, W. 1996. *Foreign Workers and Law Enforcement in Japan*. New York: Kegan Paul International.

Hollifield, J. F. 1992. *Immigrants, Markets, and States: The Political Economy of Postwar Europe*. Cambridge, MA: Harvard University Press.

Hsiao, H.-H. M. 1992. "The Rise of Social Movements and Civil Protests." In *Political Change in Taiwan*, T.-J. Cheng and S. Haggard, eds. Boulder, CO: Lynne Rienner, 57–74.

Huntington, S. P. 1996. *The Clash of Civilizations and the Remaking of World Order*. New York: Simon & Schuster.

Izuierdo Escribano, A. 2003. "The Favorites of the Twenty-First Century: Latin American Immigration in Spain." *Studi Emigrazione* 40(149):98–124.

Joppke, C. 1998. "Why Liberal States Accept Unwanted Immigration." *World Politics* 50(January):266–293.

————. 2005. *Selecting by Origin: Ethnic Migration in the Liberal State.* Cambridge, MA: Harvard University Press.

Kántor, Z., B. Majtényi, O. Ieda, B. Vizi, and I. Halász, eds. 2004. *The Hungarian Status Law: Nation Building and/or Minority Protection.* Sapporo, Japan: Slavic Research Center.

Kindleberger, Charles Poor. 1967. *Europe's Postwar Growth: The Role of Labor Supply.* Cambridge, MA: Harvard University Press.

Klein, H. S. 1983. "The Integration of Italian Immigrants into the United States and Argentina: A Comparative Analysis." *American Historical Review* 88(2):306–329.

Lee, C.-W. 2003. "'Us' and 'Them' in Korean Law: The Creation, Accommodation and Exclusion of Outsiders in South Korea." In *East Asian Law: Universal Norms and Local Cultures,* A. Rosett, L. Cheng, and M. Y. K. Woo, eds. New York: Routledge Curzon, 106–136.

————. 2004. "The Transnationalisation of Citizenship and the Logic of the Nation-State." Paper presented at the Sixth Conference of the Asia-Pacific Sociological Association on Asia-Pacific Societies in Globalization and Localization, Seoul, South Korea, September 17–19.

Levy, D. 2002. "Integrating Ethnic Germans in West Germany: The Early Postwar Period." In *Coming Home to Germany? The Integration of Ethnic Germans from Central and Eastern Europe in the Federal Republic,* D. Rock and S. Wolff, eds. New York: Berghahn Books, 19–37.

Lie, J. 2001. *Multi-Ethnic Japan.* Cambridge, MA: Harvard University Press.

Lim, T. J. 2002. "The Changing Face of Korea: The Emergence of Korea as a 'Land of Immigration.'" *Korea Society Quarterly* 3(summer/fall):16–21.

Louie, A. 2001. "Crafting Places Through Mobility: Chinese American 'Roots-Searching' in China." *Identities* 8(3):343–379.

Martin, P. L. 2004. "Germany: Managing Migration in the Twenty-First Century." In *Controlling Immigration,* Cornelius et al., eds., 221–253.

Massey, Douglas S., Joaquin Arango, Graeme Hugo, Ali Kouaouci, Adela Pellegrino, and J. Edward Taylor. 1998. *Worlds in Motion: Understanding International Migration at the End of the Millennium.* Oxford, UK: Clarendon Press.

Min, Pyong Gap. 1992. "A Comparison of Korean Minorities in China and Japan." *International Migration Review* 26:4–21.

Mori, H. 1997. *Immigration Policy and Foreign Workers in Japan.* New York: St. Martin's Press.

OECD. 2006. *International Migration Outlook: Annual Report, 2006 Edition.* Paris: OECD.

Oka, T. 1994. *Prying Open the Door: Foreign Workers in Japan.* Washington, DC: Carnegie Endowment for International Peace.

Ong, A. 1999. *Flexible Citizenship: The Cultural Logics of Transnationality.* Durham, NC: Duke University Press.

Park, J.-S., and P. Y. Chang. 2004. "Contestation in the Formation of National and Ethnic Identities in Global Context: The Case of the Overseas Koreans Act." Paper presented at the conference "Korean Identity: Past and Present," Yonsei University, Seoul, South Korea, October 27–28.

Pastore, F. 2001. "Nationality Law and International Migration: The Italian Case." In *Towards a European Nationality: Citizenship, Immigration, and Nationality Law in the EU*, R. Hansen and P. Weil, eds. Houndsmills, UK: Palgrave, 95–117.

Pempel, T. J. 1999. "Democratization and Globalization: A Comparative Study of Japan, South Korea, and Taiwan." In *Democratization and Globalization in Korea*, C.-I. Moon and J. Mo, eds. Seoul, South Korea: Yonsei University Press, 369–399.

Richardson, B. 1997. *Japanese Democracy: Power, Coordination, and Performance*. New Haven, CT: Yale University Press.

Sautman, Barry. 1997. "Racial Nationalism and China's External Behavior." *World Affairs* 160(fall):78–95.

Seol, D.-H. 2005. "Global Dimensions in Mapping the Foreign Labor Policies of Korea: A Comparative and Functional Analysis." *Development and Society* 34(1)(June):75–124.

Seol, D.-H., J.-H. Lee, June J. H. Lee, K.-T. Yim, Y.-T. Kim, and U.-S. Seo. 2004. *Gakgukui Oegukingeunroja Goyonggwanrichegye Saryeyeongu* [Comparative study of international labor migration management in Germany, Singapore, Taiwan, Hong Kong, Japan, and Korea]. Seoul, South Korea: Republic of Korea Ministry of Labor.

Seol, D.-H., and J. D. Skrentny. 2004. "South Korea: Importing Undocumented Workers." In *Controlling Immigration*, Cornelius et al., eds., 475–513.

Shimada, H. 1994. *Japan's "Guest Workers."* Tokyo: University of Tokyo Press.

Skeldon, Ronald. 1997. *Migration and Development: A Global Perspective*. Edinburgh Gate, UK: Addison Wesley Longman.

Skrentny, J. D. 2002. *The Minority Rights Revolution*. Cambridge, MA: Belknap Press.

Thuno, M. 2001. "Reaching Out and Incorporating Chinese Overseas: The Trans-Territorial Scope of the PRC by the End of the 20th Century." *China Quarterly* 168:910–929.

Tsuda, T. 2003. *Strangers in the Ethnic Homeland: Japanese Brazilian Return Migration in Transnational Perspective*. New York: Columbia University Press.

Tsuda, T., and W. A. Cornelius. 2004. "Japan: Government Policy, Immigrant Reality." In *Controlling Immigration*, Cornelius et al., eds., 439–476.

Tsuzuki, Kurumi. 2000. "Nikkei Brazilians and Local Residents: A Study of the H Housing Complex in Toyota City." *Asian and Pacific Migration Journal* 9(3):327–342.

Tu, W.-M. 1994. "Cultural China: The Periphery as the Center." In *The Living Tree: The Changing Meaning of Being Chinese Today*, W.-M. Tu, ed. Stanford, CA: Stanford University Press, 1–34.

———. 2000. "Implications of the Rise of 'Confucian' East Asia." *Daedalus* 129:195–218.

von Koppenfels, A. K. 2002. "The Decline of Privilege: The Legal Background to the Migration of Ethnic Germans." In *Coming Home to Germany? The Integration of Ethnic Germans from Central and Eastern Europe in the Federal Republic*, D. Rock and S. Wolff, eds. New York: Berghahn Books, 102–118.

Wallace, C., and D. Stola, eds. 2001. *Patterns of Migration in Central Europe*. Houndsmills, UK: Palgrave.

Wang, G. 1994. "Among Non-Chinese." In *The Living Tree: The Changing Meaning of Being Chinese Today*, W.-M. Tu, ed. Stanford, CA: Stanford University Press, 127–146.

Yamanaka, K. 1993. "New Immigration Policy and Unskilled Foreign Workers in Japan." *Pacific Affairs* 66(1):72–90.

———. 2004. "Citizenship and Differential Exclusion of Immigrants in Japan." In *State/Nation/Transnation: Perspectives on Transnationalism in the Asia-Pacific*, B. S. A. Yeoh and K. Willis, eds. New York: Routledge, 67–92.

3 Contesting Ethnic Immigration

Germany and Israel Compared

Christian Joppke and Zeev Rosenhek

FATEFULLY ENTANGLED as victim and perpetrator during the twentieth century's darkest hour, Israel and Germany adopted curiously similar policies of ethnic immigration after World War II. Both states welcomed newcomers as "immigrants" for permanent settlement and membership in the national community only if they qualified ex ante as co-ethnics, that is, as members of the state-defining majority nation. This sets an interesting counterpoint to the reverse development in the new settler nations, such as Australia or the United States, which shifted after World War II from ethnicity and race to culturally neutral criteria of immigrant admission, most notably individual skills and family unification. This is not to deny the fundamentally different perceptions of these immigrations in both cases, most notably the denial by Israel and Germany that their ethnic immigrations were immigration at all but rather the "return" of co-ethnics. However, this self-perception conflicts with the fact that in each instance we are dealing with the admission of noncitizens (or "aliens") by a state for more than temporary stays in its territory, which in common sense, as well as in international migration law (Plender 1988), constitutes immigration.

Despite basic similarities, ethnic immigration in Israel and Germany is marked by sharply differing trajectories. Whereas Jewish immigration to Israel shows no sign of weakening, the parallel return of ethnic Germans to Germany has, in principle, come to an end; a 1993 law limits the status of ethnic Germans to individuals born before 1993. The purpose of this chapter is to account for this variation, emphasizing differently structured political spaces for contesting ethnic immigration as an explanatory variable. We thus offer an interpretation of ethnic immigration that differs from the conventional perspective on this type of immigration policy, which links ethnic immigration directly to deep-seated and relatively fixed ethnic conceptions of nationhood (for Germany, see Brubaker 1992; for Israel, see Weiss 2002). Our stress on the political mechanisms that either shore up or undermine ethnic immigration is not to deny the important role of ethnic understandings of nationhood in the setting-up of ethnic immigration policies; however, they tell us little about the further course and the sources of possible contention surrounding ethnic immigration policies.

First, we offer a brief phenomenology of ethnic immigration policies and identify some shortcomings of linking them too closely to ethnic conceptions of nationhood. Second, we trace the different origins and justifications of ethnic immigration in Israel and Germany. Although ethnic conceptions of nationhood were clearly involved in the ideological articulation and legitimization of ethnic immigration in both cases, geopolitical factors were no less important for getting ethnic immigration started—the perceived demographic need for Jewish immigrants in the context of the Arab-Israeli conflict in Israel, and the consequences of World War II and the cold war in Germany. In a third step, we argue that the change or persistence of this geopolitical context and different historical connotations of ethnic immigration in both cases explain the different directions that ethnic immigration took in the 1990s. As a result of these factors, there was more political space in Germany than in Israel for an effective contestation of ethnic immigration policies.

Describing and Explaining Ethnic Immigration Policies

Although the determinants of "normal" immigration policies, such as interest-group pressure (Freeman 1995), autonomous legal systems (Joppke 1998), sub-national mobilization (Karapin 1999; Money 1999), and supranational norms and regimes (Jacobson 1996), have been recently theorized to a great extent, the specificities of ethnic immigration policies have largely escaped scholarly attention. Hence it may be worthwhile to delineate some characteristics of this type of immigration policy.

Israel's and Germany's policies of ethnic immigration are part of a larger family of immigration policies that screen newcomers according to ethnic, racial, or national origin criteria. Such schemes differ along at least three dimensions. First, some immigration policies screen according to the formal citizenship of the would-be immigrant, whereas others select on ethnicity proper. Selecting on citizenship is categorical and generic, based on the simple presence or absence of the requisite state nationality. By contrast, selecting on ethnicity proper draws the state into the murky terrain of examining individual "identity" claims, which is an altogether more elaborate—and problematic—procedure. Moreover, selecting on ethnicity creates an incentive on the part of would-be migrants for "creative ethnic reidentification" (Brubaker 1998a: 1053). In fact, the multiplication of "false" co-ethnics posed a serious challenge to both the German and Israeli ethnic immigration policies in the 1990s and opened the space for what we call restrictive contestation.

Second, some ethnic immigration policies preference certain ethnic or national origin groups according to their putative proximity (but essential differentness) to the state-bearing nation, whereas others are based on the putative sameness of the immigrant group and the state-bearing nation. Examples of proximity are the U.S. national origins quota of 1924 (see King 2000) and the preference for Italians in early postwar French immigration policy (see Viet 1998). An example of sameness is ethnic Germans and Jews, who are believed to be not similar to but identical with the state-bearing nation. Proximity schemes are justified in terms of homogeneity and assimilation and thus in terms of state and society interests, but sameness schemes are couched as the right of the ethnic migrant, to be held against the receiving state.

Finally, some ethnic policies restrict eligibility according to the time and place in which ethnic claims are raised, whereas others do not. On this dimension the German and Israeli cases finally take opposite positions. The laws governing ethnic return migration in Germany were designed as a temporary remedy for the consequences of war and expulsion, covering only ethnic Germans caught in the Soviet empire, who were deemed to be persecuted for their Germanness. By contrast, Israel's Law of Return is a permanent state-constituting provision that applies to every Jew in the world, independent of their individual or group-specific persecution.

This difference in ethnic immigration policy introduces the main objective of this chapter: to account for the resilience of Israel's ethnic immigration and the demise in principle of Germany's. The fact of divergent outcomes in Israel and Germany casts doubt on a culturalist account of ethnic immigration, which links this type of immigration policy to deep-seated and relatively static "ethnic," as against "civic," understandings of nationhood. Even the stellar and highly differentiated analysis by Brubaker (1992) succumbs to the pitfalls of a culturalist explanation when he claims that Germany's "marked openness toward ethnic Germans" (p. 165) derives from the German ethnocultural idiom of nationhood. Brubaker links the emergence of different idioms of nation-hood to specific historical conditions of state-building processes, but once crys-tallized, these cultural understandings of nationhood become rather rigid and function in his model as all-powerful causal factors.

The problem is not the insistence on the cultural conditioning of a state's immigration policies—this conditioning exists (as we shall see). Rather, the problem is the assumption of a straight line between reified and fixed identi-ties and policies, which leaves out other important variables that may influence these policies. Drawing a direct linkage between (ethnic or civic) conceptions of nationhood and immigration policy suffers from what Brubaker (1998b: 274) himself later called the "realism of the group," that is, the misconception of political communities or nations as real entities with wills and intentions. Na-tional identities may be invoked, Bourdieuian style, by individuals and groups who try to impose their preferred immigration policies, but identities do not as such generate the policies commensurable with them.

Cultural accounts of ethnic immigration revolve around a reified opposi-tion between ethnic and civic nationhood. In this they follow a central streak in the nations and nationalism literature, from Hans Kohn (1944) to Liah Green-feld (1992) and Rogers Brubaker (1992). This literature has classified Israel and Germany (along with Japan) as proverbially ethnic states, with a preconstituted "nation" conceiving of the state as its tool of representation and protection, as opposed to "civic" states, in which the nation is a creature of the state and thus is politically and territorially conceived. As writers such as Anthony Smith (1986: 149) have long argued, this dichotomy does not hold at the empirical level (see also the good critiques by Yack [1996] and by Brubaker [1999], where he cautiously qualifies his own earlier work of 1992).

Certainly, there are ethnic components to the German and Israeli states' self-conceptions, and their respective laws of return are primary expressions of them. These laws indicate that state and nation do not overlap, as is typically the case in civic states, but that the nation is prior to and wider than the state. How-ever, these ethnic components are strongly counteracted by civic components. Civic components *maximally* derive from competing, more inclusive models of nationhood; *minimally* they are inherent in the logic of liberal stateness, which revolves around the precepts of equality, public neutrality, and the universalis-tic rule of law. Minimal or maximal, civic-liberal precepts can be found in Israel and Germany alike, and they provide resources that can be—and have been—mobilized against an ethnic self-conception and related policies of the state.

What we shall call the "liberal" challenge to ethnic immigration articulates the tension between ethnic and civic stateness, bringing out that the state's preferencing of one ethnic group (even if it coincides with the majority nation) entails discrimination against the nonpreferenced group(s). However, an additional source of conflict surrounds ethnic immigration, which we call the "restrictive" challenge. Instead of deriving from a tension between ethnic and civic stateness, the restrictive challenge takes ethnic stateness for granted and attacks an overly extensive implementation that allows the entry of "false" or "diluted" co-ethnics.

Although the possibility of liberal and restrictive contention surrounding ethnic immigration is—in principle—available in Germany and Israel alike, the political space for their articulation and mobilization differs according to geopolitical context and different historical connotations of ethnic immigration. In Germany changes in the geopolitical context (i.e., the end of the cold war) along with this country's privileged location in uniting Europe contributed to a decline in the legitimacy of ethnic immigration and broadened the political space for its (liberal and restrictive) opponents. In Israel the persistence of its specific, less privileged geopolitical context (i.e., the conflict with the Palestinians) and of the concomitant material state interest in peopling the land with loyal Jews, helped to shore up ethnic immigration against the political forces opposing it in principle or in actual operation.

Origins and Justifications of Ethnic Immigration in Israel and Germany

A frequent fallacy in cross-national comparisons is to ignore the different physical sizes of the compared objects and the different scopes of their compared characteristics. In our cases the meaning and impact of numerically and typologically similar (ethnic) immigration are radically different in two countries of vastly different territory and population sizes, and these differences are bound to be even more extreme if one such immigration is entirely constitutive of state and society (as in Israel) and the other immigration remains rather peripheral to it (as in Germany). Accordingly, interpreting Jewish and ethnic German immigration exclusively in the light of ethnic statehood and nationhood in Israel and Germany obscures more than it reveals. In the German case this linkage is at best an indirect one, and far more relevant has been the political and only temporary imperative of mastering the consequences of World War II, in the context of the cold war confrontation with the Communist East. In Israel there is a more direct and openly promulgated link between Jewish immigration and ethnic statehood and nationhood; however, the full significance of Jewish immigration derives from a conflictive geopolitical environment in which demography is seen as destiny.

Demography as Destiny in Israel

The principle of unrestricted Jewish immigration was legally enshrined in the Law of Return of 1950, whose first article declares that "every Jew has the right to come to this country as an *oleh* [a Jewish immigrant to the Land of Israel]." The Law of Return—one of the few Israeli laws that explicitly references Jewishness as the basis for a special privilege—is perhaps the major legal expression of the definition of Israel as a Jewish state (see Klein 1997; Shachar 2000). By framing Jewish immigration as "return," the law provides statutory enunciation of the link between the state and the Jewish Diaspora. Tellingly, the right of return was framed not as an entitlement granted by the state but as a "natural" right of every Jew in the world that precedes and constitutes the state. Accordingly, the state only recognizes and endorses, but does not create, this right.

Part of the legitimation of Israel as a Jewish state is that it should provide a shelter for Jews threatened by persecution. This motif was mentioned in the presentation of the Law of Return in the Knesset. Yet the principle of unrestricted Jewish immigration did not only apply to those Jews suffering from discrimination or persecution; instead, the right of return was conceived of as belonging to every Jew willing to settle in Israel. Hence, in sharp contrast to Germany, the right to freely immigrate to Israel was ideologically framed as based on membership in the ethnonational community per se and not merely as a remedy for persecution or discrimination.

However, Jewish immigration is grounded not only in the ethnocultural idiom that defines the Israeli polity but also in material state-building imperatives. The Zionist colonial project was from the start founded on immigration flows, and the existence of a prestate Zionist community in Mandatory Palestine was entirely the result of successive waves of Jewish immigration. After the establishment of the state, Jewish immigration continued to play a fundamental role in the demographic makeup of Israeli society. According to the first census carried out in November 1948, 65 percent of the Jewish population was foreign born. As a consequence of massive immigration, this proportion significantly increased over the first years of statehood, reaching 75 percent in 1951. Since then and until the 1990s the percentage of foreign-born individuals among the Jewish population decreased but still remained at very high levels (36 percent in 1989). The large wave of immigration from the former Soviet Union during the 1990s caused a temporary halt in the downward trend (see Central Bureau of Statistics, various years).

Jewish immigration has played an instrumental role in the conflict between the Zionist settlers and the Arab population of Palestine and in the external confrontation with the Arab countries since 1948. Since the beginning of Zionist settlement and over the entire prestate period, the demographic ratio between the Zionist settlers and the Arab population was one of the central dimensions of the conflict between the two national movements. Both sides recognized that demography would be a central factor in the determination of the political future of Palestine and its two national communities. Accordingly, Palestinian attempts to halt, or at least limit, Jewish immigration and Zionist efforts to enlarge it as much as possible were key components in their respective political strategies.

The dependence on immigration for the consolidation of the Zionist project continued after the establishment of the Israeli state, especially during its first decade of existence. Following the 1948–1949 war, the national composition of the population residing in Israeli territory changed dramatically. First, because of flight and expulsion, only about 170,000 of an estimated 700,000–900,000 Palestinians who had lived in the territory before the founding of Israel remained (Peretz 1958: 95). In addition, as a consequence of the enormous wave of immigration following the establishment of the state, the Jewish population doubled within three years. Despite this sweeping demographic transformation, the Israeli state continued to define the ratio between the Jewish and Arab populations as a matter of national security and survival, and Jewish immigration remained the main tool to maintain the demographic superiority of the Jewish population over the Palestinian minority. This demographic superiority is seen by the state and most political forces as a precondition for holding the Palestinian minority in a subordinate status, especially given the fact that as citizens they enjoy full formal political rights (e.g., voting rights).

The demographic motif in the management of the national conflict became more acute after the 1967 war, when the occupation of Arab territories significantly enlarged the Palestinian population under Israeli control, providing new fuel to the "demographic threat" to the Jewish character of the Israeli state (see Lustick 1999). By then the reservoir of potential Jewish immigrants from Muslim countries was practically exhausted, and the Jewish communities in the Soviet bloc were banned from emigration by their respective governments, except for a brief period during the early 1970s. Under these aggravated conditions, the framing of Jewish immigration as imperative for ensuring Israel's survival remained salient and broadly consensual among Zionist political forces. As we will elaborate later, when the collapse of the Soviet Union in the early 1990s opened up a huge new reservoir of Jewish immigrants for Israel, the iron link between Jewish immigration, demography, and the protracted national conflict helped shore up the principle of ethnic immigration against its liberal and restrictive challengers.

Although the Law of Return stands for the ethnic self-definition of Israel as a Jewish state, civic principles also have a place in the legitimation and functioning of the Israeli state. For example, the Nationality Law incorporates significant civic elements; it sanctions the acquisition of citizenship by birth on territory and by residence (Gouldman 1970: ch. 5). Civic principles in the operation of state agencies, and in the political arena in general, have become more prominent over the last two decades, although they are still subordinated to ethnonational notions (Shafir and Peled 1998). The simultaneous operation of both ethnic and civic principles and the tensions between them are manifest especially in the relations between the state and its Arab-Palestinian citizens. As Peled (1992) notes, although excluded from the ethnically defined national community, Palestinian citizens enjoy formal civil and political rights, which allow them to participate, albeit in a restricted form, in the political process. These civic notions would be mobilized during the 1990s by the Palestinian leadership and "post-Zionist" Jews to advance their liberal challenge to the principle of ethnic immigration.

Mastering the Consequences of World War II in Germany

In contrast to Israel, Germany's ethnic immigration has remained peripheral and temporary rather than a state- and society-constituting device. This is not to belittle the magnitude of the German expellee issue. Expellees from the lost eastern territories and beyond constituted some 20 percent of the West German population in 1950. Their swift and generous integration was the single biggest challenge to the fledgling West German democracy, because expellees represented a considerable source of revanchism and right-wing radicalism. Public order perhaps more than "identity" considerations conditioned the setup of the legal framework for Germany's ethnic immigration in the 1950s. This suggests the centrality of the consequences of World War II for (re)activating the ethnocultural tradition, which was not automatically available for indiscriminate co-ethnics. Accordingly, the link between ethnic immigration and the ethno-cultural tradition of German nationhood is less straightforward and direct than conventional wisdom would have it (e.g., Brubaker 1992).

It is still important to point out, in line with the argument of ethnocultural tradition, that postwar Germany, like Israel, has always denied that its ethnic immigration is immigration at all but the return of co-ethnics to their homeland. This points, in both cases, to an ethnocultural relationship between people and "their" states: not states building citizenries in their image, and thus the state preceding the citizenry, but preconstituted peoples forming states for their self-representation and protection. Is Germany the "state of Germans" as Israel is a "Jewish state," then? A crucial difference between the two is that, as a result of the confrontation between Germans and Jews under Nazism, the German ethno-cultural idiom of nationhood has in principle been delegitimized, whereas the idea of Israel as a Jewish state has been powerfully reaffirmed. In addition, the ethnic homogeneity of the resident population in Germany prevented the rise of an Israeli-style demographic imperative in its policy toward ethnic Germans—there was no rebellious minority to hold down by peopling the country with loyal "Germans." In contrast to Israel, whose ethnic texture is internally visible in the rift between Jews and Arabs, the ethnic dimension of the (West) German state became internally invisible, as it was transferred into the future (as the mandate of national reunification) and extraterritorialized (as the mostly virtual commitment in the cold war period to admit co-ethnics).

Daniel Levy (1999: 22) has succinctly argued that the ethnic German expellees allowed the "rehabilitation" of Germany's otherwise delegitimized ethnocultural self-understanding after World War II; through reference to the "victimhood" of expellees, ethnocultural nationhood could be "dissociated from Nazism" (p. 49). Was (West) Germany, at least in this indirect way, a state of Germans as Israel is a state of Jews?

Turning to West Germany's founding document, the Basic Law, one can observe a tension between ethnic and liberal elements. The ethnic elements are tellingly tied to the temporariness and incompleteness of the West German state. Accordingly, the preamble of the Basic Law states that it was to apply only for a "transition period" (*Übergangszeit*), until the "unity and liberty of Germany was completed." Moreover, the "German people," in crafting this constitution, had "acted also for those Germans, who were denied participation"—the German division obviously reactivated the traditional noncongruence between state and nation. On the liberal side, the Basic Law's preamble commits the new state to a "united Europe" and "to serve peace in the world," and the constitution's first seven articles protect universal human rights independently of citizenship—all commitments that, in contrast to the ethnic ones, were conceived of as not just temporarily valid.

A cornerstone of postwar Germany's ethnic orientation, and the constitutional foundation of its ethnic immigration, is Article 116(1), which defines who is a German. This article contains a liberal element in simply stating that a "German" is someone who "possesses German citizenship," leaving the determination of citizenship to the political process. Accordingly, the German Basic Law never prescribed an ethnic citizenship law such as the one that was in force until 1999. However, Article 116(1) contains an ethnic element in adding that a "German" is also someone who "as refugee or expellee of German origins [*Volkszugehörigkeit*] or as his spouse or descendant has found reception in the territory of the German Reich according to its borders of 31 December 1937." This meant that (West) Germany was the state not only of its citizens but also of certain noncitizens, if they qualified as co-ethnics. However, as in the unity mandate in the preamble, this ethnic commitment was to be temporary—this is expressed in the facts that Article 116 was put under a statutory proviso and that it appears only in the last section of the Basic Law, which dealt with "Transitory and Concluding Regulations."

Article 116 points to the fundamental difference between Jewish and ethnic German immigration. Jewish immigration was an invitation to every Jew in the world, but ethnic German immigration applied only to those ethnic Germans who were refugees or expellees. From Article 116 alone one might conclude that the pool of potential claimants was both wider and more narrowly conceived than the actual ethnic immigration engendered by it: wider because there was no geographic specification attached but narrower because in common understanding a refugee or expellee is someone who is actually forced to leave one's homeland by a persecuting power. The Federal Expellee and Refugee Law (FERL) of 1953, which spells out the statutory framework for Germany's ethnic immigration, reversed this constellation. Article 1(2)(3) of the FERL stipulates that "an expellee is also who as German citizen or as German *Volkszugehöriger . . . after the end of the general expulsion measures* has left or leaves the former eastern territories, Danzig [the Baltic States], the Soviet Union, Poland, Czechoslovakia, Hungary, Romania, Bulgaria, Yugoslavia, Albania, or China" (emphasis added). This peculiar expellee, who was not actually expelled but who had to originate from a Communist country, was labeled a "resettler" (*Aussiedler*). Interestingly, this geographic restriction of expellee/resettler status, which denied resettler status to German minorities in Denmark, France, or Italy, occurred "with respect to the western Allied powers"; that is, it was mandated by the winners of war (Münz and Ohliger 1998: 13). In addition, it is curious that among the listed territories for resettlers are China and Albania—not known for harboring any German minority groups. This reveals, as the administrative Expulsion Pressure Guidelines of 1986 put it, the "regime- and ideology-reference" of the notion of resettler. In other words, only ethnic Germans under Communism qualified for resettler status. By the same token, one could forfeit one's claim by "special tie(s) to the political regime of the state of origin." Communists could not become resettlers. Theirs was obviously not only an ethnic status but also a political status, betraying the pivotal role of the cold war in shaping German ethnic immigration.

Resettlers, most of whose ancestors had left the "German" lands before there even was anything akin to a German national consciousness, let alone a German nation-state, have formed the bulk of ethnic German immigration since World War II. Accordingly, what had started as a temporary measure to integrate the millions of ethnic Germans who were actually forced to leave their homeland by the advancing Red Army and retaliatory expulsion was turned around by the FERL and its—rather generous—subsequent administrative implementation into an open-door policy for anyone from Eastern Europe and the Soviet Union who could claim, however remotely, German origins (Brubaker 1998a: 1050). It is therefore not far-fetched to assume that, much like the Israeli Law of Return, German policy quite literally produced the "co-ethnics" whose existence it notionally presupposed, who were lured by the prospect of moving into a country with vastly better living conditions.

Liberal and Restrictive Challenges in the 1990s

In the 1990s both Jewish and ethnic German immigration came to face serious social and political challenges. The external causes for this are similar: the removal of exit restrictions in the declining Communist states of Eastern Europe and the Soviet Union. This greatly increased the number of ethnic claimants, many of whose truthfulness was questionable. In response, Israel and Germany alike have faced a dual liberal and restrictive challenge to ethnic immigration. The existence of a liberal challenge sets ethnic immigration apart from "normal" (labor, family, or refugee) immigration, opposition to which has been restriction minded only. The liberal challenge to ethnic immigration articulates the point of view of other migrant or minority groups disadvantaged by, or with respect to, the ethnic preference policy. The liberal challenge is usually not against the entry of putative co-ethnics as such but against their *exclusive* or *preferential* entry, opting instead for an ethnically neutral immigration policy. By contrast, the restrictive challenge articulates the point of view of (certain groups among) the majority population, which sees itself threatened by the cultural and economic consequences of immigration. Ethnic immigration, after all, is still immigration. In the specific case of *ethnic* immigration, the restrictive challenge is either premised on (as in Germany) or directly addresses (as in Israel) a questionable truthfulness of claims for co-ethnicity. This questioning entails the cognitive and evaluative transformation of "returning" co-ethnics into ordinary "immigrants." The restrictive position is usually not about seeking to keep out "true" co-ethnics but about keeping in check "creative" re-identifiers.

Whereas the duality of liberal and restrictive challenges has been the same, the nature of the restrictive challenge has been rather different in both cases considered here: religious in Israel, populist in Germany. In addition, the liberal-*cum*-restrictive challenges have yielded sharply different outcomes: the resilience of Jewish immigration in Israel and the closing down in principle of ethnic German immigration in Germany.

Resilience in Israel

Although still supported by a large majority of the Jewish population in Israel, the Law of Return came under significant pressures during the 1990s. The challenges emanated from two opposite ideological sources. The first objects to the notion of Israel as a Jewish state, proposing instead a nonethnic definition of the polity. The second challenges the (de facto) expansive secular definition of the Jewishness of the state, offering instead a more restrictive, ethnoreligious conception of membership.

The Liberal Challenge   The thrust of the liberal challenge is to bring out the fundamental contradiction in the self-definition of Israel as both a Jewish and a liberal-democratic state (see Rouhana 1998), targeting the Law of Return as a major expression of the ethnic character of the state. In Israel the liberal challenge builds on a minimal sense of civic stateness, with a religious-culturally neutral plurinational *state* as the goal. In contrast to Germany, no significant political actors are pursuing the building of a more inclusive, ethnically neutral Israeli *nation*. Tellingly, the Israeli liberal challenge is mainly, although not exclusively, articulated by the political and cultural elites of the Palestinian population in Israel. For example, the celebrated Palestinian writer in the Hebrew language, Anton Shammas, denounced the Law of Return as a "racist law" (1988: 49). According to Shammas, the Law of Return may have been justified in the immediate wake of the Holocaust and if applied to *persecuted* Jews, but the indiscriminate granting of immigration rights to every Jew in the world is surely indefensible today (Shammas 1988). In addition, Palestinian members of the Knesset have picked up the notion of "a state of all its citizens," and they question and challenge the ethnic character of the Israeli state and its exclusion of the Palestinian minority. In this context, the Arab political parties openly raised the demand to abolish the Law of Return. Their basic claim is that so long as the definition of Israel as a Jewish state stands, with the Law of Return as its key symbolic and institutional component, this state cannot be regarded as a genuine democracy.

To highlight the discriminatory character of the law, Palestinian leaders often contrast the right of return granted to Jews with the dismal situation of the Palestinian refugees. In sharp contrast to the unrestricted immigration of Jews, the Palestinian population displaced and expelled during the 1948–1949 war were never allowed to return to their homeland by the Israeli state. This comparison is drawn by Knesset member Talab El-Sana from the United Arab List: "If the Jewish people have the right, according to the Law of Return, to come to the State of Israel, and this on the basis of a historical claim from 2,000 years ago, why is this right denied to those Palestinians who were forced to leave their towns and villages, not 2,000 years ago, not 1,000 years ago and not 100 years ago, but only 51 years ago?" (*Knesset Records*, July 7, 1999).

The liberal critique of the Law of Return has recently been adopted by "post-Zionist" Jews. Post-Zionism, originally an intellectual and academic preoccupation, has gained considerable public attention, particularly through its popularization in the media. It claims that the Israeli state should cease to be defined according to ethnic principles and be transformed into a "normal" liberal democracy based on the notion of ethnically neutral citizenship (see Ram 1999). Like other Zionist notions, the principle of unrestricted and exclusive Jewish immigration is viewed by many post-Zionists as an anachronism that impedes the transformation of Israel into a democratic state of all its citizens. Hence they urge the abolishment of the law (Silberstein 1999: 8, 123). Post-Zionist ideas are slowly sinking into the liberal wing of Zionist parties. For instance, Knesset member Zahava Gal-On from Meretz, a "left-wing" Zionist party, stated: "It is possible to sincerely recognize that in the Law of Return there are also racist elements, because it is based on origin and membership in a group. . . . It is a law that discriminates between those that want to immigrate to Israel and also between Jewish and non-Jewish citizens." Interestingly, she proposed implementing a German-style restriction of the right of return as applying only to Jews suffering persecution, and establishing a "normal law of immigration such as those existing in Western countries" for nonpersecuted Jews (*Knesset Records*, December 1, 1999).

No doubt the liberal critique of the Law of Return is at the moment weak politically, and the likelihood that it will effect a basic change in Israel's ethnic immigration regime in the foreseeable future is extremely low. Yet the appearance of this challenge and its growing legitimacy reveal the emergence of cracks in the ideological foundations of the ethnic character of the Israeli state.

The Restrictive Challenge   The restrictionist attack on the Law of Return also emerged during the 1990s, as a response to the ethnic composition of the large immigration wave from the Soviet Union and its successor states. As a result of a 1970 amendment to the Law of Return that made non-Jews with family ties to Jews eligible for immigration and automatic citizenship, nearly 20 percent of the immigrants arriving between 1990 and 1994 were halachic non-Jews (i.e., non-Jews according to religious law) (Tolts 1997: 150). The proportion of non-Jews even increased considerably in the following years (DellaPergola 1998: 86). Based on figures published by Israel's Central Bureau of Statistics in 2000, roughly 300,000 of all immigrants arriving in the country during the 1990s were registered as non-Jews. An unknown but probably large number of them are non-Jews not only according to the halachic definition but also according to their religious and ethnic self-identification.

Especially (but not exclusively) ultra-Orthodox religious circles view the growing number of non-Jewish immigrants as a severe threat to the Jewish character of Israel. This concern was first raised in 1990, just one year after the beginning of the new immigration wave. The minister of interior, Arye Deri, and the minister of immigration and absorption, Yitzhak Peretz, both from the ultra-Orthodox Shas Party, proposed changing the law to reduce the number of non-Jewish immigrants (*Jerusalem Post*, July 20, 1990; November 28, 1990). Other ministers and Knesset members from the ultra-Orthodox parties explicitly depicted the non-Jewish immigrants as a threat to Israel's existence (Knesset Committee on Immigration, Absorption, and Diaspora Affairs, January 24, 2000; *Knesset Records*, November 24, 1999). Even some members of Zionist secular parties expressed concern about the future of the Jewish definition of Israel (Knesset Committee on Immigration, Absorption, and Diaspora Affairs, December 6, 1999; January 24, 2000). The print media also became involved in the mounting campaign for a more restrictive immigration policy. For example, an opinion article in the *Jerusalem Post* stated: "Has the Law of Return, Zionism's ultimate instrument for the ingathering of the exiles, inadvertently become a mechanism for the creeping de-Judaization of Israel? The answer is yes, and therefore it is time, alas, to amend the law. . . . Ironic, isn't it? A Zionist cornerstone, out of control, is contributing to the diminishment of Israel's Jewish character" (*Jerusalem Post*, December 5, 1999).

Up to now, however, all attempts to limit the immigration of halachic non-Jews have failed. To understand why, we must consider the reasoning behind the defense of the law, which—in the order presented here—makes reference to the Holocaust, demographic fears, and the risk of a cataclysmic (restrictive-*cum*-liberal) challenge to the Law of Return as such. The first line of defense was to frame the eligibility criteria in the Law of Return as a response to anti-Semitic ideology in general and to Nazism in particular. To legitimize the granting of immigration rights and automatic citizenship to the non-Jewish grandchildren of Jews, many of the supporters of the Law of Return in its present form link the law to the definition of Jewishness practiced by the Nazi regime during the Holocaust. For instance, an editorial opposing any change in the law claims: "Providing a safe haven was our raison d'etre. But now we are considering changing the message. And the dangers inherent in doing so are vast. Legislators beware. . . . Nothing could be more immoral for the Jewish state than to deny a home to the same category of Jew that Hitler had wanted to exterminate" (*Jerusalem Post*, December 3, 1999).

A second defense of the Law of Return in its presently expansive version relates to the demographic functions of immigration within the context of the Israeli-Palestinian conflict. As Ian Lustick (1999) pointed out, maintaining the demographic advantage over the Palestinian minority—whether in the whole "Land of Israel" (including the occupied territories) or only within the state of Israel's recognized borders—has been the main reason for the unwillingness of most political forces to amend the law in a restrictionist direction. In this vein, Knesset member Moshe Arens, a former minister of defense and of foreign affairs from the Likud Party, explains his opposition to limiting the number of non-Jewish immigrants from the former Soviet Union: "I'm afraid that if we accept the proposal of Knesset member Halpert [to restrict the eligibility of non-Jews], . . . we might put at risk the Jewishness of the state, because today we have 20 percent of Arabs in the country. The natural increase of the Arab population is higher than the natural increase of the Jewish population. . . . If we don't succeed in increasing the percentage of Jews in the population, in not too many years we will face a huge demographic problem" (Knesset Committee on Immigration, Absorption, and Diaspora Affairs, November 9, 1999). Expressing a mainly secular notion of membership in the Jewish people, the defenders of halachic non-Jewish immigration for demographic purposes hold that the newcomers would eventually be integrated into the Jewish majority through their participation in central Jewish-Israeli institutions, such as the educational system and the army.

The third line of reasoning by the opponents of restricting the Law of Return interestingly reconnects to the liberal challenge to the law. Former prime minister Ehud Barak was not only unwilling to change the Law of Return but also unwilling to allow any discussion of it in the cabinet. This was driven by the fear that an amendment to the law limiting the eligibility of non-Jews or even a discussion of such an option might open a Pandora's box of a thorough public debate on the principle of ethnic immigration as such, enlarging the political opportunities also for the *liberal* challengers to the Law of Return. This is intimated by the minister of immigration and absorption, Yael Tamir: "We would throw ourselves into a very painful and unnecessary debate, in which the claim will be raised—that I do not want to see raised—that the Law of Return should be abolished completely" (Knesset Committee on Immigration, Absorption, and Diaspora Affairs, January 24, 2000).

The challenge to the Zionist principle of Jewish immigration, whether from a liberal or a religious-restrictionist perspective, has failed so far. Yet the public debate on the Law of Return is in motion. The emergence of this debate, triggered by the ethnic composition of the immigration wave from the former Soviet Union, shows more generally the gradual erosion of Zionist hegemony in Israel and the increasingly confrontational politics conducted by the Palestinian minority. Should the national conflict with the Palestinians and the Arab countries come to an end (admittedly a most unlikely outcome at the present time), the controversy over the ethnic character of the Israeli state and the tensions between ethnic and civic components in its definition of membership would certainly be exacerbated. Then, with the weakening of the "demographic imperative," the political space for the questioning of Jewish immigration, from both liberal and restrictive perspectives, would widen significantly.

Demise in Germany

Between 1950 and 1987 about 1.4 million resettlers were admitted to the Federal Republic of Germany, which amounts to an annual trickle of just 37,000. Low numbers kept German ethnic immigration out of the public view. This abruptly changed in 1988, when, as a result of the liberalization of Eastern Europe and the Soviet Union, the number of admitted resettlers skyrocketed, to about 220,000 in that year alone. Between 1988 and 1997, 2.2 million resettlers were admitted—which is almost double the number from the preceding four decades (Münz and Ohliger 1998). As in the Israeli case, escalating numbers of ethnic migrants created pressure on the underlying policy. In a second parallel to the Israeli case, these pressures originated from both liberal and restrictive positions. As in Israel, the liberal challenge spoke on behalf of those migrants and minorities who were disadvantaged compared to ethnic migrants, in this case asylum seekers and (Turkish) guest worker immigrants. However, the restrictive challenge was different. There could be no ideological challenge and concomitant plea to return to the original spirit of Germany's law of return because the rationale of this policy—mastery of the consequences of World War II—was simply no longer valid. There was no original spirit to recapture. Instead of an ideological challenge, Germany's restrictive challenge was a populist challenge, in which the economic and social privileges attached to expellee status lost their public support.

The Liberal Challenge   Just about when the center-right government celebrated the reception of ethnic German resettlers as an "act of national solidarity" (Chancellor Kohl, quoted by Levy 1999: 132), the same government responded to a swelling number of asylum seekers by trying to renege on the constitutional asylum right, as guaranteed by Article 16 of the Basic Law. This inequity was doubly scandalous, because both asylum seekers and ethnic resettlers (who were officially assumed to suffer from "expulsion pressure") were notionally refugees. However, how could ethnic resettlers from post-Communist Poland, Hungary, or Romania still be subject to expulsion pressure when, according to the new "safe country of origin" rule in asylum policy, the same states were officially labeled "free of persecution" (*verfolgungsfrei*), so that asylum requests by people originating from these states were generally denied? The contradictory treatment of both types of refugees was first attacked by a leading Social Democratic Party (SPD) politician, Oscar Lafontaine. Calling the center-right government's preference for ethnic German over non-German refugees *Deutschtümelei* (an untranslatable term denoting ethnic nationalism), Lafontaine declared: "I have certain problems to admit German-origin people in the fourth and fifth generation, while colored people whose lives are at risk are rejected" (*Frankfurter Rundschau*, November 7, 1988). Chancellor Kohl, known externally for his commitment to unifying Europe but on the domestic scene a long-standing proponent of a strengthened ethnic sense of national community, derided this statement as "disgusting," and he thundered that Germans would be a "morally deprived people" if they did not stand by their "compatriots" (*Frankfurter Rundschau*, November 7, 1988).

As in Israel, this was a struggle between liberal and ethnic interpretations of the German state, with liberals rallying around the defense of the constitutional asylum right (Article 16) and ethnics pointing to the commitments enshrined in the Basic Law's ethnic German expellee clause (Article 116). A first difference, however, was that the commitment to asylum seekers was an abstract human rights commitment, directed at people outside Germany's territorial and national boundaries, whereas the Israeli liberals' reference to disadvantaged Palestinians meant a group that was not only within the state's borders but also considered its territory their ancient homeland, much as Jews did. In this regard, the structural equivalent to Palestinians in Israel is the descendants of non-European guest workers (especially Turks). They were kept out of the citizenry by archaic citizenship laws that favored ethnic resettlers, even though the ethnic resettlers were without any concrete ties to German society. This was a much more powerful comparison, because it pointed to a discriminated group in, rather than outside, German society. Calling those Polish, Russian, and Romanian newcomers "Germans who want to live among Germans" (Liesner 1988: 3) while calling those who were born and raised in Germany foreigners showed in extremis the obsoleteness of the ethnic idiom of nationhood. Liberal challengers of ethnic immigration, in fact, were drawing references both to disadvantaged asylum seekers and guest worker immigrants. If the asylum seeker reference was somewhat more prominent, this was simply because this was the largest migrant group in the early 1990s, singled out by the resettler-friendly center-right government for restrictive measures.

The notion of *Deutschtümelei* and the inclination of the German liberal challenge to associate the conservative government's ethnic return policy with the Nazist *Heim-ins-Reich-Politik*, which had a basis in some questionable administrative practices, indicates a second difference from the Israeli case—the obvious delegitimization and decline of an ethnic understanding of nationhood. Positively phrased, the German liberal challenge to ethnic immigration could rely not only on a minimal sense of civic stateness, based on the procedural logic of representative democracy and legal universalism, but also on a thicker sense of civic nationhood, according to which it has become anachronistic to define Germanness on the basis of ethnic genealogy (for details see Levy 1999). This made the German liberal challenge potentially much stronger than its Israeli counterpart, which remained limited to a few (Arab and post-Zionist) fringe voices outside the political and societal mainstream.

At the discursive level, the German liberal challenge came in two variants. One variation considered ethnic resettlers as just one of several immigrant groups and called for a comprehensive and self-declared immigration policy to take care of all of them. As a Green member of parliament put it, "Resettlers are immigrants and refugees, independently of their ethnic origins" (*Das Parlament*, August 25, 1989). The other variant was to take sides, particularly with asylum seekers against resettlers, as in the Lafontaine response. Behind these responses were different images of resettlers: as what they were, a sociological minority (e.g., asylum seekers eager to escape poverty and state breakdown); or as what they were made to be in official discourse, co-ethnics, and thus unloved relics of ethnic nationhood.

The Restrictive Challenge   In the context of a center-right party coalition in power during most of the 1990s, the restrictive challenge had to be more immediately effective than the liberal challenge to ethnic German immigration. Its focus became the economic and social benefits bestowed on ethnic newcomers by the state. The FERL of 1953, the legal basis of ethnic immigration, was, first, a social integration law that provided for a long list of positive discrimination measures. Elderly resettlers, for instance, received fictionally wage- and employment-based pensions that equaled and sometimes even exceeded those of comparable native Germans, even though they had never worked in Germany and thus had not contributed to the public pension funds. "Who has lost his home and property because of his Germanness may well expect that the great insurance community of West Germany will compensate him for this," said the minister responsible during the crafting of the FERL (German Parliament, BT-Drs., Stenographische Berichte 260, Sitzung vom, April 4, 1953). This reasoning may have been appropriate in 1953, when the number of resettlers was down to a trickle of 4,000 per year. It was anachronistic when more than 20 times as many arrived in 1988, with a rather lesser sense of obligation on the part of West Germany's "great insurance community." Against the backdrop of increasing mass unemployment and slimming welfare benefits for natives, the generous benefits bestowed on the ethnic resettlers had to stir massive resentment and social envy. By 1990, more than 80 percent of the public was in favor of restricting ethnic immigration, which was deemed by most to be economically rather than ethnically motivated (Levy 1999: 143).

In response to the dramatic collapse of public support for ethnic German immigration, the center-right government quickly retreated from its initial approach to make the newcomers' swift integration a 1950s-style "national task." Just one year after passing the ambitious Special Programme for Integrating Resettlers in 1988, the focus shifted toward keeping resettlers in their places of origin, by means of development aids and by securing in situ minority and self-government rights (Puskeppeleit 1996: 104). For those still bent on immigrating, a series of laws passed since 1989 made this both less lucrative and more difficult. The Integration Adjustment Act of January 1990, among other things, replaced wage-based unemployment benefits with a standardized and more modest "integration money," which is limited to one year. Six months later, the Resettler Reception Law, in a copy of the British "entry clearance" system, shifted the application procedure to the countries of origin. This amounted to an unofficial quota system (and approximation of ethnic return to "normal" immigration), almost halving the number of admitted resettlers, from 400,000 in 1990 to 220,000 in 1991.

The restrictive trend culminated in the Law on Settling the Consequences of the War (*Kriegsfolgenbereinigungsgesetz*) of 1993, which phased out all special laws dealing with World War II consequences, thus signaling the official end of the postwar period. This law was a compromise between the ruling Christian Democratic Union (Christlich-Demokratische Union, CDU) and the oppositional SPD. The SPD wanted to put an end to ethnic German immigration as such by means of a "fixed day" (*Stichtag*), after which no further applications were to be accepted, arguing that after the liberalization of Eastern Europe there was no longer any expulsion pressure. On the other side, the CDU rejected such a deadline rule, but, interestingly, with the defensive argument that the resulting "exit panic" would further increase rather than decrease ethnic immigration (Alexy 1993); the wish to decrease ethnic German immigration had evidently become consensual by then. The SPD demand had a particular bite because the parliamentary opposition's consent was needed for the center-right government's plan to curtail the constitutional asylum right. In the so-called

Asylum Compromise of December 1992, the SPD gave in to restrict asylum, but only at the price of restricting ethnic German immigration. Accordingly, the *Kriegsfolgenbereinigungsgesetz*, which (among other things) implements the *Aussiedler* component of the Asylum Compromise, bears the mark not only of the restrictionist but also of the liberal challenge to ethnic immigration.

The crucial novelty of the new law is to deny the status of ethnic resettler to all individuals born after January 1, 1993. This means that ethnic German immigration has in principle come to an end. For those still eligible to apply, the procedure has been fundamentally reshuffled. First, a formal quota restriction of 200,000 admissions per year (reduced to 120,000 in the late 1990s) has been instituted. Second, except for applicants from the former Soviet Union, the existence of expulsion pressure (which is one of two prerequisites for being granted the status of *Aussiedler*) is no longer presumed but has to be proved by the applicant. Third, the criteria for ethnic membership (*Volkszugehörigkeit*, which is the second prerequisite for *Aussiedler* status) have been tightened for applicants born after December 31, 1923. Most important, the active mastery of the German language is now key to the proof of one's *Volkszugehörigkeit*. This change, innocent as it seems, marks a fundamental departure from previous recognition practice, in which the absence of German language skills was taken as a sign of oppression and forced assimilation and thus held in favor of the ethnic claimant.

Discussion

A common feature of co-ethnic immigration is to force the state into the difficult business of checking individual identity claims—interestingly, not unlike asylum policy, in which individual biographic claims are the subject of an excruciating recognition procedure. These classificatory practices by states are not determined by a fixed sense of identity but instead are moldable, subject to conflict, and injected with a heavy dose of political exigency. In Israel the question "Who is a Jew?" has been anything but clear, and the eligibility criteria of the Law of Return have been the source of permanent conflict between secular and religious understandings of Jewishness (see Samet 1985). In Germany the most recent emphasis on language in determining ethnic Germanness is entirely the result of state interests. It responds to the oddity of sociological non-Germans entering as official co-ethnics, which brought the public up against the policy and found concrete manifestation in obvious problems in socially integrating the latest wave of *Spätaussiedler*, particularly from ex-Soviet Eurasia (e.g., Dietz and Hilkes 1994). In radically changing the role of language in the recognition procedure, the German government has de facto admitted that the status of ethnic Germans is more the result of its own policy than of some underlying ethnic Germanness.

This indicates a second feature of immigration policies based on co-ethnicity: the production of ethnicity by the very policies that are meant to presuppose and passively register this ethnicity. Ethnic immigration policies are performative; they help create the (ethnic) reality that they nominally presuppose. In our cases the receiving states' production of ethnicity is also favored by some objective demographic features of the sending regions. The pool of applicants for ethnic German or Jewish status in Eastern Europe and the former Soviet Union is anything but sharply bounded; instead, it is characterized by high degrees of intermarriage with and cultural and linguistic assimilation into their local environments (see Münz and Ohliger 1998). It is therefore not far-fetched to assume that the "official" ethnicity, not the "real" ethnicity, of the state is driving this strangely non-Euclidian immigration in which "outmigrations may increase rather than decrease the reservoir of potential ethnomigrants" (Brubaker 1998a: 1053).

A third feature of ethnic immigration policies is their susceptibility to a liberal challenge, even in such proverbially ethnic states as Israel and Germany. This is because such policies conflict with constitutive principles of liberal stateness, such as public neutrality and equality (see Dworkin 1978). At the academic level liberals have usually argued in favor of open borders (Carens 1987), and a policy that makes closed borders more permeable for some should not further outrage them—if those "some" had not been singled out according to ascriptive group criteria, which entails discrimination against other immigrant and minority groups. Because ethnic immigration is, after all, immigration, it has also provoked a restrictive challenge, which addresses the economic and cultural costs of immigration; in particular, the restrictive challenge is premised on questioning the veracity of co-ethnicity claims, as a result of which returning co-ethnics are refashioned as ordinary immigrants. Interestingly, although obviously differently motivated, the liberal and restrictive challenges have synergetic effects, one reinforcing the other. The liberal position is usually not against the entry of putative co-ethnics as such but is against their *exclusive* or *preferential* entry, opting instead for an ethnically neutral immigration policy. In turn, the restrictive position is usually not about seeking to keep out "true" co-ethnics but about keeping in check "creative" re-identifiers and the resentment that arises from giving them entitlements that exceed those of the domestic population, particularly in the context of slimming welfare states. However, in their synergetic confluence the liberal and restrictive challenges can grow into a severe threat to ethnic immigration as such. This has been the German experience, in which the combination of the restrictive and liberal challenges in the Asylum Compromise of 1992 led to the death in principle of ethnic German immigration. Likewise, the unwillingness of mainstream political forces in Israel to change the Law of Return in a restrictive direction (as wanted by Orthodox religious circles) was encouraged by the fear that this might also promote a full-scale liberal attack on the Law of Return as such and thus endanger the Jewish character of the state.

To explain divergent outcomes in Israel and Germany, we have argued that for historical and geopolitical reasons the political space for raising the liberal and restrictive challenges was differently developed in both cases. *Historically*, the encounter between Germans and Jews under Nazism compromised ethnic statehood in Germany, permitting only a temporally and spatially qualified ethnic immigration policy. By contrast, the Holocaust provided a powerful founding myth for Israel as the place for the "ingathering of the exiles" without any temporal or spatial limitations. As we saw, the Holocaust motif was also effectively used to deflect the restrictive religious challenge to the Law of Return in its current, expansive form. *Geopolitically*, Israel's interest in Jewish immigration is enduringly tied up with the protracted national conflict with the Palestinians, whereas the geopolitical interest of the German state in ethnic immigration was temporally limited to the cold war context. One difference with Israel is that in Germany ethnic immigration has never had to be at the service of a state whose territory is permanently contested by rival ethnonational groups. The absence of territorial disputes between rival ethnonational groups deprived ethnic immigration of all secondary strategic purposes, next to complying with an individual right of the ethnic claimant. And the legitimacy of claims for co-ethnicity became ever more doubtful as national self-understanding moved from an ethnic to a civic orientation. When the massive entry of notionally co-ethnic but sociologically Russian or Eastern European immigrants in the 1990s created adjustment and integration problems similar to those of "normal" immigrants, an obvious opening was provided also for the restrictive challenge, which at that point was no longer kept in check by the cold war division of the European continent. By contrast, the persistence of the conflict between Jews and Palestinians over the same territory gave rise to a demographic imperative of such magnitude that all liberal or restrictive challenges to ethnic immigration in Israel have (so far) come to nil. Given its historical roots in an ethnonational colonial project, Israel is determined to be, perhaps permanently, a strong "nationalizing state" (Brubaker 1996) that seeks to strengthen the Jewish majority against the Palestinian minority by admitting more (and in principle only) Jewish immigrants. This demographic imperative has constricted the political space not only for the liberal challenge but also for the restrictive challenge to ethnic immigration—a doctrinary, narrow definition of Jewishness is simply luxurious in the Hobbesian zone of war, into which Israel seems precariously and permanently locked.

The full scale of Germany's turning away from ethnic German immigration and of Israel's continued commitment to Jewish immigration is evident in Germany's recent preferential admission of Jewish immigrants and in Israel's continued rejection of the right of return for Palestinians. Just about when the German government restricted the admission of ethnic Germans, it opened the doors wide for Jewish immigrants from the former Soviet Union. Since the passing of the 1991 Quota Refugee Law, 115,000 Russian Jews have seized the opportunity to immigrate freely (without numerical restrictions and without individual screening) to Germany, quadrupling the size of the small Jewish community in the *Land der Täter* (Laurence 2000). In a delicate twist, the Israeli government has repeatedly urged the German government not to grant automatic refugee status to Russian Jews, claiming them for its own nation-building purposes. Admitting Jewish immigrants is the latest instance in the country's politics of *Wiedergutmachung* (reparations), in which Jews obviously take a higher order of priority than co-ethnics.

A partial structural equivalent on the Israeli side would be restrictions on Jewish immigration and an open-door policy for Palestinians. The right of return for the 3.5 million Palestinian refugees actually was a central stake in the aborted peace negotiations between former prime minister Barak and the Palestinian leadership. It was overwhelmingly rejected even by liberal Israeli intellectuals and peace activists.

The wholesale rejection of the Palestinian right of return invokes the demographic imperative not to be outnumbered by Palestinians, which has been a central element in the resilience of Jewish-priority immigration in Israel. It also shows that the definition of Israel as a Jewish state prevails; no civic transformation of Israeli nationhood is in the making. By contrast, the decline of ethnic German immigration is closely linked to the rise of a new civic-territorial identity in postwar Germany (see Levy 1999). If there still is an "ethnocultural idiom of nationhood" (Brubaker 1992) in Germany, it is not readily visible in the disparate treatment of ethnic Germans and Jews for immigration purposes, and at best it has taken on strangely inverted forms.

In this chapter we have considered ethnic immigration policies as a dependent variable that is shaped not only by ethnic national idioms but also by geopolitical context and countervailing (liberal and restrictive) forces. However, the dynamics of ethnic immigration may also be looked at as an independent variable that affects the boundaries and the constitution of the national community. Once a policy has been set, it in turn affects the boundary definitions that it partially reflects. After the demise of ethnic German immigration, which will be complete in only a generation or so, a major institutional expression of ethnic stateness will have disappeared in Germany. The default result of this must be the further strengthening of civic nationhood. In the same vein, Daniel Levy (1999) argued that the scaling down of ethnic German immigration both reflects and reinforces the rise of a civic identity in contemporary Germany. Conversely, the resilience of Jewish immigration is not just expressive of but also reproduces the ethnic self-definition of the Israeli state as a Jewish state. Note the superb irony that this is attained through admitting also halachic or even self-defined non-Jews, which might eventually lead to the rise of a minority identity of the Russian newcomers and thus add to the already considerable challenges to the Jewish definition of Israel. Conditioning and conditioned at the same time, the boundaries of the national community are not fixed but fluid as a result of, among other things, a state's ethnic immigration policies.

Note

This chapter is an abbreviated version of an article that first appeared in *Archives européennes de sociologie* 43(3):301–335 (2002).

References Cited

Alexy, Hans. 1993. "Zur Neuregelung des Aussiedlerzuzugs." *Neue Zeitschrift für Verwaltungsrecht* 12:1171–1173.

Brubaker, Rogers. 1992. *Citizenship and Nationhood in France and Germany.* Cambridge, MA: Harvard University Press.

———. 1996. *Nationalism Reframed.* New York: Cambridge University Press.

———. 1998a. "Migrations of Ethnic Unmixing in the 'New Europe.'" *International Migration Review* 32(4):1047–1065.

———. 1998b. "Myths and Misconceptions in the Study of Nationalism." In *The State of the Nation,* John Hall, ed. Cambridge, UK: Cambridge University Press, 272–306.

————. 1999. "The Manichean Myth: Rethinking the Distinction Between 'Civic' and 'Ethnic' Nationalism." In *Nation and National Identity*, Hanspeter Kriesi, Klaus Armingeon, Hannes Siegrist, and Andreas Wimmer, eds. Zurich: Ruegger, 55–71.

Carens, Joseph. 1987. "Aliens and Citizens: The Case for Open Borders." *Journal of Politics* 49(2):251–273.

Central Bureau of Statistics. Various years. *Statistical Abstract of Israel.* Jerusalem: Central Bureau of Statistics.

DellaPergola, Sergio. 1998. "The Global Context of Migration to Israel." In *Immigration to Israel,* Elazar Leshem and Judith Shuval, eds. New Brunswick, NJ: Transaction, 51–92.

Dietz, Barbara, and Peter Hilkes. 1994. *Integriert oder Isoliert?* Munich: Olzog.

Dworkin, Ronald. 1978. "Liberalism." In *Public and Private Morality*, Stuart Hampshire, ed. Cambridge, UK: Cambridge University Press, 113–143.

Freeman, Gary. 1995. "Modes of Immigration Politics in Liberal Democratic States." *International Migration Review* 29(4):881–902.

Gouldman, M. D. 1970. *Israel Nationality Law.* Jerusalem: Institute for Legislative Research and Comparative Law, Hebrew University of Jerusalem.

Greenfeld, Liah. 1992. *Nationalism.* Cambridge, MA: Harvard University Press.

Jacobson, David. 1996. *Rights Across Borders: Immigration and the Decline of Citizenship.* Baltimore: Johns Hopkins University Press.

Joppke, Christian. 1998. "Why Liberal States Accept Unwanted Immigration." *World Politics* 50(2):266–293.

Karapin, Roger. 1999. "The Politics of Immigration Control in Britain and Germany." *Comparative Politics* 31(4):423–444.

King, Desmond. 2000. *Making Americans.* Cambridge, MA: Harvard University Press.

Klein, Claude. 1997. "The Right of Return in Israeli Law." *Tel Aviv University Studies in Law* 13:53–61.

Kohn, Hans. 1944. *The Idea of Nationalism.* New York: Macmillan.

Laurence, Jonathan. 2000. "(Re)constructing Community in Berlin." Unpublished manuscript.

Levy, Daniel. 1999. "Remembering the Nation." Ph.D. dissertation, Columbia University, New York.

Liesner, Ernst. 1988. *Aussiedler.* Herford, Germany: Maximilian.

Lustick, Ian. 1999. "Israel as a Non-Arab State: The Political Implications of Mass Immigration of Non-Jews." *Middle East Journal* 53(3):417–433.

Money, Jeannette. 1999. *Fences and Neighbors.* Ithaca, NY: Cornell University Press.

Münz, Rainer, and Rainer Ohliger. 1998. "Deutsche Minderheiten in Ostmittel- und Osteuropa, Aussiedler in Deutschland." Berlin: Humboldt University (hectograph).

Peled, Yoav. 1992. "Ethnic Democracy and the Legal Construction of Citizenship: Arab Citizens of the Jewish State." *American Political Science Review* 86(2):432–443.

Peretz, Don. 1958. *Israel and the Palestine Arabs.* Washington, DC: Middle East Institute.

Plender, Richard. 1988. *International Migration Law,* 2nd ed. Dordrecht, Netherlands: Nijhoff.

Puskeppeleit, Juergen. 1996. "Der Paradigmenwechsel der Aussiedlerpolitik." In *Forschungsfeld Aussiedler,* Inge Graudenz and Regina Roemhild, eds. Frankfurt am Main: Peter Lang, 99–122.

Ram, Uri. 1999. "The State of the Nation: Contemporary Challenges to Zionism in Israel." *Constellations* 6(3):325–338.

Rouhana, Nadim. 1998. "Israel and Its Arab Citizens: Predicaments in the Relationship Between Ethnic States and Ethnonational Minorities." *Third World Quarterly* 19(2):277–296.

Samet, Moshe. 1985. "Who Is a Jew? (1958–1977)." *Jerusalem Quarterly* 19(2):277–296.

Shachar, Ayelet. 2000. "Citizenship and Membership in the Israeli Polity." In *From Migrants to Citizens: Membership in a Changing World,* Alexander Aleinikoff and Douglas Klusmeyer, eds. Washington, DC: Carnegie Endowment for International Peace, 386–433.

Shafir, Gershon, and Yoav Peled. 1998. "Citizenship and Stratification in an Ethnic Democracy." *Ethnic and Racial Studies* 21(3):408–427.

Shammas, Anton. 1988. "The Morning After." *New York Review of Books* 35(14):47–52.

Silberstein, Laurence. 1999. *The Postzionism Debate: Knowledge and Power in Israeli Culture.* New York: Routledge.

Smith, Anthony. 1986. *The Ethnic Origins of Nations.* Oxford, UK: Blackwell.

Tolts, Mark. 1997. "The Interrelationship Between Emigration and the Socio-Demographic Profile of Russian Jewry." In *Russian Jews in Three Continents,* Noah Lewin-Epstein, Yaacov Ro'i, and Paul Ritterband, eds. London: Frank Cass, 147–176.

Viet, Vincent. 1998. *La France immigrée.* Paris: Fayard.

Weiss, Yfaat. 2002. "The Golem and Its Creator, or How the Jewish Nation-State Became Multiethnic." In *Challenging Ethnic Citizenship: German and Israeli Perspectives on Immigration,* Daniel Levy and Yfaat Weiss, eds. New York: Berghahn, 82–104.

Yack, Bernard. 1996. "The Myth of the Civic Nation." *Critical Review* 10(2):193–211.

Ethnic Return Migration to Europe

From Germans to Migrants

Aussiedler Migration to Germany

Amanda Klekowski von Koppenfels

The German government is aware of its historical responsibility toward the German minorities in Eastern Europe and, in particular, toward those in the former Soviet Union. In light of this background, the government respects the decision of each individual to either make his future in his current home or to come to Germany within the framework of the legally defined conditions of admittance. The government will make sure that this migration is socially acceptable. *This presupposes integration. Integration is therefore the central focus of* Aussiedler *policy.*

Federal Republic of Germany, Federal Ministry of the Interior (n.d. (b)) (emphasis added)

NOT QUITE 20 YEARS AGO, the *Aussiedler*—ethnic Germans living in the former Soviet Union and Eastern and Central Europe and eligible to be accepted as citizens in Germany—were presented by the German government as "our own countrymen" (*unsere eigene Landsleute*) (Waffenschmidt 1988: 1). Today, they have become immigrants accepted for historical reasons whose integration, the German government assures its citizens, will be made as "socially acceptable" as possible. Once, "the German *Aussiedler* [were] welcome here" and they were touted as "a large and varied net gain for our country and for us all," which could be "verif[ied]" with "quantifiable data" (Pressemitteilung 440/89, 1989). Today, the Immigration Law (2005) has a provision for integration courses—"a fundamental building block for integration in Germany"—which is intended for *Aussiedler* and their spouses and children as well as for noncitizen migrants, clearly indicating that *Aussiedler* are seen to be facing the same integration challenges that any new migrant faces (Federal Republic of Germany 2004; Federal Republic of Germany, Federal Ministry of the Interior, n.d. (a)).

In the post–cold war era momentous changes surrounding *Aussiedler* migration have occurred. One of the most fundamental changes is the makeup of the *Aussiedler* migration flow itself, which shifted from a pre–cold war makeup of Germans from Poland and Romania to one made up largely of migrants from mixed German-Russian marriages in the former Soviet Union. The reasons for migration have also arguably shifted, from co-ethnic return migration on the basis of discrimination to economically motivated migration. *Aussiedler* policy has largely been reactive, as has much of overall German migration policy and legislation, rather than being a proactive and coherent strategy.

Significantly, the context of *Aussiedler* migration has also shifted, as has the political context of migration to Germany in toto. Although the change in policy rhetoric indicates a substantive shift both in the political context of *Aussiedler* migration and in the status of *Aussiedler* themselves, other changes in German legislation, policy, and rhetoric demonstrate a parallel liberalization of broader naturalization and immigration policy. *Aussiedler* are now increasingly seen as immigrants like any others; and, indeed, conversely, other immigrants are increasingly welcome as citizens in the German polity, whereas *Aussiedler*— or immigrant citizens—suffer from increasingly negative public opinion. This shift has, in turn, had a negative effect on the integration and self-identity of *Aussiedler*, who increasingly view themselves as neither Germans nor Russians but as a distinctly separate group.

What has been behind this shift? I argue here that, paradoxically, two related aspects of *Aussiedler* migration itself were the driving force behind the dramatic change in German immigration and citizenship policy in the 1990s: *Aussiedler*'s surprisingly poor—compared to the level expected—sociocultural and economic integration and their own self-understanding and German public perception of their poor integration against the background of what had been expected (compare Chapter 1).[1] Finally, but no less significantly, are the numbers involved. *Aussiedler* migration, which averaged 40,000 per year from 1950 to the mid-1980s, peaked at nearly 400,000 in 1990 as the cold war drew to an end. As a result of these three developments, *Aussiedler* migration was severely restricted. At the same time, a more open policy toward non-German residents in Germany was developing—the result, I argue, of an increasing conviction among German policymakers that noncitizen denizens were a more fundamental part of German society than immigrant citizens; again, this was a reactive shift, but one whose significance should not be underestimated. Ultimately, by the turn of the twenty-first century, *Aussiedler* were disadvantaged compared to non-German residents in Germany, in terms both of migration and their lack of social integration, and Germany's migration policy had shifted from one of ethnic privilege to a more open one (see Chapter 3) in response to the deteriorating *Aussiedler* situation and changes in geopolitics.

The Development and Changing Political-Ideological Interpretation of *Aussiedler* Policy

Ethnic German migrants from Eastern and Central Europe and the former Soviet Union who enjoy a special legal status, *Aussiedler*, become German citizens and receive assistance (now cut back substantially) in integrating into German society and economy (for more information see von Koppenfels 2002). The post–World War II *Aussiedler* policy arose from a primarily ideological basis. Rather than being open to all those of German origin, as is often believed, the *Aussiedler* program was open only to ethnic Germans from Communist countries (and, since 1993, only to those from the former Soviet Union).[2] The policy was based on the supposition of ethnically based discrimination or persecution of Germans in Eastern and Central Europe and not on German ethnic belonging as such. It was based on two legal texts: Article 116 of the Basic Law and the Federal Expellee and Refugee Law (FERL) of 1953.[3] These two laws were developed in reaction to two crucial policy decisions made during and after World War II. These decisions—made by the Allies and by the Soviet Union—did draw on German ethnicity: When Hitler invaded Russia in 1941, Stalin feared that ethnic Germans, living in Russia since the eighteenth century, might place their loyalty to Germany above their loyalty to Russia. Solely on the basis of their German ethnicity, Stalin therefore ordered 500,000 ethnic Germans deported eastward to Kazakhstan and Siberia, where they remained in internment camps until 1956.[4] Similarly, the Allies' decision to expel 8 million Germans from former German territories ceded to Poland and Czechoslovakia, westward this time, also played a role.[5] In both cases, German ethnicity (determined by such factors as family name, native language, or religion) was the decisive factor in the expulsion or deportation decision.

The citizenship status of the 8 million expellees in postwar West Germany was legally unclear, with some holding Polish or Czech passports and others holding German ones; likewise, there was also ideologically based concern for the 3 to 4 million Germans in Eastern and Central Europe and the Soviet Union[6] as well as the 16 million in East Germany. Responding to the use of ethnicity in the decisions made at Potsdam and made by Stalin, ethnicity was

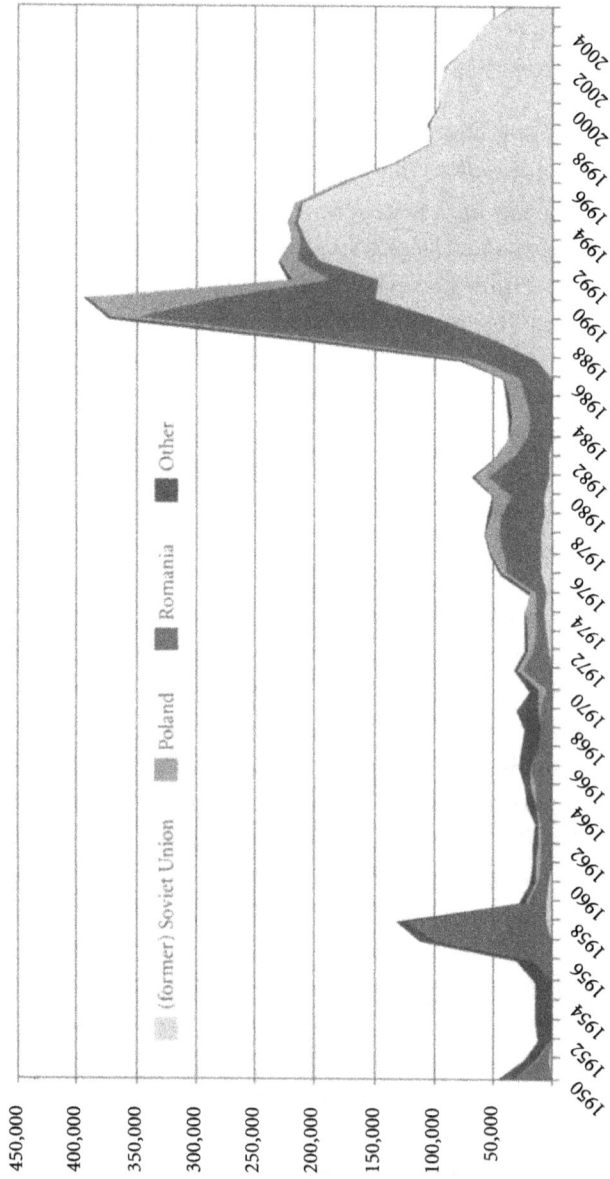

Figure 4.1 *Aussiedler* migration to Germany, 1950–2006. Data from "Zuzug 1950–1996" (1996) and Statistisches Bundesamt (2008).

correspondingly introduced into these two German laws to ensure the inclusion of these Germans. Article 116 removed any uncertainty, including expellees as full members in the German polity and making no legal differentiation between expellees and native Germans.[7] Article 116 included the phrase *deutsche Volkszugehörigkeit*, roughly translated as "German ethnicity," but literally meaning "belonging to the German people," to assure this legal equality (Parlamentarischer Rat 1949: 596). It should be noted that at the same time, the right to asylum for political and other refugees was equally enshrined in Article 16 of the Basic Law.

The FERL, passed in 1953 after heavy lobbying by expellees, established a legal basis for the integration and equality of the expellees as well as for the continued acceptance of *Aussiedler* from Central and Eastern Europe and refugees from East Germany. The provisions for the continued acceptance of *Aussiedler* and refugees from East Germany reflected West Germany's political positioning during the cold war and were justified as such. In February 1953 Minister for Expellees Lukaschek said in the German Parliament that the refugees from East Germany who would benefit under this law "are victims of the Cold War. The flight from the Soviet Zone of Occupation is a clear political vote of the German people for the free West" (Deutscher Bundestag, 250th Session, February 25, 1953: 11,972B). Or, from a different angle, drawing an explicit comparison to the liberal German asylum policy that accepted nearly all those fleeing the Communist bloc,[8] one member of Parliament noted that it should likewise be "a matter of course that our . . . German brothers and sisters [from Communist countries] may come here unhindered" (Parlamentarischer Rat 1950: 1756).

As argued later, however, the post–cold war migration was qualitatively different, which had significant results for German migration policy. Broadly, the door to Germany from the Soviet bloc was wide open during the cold war. However, during that time, the door out of the Soviet bloc was, for the most part, closed. As that door began to open with Mikhail Gorbachev's liberalization at the end of the 1980s, the raison d'être of the German policy lost its validity, and the Germans began to close their doors to their German countrymen (see Figure 4.1). This restriction was hastened by the poor integration and social marginalization of *Aussiedler*, which in turn led to increasing negative public opinion (see opening quote of this chapter). These domestic political factors undoubtedly played a role in the changes in *Aussiedler* policy.

Political-Ideological Interpretation of Aussiedler *Policy*

Because *Aussiedler* are accepted in Germany on the basis of presumed ethnic discrimination[9] rather than ethnicity per se, potential *Aussiedler* must therefore see themselves as German in the former Soviet Union and represent themselves as German to others (FERL, §6). The legal assumption of this representation is then that they have suffered discrimination on the basis of being members of the German minority and are, on the basis of that presumed discrimination, eligible for *Aussiedler* status. Logically, then, it follows that the relevant laws require potential *Aussiedler* to show that they have maintained German linguistic,[10] cultural, and/or social characteristics in order to qualify for *Aussiedler* status. In other words, to have suffered ethnic discrimination, they must have been identifiable as members of the German ethnic minority. If they were not identifiable as such, they cannot have been singled out for ethnically based persecution or discrimination.

This requirement was initially—in the 1950s, 1960s, and early 1970s—interpreted rather loosely both by officials and by courts deciding disputed cases. However, as the political landscape changed in the Eastern bloc, this situation did not continue to hold true. In 1975, with the signature of the Helsinki Final Act and the establishment of the Commission on Security and Cooperation in Europe (CSCE), human and minority rights were protected in signatory states, which included Romania, Poland, and the Soviet Union—the states with the bulk of ethnic Germans in Central and Eastern Europe. Thus the purpose of the *Aussiedler* policy, that of protecting the minority and human rights of one particular ethnic minority, was to some extent rendered superfluous.[11] This development was reflected in court decisions that tightened requirements for ethnic German return migration.

Cold War Versus Post–Cold War Aussiedler

When *Aussiedler* migration and integration is analyzed, the cold war–era *Aussiedler* are, for the most part, widely seen as unproblematic and successful, whereas the integration of those who migrated in the post–cold war era increasingly deteriorated. *Aussiedler* who migrated during the cold war were, it is nearly universally agreed, unproblematic in terms of integration. They worked hard, learned hard, were willing to integrate, and were accepted as Germans. They largely came from Poland and Romania, with just under 5 percent coming from the Soviet Union in the 1950–1987 period. They had maintained ties with German culture, including strong German language skills, and had education and professional training that were relatively close to German standards. Furthermore, those *Aussiedler* who migrated during the cold war appear to have been those who had both closer ties to Germany and a stronger will to emigrate—when emigration was quite difficult—and to integrate.

With the coming of the post–cold war *Aussiedler*, the situation in Germany changed as well. The origin of the *Aussiedler* was radically different, with about 75 percent (1988–2005) coming from the former Soviet Union—with different language and professional skills—a situation that was exacerbated by German legislation passed in 1992 limiting migration to the former Soviet Union.

At the same time, public opinion began to turn against *Aussiedler*. This negative public opinion was one of the key factors in the severe reduction of integration benefits—which in the early 1990s included job training, language courses, loans, pension benefits (now reduced to well below native German levels), and lump sum "compensatory" payments (FERL, §§9, 13; "Hilfen für Spätaussiedler," 1998: 38–53; "Sonderprogramm zur Eingliederung der Aussiedler," 1988: 5–18). Not only was the increasing scale of *Aussiedler* migration (peaking at 400,000 in 1990) significant, but the strengthening "social envy" of native Germans toward *Aussiedler* increasingly made *Aussiedler* benefits a domestic political quagmire. The seemingly poor integration that followed, regardless of the payment of integration benefits, likewise had a negative effect on German public opinion.

An October 2005 press release (Federal Republic of Germany, Federal Ministry of the Interior, 2005) from the German Ministry of the Interior clarified what benefits *Aussiedler* could or could not receive and also noted disadvantages that ethnic Germans in the former Soviet Union have faced since World War II. The press release went on to say that integration had become increasingly difficult, because of the decrease in language skills, and that "the federal government therefore reacted with the Immigration Law," which requires language tests for all *Aussiedler* and their family members to ensure that "[*Aussiedler*] migration remain[s] socially tolerable." In other words, the logistics of *Aussiedler* migration were changed directly, if not solely, as a reaction to negative public opinion in Germany.

Makeup of Aussiedler *Flow*

A 1992 law (the Act Dealing with the Consequences of the War [ADCW], discussed later) introduced different categories of *Aussiedler*, with those who qualified as *Aussiedler* being treated under §4 of the law. Spouses and children are subject to the regulations of §7, and other family members, such as step-children, non-*Aussiedler* children-in-law, and grandchildren, are subject to §8 of the ADCW. Different bundles of rights are linked with each category.

The makeup of the flow has shifted significantly, largely because of mixed marriages; in 1993 *Aussiedler* themselves made up nearly three-quarters of the migrants (§4), but by 2004 they made up one-fifth. The increasing number of non-*Aussiedler* also lends credence to the argument that the post–cold war *Aussiedler* are moving more for economically instrumental reasons than for reasons of ethnic solidarity. This development—and the rights associated with each status—has important implications for integration and, indeed, led to the inclusion of *Aussiedler* in the 2005 Immigration Law and its mandate that all *Aussiedler* and family take language tests.

Social Integration Problems and Negative Public Opinion

As with so many other return migrants, an easy and seamless integration was expected by the host government and population alike. These high expectations (compare Chapter 1) made the following poor integration seem all the worse. Indeed, it led to a crisis of identity, both for *Aussiedler* and for Germany itself, and also negatively affected governmental and host population attitudes toward *Aussiedler*. All three elements are closely linked, as we will see.

Linguistic Integration: Increasingly Problematic

Partly explained by the increase in mixed German-Russian marriages, the poor language skills—an element of the poor integration—of the post–cold war *Aussiedler* has been one of the significant factors in a downward trend in public opinion, beginning in the late 1980s. By 1988, when 200,000 *Aussiedler* came to Germany, 60 percent of Germans named "speaking poor German" as a characteristic they associate with *Aussiedler* (Noelle-Neuman and Köcher 1993: 524), an association that has only strengthened. A 1996 survey of young *Aussiedler* who had arrived in Germany between 1990 and 1994 showed that only 3 percent characterized their German as "very good," another 30 percent as "good," 52 percent as "mediocre," and 14 percent as "bad" or "very bad" (Dietz and Roll 1998: 178).

Indeed, in 1996, ostensibly to meet legal requirements for admission but perhaps, more realistically, to test for integrative capacity, language tests were introduced as part of the admission process. Failure rates were staggering. Success rates decreased from a high of 69.3 percent in 1996, when the test was not yet fully obligatory, to 42.1 percent in 2003, with more than half failing (Bundesverwaltungsamt, personal communication, 2003). The slightly higher success rates in 2004 and 2005 may be due to significantly fewer applications, with those whose language abilities are not strong enough simply not applying.

The language test requirement in the Immigration Law of 2005 was justified in a Ministry of the Interior press release: "The Immigration Law makes the integration of *Aussiedler* families easier in that non-German family members must acquire and demonstrate basic knowledge of German in their countries of origin" ("Neun Monate Zuwanderungsgesetz," 2005: 12). Again we see the emphasis on social acceptance of the *Aussiedler* migration; negative public opinion has an impact not only on *Aussiedler* themselves but also on policymakers. Of 1,500 *Aussiedler* family members invited to take a test in 2005, 60 percent took the test and just 25 percent passed (Federal Republic of Germany, Federal Ministry of the Interior, 2006b: 238). In May 1999 the *Aussiedler* commissioner exhorted *Aussiedler* to "Speak German! . . . If you speak Russian here in Germany, what will identify you as German?" (Welt 1999: 4), and in September 1999 he noted that "in the interests of integration, it would be ideal if family members were also required to demonstrate their German abilities through a language test" ("Aktuelle Einschätzung der Lage," 1999: 6).

Socioeconomic Marginalization: The "Integration Industry"

The majority of *Aussiedler* hold a German passport and are thus, from a legal (formal) standpoint, on an equal footing with German citizens, yet many are unemployed, thus further reducing opportunities to interact with the native population. Unemployment statistics for *Aussiedler* are calculated only for five years after migration, based on the assumption that they will be "integrated" after five years. However, the German microcensus does offer a means of statistically isolating *Aussiedler*. Birkner (2007) recently carried out that analysis and concluded that unemployment in 2005 among *Aussiedler* was 27 percent, versus 10 percent for native Germans, indicating that long-term unemployment is an even more significant problem than initial unemployment. Other recent research indicates that *Aussiedler* are, at least in one city (Ingolstadt), often hired through temporary agencies. They often remain isolated from German workers or other migrant groups both at work and at home. According to the findings of this study, *Aussiedler* often speak Russian together at work, which leads to a further feeling of separation and distance (Siebenhüter 2007).

Many *Aussiedler* are also underemployed, accepting, for instance, positions as *Bauhelfer* (building site assistant), whereas once they were engineers (interview, November 28, 1996), and as nurse's aides, whereas once they were physicians (interview, December 13, 1997). Educated *Aussiedler* can become social workers or translators in place of almost anything (interviews, November 25, 1996, and February 27, 1997)—although here, too, supply far outweighs demand—whereas uneducated *Aussiedler*, or those with nontransferable skills, often find only janitorial or recyclable-sorting positions. *Aussiedler* counselors proudly report that "their" *Aussiedler* have no trouble finding jobs, because they work hard and will accept any employment (interviews, November 28, 1996, February 27, 1997, and March 5, 1997), yet underemployment is particularly difficult for educated workers who have been trained to a much higher level and who must choose between unemployment and taking work well below the level of their training.[12]

In some regions, only low-paid "Hartv IV" jobs are available.[13] For instance, in Marzahn, a district of Berlin with a high *Aussiedler* population, there is a veritable "integration industry" of integration counselors (Soboczynski 2006: 20) but no jobs—and an unemployment rate of 21 percent.

The repeated emphasis that *Aussiedler* are ready to work at any job raises some interesting questions. They sound much more like traditional immigrants to a classical immigration country than ethnic return migrants. Indeed, one study found that the primary reason for migration was to ensure a future for their children, mentioned by 68 percent of *Aussiedler*; this same study found that less than half—47 percent—named living in their ancestors' home (Ködderitzsch 1996: 143).

My own interviews show approximately equal emphasis on better material circumstances, living near immediate relatives, living with Germans, and a better future for the children. Despite earlier governmental protestations to the contrary—that most *Aussiedler* come to Germany to "live as Germans"—most come for a better life, either for themselves or, more often, for their children. Consequently, finding work, any work, is a means to achieving a goal that is dear to most immigrants—their children's future—but it does hinder first-generation migrants' integration.

Regardless of the reasons for the migration, the outcome of unemployment or underemployment is disappointing in the country that was supposed to provide a new (ancestral) home and/or a new start in life. Living on welfare is a hard blow to one's pride, even if the material circumstances are the same as or even slightly better than those in Kazakhstan. Moving from self-reliance to being a government dependent is a bitter pill to swallow for people who are "returning home." Although there is a certain philosophical acceptance of the situation—"It could be worse," said many of those I spoke with—other problems such as alcoholism, drug addiction, and depression are considerably higher among *Aussiedler* than among the general population (Soboczynski 2006; "Interkulturelle Kompetenz," 2006: 20).

Education: A Way Out or Confirming Segregation?

In Germany, young people are required to go to school until they turn 16, making the most at-risk group, according to social workers, the group of teenagers who migrated to Germany when they were about 12 to 17 years old: those who were too young to be able to choose to stay but too old to benefit from the socializing influence of the German educational system.[14] Instead, these young people—often unhappy with the family's decision to leave for Germany, perhaps having had to leave a first boyfriend or girlfriend—are not required to attend school or are required to do so for only one or two years; consequently, they are not able to compete in the labor market with native German youth or noncitizen youth who have attended German schools since childhood. Social workers I interviewed even spoke of this group as a "lost generation," and they are not the only ones expressing this opinion (Soboczynski 2006: 18). These young people—those of school age—are also not eligible for the language or integration course, even under the 2005 Immigration Law. Although the crime rate among *Aussiedler* youth has declined somewhat in recent years, perhaps linked to lower numbers of migrants, it is still disconcertingly high, and rates of drug use and alcoholism are also still high (Soboczynski 2006: 18).

Despite legal steps to enforce an equal distribution of *Aussiedler* across Germany (see later discussion on the Residence Assignment Act), some districts and city neighborhoods have a high concentration of *Aussiedler*. In some school systems—for instance, in Marzahn in Berlin or in some areas in Lahr in Baden-Württemberg—*Aussiedler* children can make up one-third to one-half of some school classes, particularly where special classes have been introduced for *Aussiedler*. In these cases *Aussiedler* do not speak German with their classmates but continue to speak Russian, thus further hindering their German language acquisition. Adding to this situation is the statistical reality that about one-third of *Aussiedler* are 18 years of age or younger, whereas only 18 percent of the indigenous German population is under the age of 18 ("Altersstruktur der Aussiedler," 1999; Statistisches Bundesamt 2008: 63). According to one survey, 67 percent of *Aussiedler* youth speak Russian with their friends rather than German (Dietz and Roll 1998: 180). Because of their poor German skills, when they arrive in Germany, most *Aussiedler* children do not attend the grade level that would correspond to their age but are placed in a different (lower level) school or in a lower grade level. Thus *Aussiedler* who arrive in Germany during the last years of secondary school are generally at a lower educational level than other students in Germany, which places them at a disadvantage for the rest of their lives.

German Public Opinion

From an initial positive impression in the 1970s and 1980s, German public opinion of *Aussiedler* has declined as *Aussiedler* numbers have increased and their language skills and integration have worsened. In November 1988, before the financial strain of unification and after just one year of a heavy inflow of *Aussiedler*, 35 percent of those Germans asked had a "good opinion" of *Aussiedler*, whereas 14 percent did not (Noelle-Neumann and Köcher 1993: 524). However, starting in 1991, when asked whether *Aussiedler* migration should be restricted, 68 percent agreed and 10 percent said it should be discontinued. Just 22 percent said it should continue without restriction, with only 14 percent agreeing by 2000. Since 2000, regular press releases by the German Ministry of the Interior have touted the lower *Aussiedler* numbers, and the lack of any public opinion poll since 2000 on the question of public attitudes toward *Aussiedler* is telling.

The public distaste for Russian-speaking *Aussiedler* is such that a Russian woman, who had emigrated in the 1970s to Germany and who was accustomed to speaking Russian in public with her mother, stopped doing so in the mid-1990s for fear of being seen as an *Aussiedler* (interview, June 5, 2005).

German government representatives (as well as government policy) kept pace with the changing public opinion. Their press releases increasingly reflected a changing focus. The first commissioner for *Aussiedler* affairs talked of helping "our" German brothers and sisters, with one of the bases of *Aussiedler* policy being that "the door to Germany will remain open for German *Aussiedler*!" ("Wir lassen die Deutschen," 1993: 1); he went on to say, "In the long run, the German *Aussiedler* with their large young families are a multi-faceted gain for our country" ("Aussiedlerpolitik 1993," 1993: 7). As early as 1993, public campaigns were run, with distribution of brochures and TV series about the history of *Aussiedler* and individual stories helping native Germans learn more about *Aussiedler*.

The second commissioner spoke more paternalistically of assisting *Aussiedler* to integrate, and the third commissioner had the following exchange in an interview in December 2004 shortly after his appointment:

> *Die Welt*: Who is better integrated: immigrants from Turkey or from Russia?
>
> Kemper: That is difficult to say. At a meeting with domestic politicians, young Turks and Russians, there was an astonishing outcome. The Turks, who have no German citizenship, spoke good German and said "Send the foreigners home!" The *Russians* had a German passport, but barely understood *our* language. This shows that different immigrant groups compete with one another. (Federal Republic of Germany, Federal Ministry of the Interior, 2004; emphasis added)

This quote shows far more than that; it indicates a real change in official attitude toward *Aussiedler*. Whereas *Aussiedler* were earlier welcomed as co-ethnics suffering under discriminatory regimes and were seen as Germans, today the government representative responsible for their welfare calls them Russians and notes that they barely understand "our" language. On the other hand, Turkish residents in Germany who do not hold German passports are seen as well integrated into German society. The fourth and current commissioner, now the commissioner for *Aussiedler* and minority affairs, has continued to emphasize the importance of the German language and of integration.

The media has also kept up a steady series of negative articles. Only rarely, if ever, are positive articles printed about *Aussiedler*; when these are printed, they are often the result of good public relations work by a nongovernmental organization involved in *Aussiedler* integration work. Government-sponsored initiatives, such as contests for the best integration strategy, are also increasing. However, the most common articles continue to be about integration problems. Articles about clashes between gangs of young "Turks" and "Russians," increasing drug use among adolescent *Aussiedler*, the appearance of "Little Moscow" neighborhoods and grocery stores importing goods from Russia, and the problems of schools in which 50 percent of the classes are "Russians" are typical.

Identity and Integration: Does One Affect the Other?

German? Russian? Outsider? Identity and Belonging

For those who migrated to Germany to live as Germans among Germans, then, it is clear that this dream has not come true. *Aussiedler* lag behind native Germans in the areas of language skills, education, and socioeconomic status.

Such uniformly poor success in the hard-won "homeland"—with immigration achieved often only after a long, bureaucratic process—is particularly demoralizing and causes *Aussiedler* to look again at their own self-worth and identity. Even the German office of the International Organization for Migration (IOM), which, among other undertakings, organizes voluntary return for rejected asylum seekers, has been approached by penniless and desperate *Aussiedler* who hope that IOM can help them return "home"—to Kazakhstan (Bernd Hemingway, Chief of Mission, IOM Berlin, personal communication, March 23, 2006). Social workers also note that they are seeing increasing numbers of *Aussiedler* returning to the former Soviet Union because they see no future in Germany (Soboczynski 2006: 19).

Aussiedler were regarded as foreigners or as outsiders in Eastern and Central Europe, and many emigrated in search of the one country where they thought they would be accepted as insiders. This acceptance has not been forthcoming, however—not by the government or the host population and not in terms of the economy and society. An increasingly negative public pressure has had its own impact on *Aussiedler*: Although *Aussiedler* felt welcome in the 1970s, in the 1990s they increasingly felt "foreign" in Germany. In interviews I conducted, many Russian Germans complained that "there we were the fascist pigs; here we are the Russians."

A growing body of evidence suggests that, although *Aussiedler* were not accepted in their countries of origin, neither are they accepted in Germany as Germans. One 1995 study of Russian Germans and Polish Germans showed that 35 percent of Russian Germans surveyed faced discrimination, whereas only 21 percent of Polish Germans felt the same (Graudenz and Römhild 1995: 50). In a 1992 study, nearly 40 percent of *Aussiedler* felt unwelcome in Germany (Dietz and Hilkes 1994: 85). A 1990–1991 study showed that nearly 75 percent had experienced discrimination (Saring 1993: 133). These numbers are substantiated by surveys of indigenous Germans: 57.1 percent of German youth thought that *Aussiedler* were only partly welcome in Germany and 29.4 percent thought that *Aussiedler* were not welcome at all (Dietz and Roll 1998: 173). Many of the *Aussiedler* I spoke with reported that, although they were called Germans in the former Soviet Union, they are now called Russians in Germany (interviews, winter 1996 and spring 1997). In answering a question about how he identifies himself, one man I spoke to said, "And why would I want to be seen as a German? I've had it up to here with Germans!" (interview, June 2, 1997). He drew a clear connection between his social and economic marginalization and the way he identifies himself—as Russian. He is not the only one; increasingly many adults see themselves as "foreign Germans" or even as the hated Russians, and youngsters at school often retreat to their Russian or Kazakh origins in order to distinguish themselves from their German peers (Dornseifer-Seitz 2006: 181).

Indeed, interviews collected in the book *We Are Always the Strangers* express this view again and again (Ferstl and Hetzel 1990). The social situation of *Aussiedler*—segregated living areas, poor language skills, low educational level, and high unemployment—is both a factor in the *Fremdsein* (being foreign) identity creation of *Aussiedler* and a result of socioeconomic and cultural marginalization of *Aussiedler*. More worrisome is the fact that *Aussiedler* have been the victims of xenophobic violence in Germany, as reported in newspapers and police bulletins. The fact that *Aussiedler* hold a German passport is of no interest to right-wing thugs, who call them Russians; here, too, the line between a "returning" German and a naturalized German is blurring.

At a Christmas party I attended with social workers and *Aussiedler*, we sang Christmas carols. We sang traditional German songs, with the two social workers (one a Polish *Aussiedler* who had come in 1987) valiantly leading a group of tonelessly mumbling *Aussiedler*. Finally, brightly smiling, one said to the *Aussiedler*, "Would you like to sing one of *your* songs now?" Sitting up straight, suddenly animated, the *Aussiedler* happily sang one Russian song after another. Anyone passing in the street, not knowing these were German citizens—or even knowing that they were—would have been able to know within one line of the song that these were immigrants. In terms of identity, these women were more Russian than German, yet in the Soviet Union they had been known as the Germans. The linguistic, socioeconomic, and attitudinal exclusion experienced by *Aussiedler* keeps them separate from the mainstream society and maintains a distinct identity.

However, this type of episode also leads to other mistaken identities. I was at the home of an *Aussiedler* man and his Russian wife. After discussing contemporary Germany and the loss of values among "young people," the couple presented me with a delicacy: blini. Proudly telling me that "we learned things from the Russians too," the man explained to me that the blini, already folded in quarters, should be folded once more, then dipped into honey or sour cream, and eaten with the fingers. Just then, the doorbell rang. It was a well-meaning representative from the Protestant Church who had come to check on the new immigrants. Catching a glimpse of the lovingly prepared blini, the man reached out, took one, shook it out into a circle, exclaiming as he did so, "Ah, crêpes suzette! You eat them like this!" The *Aussiedler*, earlier animated and excitedly telling me about "what we learned from the Russians," sank back onto the sofa, letting the German authority figure tell him how to eat "crêpes suzette" that his Russian wife had made. While clearly identifying as a German, the man showed a pride in other elements of his country of origin; these were disregarded by the representative of the German church who was focused on complete as-similation. Such events could have an impact on identity, leading *Aussiedler* to identify less and less with Germans and Germany.

The question of identity is a difficult one for many *Aussiedler*. Of the *Aus-siedler* I spoke with, nearly half of them either felt Russian or simply "foreign" upon their migration to Germany, but most felt German in their country of origin—their old identity had been lost, but a new one had not yet emerged in its stead. The image that most *Aussiedler* have of Germany, recounted by parents or grandparents, is of a prewar traditional Germany, an image that is dispelled almost immediately upon entry into Germany. One social worker told me of an *Aussiedler* who came to her office bearing her papers in a beautiful leather folder, with an embossed gold design on the front. The design was a Nazi swastika. The woman cherished the folder as something that had belonged to her (German) father but simply did not understand why this design could not be shown in contemporary Germany. To her, something German was German. Like other immigrants, she had not been socialized in the postwar German cul-ture—an omission that the German naturalization test, introduced in October 2008, attempts to rectify.

For *Aussiedler* as ethnic return migrants, norms and social expectations in Germany are different than expected, requiring a mental readjustment for them to participate fully. This attitude differs from the expectations of more traditional migrants, who anticipate a different culture. Most damaging of all for identity and successful integration, ethnic Germans have often been raised in the belief that they are Germans and that their true home is Ger-many. Brought up on stories of the ancient German homeland and raised in an German ethnocultural tradition, *Aussiedler* often arrive in Germany only to experience, once again, exclusion and negative public opinion, leading them to determine that, although they may not be Russian, neither are they German; they do not receive the recognition or the jobs they had hoped for, and the lan-guage is difficult to learn and society is not as welcoming as hoped. *Aussiedler* undergo serious problems of adjustment when they arrive in Germany only to discover that they fit in better in Kazakhstan than in Kassel and that jokes are told about them. In one study, 76.3 percent of the respondents felt German before their migration, and only 57.9 percent felt German after their migration (Findeis and Botzian 1996: 174, 185). Although *Aussiedler* did not feel Russian before their migration, now they do not feel German, yet they hesitate to be identified as Russian; a new mixed identity seems to be emerging, one that as yet has no real home. At the same time, Germans' concept of what a German is has also shifted over time, moving away from an ethnically defined concept and toward one based on social integration.

From the perspective of identity and feelings of acceptance, it is clear that the attitude of the host country has a major influence on the successful integration of any immigrant group. Following Alejandro Portes and Ruben Rumbaut's model of contexts of reception (Portes and Rumbaut 1996: 84–92), one can easily argue that until the late 1980s, *Aussiedler* enjoyed a reception context of "active encouragement" but that their reception shifted over the course of the 1990s to one of passive acceptance (or what Portes earlier called a neutral context) (Portes and Böröcz 1989) and even, in some ways (see later discussion on the Residence Assignment Act), to a status of exclusion. This context of reception in the homeland is especially crucial for a diasporic return migration, where, as noted, thoughts of home have been maintained throughout the years of diaspora, often in the face of ethnically based discrimination.

Germans into Migrants . . . :
Increasing Policy Restrictions on *Aussiedler* Migration

As mentioned, as the walls of the Soviet bloc quite literally tumbled down, starting in 1989, the political-ideological rationale of the *Aussiedler* policy became obsolete. Nonetheless, the political rhetoric—and oft-quoted phrase—was, "The door will remain open!" Despite this stated rhetoric, policy became increasingly restrictive and Germany became increasingly open to including other immigrants as citizens. Another oft-quoted phrase, "Germany is not an immigration country," was itself finally laid to rest in 2000, along with the phrase "The door remains open." How can this dichotomy be explained?

The recent shift to equating *Aussiedler* and noncitizen migrants on the level of integration not only is a clear sign of the paradigm shift in German immigration policy but also sends a clear signal to *Aussiedler*: They are not returning "home" but are being accepted for a historical reason in an immigration country. Not only have admissions requirements for *Aussiedler* been tightened, but integration assistance and other benefits have also been severely cut back. At the same time, press releases from the German Ministry of the Interior proudly announce how many fewer asylum seekers or *Aussiedler* there were compared to last month or last year. Every press release also contains an appeal from the ministry to future applicants that they and their family members should learn German: "After arrival in Germany, [German] language skills will make integration considerably easier and also assure the continued acceptance of Aussiedler migration by the native population," and, further, "I believe that this effort can be expected of applicants—as future German citizens" (Federal Republic of Germany, Federal Ministry of the Interior, 2006a). The emphasis on integration and the importance of acceptance by the German population is clear. The repercussions for the *Aussiedler* population currently in Germany and for new arrivals can be anticipated.

German government actions to both restrict the admission of *Aussiedler* and to reduce integration packages in Germany and the passage of other restrictive laws resulted not only in fewer resources but also in *Aussiedler* increasingly feeling excluded by the German government. Referring to the introduction of language tests for *Aussiedler*, one man remarked to me, "We were afraid to be Germans in Russia. Now they [the German government] tell us we have to already speak German?! Bah!" (interview, November 27, 1996). Another noted that being on welfare rather than receiving a special integration package left a bad taste in the mouth: "They should give us more money, more support at the beginning, as it was earlier. Integration should be stronger; [it makes a difference] where the same money comes from. Getting welfare . . . that makes us feel bad" (interview, June 1, 1997). These two respondents clearly indicated that the changes made to *Aussiedler* policy made them feel less comfortable in Germany, with both drawing an explicit comparison to the earlier policies. Yet on what bases were these policy changes made?

As noted, several factors played a role, among them the increasing numbers, the end of the cold war, and the poor integration of *Aussiedler* themselves. As the cold war ended, it was clear, for both domestic political reasons and simply the concept of fair play, that *Aussiedler* policy could not simply be shut down overnight. Instead, restriction after restriction came into effect, with numbers dropping precipitously—and each drop identifiably related to each law.

The Aussiedler Acceptance Act of 1990 required that potential *Aussiedler* apply before migrating to Germany and take a German language test upon arrival in Germany—and *Aussiedler* could be required to return to their countries of origin if it appeared that they had misrepresented their German abilities on the application. This act was passed one year after the Residence Assignment Act (see later discussion), which was intended to prevent the creation of compact ethnic communities. From 1990 on, ethnic Germans who migrated to Germany on tourist visas, rather than following the prescribed path, forfeited their *Aussiedler* status. The reasoning was that the situation for minorities was not as bad as it had been and that it was not "unreasonable" to ask Germans to wait several months more. The introduction of the application procedure proved effective immediately; the number of *Aussiedler* dropped from nearly 400,000 in 1990 to about 222,000 in 1991 and 230,000 in 1992.

The ADCW[15] of 1992 was part of the so-called asylum compromise, which was the concession of the political left to restrict the previously liberal right to asylum (amendment of Article 16 of the Basic Law) and the concession of the political right to restrict *Aussiedler* migration (passage of the ADCW). Both restrictions reflect the obsolete quality of the original political-ideological underpinning of the two policies—and are a reaction to the high numbers. The ADCW restricts *Aussiedler* migration to those living in the former Soviet Union and the Baltic states, with a few exceptions;[16] all others must prove explicitly that they still suffer ethnically based discrimination or the aftereffects of earlier discrimination (see Figure 4.1 for the origins of *Aussiedler*), but such discrimination is, unless proven otherwise, assumed to no longer exist. Different categorizations of *Aussiedler* were introduced, with distinctions in legal rights among categories, and these categories had significant repercussions for integration, as discussed earlier. Perhaps most significant, building on court decisions that noted that ethnically based discrimination can no longer be treated as synonymous with ethnicity (BVerwGE 9 C 392.94; BVerwGE 9 C 391.95),[17] reasons for exclusion from *Aussiedler* status are now explicitly included in the law.[18] Even after the end of the cold war, the political-ideological background to this policy is clearly visible. Finally, the ADCW introduced a quota of about 220,000, later reduced to 100,000 by a complicated and well-hidden amendment to the law (Federal Budget of 2000: 2535).[19] In retrospect, the quota, rather than the restriction to the former Soviet Union, was the more significant aspect of the act. Poor integration and chain migration within Germany were clearly factors in the decision to restrict migration.

Language tests in the *country of origin* were introduced in 1996, ostensibly to verify that German was the language of the home and not learned at the Goethe Institute. Nearly 60 percent of applicants failed in 2003 and 2004, with just over 50 percent failing in 2005. The test also resolved the problem of those individuals whose demonstrated language skills on arrival in Germany failed to match the language skills stated on the application ("Informationen zur Durchführung von Sprachtests," 1997: 5). In addition, however, the integration capacity of *Aussiedler* in Germany—already quite problematic by the mid-1990s—was strengthened. The transition from German to immigrant was well under way. The language tests also significantly reduced the number of *Aussiedler*, from 177,751 in 1996 to 103,080 in 1998—the figure on which the new quota was based.

The German government maintained for quite some time that the primary purpose of the test was to check for identity, but it has become clear that integration is, if not the primary purpose, certainly an important secondary one. *Aussiedler* are, in more than one way, treated as immigrants who must be socially integrated and accepted. These policies clearly treat *Aussiedler* as objects of policy, which has an impact on their identity as Germans. More stunning still in this regard is the restriction on *Aussiedler* freedom of movement introduced in 1989.

The 1989 Residence Assignment Act responded to the large influx of 380,000 *Aussiedler* migrating to Germany in that year alone. Because most *Aussiedler*, like other migrants, draw on their social networks when deciding where to live in Germany, the government moved quickly to prevent *Aussiedler* from further concentrating in particular regions of the country. The government sought to establish an even distribution throughout Germany, based on the same quota system used for postwar expellees and contemporary asylum seekers. Purportedly serving two purposes—integrating *Aussiedler* and reducing burdens on particular municipalities (responsible for welfare payments)—the aspect of the burden on municipalities is the more significant. It reinforces and even predates the German government's call for a "socially acceptable" migration—a message that is not lost on *Aussiedler* and further inhibits their integration.

Initially valid for three years but extended repeatedly, the Residence Assignment Act is applied to all newly arrived *Aussiedler* on any form of public assistance—in other words, nearly all *Aussiedler*—and requires them to stay in their assigned federal state for three years, unless they can demonstrate that they have a job or apprenticeship or have been accepted as a student elsewhere. As of 1992, moving is associated with sanctions, including forfeiting all social services, such as language courses, welfare, unemployment benefits, and job retraining programs. No other definable group of German citizens[20] and no noncitizen (with the exception of asylum seekers whose applications are still pending) are subject to such restrictions on freedom of movement. This act has been successful in preventing *Aussiedler* from moving.

However, the Residence Assignment Act clearly restricts the freedom of movement of *Aussiedler*. A 2004 decision by the German Constitutional Court concluded that the law does not violate the constitution, although it notes that freedom of movement is, in fact, severely restricted for *Aussiedler* (for more on the constitutionality of the law, see von Koppenfels 2004). Indeed, the Court, in its decision, stated that there would be issues of constitutionality for this law in the future if hardship cases were not taken into account in a future version of the act (BVerfG, 1 BvR 1266/00, March 17, 2004, para. 51);[21] these considerations were taken into account in the 2005 amendments made to the act. Examinations of the *Aussiedler* situation as well as general migration research show that network migration is a help, rather than a hindrance, to integration, indicating that this law is primarily in place to maintain social peace in the communities. Indeed, one academic, Barbara Dietz, quoted in the Court decision, notes that "the assignment to a place of residence has no influence on entry into the labor market" and furthermore that "the assignment hinders access to *Aussiedler* networks, which are useful for integration, finding a place to live and finding work." Dietz further noted that a "disproportionate migration would lead to complaints on the part of the native population." Her testimony concludes with the statement that "regardless of where *Aussiedler* families live, they continue to speak Russian for a long time" (BVerfG, 1 BvR 1266/00, March 17, 2004, para. 22).

A study analyzing the impacts of the Residence Assignment Act on employment, mandated by the Court decision (BVerfG, 1 BvR 1266/00, March 17, 2004, para. 43), found that the level of unemployment in the place of residence was an important factor in *Aussiedler* unemployment; in other words, if *Aussiedler* were settled in areas with high unemployment, they had lower chances of finding a job (Haug and Sauer 2007). The study has not yet analyzed the effect of distribution on language and other aspects of integration. Recall the comment on the Ministry of the Interior Web site: "The government will make sure that this migration is socially acceptable." This objective is clearly the focus of the Residence Assignment Act, indeed much more so than any improved integration for *Aussiedler*. It seems obvious that *Aussiedler* are not returning Germans but are migrants, indeed ones who are even more restricted than other, non-German migrants, who may live where they choose. If the postwar migration policy had aspects privileging German migrants, it has now moved solidly away.

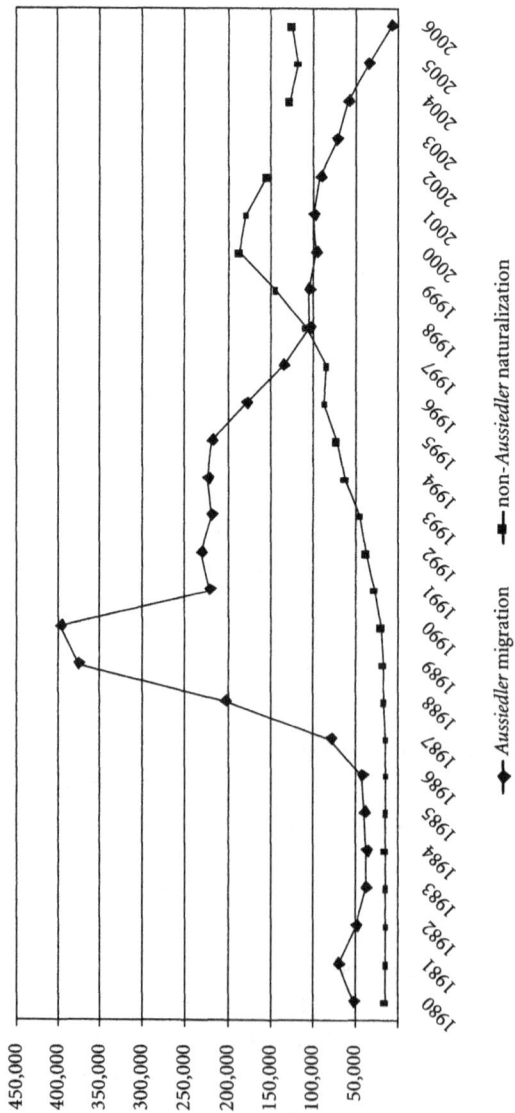

Figure 4.2 *Aussiedler* migration and (non-*Aussiedler*) naturalization, 1980–2006. Data from Statistisches Bundesamt (2005, 2007, 2008) and "Zuzug 1950–1996" (1996).

. . . and Migrants into Germans:
How Germany Became an Immigration Country

As *Aussiedler* migration was becoming more restrictive, the German polity was, on the other hand, opening up to non-German migrants. So-called guest worker migration of the 1950s and 1960s had gradually become permanent, yet these migrants had not been offered an easy and welcoming path to citizenship.[22] More integrated into society in many ways than post–cold war *Aussiedler*, these "denizens" became recognized as substantive members of German society, even as *Aussiedler* increasingly were not.

The noncitizen resident population in Germany reached 5.9 million (7.3 percent of the population) by 1991 and 7.3 million (8.9 percent) by 2003. The 1990 revision of the Foreigners' Law, followed by a 1993 government decree, had the effect of making naturalization for those ages 16 to 23 automatic upon application; eight years' residence and six years' attendance in German schools were the basic requirements for youth naturalization. In 1992 the ADCW was passed, restricting *Aussiedler* migration. Until January 1, 2000, a 10-year residence requirement was still required for discretionary naturalization for adults (i.e., authorities may or may not grant the application), and 15 years' residence was necessary for an absolute right to naturalization (i.e., an applicant cannot be denied). The 2000 citizenship law reduced these requirements to eight years for a right to naturalization and introduced limited jus soli, whereby a child born to foreign parents (of whom at least one has lived in Germany for eight years and has had an unlimited right of residence for three years) receives German citizenship but would have to choose by age 23 between German citizenship and that of his or her parents.[23] In 2000 the Residence Assignment Act was extended. Thus German citizenship approaches the most liberal states in the European Union and surpasses the most restrictive. The Residence Assignment Act also incorporated the naturalization of *Aussiedler*, which had previously been addressed in separate legislation.

It is often said by critics that Germany permits more *Aussiedler* to migrate than noncitizens to naturalize. Many more noncitizens have always been eligible to naturalize (particularly after reforms to the Foreigners' Law in 1990 and 1993) than have done so. However, even taking note of that aspect, in 1998 the point was reached where there were more naturalizations (excluding *Aussiedler*) than there were *Aussiedler* migrating to Germany (Figure 4.2). The decline after 2000 is arguably not a decline; rather, 2000 was an artificial high, when jus soli was being applied retroactively to those born after 1990.

The 2005 Immigration Law in Germany introduced language tests for family members of *Aussiedler* and provided for integration seminars for all newcomers to Germany, whether German citizens (*Aussiedler*) or noncitizens. It also institutionalized immigration to Germany, albeit at lower levels than initially hoped for by the center-left government.

Conclusion

The case of *Aussiedler*—perhaps the world's best-known case of co-ethnic return policy—demonstrates that neither ethnic belonging nor the possession of a passport automatically translates into successful cultural or socioeconomic integration. Indeed, the obverse appears to be true: Successful socioeconomic integration plays a more significant role in belonging and membership in a society regardless of ethnic origin.

Although *Aussiedler* migration in earlier years resulted in successful integration, post–cold war *Aussiedler* migration has unmistakably resulted, for the most part, in an unintegrated group of migrants and an increasingly hostile host population, which, in turn, has resulted in ongoing restrictions to *Aussiedler* migration. Cold war–era *Aussiedler* had better German language skills at the time of migration and more applicable professional training, and they had faced the hurdle of leaving the Communist bloc, after which the challenge of integrating into Germany must have seemed entirely surmountable and a goal that had already been fought for. Those who migrated after the cold war, however, with their poorer German language skills and less relevant training, were able to leave the former Soviet Union relatively easily; the first true challenge came only with the integration process in Germany. Having expected a warm welcome and an uncomplicated improvement in living standards, post–cold war *Aussiedler* received neither, and their identity, already somewhat tenuous, became more so.

From the perspective of the receiving society, the situation was similar. During the cold war, anti-Communist rhetoric was daily fare and accepting refugees from Communist regimes, whether German *Aussiedler*, East German refugees, or non-German asylum seekers from Communist countries, was an unremarkable aspect of the cold war. In the post–cold war era, however, ethnic German migrants, who, in addition to special privileges, increasingly spoke no German, were no longer seen as the deserving and wronged fellow Germans they once had been but were rather seen as poorly integrated economic migrants and a drain on an increasingly strained system.

Ultimately, *Aussiedler*'s poor integration, their self-identity and the identity ascribed to them by the German population, and increasing non-German migration resulted in major policy shifts in Germany. These policy shifts, again largely reacting to both domestic opinion and changes in geopolitics, reveal a fundamentally changed Germany. It cannot be argued that German policymakers intentionally shifted toward a proactive policy of immigration. However, it can be argued that the many reactive changes made in the postwar and, especially, post–cold war era did ultimately result in a situation in which there was a fundamental realization that Germany was an immigration country. Those "countrymen" who came to Germany because of lingering outcomes of World War II were immigrants all along, despite initial policy rhetoric to the contrary; their migration has altered Germany accordingly.

As in other cases of ethnic return migration, it must be concluded that ethnicity and a sense of "imagined community"—indeed, often a mistaken one—are not enough. Once regarded as Germans, *Aussiedler* today are a migrant group among many others: In 2005, 120,000 noncitizens (and non-*Aussiedler*) naturalized as Germans; 35,000 *Aussiedler* came to Germany; 55,000 noncitizen, non-*Aussiedler* spouses and children joined their (non-*Aussiedler*) families in Germany; and nearly 7 million noncitizens were living in Germany.

Notes

1. It is important to bear in mind, however, that poorly integrated migrants are considerably more visible than well-integrated migrants.

2. Beginning in May 2007, potential *Aussiedler* living in Estonia, Latvia, or Lithuania, now member states of the European Union, were no longer eligible.

3. Federal Republic of Germany, "Gesetz über die Angelegenheiten der Vertriebenen und Flüchtlinge (Bundesvertriebenengesetz—BVFG)" [Federal Expellees' and Refugees Law, FERL], May 22, 1953, *Bundesgesetzblatt* I, 201.

4. Members of other ethnic groups were also deported, such as Ingrian Finns, who also have been granted a privileged migration status to Finland. Some 25,000 returned to Finland between 1990 and 2003. They have had integration problems similar to those of *Aussiedler* (Tanner 2004). Poles, Ukrainians, and others were deported as well. Poland has a small-scale return migration program. It should also be noted that, at the same time (1942–1945), 120,000 Japanese Americans (most of them American citizens) were placed in detention camps in the United States for the same reason.

5. The Allies, fearing instability and ethnic conflict in Central and Eastern Europe, determined at the Potsdam Conference in July 1945 that the 2 to 3 million ethnic

Germans remaining to the east in the four occupied zones of Germany, Poland, East Prussia, and Czechoslovakia were to be expelled in an "orderly and humane fashion" to Germany between 1945 and 1949. The number was underestimated: 12 million ethnic Germans were expelled (8 million to West Germany and 4 million to East Germany). Poles were also expelled from territory that was ceded to the Soviet Union and were resettled in the areas from which Germans had been expelled.

6. Some areas (Romania, Hungary, Soviet Union) were not subject to widespread expulsions. In addition, a number of ethnic Germans were able to escape expulsion in Poland and Czechoslovakia; those who were of use to the Communist governments, such as miners or skilled craftsmen, were not permitted to leave, and those who had Polish or Czech spouses could also often avoid expulsion, as could Catholics in Poland.

7. Article 116, para. 1: "Unless otherwise provided by law a German citizen within the meaning of this Basic Law is a person who possesses German citizenship or who has been admitted to the territory of the German Reich within the frontiers of 31 December 1937 as a refugee or expellee of German ethnic origin or as their spouse or descendant."

8. During the cold war, nearly all asylum seekers from Eastern Europe were accepted, either as refugees or with subsidiary protection, that is, protection from deportation.

9. The discrimination against Germans in the former Soviet Union stems from a transference of hostility toward the Nazis to hostility toward ethnic Germans in the postwar period.

10. Starting in 1996, this knowledge had to be demonstrated through a language test.

11. The asylum policy likewise began to undergo drastic shifts, most clearly demonstrated by the sharp drop in asylum recognition rates over the succeeding years.

12. The relevant law states that *Aussiedler*'s professional qualifications are to be recognized, provided that there is an equivalent in Germany (FERL, §10); yet often the exact equivalent does not exist and the qualifications are thus not accepted.

13. The Hartz IV reforms in 2005 were intended to integrate the unemployed into the labor market. Those on unemployment benefits (now combined with welfare) had the option of taking on employment paying 1.00 euro per hour.

14. The educational system is an important factor in integration. In earlier requirements for naturalization, Germany, like other countries, linked the requirement of a certain number of years in a German school to easier naturalization.

15. *Kriegsfolgenbereinigungsgesetz*, or, literally, "Act Cleaning Up the Consequences of the War."

16. From 1992 to 2005, 95.7 percent of all *Aussiedler* were from the former Soviet Union. Following the accession of Estonia, Latvia, and Lithuania to the European

Union, a further amendment to the act, which took force in May 2007, no longer permitted *Aussiedler* migration from the Baltic states.

17. Bundesverwaltungsgericht, BVerwGE 9 C 392.94 (June 13, 1995); Bundesverwaltungsgericht, BVerwGE 9 C 391.95 (August 29, 1995).

18. These include, for instance, having held a high position in the Communist regime; discrimination clearly did not exist in such cases.

19. In the federal budget of 2000, which includes a number of amendments to various laws, an amendment to the Federal Expellees' and Refugees' Law was included as well: In §27, para. 3, sentence 1, the statement "average of 1991 and 1992" was replaced with "in the year 1998." This amendment changes the quota of *Aussiedler* migrating to Germany from 122,780 (+/–10 percent) to 103,080 (+/–10 percent). Federal Republic of Germany, "Gesetz zur Sanierung des Bundeshaushalts (Haushaltssanierungsgesetz—HsanG)" [federal budget], December 22, 1999, *Bundesgesetzblatt* I, December 28.

20. Except for those in the military.

21. Bundesverfassungsgericht (BVerfG), 1 BvR 1266/00 (March 17, 2004). http://www.bverfg.de/entscheidungen/rs20040317_1bvr126600.html.

22. The majority were in fact eligible for German citizenship, but such factors as cost, lack of identification with "being German," and the prohibition of dual citizenship prevented many from naturalizing.

23. This clause is widely expected to be challenged in the courts.

References Cited

"Aktuelle Einschätzung der Lage." 1999. *Info-Dienst Deutsche Aussiedler* 103(September):2–4.

"Altersstruktur der Aussiedler." 1999. *Info-Dienst Deutsche Aussiedler* 104(September):28.

"Aussiedlerpolitik 1993." 1993. *Info-Dienst Deutsche Aussiedler* 38(January):5–23.

Birkner, Elisabeth. 2007. "Aussiedler im Mikrozensus 2005: Identifizierungsprobleme und erste Analysen zur Arbeitsmarktintegration." Paper presented at the conference "Integrationschancen von Aussiedlern," Nürnberg, Germany, March 29–30. http://doku.iab.de/veranstaltungen/2007/spaetauss2007_birkner.pdf. Accessed June 11, 2007.

Dietz, Barbara, and Peter Hilkes. 1994. *Integriert oder Isoliert? Zur Situation Rußlanddeutscher Aussiedler in der Bundesrepublik Deutschland.* Munich: Olzog Verlag.

Dietz, Barbara, and Heike Roll. 1998. *Jugendliche Aussiedler: Porträt einer Zuwanderergeneration.* Frankfurt: Campus.

Dornseifer-Seitz, Adelheid. 2006. "Gesellschaftspolitische Integration von Spätaussiedlerinnen und Spätaussiedlern." In *Politische Bildung in der Einwanderungsgesellschaft*, Heidi Behrens and Jan Motte, eds. Schwalbach, Germany: Wochenschau, 179–193.

Federal Republic of Germany. 2004 (December 13). "Verordnung über die Durchführung von Integrationskursen für Ausländer und Spätaussiedler." *Bundesgesetzblatt* I,
December 17.

Federal Republic of Germany, Federal Ministry of the Interior. 2004. "Aussiedlerbeauf-
tragter kritisiert Aufsplittung der Zuständigkeiten bei der Integration." December 17. http://www.bmi.bund.de/nn_898278/Internet/Content/Nachrichten/Archiv/
Medienspiegel/2004/12/Aussiedlerbeauftragter__Interview__DIE__WELT.html.

————. 2005. "Welche Leistungen erhalten Spätaussiedler?" Press Release. http://www
.bmi.bund.de/cln_028/nn_122688/Internet/Content/Themen/Vertriebene__Spaet
aussiedler/DatenundFakten/Welche-Leistungen-erhalten-Spaetaussiedler.html.

————. 2006a. "2005—Spätaussiedler Zahl weiter rückläufig." Press release, January 10. http://www.bmi.bund.de/cln_012/nn_122052/Internet/Content/Themen/
Aussiedlerbeauftragter/Pressemitteilungen__nur__BA__Seite/2005__Spaetaussied
lerzuzug.html.

————. 2006b. "Praktiker-Erfahrungsaustausch im Rahmen der Evaluierung des Zu-
wanderungsgesetzes am 30. und 31. März 2006 im Bundesministerium des Innern
in Berlin." http://www.bmi.bund.de/Internet/Content/Common/Anlagen/Themen/
Auslaender__Fluechtlinge__Asyl/DatenundFakten/Anlage__1__Evaluierungsbericht
__Zuwanderungsgesetz,templateId=raw,property=publicationFile.pdf.

————. n.d. (a). "Integration der bei uns lebenden Ausländer." http://www.bmi
.bund.de/nn_759140/Internet/Content/Themen/Integration/PolitischeZiele/Inte
gration__der__bei__uns__lebenden__Id__19051__de.html. Accessed February 23,
2006.

————. n.d. (b). "Schwerpunkte der Aussiedlerpolitik." http://www.bmi.bund.de/
cln_007/nn_165002/Internet/Content/Themen/Vertriebene__Spaetaussiedler/Politi
scheZiele/Schwerpunkte__der__Aussiedlerpolitik__Id__19809__de.html. Accessed
May 2, 2005, and February 23, 2006.

Ferstl, Lothar, and Harald Hetzel. 1990. *"Wir sind immer die Fremden": Aussiedler in
Deutschland.* Bonn: Dietz Taschenbuch.

Findeis, Albrecht, and Peter Botzian. 1996. "Sozialarbeit mit Aussiedlern: Leben hinter'm
Zaun: fürsorgliche Isolation oder mißlungene Integration? Eine Bestandsaufnahme
des Landes Berlin für Aussiedler in Berlin-Marienfelde." Masters thesis, Evangelische
Fachhochschule, Berlin.

German Parliament. 1953 (February 25). *Stenographische Protokolle* 1/250. Bonn:
Deutscher Bundestag.

Graudenz, Ines, and Regina Römhild. 1995. "Grenzerfahrungen: Deutschstämmige Migranten aus Polen und der ehemaligen Sowjetunion im Vergleich." In *Forschungsfeld Aussiedler: Ansichten aus Deutschland,* Ines Graudenz and Regina Römhild, eds.
Frankfurt: Peter Lang, 29–67.

Haug, Sonja, and Lenore Sauer. 2007. "Projekt zur Erstellung eines Berichts zur Ermittlung und Bewertung der Auswirkungen des WoZuG." http://doku.iab.de/veran-stal tungen/2007/spaetauss2007_haug_sauer.pdf. Accessed June 10, 2007.

"Hilfen für Spätaussiedler." 1998. *Info-Dienst Deutsche Aussiedler* 97(June):38–55.

"Informationen zur Durchführung von Sprachtests." 1997. *Info-Dienst Deutsche Aus-siedler* 88(April):5–9.

"Interkulturelle Kompetenz: (Polizeilicher) Umgang mit Aussiedlern aus Osteuropa; Deutschrussen, Russlanddeutsche, Migranten und Aussiedler mit russischem Hintergrund—eine Bedrohung?" 2006. *Polizeispiegel,* November. http://www.dpolg -brandenburg.com/new/dpolg/upload/polizeispiegel/2006/pdf%202006/11_bund .pdf. Accessed June 24, 2007.

Ködderitzsch, Peter. 1996. *Studie: Zur Lage, Lebenssituation, Befindlichkeit und Integra-tion der rußlanddeutschen Aussiedler in Berlin.* Berlin: Forschungsstelle Sozialanaly-sen Berlin e.V., 143.

"Neun Monate Zuwanderungsgesetz." 2005. *Info-Dienst Deutsche Aussiedler* 118(No-vember):12–13.

Noelle-Neumann, Elisabeth, and Renate Köcher, eds. 1993. *Allensbacher Jahrbuch der Demoskopie 1984–1992.* Munich: K. G. Saur.

Parlamentarischer Rat. 1949 (January 19). *Stenographische Berichte über die Verhand-lungen im Hauptausschuß.* 45th sitting. Bonn: Parlamentarischer Rat.

———. 1950 (January 18). *Stenographische Berichte über die Verhandlungen im Plenum.* 20th sitting. Bonn: Parlamentarischer Rat.

Portes, Alejandro, and Jozsef Böröcz. 1989. "Contemporary Immigration: Theoretical Perspectives on Its Determinants and Mode of Incorporation." *International Migra-tion Review* 23:606–630.

Portes, Alejandro, and Ruben Rumbaut. 1996. *Immigrant America.* Berkeley: University of California Press.

Pressemitteilung 440/89. 1989 (September 22). *Info-Dienst Deutsche Aussiedler* 8(No-vember):4–7 (in German).

Saring, Alexander Johannes. 1993. "Empirische Untersuchung zur Primären Integra-tion deutscher Spätaussiedler im Raum Weilburg." Ph.D. dissertation, University of Gießen.

Siebenhüter, Sandra. 2007. "Aussiedler in der Arbeitswelt: Wenn deutsche Kollegen nur russisch sprechen." Paper presented at the conference "Integrationschancen von Aussiedlern," Nürnberg, Germany, March 29–30. http://doku.iab.de/veranstaltun gen/2007/spaetaussiedler2007_siebenhueter_abstract.pdf. Accessed June 11, 2007.

Soboczynski, Adam. 2006. "Fremde Heimat Deutschland." *Die Zeit,* October 12.

"Sonderprogramm zur Eingliderung der Aussiedler." 1988. *Info-Dienst Deutsche Aus-siedler* 1(November):5–19.

Statistisches Bundesamt. 2005. *Bevölkerung und Erwerbstätigkeit* [Population and em-ployment]. Fachserie 1, Reihe 2.1. Wiesbaden: Statistisches Bundesamt.

————. 2007. *Bevölkerung und Erwerbstätigkeit* [Population and employment]. Fachserie 1, Reihe 2.1. Wiesbaden: Statistisches Bundesamt.

————. 2008. *Statistisches Jahrbuch 2007.* Wiesbaden: Statistisches Bundesamt.

Tanner, Arno. 2004. "Finland's Prosperity Brings New Migrants." http://www.migration information.org/Profiles/display.cfm?ID=267. Accessed May 14, 2005.

von Koppenfels, Amanda Klekowski. 2002. "The Devolution of Privilege: The Legal Background of the Migration of Ethnic Germans." In *Coming Home to Germany? The Integration of Ethnic Germans from Central and Eastern Europe in the Federal Republic,* David Rock and Stefan Wolff, eds. Oxford: Berghahn Books, 102–118.

————. 2004. "Second-Class Citizens? Restricted Freedom of Movement for Spätaussiedler Is Constitutional." *German Law Journal* 5(7): 761–789. http://www.german lawjournal.com.

Waffenschmidt, Horst. 1988. "Liebe Leserinnen und Leser . . ." *Info-Dienst Deutsche Aussiedler* 1(November):1.

Welt, Jochen. 1999. "Die Aussiedlerpolitik der Bundesregierung." *Info-Dienst Deutsche Aussiedler* 101(May):2–10.

"Wir lassen die Deutschen in den Aussiedlungsgebiete nicht im Stich." 1993. *Info-Dienst Deutsche Aussiedler* 38(January):1–4.

"Zuzug 1950–1996" [Migration 1950–1996]. 1996. *Info-Dienst Deutsche Aussiedler* 91(September):2–5.

5 Imagined Homecomings

The Problem with Similarity Among Ethnic Return Migrants in Spain

David Cook-Martín and Anahí Viladrich

POPULAR AND SCHOLARLY CURIOSITY has recently been piqued by official policies that give a privileged migratory or citizenship status to individuals abroad because of presumed common origins with a granting state's people. The *Aussiedler*, or ethnic Germans, and members of the Jewish Diaspora are among the best known examples of people affected by these ethnic affinity policies (Joppke 2005; Levy and Weiss 2002), but, as Tsuda notes in the introduction to this volume, there are many other instances: Latin Americans descended from Italian, Japanese, and Spanish emigrants, ethnic Hungarians in Eastern Europe, descendants of the Irish in the Americas, and Estonian-descent West Siberians (Brubaker 1998; Corcoran 2002; Fox 2006; Kulu 1998; Rhi Sausi and García 1992; Tsuda 2003). Despite policymakers', hosts', and migrants' tacit assumption that ethnic affinity facilitates social and economic integration, a search of the literature reveals an expectations mismatch between new arrivals and natives in virtually every case. When anticipated opportunities and social acceptance do not materialize, ethnic return migrants and their hosts become frustrated with each other. They often reappraise supposed commonalities, and newcomers may return to their previous country of residence or move to another destination. In other instances these migrants find jobs but not the expected social welcome. Existing studies document a range of frustrated expectations and related consequences but fail to offer an explanation.

What accounts for the expectations gap between people legally and popularly presumed to enjoy considerable affinities and good prospects for mutual acceptance? Drawing on a study of Spanish-descent Argentines in Spain, we argue that contrary to conventional knowledge, the effect of perceived ethnic resemblance varies across social contexts. It can be an asset for Spanish-descent Argentines looking for housing, access to education, friends, dates, or even a marriage partner in Spain, but it can be a liability in the labor market, where access to the first rungs of the occupational ladder is often reserved by employers for newcomers valued precisely because their work orientations differ from those of natives. A willingness to endure low wages and subpar working conditions in view of a potential economic and status payoff in the homeland—what social scientists have called a dual frame of reference—has made new immigrants appealing to employers. To the extent that ethnic return migrants are oriented primarily to the local economic and status structure, employers may not view them favorably and their access to entry-level jobs may be hindered and/or they may be forced to compete with better-positioned natives for skilled or professional jobs. Herein lies the problem of assuming that similarity offers benefits across the board.

In the next section we describe what we mean by ethnicity and how it can shape job market orientations and employers' evaluations of prospective workers. We then explain the rationale for including two cases of ethnic return migration to Spain and delve into the historical and institutional bases of presumed commonalities. An analysis of these two cases is the empirical core of our argument. In a discussion section we compare key insights gleaned from the Spanish cases with observations from studies of ethnic Germans in Germany and Japanese-descent Brazilians in Japan. We conclude that ethnic return migrants' orientations are shaped by the terms of the policies that give them access to the destination country's labor markets and citizenship.

Ethnic Affinity, Job Market Orientations, and Tractable Labor

In this chapter we use the term *ethnicity* to refer to social relations premised on a "subjectively believed community of descent" or origins (Weber 1978: 387). This belief is based on, among other things, phenotype, customs, or memories of colonization and migration. However contrived the foundations of ethnicity, if people believe in them, they are real in their consequences (Thomas and Thomas 1928: 572). We use ethnicity, then, to analytically capture this subjective belief in common origins, associated relations, and putative affinity but not in reference to any substantial group (recall Tsuda's introduction to this volume). In the case at hand, Spanish policies reflect a belief in common origins with (1) descendants of former colonial subjects that at times have been viewed as belonging to a state-transcending community of Hispanic nations[1] and/or (2) descendants of Spanish emigrants to the Americas, Africa, and Europe. Ethnicity can be the means to effect monopolistic closure around scarce goods, in this instance Spanish (and European) labor markets, and social welfare resources. Ethnic affinity policies are laws and related official practices through which one state (e.g., Spain) gives prospective migrants living in other countries (e.g., Spanish-descent Argentines) a privileged migration or citizenship status based on perceived common origins. Ethnic return migrants—the beneficiaries of these policies—have access to much the same social and economic goods as their legally defined co-ethnics, at least on paper. Ethnic affinity laws are part of an official discourse to bring into existence the very distinctions they treat as natural and self-evident (Bourdieu 1991: 223). For instance, the legal category of emigrant returnee, which applies to people who may never have set foot in Spain and who have another nationality, represents a claim on these individuals by virtue of history and familial ties. It is analytically important to recognize that these policies and related categories are used by participants in struggles to define national insiders and, by default, outsiders and do not reflect obvious or "objective" distinctions.

State actors in developed economies are often caught between two competing impulses. On the one hand, maximizing social cohesion within a territorially circumscribed population is persistently emphasized and often entails state efforts to minimize difference. On the other hand, embeddedness in an economic system that relies on the availability of ever cheaper labor means that workers must often come from abroad. Ethnic return migrants appear to reconcile these contradictory impulses. They are more likely to share linguistic competencies, religion, customs, orientations, and possibly phenotype with natives, and they would presumably fill entry-level jobs not taken by natives, at least for a time. The tacit assumption of participants and observers is that ethnic affinity refers to similarities among natives and newcomers that traverse multiple social contexts and ease mutual acceptance among migrants and co-ethnic hosts.

Economic scholarship on migrants, however, suggests that similarity may actually be problematic in the work domain. Employers who hire for jobs commonly available to new arrivals expect a deferential disposition unlikely to be found among co-ethnics who share with natives social characteristics, expectations, and legal rights. Analysts have long argued that what makes migrants desirable as workers is their tendency to use a dual frame of reference to interpret their experience and orient their action (Massey et al. 1987; Piore 1979; Waldinger and Lichter 2003).[2] This dual frame consists of a willingness to accept low-status and poorly paid jobs in the receiving context in view of expected financial and social status returns in the homeland. Employers interpret this disposition as deference, and it becomes part of their assessment of workers' suitability for particular jobs. Employers also understand that natives oriented to the local status structure are unwilling to fill entry-level positions. Because migrants often think of the here and now in terms of the there and then, they also tolerate living quarters and everyday hardships they might not have endured in the homeland (Piore 1979). To be sure, migrants' orientation to the context of settlement changes, but this is a process that unfolds over time.

So long as the supply of foreign tractable workers is steady, employers are likely to continue to hire them. Indeed, economic sociologists argue that, all things being equal, employers are likely to hire the same people today that they hired yesterday (Tilly and Tilly 1998: 195). However, if workers' tractability in a particular sector is diminished in noticeable ways—say, through unionization—employers may replace them with a new category of workers. This is what has been happening, for instance, in the strawberry sector in southern Spain: Male Maghrebian workers who had harvested this "time-sensitive" product since the late 1980s became politically mobilized, and employers began to replace them with Eastern European and Latin American female workers touted as more reliable, deferential, and "better suited" to this delicate crop ("Inmigración en España," 2001; "Southern Europe," 2002; cf. Pedreño Cánovas 2000). Tractability is of utmost importance to employers and, when it is threatened, they are likely to replace one category of newcomers with another composed of more deferential workers.

Ethnic return migrants have all the makings of less pliable workers. They have the same formal rights and privileges as their native hosts, access to similar jobs, and likely similar work expectations. Even when they do not, prospective hosts may assume that they do and conclude that they are unlikely to be compliant workers. Native employers do not, for the most part, want to hire ethnic kin to do the dirty, dangerous, and difficult (3D) jobs they have to offer at low wages; they prefer strangers. This is why we argue that, although ethnic similarity may suggest mutual acceptance in some domains, it is not necessarily so in the sphere of work.

Data and Methods

We support our argument by examining two case studies of Argentines whose migration to Spain has been facilitated by ethnic affinity policies. These are key cases because observers and participants alike generally assume a high degree of affinity between these migrants and their supposed Iberian kin and expect that this affinity will facilitate mutual acceptance and ease the transition to Spain. These presuppositions are understandable given the historical, cultural, and organizational links between Spain and Argentina since the mid-nineteenth century. If anywhere, ethnic return migration should work here as conventionally anticipated.

To establish the baseline of conventional knowledge with its implicit expectation of mutual acceptance, we examine the discursive construction of the case of Spanish-descent Argentines and their hosts in Aguaviva, a small town in the rural Spanish region of Aragon. The analysis rests on a close interpretive reading of 257 articles compiled by us between 2000 and 2005 from the Spanish, Argentine, North American, and European press. We collected articles with specific references to ethnic return migration from Argentina to Spain and those that specifically referred to Aguaviva (a fifth of all items compiled). Our interpretive approach situates authors, characters, plot, and language in their respective local, regional, national, and supranational contexts, notes common assumptions, and contrasts implicit and changing claims about ethnic migrants. This case serves as a window onto the sometimes conflicting expectations of Spanish-descent Argentines and their co-ethnic hosts, as viewed by journalists from different national standpoints who take for granted the commonality between people in these categories and what this implies for mutual acceptance. Aguaviva is also a strategic site because it reflects broader Spanish and European concerns about declining populations and about immigration as a solution to demographic dilemmas.

To examine on-the-ground dynamics between natives and ethnic migrants, and in particular their mutual acceptance in a range of contexts, we turn to a qualitative account that draws on observations and interviews carried out between June 2001 and September 2003 among Spanish Argentines in Ría, a pseudonym for an industrial port city in Galicia, Spain. One of us (Cook-Martín) carried out fieldwork that consisted of a dozen intensive interviews with ethnic return migrants. Cook-Martín selected initial participants from a list of names given by three independent contacts in the community. In turn, these initial contacts each provided a list of other potential interviewees from which additional names were drawn with an eye for maximizing differences in participant characteristics and experiences.[3] Fieldwork also included observations and less formal interviews with participants at work, home, and recreational venues (e.g., a local café patronized by Argentines and cultural events that attracted people who had lived in Argentina).

The selection of an urban locale (Ría) and a rural one (Aguaviva) allows us to rule out the possibility that the observed expectations mismatch is an effect of rural-urban differences among newcomers and natives. More important, it underscores that, although two distinct types of ethnicity are at work in these cases, they both shape expectations in remarkably similar ways.[4] In Aguaviva the belief in common origins is sustained loosely by a narrative of *hispanidad* steeped in Spain's history of emigration. Institutionally, this "historical legacies" flavor of ethnicity has informed Spanish immigration policies that contain preferential provisions for Latin Americans and, more recently, nationality policies that give preferential status to anyone who can support links to a Spanish parent or grandparent with official documentation (Reino de España 2002). In Ría ethnicity is conceptualized in terms of concrete kinship ties among newcomers and natives thanks to migration flows that linked Galicia and Argentina well into the 1970s. This conception is taken for granted, if not validated, by regional official policies for *retornados* (returnees) that offer assistance to Galician emigrants or their descendants. Thus, a third methodological component of this study is an analysis of policies that reflect and shape relevant notions of ethnicity.

The Foundations of Ethnic Affinity

More than a century of substantial migration between Argentina and Spain, related cultural and organizational links, and legal mechanisms have sustained the widely held assumption of common origins. As part of a larger wave of European migration, 3.17 million Spaniards migrated to Argentina between 1857 and 1975 and just over half remained. The people who moved back and forth between the two countries built the networks characteristic of most migrations (Tilly 1990). These included hometown and/or mutual assistance associations that were especially prevalent among Galicians—more than 45 percent of Spanish migrants to Argentina (Álvarez Silvar 1997). By the 1920s there were a sufficient number of associations to justify a Federation of Galician Societies (FGS) (Fernández Santiago 2001). These associations not only met migrants' material and cultural needs in Argentina but also linked them to sending areas and channeled crucial resources to the homeland. In recent years associations have served as sources of homeland information for those interested in the possibility of migrating to Galicia. In Buenos Aires the FGS has continued to bridge the cultural and political lives of its members and Galicians in the homeland. In fact, it was through an FGS-sponsored radio program—*Galicia Oxe*—that Argentines first heard of the opportunities in Aguaviva discussed later.

The possibility of reclaiming Spanish citizenship a generation or more after the last emigrants arrived in Argentina speaks to the tenor of legal mechanisms developed under particular circumstances. Specifically, migration between Argentina and Spain coincided with nation-state building and consolidation processes in each country. Central to these processes were efforts to constitute national populations by identifying people as members subject to official administration and by gaining people's allegiance to a *patria*. Vastly underpopulated, Argentina faced the challenge of attracting people to feed labor demand and to call its own; Spain had to make Spaniards out of a highly mobile and diverse population. Migration and nationality law were concrete mechanisms through which these countries competed over the same migrants and their children. The outcome of these struggles has been a pattern of ethnic affinity policy, as defined earlier.

Argentine expressions of this policy pattern include long-standing dual nationality agreements and official preference for Spanish migrants, especially in the inter- and postwar years (Cook-Martín 2008). Dual nationality agreements have allowed citizens of Argentina and Spain to maintain legal affiliations with both countries without the effects of conflicting citizenship obligations. Commercial and migration treaties have made possible the entry of Spaniards on privileged terms, especially since the 1940s (Quijada Mauriño 1989). Spanish manifestations of ethnic affinity policy include right of blood (jus sanguinis) nationality laws and, more recently, central-state and regional migration policies. Since the nineteenth century, the Spanish Civil Code has conferred citizenship on the children of Spaniards[5] regardless of birthplace, provided that prescribed administrative procedures were carefully followed. Modifications to the code introduced in 2002 have made nationality provisions even more expansive toward the descendants of Spaniards (Reino de España 2002).

Since its inception, Spanish immigration law has included positive preferences for "Ibero-Americans," other former colonials, historically wronged communities, and citizens of strategic regions (Reino de España 1985). Despite a recent convergence toward a liberal-democratic norm, with its emphasis on universalistic admissions criteria (Joppke 2005), some positive preferences persist in the most recent iteration of Spanish immigration law (Reino de España 2003).[6] More important, preferences have migrated to nationality law and are still operative in immigration administrative practices.

Flows and stocks of immigrants in Spain support this last point. Although the supply of North African migrants is plentiful, it is the stock of Latin Americans that has grown fastest in Spain over the last five years. Until recently, Moroccans and other North Africans have constituted the main contingent of migrants to Spain. In 2003 Moroccans accounted for just over 20 percent and all Africans for just over 26 percent of immigrants in Spain (Reino de España 2004). However, recent figures show that registered Ecuadorans, documented or otherwise, have surpassed Moroccans as the largest group of foreigners in Spain. The total number of foreigners in Spain was estimated at 2.6 million in 2003, or 6.2 percent of the total population. According to these data, Ecuadorans and Colombians account for almost one-fourth of all foreigners in Spain. Spanish social security data show that Ecuadorans number almost 250,000 registered workers, and Colombians approximately 130,000 (Reino de España 2005). The most recent and comprehensive study of the Argentine-born in Spain shows that they number just over 250,000 (Actis and Esteban 2006). The population has been historically undercounted because of its privileged legal status and administrative treatment.

Notwithstanding the universalistic cast of immigration law, preferential treatment of Spanish-descent Latin Americans in nationality law and actual administrative practice—at the "border" and in the implementation of "regularization" programs—has resulted in an immigrant population that models Spanish ethnic preferences (Cea d'Ancona 2004; Cook-Martín 2002; Izquierdo Escribano et al. 2002; Retis 2003; Solé and Parella 2003). In a fascinating policy shell game driven largely by European Union (EU) pressures, positive preferences for Latin Americans—especially those from former emigrant-receiving areas in South America—have shifted from one legal domain to another. Because nationality policies constitute a back door to membership in EU-member polities, however, pressure is mounting to change them (Zincone 2006).

Local and regional-level migration policy also evidences positive preferences. The cases described in this chapter illustrate two patterns of ethnic affinity policy applied at the subnational level.[7] In the first pattern, municipal governments leverage the privileged migration status available to Spanish-descent foreigners through aggressive recruitment in culturally Spanish enclaves abroad. Local governments from Spain use what had been largely dormant associational ties to get the word out to prospective eligible migrants and to select according to other criteria (age, familial status, skills). Municipal-level governments work within existing central-state laws but accentuate selectivity according to local needs and preferences and even organize associations of governments with these objectives.

In the second pattern, regional governments design laws and related official practices to facilitate co-ethnic "return." Often the prospective beneficiaries are considered citizens by other states and do not necessarily identify affectively with the ancestral homeland in question. Policies of the Autonomous Region of Galicia, discussed later, are an example of this second pattern. Like central-state policies, the legal right of return is supported by invoking a historical-cultural rationale. However, the argument is specific to a Galician history of emigration and is associated with access to material and symbolic resources. The symbolic resources include officially sanctioned identification with Galicia (Parlamento de Galicia 1983), and the material resources are resources for returning emigrants (Conseillo de Emigración 2006). In this case ethnic selectivity is bolstered by regional government institutional, financial, and organizational resources.

This brief overview underscores the historical and institutional bases of a widespread presumption of affinity among Spaniards and Latin American migrants, especially Argentines. In the following sections we demonstrate the shortcomings of the underlying family-resemblance-facilitates-integration rationale, particularly as Spanish-descent Argentines try to break into labor markets in Spain.

Aguaviva: Frustrated Expectations and Ethnic Redefinitions

A small town located midway between Madrid and Zaragoza, Aguaviva has gained notoriety since the turn of the millennium as the site of an innovative program to fight depopulation through selective recruitment of Spanish-descent migrants in South America. Its experiment with immigration by design has received considerable attention from the Spanish, European, and Argentine press because it resonates with broader concerns of European states perceived to be in demographic decline or in a so-called second demographic transition (Kligman 2005; Pérez Leira 2002) and concerns of relatively new, economically ailing emigration countries such as Argentina (Actis and Esteban 2006; Lattes et al. 2003). The Aguaviva story is captivating precisely because it purports to be a win-win encounter of sending and receiving country needs. From the sending country viewpoint, under- and unemployed citizens are able to access European labor markets and perhaps even send remittances (Calvo 2005). From the receiving country perspective, a diminishing population is replenished with people who make possible the reproduction of European polities and economies. The crucial point is that these newcomers presumably bear a family resemblance to natives and are therefore thought more likely to fit in easily. Tacit in this understanding is a comparison with other prospective migrants who are linguistically, religiously, racially, and culturally more distant from the native norm and thus less amenable to integration (Gil Araujo 2004). Thus the selective immigration program undertaken by Aguaviva is newsworthy because it is a proactive and innovative approach to dilemmas faced by European receiving and Latin American sending states, not because of its exceptionality.

Contrary to expectation, however, family resemblance has not ensured relatively easy acceptance. Many Spanish-descent Argentines recruited to Aguaviva have shunned the jobs and accommodations offered to them. Native hosts, on the other hand, have been happy with the demographic replenishment but have questioned newcomers' work ethic and have compared them to Romanian immigrants who unexpectedly met and exceeded local hopes. For observers and participants this has been a puzzling turn of events that motivates print media narratives. To explain this outcome, we review the Aguaviva case in detail and make the argument that ethnic affinity varies in the extent to which it eases mutual acceptance across social contexts.[8]

By the late 1990s, Aguaviva's mayor, Luis Bricio, had concluded that, absent drastic measures, small towns like his would disappear within a generation. Aguaviva had the lowest birth rate in a country with the lowest birth rate in the world (Álvarez Álvarez 1999; Carricart and Litvak 2000; Fernández Cordón 2001). With other mayors from his region, Bricio founded the Spanish Association of Municipalities Against Depopulation (AEMCD), of which he has remained president. The objectives of the AEMCD were to foster economic development while promoting selective immigration (Bricio Manzanares 2004). Concretely, towns would sponsor preferably large Latin American families of Spanish descent. Interest settled especially on Argentina because many of its Spanish-descent citizens had begun to apply for Italian or Spanish citizenship in the wake of economic crisis. Migrants would enter a contract with each municipality, committing to stay for a period of five years. For their part, municipalities would front relocation costs and provide housing and work.

In July 2000 Bricio traveled to Argentina to select a dozen pioneer families. Working through local chapters of the Spanish conservative Partido Popular in Buenos Aires, Rosario, and Mar del Plata, he announced several blue-collar openings for couples younger than age 40 with at least two children (Carricart and Litvak 2000; Monserrat 2000). Bricio appeared on a local radio program,

Galicia Oxe, and at least two large media outlets picked up the story. The widely disseminated announcement received an overwhelming response, and within two days the Partido Popular offices processed the inquiries of more than 5,000 people (Ortega 2001). By April 2001, 10 Argentine and 2 Uruguayan families had settled in Aguaviva, adding 34 children to the local primary school with a previous enrollment of 50 children. They were mostly from middle-class urban backgrounds, and many had managed small businesses during the most recent economic crisis in Argentina. The families arrived with much fanfare, and rosy assessments of Bricio's initiative were the order of the day. Newcomers to Aguaviva celebrated their good fortune and the generosity of their hosts in multiple interviews with the Spanish and Argentine press. It seemed that there had been a happy meeting between the demographic needs of rural Spain and the economic needs of Spanish-descent Argentines. Subsequently the repopulation program was expanded to include families from other Latin American countries and Eastern Europe, primarily Romania. In all, about 25 families arrived in Aguaviva, raising its total population to more than 700 people ("Aguaviva," 2005) and doubling its school-age population (Daly 2003).

Despite the auspicious beginnings of the Aguaviva initiative, half the Argentine families had left or were considering leaving within a year of arriving. They all had Argentine and Spanish nationality, which allowed for movement within the European Union. Most claimed that Aguaviva had not met its promises of providing adequate housing and, especially, work. New arrivals felt entitled to the same treatment as natives, for which they adduced two entwined rationales. The first was historical. Newcomers invoked narratives of aid rendered by Argentina to Spain's past emigrants, including their own ancestors, to imply that contemporary Spaniards maintained an outstanding debt with Argentina that could be repaid by giving its citizens a comparable hand. Jorge López (age 40, laid off as a technician with 3M in Buenos Aires) held that "my grandfather left Spain because he was going hungry. And he arrived in Argentina looking for a better life. Now, history repeats itself, but the other way around" (Carricart and Litvak 2000: 2).

The second rationale for treatment on a par with natives was legal. Because many migrants had or were in the process of acquiring dual Argentine and Spanish citizenship, they felt entitled to the same rights and privileges as other Spaniards. Therefore dual nationals were not willing to take menial, dangerous, or poorly paid jobs just because they offered nominally more compensation than those available in Argentina. When access to other jobs proved problematic, newcomers felt duped. For instance, several participants in the repopulation program complained that the jobs they had been promised before coming to Aguaviva required Spanish certifications, such as a commercial driver's license, at a significant cost. Unable to complete the coursework and pay the fees, they were forced to consider jobs at the local sandpit that were from their perspective underpaid and dangerous (Monserrat 2002; Webster 2001). In addition, most newcomers came from urban contexts and thought that the housing supplied by locals was substandard and lacking in basic amenities.

The townspeople shared with Spanish-descent migrants a sense of cultural affinity and the expectation that it would facilitate the settlement process. "If it were simply a matter of finding workers," Mayor Bricio had said of his program, "we wouldn't have travelled so far to find Hispano-Argentines" (Carricart and Litvak 2000: 2). Indeed, as mentioned, many migrants from other parts of Latin America and from North Africa were available for employment in Spain (see Gil Araujo 2004). "But it's a matter of finding people who will come to Aguaviva with the intention of staying forever," Bricio continued. "For this, the capacity to integrate and adapt to our customs are key, so the natural candidates should be the descendants of Spaniards." From the community's perspective it was important to find the right *kind* of workers: those similar to Aguaviva's residents and who could presumably reproduce their way of life. Moreover, townspeople underscored their willingness to settle a historical debt with Argentina, a country that in the past had dealt generously with Spain by receiving its emigrants.[9]

However, when it came to work and housing, Aguaviva natives held the same expectations of Spanish-descent Argentines as they did of immigrants generally, a point amply illustrated by frequent comparisons with Romanian immigrants. After the municipality sued several newcomers who left Aguaviva allegedly in breach of contract, the mayor left no doubts about native work expectations: "[We brought them] not to be princes, but to work and earn a living" ("Aguaviva," 2005). When newcomers refused to do available work, their moral orientation was called into question. In interviews shortly after the arrival of Spanish-descent Argentines, the mayor noted that the Latin Americans had "a different concept of work" than local residents (Webster 2001: 24). In this and other interviews, natives invariably contrasted Romanian and Argentine migrants and presented the Romanians as examples worthy of emulation. Locals observed that despite religious and linguistic differences, Romanian immigrants were "more like us" than the Latin American newcomers in their ethic of hard work and modest expectations (Daly 2003; Voss 2003). Indeed, Romanians' willingness to do hard manual labor and to live in what their urban-origin Argentine counterparts considered substandard housing emerged repeatedly in native narratives. Interestingly, however, the jobs and homes alluded to by natives were ones they were not filling or inhabiting. The upshot of the Argentine-Romanian comparison is that, although natives were willing to overlook linguistic and religious differences, they were less forgiving with unmet expectations in the occupational realm and reassessed the "real" bases of affinity accordingly.

In this reassessment cultural affinity was not discarded but rather moved down the list of factors likely to enhance natives' and newcomers' mutual acceptance (Bricio Manzanares 2004). Status as a Spanish national allows prospective migrants to make the first cut, but their disposition toward work and possession of skills to match available jobs head the list of favorable factors. Family size, rural origins, and a disposition for "peaceful coexistence" follow as other criteria considered important in the aftermath of Aguaviva's first experience with selective immigration. Mayor Bricio and town residents have come to advocate a more exhaustive vetting process at the point of origin that pays particular attention to skills and work disposition.

According to Bricio, "integration doesn't depend on the language, nor is it guaranteed by a shared Spanish heritage. . . . *What really matters is the work ethic and that the skills they come with match the sort of jobs we can offer here*" (emphasis added; Voss 2003: 2). In this reconsideration of factors likely to facilitate integration, the limits of similarity are implicitly recognized. The point is not that newcomers should be like natives linguistically or culturally but that they should match available jobs both in skills and in a disposition to do them, as perceived by native employers. It is all well and good to prefer people who speak the same language, worship at the same altar, and share historical experiences of solidarity, but these do not make for desirable workers. As the evaluation of Romanians suggests, what constitutes a good or desirable worker is a willingness to do jobs that natives are not doing. Notwithstanding natives' moral discourse about work orientation, they actually share with their Argentine brethren an aversion to the types of jobs now filled by Romanians. The "problem" from a work perspective is not that they are different in their attitudes toward particular jobs but that they are too similar.

If this interpretation is correct, then selecting migrants who are like their prospective hosts in every respect would not help and could hinder the matching of ethnic return migrants to jobs generally available to newcomers, unless, as we argue in another section, some basis exists for limiting labor market expectations. To probe this claim further, in the next section we recount the experience of Spanish-descent Argentines in Ría, a pseudonymous city in the ancestral homeland and traditional emigrant-exporting region of Galicia. Ethnic return migrants in this instance more closely resemble natives along several dimensions, and from a conventional perspective this would suggest better integrative prospects. And yet, although well received in most social contexts, these migrants have encountered significant problems in their job search.

Galicia: Better a Stranger Than a Distant Cousin?

The outcome of the Aguaviva story was not simply an artifact of rural-urban differences among migrants and their hosts, as some actors and observers argue. The people interviewed in Galicia shared natives' urban origins and had family ties to Galicia, arrived in a context with long-standing institutional links with Argentina, and benefited from subnational government policies favoring returnees. Despite this advantageous convergence of factors, Spanish-descent Argentine migrants to Galicia often found their expectations and aspirations at odds, if not in direct conflict, with those of natives, especially in the occupational domain.

The urban origins alluded to earlier really subsume several dimensions of possible commonality among immigrants and hosts: educational profiles, the closeness of worker-job match, and infrastructural expectations. Interviewees had similar educational attainment or skills as their hosts (Algañaraz 2006). Those with some university and professional aspirations in particular competed with similarly trained but locally credentialed natives and faced the most difficulties in finding jobs that matched their formal training and professional aspirations. Skilled workers were in greater demand but had to contend with locals whose nationality and papers were never in question. A study commissioned by the Xunta de Galicia[10] found that, although almost 35 percent of Galician-descent Argentines had a college education that prepared them for the professions, the demand in Galicia was for skilled workers (Heguy 2003). In terms of infrastructural expectations, newcomers from large cities such as Buenos Aires, Rosario, and Santa Fe were likely to find housing, transportation, and a cultural life comparable to those in Argentina. In addition to having urban profiles in common with Galicians, those interviewed often had parents and grandparents who hailed from Galicia and even Ría. Thus returnees frequently had kinship ties to natives, even if distant, and so the metaphor of relatives fallen on hard times had more literal underpinnings in Ría than in Aguaviva. A kinship network was important in helping ethnic migrants find housing or a job, although the job offers were less frequent than one might expect because native relatives were often elderly and disengaged from the labor market or had to worry about their own children's placement. At an affective level newcomers were able to connect with the place reminisced about by their parents or grandparents. This is in sharp contrast to the experience of newcomers to Aguaviva, whose links were relatively more contrived.

As mentioned, a sense of affinity among Spanish-descent Argentines and native Galicians is aided by historical, institutional, and organizational links to Argentina. The historical legacies of migration to Argentina and other Latin American countries pervade many aspects of Galicia's contemporary, social, and political life, so that a sense of connection to *retornados* is robust compared to what one might find in a place such as Aguaviva, which experienced emigration but no significant return migration. The names of city streets and businesses, schools, and cultural institutions founded with past remittances from Argentina and Cuba, the influence of Galician voters abroad as reported in the local media, and the recognition of emigrant intellectuals as architects of regional identity serve as reminders of Galicia's emigration history and its ties abroad. A sense of connection to returnees is also nurtured by the activities of associations, some with a long tradition of fostering ties to Galician communities abroad and some new. From an institutional perspective the government of Galicia has defined the very category of returnee and has developed policies and administrative structures to serve eligible individuals (Xunta de Galicia 1981).[11] These regional policies operate within the framework of central-state counterparts but dedicate financial and organizational resources to those who avail themselves of Spanish citizenship and to immigration preferences for emigrants and their descendants. The Consellería de Emigración is the administrative entity that coordinates official and nongovernmental organization support for returnees.[12] In fiscal year 2006 the regional government allocated 17 million euros to programs for return migrants, including monies to fund job placement, housing, and education (Conseillo de Emigración 2006). The most recent institutional development has been the proposed passage of a new Statute of Citizens Abroad, which would recognize rights and privileges for the estimated 1.5 million Spaniards abroad, including those of just over 900,000 Galicians (Abejón 2006; Reino de España 2006).

It stands to reason, given these linkages, that the arrival of Spanish-descent Argentines would be viewed rather like a homecoming and that their acceptance would be unproblematic. And indeed, ethnic return migrants are portrayed sympathetically in the press as co-ethnics returned from a long sojourn abroad (e.g., "Ana Martínez," 2005). For their part, ethnic return migrants report a sense of being accepted by native Galicians. Sofía (age 40, a registered nurse from Córdoba, Argentina) relates that she encountered some initial reserve among Galicians, but she attributes this to a general distrust of outsiders, including Spaniards from other regions. She cites as an example of Galician hospitality the child care assistance received from neighbors when she and her husband first arrived from Argentina in 1990. Other Spanish-descent Argentine youths and their native peers tell of the popularity of Argentines on the local party scene and in local football clubs.

However, in the realm of work, the assessments are more negative. The dedication of resources to facilitate returnees' labor market integration attests to the regional government's preoccupation with employment problems observed among Latin American returnees (Conseillo de Emigración 2006; Pérez Leira 2002; "Los retornados," 2004). Local media have also given wide coverage to returnees' downward occupational mobility ("Ana Martínez," 2005). In field interviews, Spanish-descent migrants report a range of problems in the occupational sphere. A salient complaint concerns job aspirations that overlap with those of other Spaniards. For instance, Manolo (late 20s, a student and unemployed former hotel worker) wants to find work in "administration or marketing" but has been unsuccessful since arriving two months earlier. He is part of the 23 percent of returnees who are the foreign-born children and grandchildren of Galicians and who have Spanish citizenship ("Vigo estudia el perfil," 2003). As a citizen, he thinks he should have access to the same jobs and pay as any other Spaniard. To date, the jobs offered to him are ones he considers below his abilities, experience, and pay expectations.

On the other hand, natives tacitly expect that newcomers should gratefully take available unskilled and semiskilled jobs at modest wages, because even highly skilled and credentialed native workers have had to migrate to other parts of Spain and Europe in search of work. Marisa (age 35, an employer and daughter of a prominent Galician leader in Buenos Aires) worries about the cavalier attitude of many returnees who, like Manolo, have a disposition ill-suited to someone in search of work. Some newcomers even tell demeaning jokes about their hosts and prospective employers. In her view this does not bode well for Argentine job seekers. In her assessment of Spanish-descent migrants the comparison is to other immigrants willing to humbly accept the opportunities offered to them and to Galicians who, as past emigrants, sacrificed abroad in order to make a better life for themselves and their families at home.

And yet, when ethnic migrants are willing to do jobs for which they are overqualified, employers sometimes make assumptions that exclude them from these positions. For example, Claudio (mid-20s, a truck driver and son of Galician emigrants) and his brother-in-law, Juan (mid-20s, a truck driver who is married to a Galician), are desperately seeking employment at a local union office and tell of their dilemma. On the one hand, because they have not yet received their national identification cards, employers are reluctant to hire them for highly regulated driving positions when there are other fully documented drivers. On the other hand, employers are unwilling to hire them for less qualified work once they learn that Claudio and Juan are Spanish citizens. A local union representative who helps place workers like Juan and Claudio believes that employers assume that as Spaniards, such workers will not really be willing to do unskilled, poorly paid jobs. Thus workers' own aspirations and employers' notions of who is suited to what jobs can effectively frustrate ethnic migrants' job search.

One alternative for Spanish-descent migrants is to enter an emerging ethnic employment niche. Pablo (age 55, a bartender) tells of returning to Ría after 45 years in Buenos Aires and not being able to find steady employment. He is eligible for some government assistance but is making ends meet by tending bar in a café that caters mostly to Argentine expatriates. As an older returnee, it is unlikely that employers will select him for entry-level positions, and he does not have the educational credentials to fill skilled or professional openings. However, the commercial sector that serves immigrants is still relatively small and is unlikely to offer jobs attractive to most ethnic migrants.

For the most part, ethnic return migrants face barriers to entering the local labor market because of expectations that overlap or clash with those of natives or because of employers' notions of which prospective workers dispositionally fit what jobs. The employment history of Sofía, the Spanish-descent migrant mentioned earlier, clearly illustrates these hurdles and, in particular, the crucial difference that citizenship status can make in workers' and employers' dispositions and job-matching processes. Although a registered nurse in Argentina, Sofía was hired as a nurse's aide at the local hospital, and for a few years she worked off the books. She had not revalidated her Argentine degree, and the hospital was content to have her work at lower pay. At the time she was not a Spanish citizen. When she applied for residency papers, the hospital issued a contract for the authorities confirming contributions to the social security system on Sofía's behalf. They then deducted this money, which they were contributing for native workers, from her salary each month. Sofía felt there was no alternative and thought it part of paying one's dues in a new country. Once a Spanish citizen, she was no longer dependent on the hospital's contracts to show continuous employment, a requirement for the periodic renewal of residency permits, and felt entitled to better pay, something that the hospital resisted. Sofía eventually went on disability leave and then was laid off, but she received unemployment benefits from the government. By this time, her husband had become captain of a merchant marine ship and they were able to make ends meet. She continued to work for local hospitals on a part-time basis because they would not hire her full-time to avoid paying benefits. Ironically, the change in expectations that accompanied Sofía's change in citizenship status put her in a precarious employment position.

The consensus among the Spanish-descent migrants we interviewed was that formal citizenship did not translate into the substantive rights they envisioned for themselves in the job market. Aspiring to the same jobs as their co-ethnic hosts, they became frustrated with settlement in Ría. Galicians found these expectations unrealistic and arrogant. To the extent that newcomers were not willing to do entry-level jobs, they were cast as undesirable workers. On the other hand, newcomers felt that even when they were willing to do low-paying and low-status jobs, employers were likely not interested or thought that these jobs were beneath newly arrived co-ethnics. It was the legally defined similarity of Spanish-descent Argentines that underlay the expectation of landing native jobs and hindered the maintenance of a dual frame of reference, which in turn led to employers' categorization of newcomers as workers ill-suited to available positions.

Shades of Similarity and Difference

A fundamental insight gleaned from this and other studies in this volume concerns the critical role of state membership and mobility policies in shaping the terms on which ethnic return migrants and natives approach the labor market, a crucial sphere of integration. Indeed, a comparison with other instances of ethnic return migration shows that the fit between native and newcomer work expectations varies according to the extent that official policies foster or hinder a dual frame of reference. Exemplars of the East Asian and Western European patterns described by Tsuda in the introduction and conclusion of this volume support this point.

It is precisely the contour of immigration and citizenship policies in each instance that accounts for the differential labor market outcomes and suggests as a possible mechanism the impact of these laws and associated official practices on expectations brought to job-matching encounters. If these policies foster a dual frame of reference, ethnic return migrants are likely to successfully enter the job market; but if the policies hinder a dual orientation, migrants are likely to have trouble finding work. The Japanese government grants *nikkeijin* a preferential but still temporary migratory status and does not easily confer citizenship, even to co-ethnic newcomers. In addition, Japanese-descent workers are recruited abroad and come with a time-limited contract that carefully dictates the terms of work and residence. Indeed they are referred to as *dekasegi*, or temporary migrant workers (Tsuda 2003). Residential segregation of newcomers further accentuates distinctions between natives and newcomers. Combined, these factors sustain a dual frame of reference among Japanese-descent migrants that makes them willing to endure downward mobility in view of a material and status payoff in the sending country and thus more exploitable and desirable as workers. By contrast, ethnic Germans have the same rights and privileges as any other German. Although the number of people classified as ethnic Germans eligible for entry and citizenship has declined significantly over the last 15 years, those who have entered in the past have the same rights as their co-nationals and access to language training, job placement assistance, and welfare benefits (Oezcan 2004). By definition, *Aussiedler* policy fosters an orientation toward the German economic and status system. We posit that this orientation makes ethnic newcomers less like other immigrants willing to do 3D jobs and hence less pliable or exploitable from the perspective of native employers. In sum, it is the content of policies that shapes the labor market insertion of ethnic return migrants.

Conclusion

The analytic upshot of this chapter is that students of ethnic return migrations should uncover rather than take for granted what officially defined commonalities portend for the mutual acceptance of natives and newcomers. As we have shown, vague presumptions of similarity and implied social acceptance are inconsistent especially with actual experiences in the world of work. To take state-generated claims of affinity for granted not only gives scientific legitimacy to official visions of how the social world is parsed but also hinders knowledge about how and why states make such claims and with what consequences. An exclusive focus on the positive preference for co-ethnic migrants, for instance, may elide a tacit exclusionary flip side. In Spain, the dark side of ethnic affinity policies has been the replacement of North African migrants with Latin Americans. Another example includes taking at face value participants' reappraisals of ethnic affinity in the wake of conflicting expectations. Although these reassessments may contain accurate insights—Mayor Bricio's recognition that newcomers should be well suited to locally available jobs—they are simply new chapters in an ongoing struggle of who will be categorized into what class of people and to what ends. Reinterpretations of affinity are not adjustments of group definitions to more accurately reflect the boundaries of real entities. Ethnicity is, after all, about relationships, not substances (Bourdieu 1985). Analysts would do well to remember this as they interpret conflicting or unmet expectations born of the mismatch between formal and substantive rights and obligations.

Notes

This chapter is a modified and slightly expanded version of "The Problem with Similarity: Ethnic Affinity Migrants in Spain," published in the *Journal of Ethnic and Migration Studies* 35(1):151–170 (2009). It is reprinted here with permission of the publisher (Taylor & Francis Ltd., http://www.informaworld.com). Cook-Martín thanks the UCLA Center for European and Eurasian Studies, the Berkeley Institute of European Studies, and the National Science Foundation (through grant SES-0512080) for their support. Viladrich thankfully acknowledges the support of the Urban Public Health Program, the School of Health Sciences, and the School of the Health Professions (CUNY) and the partial support of the Russeau gift from Hunter College. Thanks also to Ödül Bozkurt, David Fitzgerald, Jon Fox, Sandra Gil Araujo, and anonymous reviewers for their invaluable comments. We are especially grateful to Takeyuki Tsuda for his intellectual engagement and editorial leadership. Above all, we thank the people who shared with us their life experiences.

1. On the historical meaning of *hispanismo* and *hispanidad*, see Balfour (1996), Diffie (1943), Gomez-Escalonilla (1991), and Rein (1991). See also Joppke's (2005: 114–117) more recent discussion with specific reference to this ideology's effect on nationality law.

2. The dual frame of reference concept has also been used productively by anthropologists and sociologists to explain differences in educational achievement between natives and newcomers (Ogbu 1990; Reese 2001; Suarez-Orozco 1987; Waters 1999).

3. This selection strategy begins with independent points of entry that serve as sources for a lengthening chain of referrals. The limit on the number of selection iterations can be determined theoretically (Charmaz 2001; Gaskell 2000) as well as statistically (Heckathorn 2002).

4. Thanks to Christian Joppke for encouraging us to draw out this distinction.

5. Until 1982, Spanish nationality was transmitted to the children of Spanish men. Gender-neutral nationality provisions were made retroactive in 2002 (Cook-Martín 2006).

6. Although these are minor and consist of exemptions from work permit fees.

7. Similar practices are at work in the Italian case and are the subject of ongoing examination by Cook-Martín.

8. After reviewing an early draft of this chapter, Garcia (2007) conducted summer field research in Aguaviva and confirmed the conclusions reached through our "once-removed" analysis.

9. This perspective is ubiquitous in Spanish public discourse about Argentines (Spanish president Rodriguez Zapatero, cited in "Leyes de inmigración," 2005; Cook-Martín 2002: 23–24; Retis 2003: 15).

10. The Xunta de Galicia is the regional government organization. Galicia is one of seventeen autonomous communities in Spain and one of four regions with special provisions of autonomy.

11. "Return migration" to Spain comes not only from the Americas but also from other European countries and North Africa (Rogers 1985; Vilar and Vilar 1999a, 1999b).

12. For a list of nongovernmental organizations that serve return migrants, see Fundación Galicia Emigración (http://www.fundaciongaliciaemigracion.es/funCastellano /noticia.php?idNoticia=12).

References Cited

Abejón, Paloma. 2006. "El Gobierno iguala los derechos de los emigrantes y los residentes en Galicia." *La Voz de Galicia*, February 3.

Actis, Walter, and F. O. Esteban. 2006. "Argentinos hacia España ('sudacas' en tierras 'gallegas'): El estado de la cuestión." In *Sur-Norte: Estudios sobre la emigracion reciente de argentinos*, S. Novick, ed. Buenos Aires: Catálogos e Instituto de Investigaciones Gino Germani, 205–258.

"Aguaviva: Alegrías y sinsabores de una aldea global y sus inmigrantes Rio Platenses." 2005. *Impulso*, April 22.

Algañaraz, J. C. 2006. "Fuerte presencia en España de argentinos con alto nivel profesional." *Clarín*, December 28. http://www.clarin.com/diario/2006/12/28/sociedad /s-03401.htm.

Álvarez Álvarez, Florentina. 1999. "La encuesta de fertilidad se publicará a fin de este año." *Revista Fuentes Estadisticas—La Familia* 37:1–5.

Álvarez Silvar, Gabriel. 1997. *La migración de retorno en Galicia (1970–1995).* Santiago de Compostela, Spain: Secretaría Xeral de Relacións coas Comunidades Galegas.

"Ana Martínez, emigrante a Argentina." 2005. *El Correo Gallego,* February 19.

Balfour, Sebastian. 1996. "'The Lion and the Pig': Nationalism and National Identity in Fin-de-Siècle Spain." In *Nationalism and the Nation in the Iberian Peninsula: Competing and Conflicting Identities,* C. Mar-Molinero and A. Smith, eds. Oxford: Berg, 107–117.

Bourdieu, Pierre. 1985. "The Social Space and the Genesis of Groups." *Theory and Society* 14(6):723–744.

———. 1991. *Language and Symbolic Power.* Cambridge, MA: Harvard University Press.

Bricio Manzanares, Luis. 2004. "Selección de nuevos pobladores." *Servicios Sociales, Debate* 10:53–67.

Brubaker, Rogers. 1998. "Migrations of Ethnic Unmixing in the 'New Europe.'" *International Migration Review* 32(4):1047–1065.

Calvo, P. 2005. "Record de ayuda de los argentinos que se fueron." *Clarín,* March 13.

Carricart, J. M., and C. Litvak. 2000. "Informe especial: Los argentinos que se van a vivir a España." *Gente,* August 8.

Cea d'Ancona, M. A. 2004. *La activación de la xenofobia en España: Qué miden las encuestas?* Madrid: Centro de Investigaciones Sociológicas.

Charmaz, Kathy. 2001. "Grounded Theory." In *Contemporary Field Research: Perspectives and Formulations,* R. M. Emerson, ed. Prospect Heights, IL: Waveland Press, 335–352.

Conseillo de Emigración. 2006. *Proxecto de Orzamentos da Comunidade Autónoma Galega Ano 2006.* Santiago de Compostela, Spain: Conseillo de Emigración.

Cook-Martín, David. 2002. "Social Classification of Latin Americans in Spanish Immigration Policy." Los Angeles: University of California, Los Angeles.

———. 2006. "Soldiers and Wayward Women: Gendered Citizenship and Migration Policy in Argentina, Italy, and Spain Since 1850." *Citizenship Studies* 10:571–590.

———. 2008. "Rules, Red Tape, and Paperwork: The Archeology of State Control over Migrants, 1850–1930." *Journal of Historical Sociology* 21:82–119.

Corcoran, M. P. 2002. "The Process of Migration and the Reinvention of Self: The Experiences of Returning Irish Emigrants." *Eire-Ireland: Journal of Irish Studies* 37(1–2):1751–1791.

Daly, Emma. 2003. "Aguaviva Journal: By Enticing Foreigners, Villages Grow Young Again." *New York Times,* July 31.

Diffie, Bailey W. 1943. "The Ideology of Hispanidad." *Hispanic American Historical Review* 23(3):457–482.

Fernández Cordón, J. A. 2001. "El futuro demográfico y la oferta de trabajo en España." *Migraciones* 9:45–68.

Fernández Santiago, M. X. 2001. "Asociacionismo gallego en Buenos Aires (1936–1960)." In *La Galicia austral: La inmigración gallega en la Argentina*, X. M. Núñez Seixas, ed. Buenos Aires: Editorial Biblos, 181–201.

Fox, Jon. 2006. "National Identities on the Move: Transylvanian Hungarian Labour Migrants in Hungary." *Journal of Ethnic and Migration Studies* 29:449–466.

Garcia, A. 2007. *Internalizing Immigration Policy Within the Nation-State: The Local Initiative of Aguaviva, Spain*. San Diego: University of California, Latin American Studies.

Gaskell, George. 2000. "Individual and Group Interviewing." In *Qualitative Researching with Text, Image, and Sound: A Practical Handbook*, M. W. Bauer and G. Gaskell, eds. London: Sage, 38–56.

Gil Araujo, S. 2004. "Inmigración latinoamericana en España: Estado de la cuestión." Working paper. Madrid: Instituto Universitario de Estudios Norteamericanos de la Universidad de Alcalá–Universidad de Alcalá and Florida International University.

Gomez-Escalonilla, Lorenzo Delgado. 1991. "Percepciones y estrategias culturales españolas hacia América Latina durante la Segunda Guerra Mundial." *Estudios Interdisciplinarios de América Latina y el Caribe* 2:1–25.

Heckathorn, D. D. 2002. "Respondent-Driven Sampling II: Deriving Valid Population Estimates from Chain-Referral Samples of Hidden Populations." *Social Problems* 49:11–34.

Heguy, Silvina. 2003. "Uno de cada tres gallegos quiere volver a España." *Clarín*, August 9, 40–41.

"Inmigración en España." 2001. *El País*, June 15.

Izquierdo Escribano, A., D. López de Lera, and R. Martínez Buján. 2002. "Los preferidos del Siglo XXI: La inmigración latinoamericana en España." In *La inmigración en España: Contextos y alternativas*, F. J. García Castaño and C. Muriel, eds. Granada, Spain: Laboratorio de Estudios Interculturales, 237–249.

Joppke, Christian. 2005. *Selecting by Origin: Ethnic Migration in the Liberal State*. Cambridge, MA: Harvard University Press.

Kligman, Gail. 2005. "A Reflection on Barren States: The Demographic Paradoxes of Consumer Capitalism." In *Barren States: The Population "Implosion" in Europe*, C. B. Douglass, ed. New York: Berg, 249–260.

Kulu, Hill. 1998. "Ethnic Return Migration: An Estonian Case." *International Migration* 36(3):313–336.

Lattes, A. E., P. A. Comelatto, and C. M. Levit. 2003. "Migración y dinámica demográfica en la Argentina durante la segunda mitad del siglo XX." *Estudios Migratorios Latinoamericanos* 17(50):69–110.

Levy, Daniel, and Yfaat Weiss. 2002. *Challenging Ethnic Citizenship: German and Israeli Perspectives on Immigration*. New York: Berghahn.

"Leyes de inmigración y los argentinos." 2005. *Clarín*, January 23. http://www.clarin.com/diario/2005/01/23/elmundo/i-01903.htm.

Massey, D., R. Alarcón, J. Durand, and H. González. 1987. *Return to Aztlán: The Social Process of International Migration from Western Mexico*. Berkeley: University of California Press.

Monserrat, C. 2000. "De Mar del Plata a Teruel: Aguaviva, un pequeño pueblo aragonés, trata de repoblarse dando trabajo a familias argentinas." *El Pais Digital*, no. 1602, September 21.

————. 2002. "De Mar del Plata al desempleo con parada en el Bajo Aragón: Seis de las ocho familias argentinas que se mudaron a Aguaviva sostienen que las promesas se han incumplido." *El Pais*, April 18.

Oezcan, Veysel. 2004. "Fewer Ethnic Germans Immigrating to Ancestral Homeland." Migration Information Source, February. http://www.migrationinformation.org/Feature/display.cfm?id=201.

Ogbu, John U. 1990. "Minority Status and Literacy in Comparative Perspective." *Daedalus* 119:141–168.

Ortega, Javier. 2001. "Nace en Aragón una asociación de pueblos para traer inmigrantes a España." *El Mundo*, January 15.

Parlamento de Galicia. 1983. *Lei 4, 1983, do 15 Xuño, de Recoñecemento da Galeguidade*, Parlamento de Galicia, ed. Santiago de Compostela, Spain: Parlamento de Galicia.

Pedreño Cánovas, A. 2000. "Inmigración y gestión empresarial de la mano de obra." Paper presented at the Conferencia sobre la inmigración en España, II Congreso de la Inmigración en España, Madrid, October 5–7.

Pérez Leira, L. 2002. "Encuesta argentinos en Galicia." Vigo, Spain: Confederación Intersindical Galega. Unpublished manuscript.

Piore, Michael. 1979. *Birds of Passage: Migrant Labor and Industrial Societies*. New York: Cambridge University Press.

Quijada Mauriño, Monica. 1989. "Política inmigratoria del primer Peronismo." *Revista Europea de Estudios Latinoamericanos y del Caribe* 47(December):43–64.

Reese, Leslie. 2001. "Morality and Identity in Mexican Immigrant Parents' Vision of the Future." *Journal of Ethnic and Migrations Studies* 27:455–472.

Rein, Raanan. 1991. "Hispanidad y oportunismo político: El caso peronista." *Estudios Interdisciplinarios de América Latina y el Caribe* 2(2):1–23.

Reino de España. 1985. "Ley Orgánica 7/1985, de 1 de julio, sobre derechos y libertades de los extranjeros en España." *Boletín Oficial del Estado* 158(July 3). Madrid.

————. 2002. *Código Civil*. Madrid: Editorial Tecnos.

————. 2003. "Ley Orgánica 14/2003 de 20 de noviembre." *Boletín Oficial del Estado* 270(November 21). Madrid.

————. 2004. *Anuario Estadístico de Inmigración*, Ministerio de Trabajo y Asuntos Sociales, ed. Madrid: Secretaría de Estado de Inmigración y Emigración, Observatorio Permanente de la Inmigración.

————. 2005. *Trabajadores extranjeros en el mercado de trabajo*, Ministerio de Trabajo y Asuntos Sociales, ed. Madrid: Observatorio Permanente de la Inmigración.

————. 2006. *Boletín oficial de las Cortes Generales, Congreso de los Diputados, VIII Legislatura, Estatuto de los ciudadanos españoles en el exterior.* Series A, no. 75-1. Madrid: Cortes Generales.

Retis, Jéssica. 2003. "Tendencias en la representación de los inmigrantes latinoamericanos en la prensa nacional española. Colombianos, ecuatorianos y argentinos: ¿iguales o diferentes?" Madrid: Instituto Universitario de Investigación Ortega y Gasset. Unpublished manuscript.

"Los retornados de Europa cobran el cuádruple que los de América." 2004. *La Voz de Galicia*, July 12.

Rhi Sausi, J. L., and M. A. García. 1992. *Gli Argentini in Italia: Una comunitá di immmigrati nel paese degli avi.* Bologna, Italy: Biblioteca Universale Synergon.

Rogers, R. 1985. *Guests Come to Stay: The Effects of European Labor Migration on Sending and Receiving Countries.* Boulder, CO: Westview Press.

Solé, C., and S. Parella. 2003. "The Labor Market and Racial Discrimination in Spain." *Journal of Ethnic and Migration Studies* 29(1):121–140.

"Southern Europe." 2002. *Migration News*, v. 8 (July).

Suarez-Orozco, Marcelo M. 1987. "'Becoming Somebody': Central American Immigrants in U.S. Inner-City Schools." *Anthropology and Education Quarterly* 18:287–299.

Thomas, W. I., and Dorothy Swaine Thomas. 1928. *The Child in America: Behavior Problems and Programs.* New York: Knopf.

Tilly, Charles. 1990. "Transplanted Networks." In *Immigration Reconsidered: History, Sociology, and Politics*, V. Yans-McLaughlin, ed. New York: Oxford University Press, 79–95.

Tilly, Chris, and Charles Tilly. 1998. *Work Under Capitalism.* Boulder, CO: Westview Press.

Tsuda, Takeyuki. 2003. *Strangers in the Ethnic Homeland.* New York: Columbia University Press.

"Vigo estudia el perfil del gallego retornado." 2003. *El Mundo*, January 10.

Vilar, J. B., and M. J. Vilar. 1999a. *La emigración española a Europa en el siglo XX.* Madrid: Arco/Libros.

————. 1999b. *La emigración española al Norte de Africa (1830–1999).* Madrid: Arco/Libros.

Voss, Michael. 2003. "Rural Spain Welcomes Immigrants." BBC News Online, June 19. http://news.bbc.co.uk/2/hi/world/europe/3002928.stm.

Waldinger, R., and M. I. Lichter. 2003. *How the Other Half Works: Immigration and the Social Organization of Labor.* Los Angeles: University of California Press.

Waters, Mary C. 1999. *Black Identities: West Indian Immigrant Dreams and American Realities.* New York: Russell Sage Foundation.

Weber, M. 1978. *Economy and Society: An Outline of Interpretive Sociology.* Berkeley: University of California Press.

Webster, J. 2001. "Aguaviva la aldea global." *El País Semenal,* December 23, 22–30.

Xunta de Galicia. 1981. *O estatuto de autonomía de Galicia.* Santiago de Compostela, Spain: Xunta de Galicia.

Zincone, Giovanna. 2006. *Familismo legale: Como (non) diventare italiani.* Rome: Editori Laterza.

Ethnic "Return" Migration to Sweden

The Dividing Line of Language

Charlotta Hedberg

MIGRATION BETWEEN Sweden and Finland, two neighboring countries in northern Europe, is nothing new. Over the centuries interaction and settlements have taken place across the sea that separates the countries (Allardt 1996; Törnblom 1993). Since the 1950s, in the postwar era of labor migration, a massive stream of migrants has entered Sweden from less economically developed Finland (De Geer and Wester 1975; Häggström et al. 1990). In the 1970s, when economic equilibrium was established between the countries, the migration process seemed to stop, and on an aggregated level the share of migrants decreased dramatically. However, within the migration stream from Finland to Sweden, a Swedish-speaking minority group was present, and it was greatly overrepresented in relation to the size of this group in Finland (Hedberg and Kepsu 2003).[1] In the 1980s and 1990s, this group, the Finland Swedes, continued to migrate to Sweden, despite decreased economic motivation. Their migration to Sweden can be approached as ethnic "return" migration, with migrants moving to the country where their ethnic mother tongue is spoken. Tangible socioeconomic relations link Finland with Sweden and are facilitated by the geographic proximity of the two countries. As a consequence, the issue of ethnic affinity plays a much more important role in the Finland Swedish case of ethnic return migration than it does for the other migrant groups discussed in this book. In fact, of these groups, only the ethnic Hungarians migrating from Romania to Hungary (Chapter 7) represent a case of migrants in which similar transnational links are present. In contrast to this case, however, the Finland Swedish migration to Sweden takes place between two countries in the developed world, with similar economic standards, as was also mentioned in Chapter 1. Consequently, this migration process is not primarily motivated by economic factors; instead the motivation of ethnic affinity is in the foreground. This makes the Finland Swedish case of ethnic return migration quite particular and highlights the role of ethnic affinity in the return migration process more distinctly than in the other cases.

Finland Swedes are an indigenous minority in Finland. Their ancestors arrived from Sweden in prehistoric times. Finland was an integrated part of the Swedish kingdom until 1809, when it came under Russian rule, and until then Swedish speakers held political power in Finland (Engman 1995). Groups of Swedish speakers represented the urban cultural and political elites, but they were also found within rural strata of fishers and farmers (Allardt and Starck 1981). When Finland came under Russian control, the Swedish speakers gradually lost their position of power in Finnish society. In the constitution of the new Finnish republic after World War I the Swedish language enjoyed equal status with the Finnish language.

To this day cultural references to Sweden and the spoken Swedish language have remained vital parts of Finland Swedish ethnic identity (Höckerstedt 2000). In parallel, however, a national identity has developed within the group that refers to Finland as the country of residence (Åström 2001). Thus a Finland Swede often has a double identity, with one foot in Finland and the other in Sweden. The response of the two countries to Finland Swedes is not always equally obliging; their privileged linguistic status in Finland is often much debated in the daily news, and in Sweden the group is relatively unknown.

The Swedish language serves as a major symbol of Finland Swedish ethnic identity in relation to the Finnish-speaking majority group in Finland (Allardt and Starck 1981; Åström 2001; Höckerstedt 2000). In fact, the linguistic difference is the only obvious deviant characteristic between Swedish and Finnish speakers, because other typical ethnic markers, such as religion or a different appearance, are the same for both groups. The Finland Swedish minority has thus built its political aspirations around the question of language and particularly the preservation of their linguistic status in the Finnish constitution. Minority rights, such as Swedish schools and services in Swedish from public sector agencies, are tied to the varying proportion of Swedish speakers within municipal populations.[2] Furthermore, the Swedish language is the element that unifies Finland Swedes as an ethnic group across Swedish Finland, that is, the heterogeneous Swedish-speaking regions of Finland.

McRae (1999) argues that the linguistic situation between Finnish and Swedish speakers in Finland is characterized by great complexity. The gap between the Finland Swedes' formal language rights and the difficulties they experience practicing these rights on an everyday basis is large. To avoid conflict, the group tends to keep quiet and to flexibly meet the expectations of the Finnish-speaking majority. This places the Swedish language in Finland in a threatened position. The opportunities to use Swedish in Finland decreased dramatically during the twentieth century.

In 1999 there were 300,000 Finland Swedes in Finland, accounting for 6 percent of the population (Finnäs 2001). They were unevenly distributed across the country, however. Most regions had almost no Swedish-speaking population, whereas the proportion of Swedish speakers in other districts ranged from 10 percent to 90 percent of the population. In those regions where Finland Swedes are in a local minority position, Swedish is predominantly used in the private sphere, whereas in regions with a Swedish-speaking majority Swedish is also spoken at workplaces and "downtown." Thus language use in Finland serves as a distinctive marker of the power position of different groups.

The Swedish language also constitutes a vital link between Finland and Sweden (Höckerstedt 2000). Until 1809 the two countries were politically and culturally intertwined, and even today Sweden is central to many Finland Swedes as an extended Swedish-speaking area, in a cultural-historical as well as a practical sense. The fact that Sweden and Finland are neighboring countries serves to keep these relations alive.

In this chapter I analyze Finland Swedish migration to Sweden as an affinity-based process of ethnic return migration to Sweden. From this point of view, I aim to explore the causes of Finland Swedish migration from Finland to Sweden and to investigate the integration process in Sweden. Special consideration is given to the linguistic minority situation in Finland and to the way language creates sociocultural linkages to Sweden as a country of both economic and geographic proximity. I argue that these factors form vital constituents of Finland Swedish ethnic identity, which plays a crucial role in the migration process to Sweden. When moving to Sweden, the group's mother tongue is transferred from a minority to a majority language. I investigate whether Finland Swedish migrants separate themselves from the Swedish-speaking majority or whether they tend to assimilate in Sweden. The common Swedish language, as a mediator of Finland Swedish ethnic affinity in Sweden, is thus assumed to play a major role in the processes of both migration and integration.

This chapter is based on a qualitative interview study conducted in 2003. Twenty-two interviews were analyzed. The interviews were conducted with migrants who defined themselves as Finland Swedes who had moved to Sweden between 1976 and 1999. Twelve interviews were conducted with migrants who still lived in Sweden, and ten interviews were conducted with Finland Swedes who had returned to Finland. The interviews were selected by means of a stratified sampling procedure. They represent the age and gender groups that were typical of migrants from the three selected case study areas. These localities in turn represented three different parts of Swedish Finland, across which the

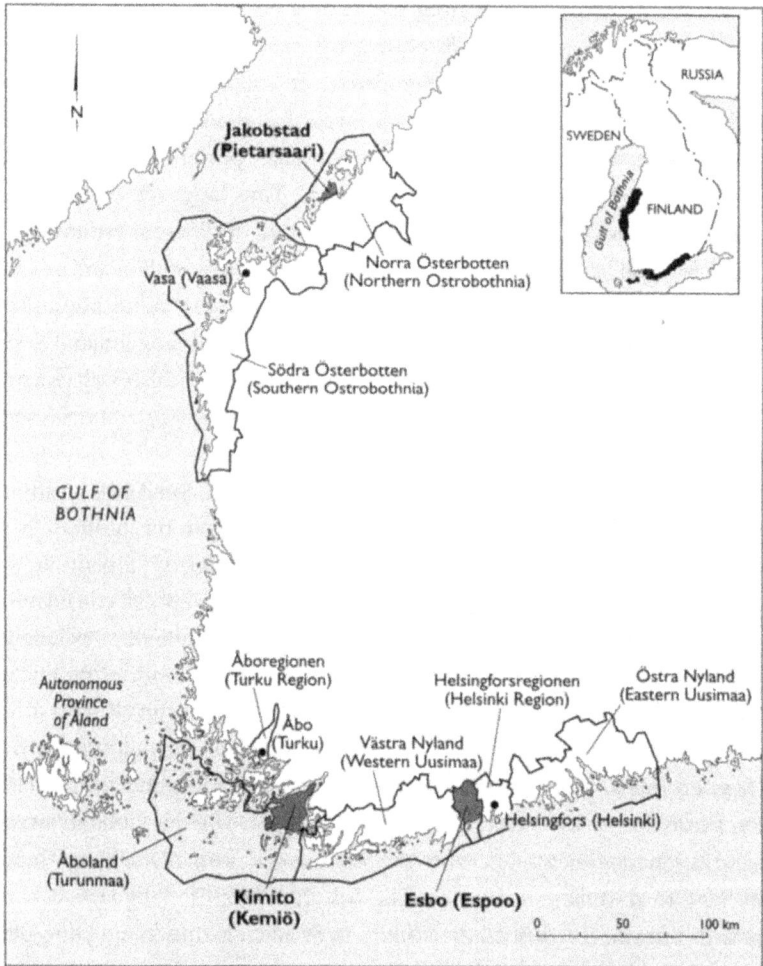

Figure 6.1 Three of the Swedish-speaking areas of Finland (Esbo, Kimito, and Jakobstad). Based on an illustration by Kaisa Kepsu, Helsinki University, 2003.

causes of migration vary as a result of large interregional differences (Map 6.1): (1) Esbo (Espoo), in the central capital area of Helsingfors (Helsinki) in Nyland (Uusimaa); (2) the rural municipality Kimito (Kemiö), in the Åboland (Turunmaa) archipelago region; and (3) Jakobstad (Pietarsaari), a small town in the Northern Österbotten (Pohjanmaa/Ostrobothnia) region.[3]

Theoretical Aspects of Identity and Migration

When a minority group moves to a country of perceived ethnic affinity, the migrants become part of a process of ethnic return migration (Brubaker 1998; Clachar 1997; Kulu 1998; Tsuda 1999, 2000, 2002). This migratory process is often repeated over generations, as a cultural expectation or norm to return-migrate develops in the community (Tsuda 1999). The process involves a particular focus on issues of ethnic identity in the form of cultural and emotional linkages to a country of perceived ethnic "belonging" before migration and in the form of the transformation of ethnic identity that occurs in the integration process after migration.

Thus it is vital to consider aspects of ethnic identity both at the initiation of the return migration process, as a part of the migration decision, and as a means of adaptation in the context of the process of integration into the new society. Ethnic identity can be viewed as a collective dimension of an individual's identity with which a person associates him- or herself and with which he or she feels an affinity (Bourgeois 2000). This occurs through relations to other ethnic groups and through alleged differences in relation to these other groups, which are constantly changing (Hall 1996). Within an ethnic group the perception of a common history and culture (Sarup 1996) and a unifying language (Giles et al. 1977) are decisive factors for the feeling of affinity. Outwardly, the relations to other ethnic groups are often established in the form of power relations between majority and minority groups (Li et al. 1995).

Ethnic identity can influence the decision to migrate because of an improved power position of the group in the new country (Li et al. 1995) and because of shared values with the country of immigration (Tsuda 1999). Shared values would be the case for ethnic return migrants who associate themselves with the country of immigration as a result of an ethnic memory of belonging. However, previous studies have shown that the migrants often encountered unexpected difficulties in their ethnic homeland and entered a process of identity transformation (Clachar 1997; Tsuda 2000). Because of the divergence in language but also because of differences in attitudes and behaviors, the migrants felt alienated when they returned to their country of ethnic affinity. Often, members of the group did not speak their "ethnic mother tongue" fluently, or at all, which created a feeling of unexpected exclusion when they returned. Instead, the migrants' affinity with the country of out-migration increased.

It is somewhat challenging to label Finland Swedish migration to Sweden ethnic return migration. The group has been present in Finland for more than 800 years and is well established as a prosperous group in a developed country. The Finland Swedes have often been described as one of the best-treated minority groups in the world, and they are officially equivalent to the Finnish-speaking majority (Similä 1992). In practice, though, Finland Swedes do occupy a minority position (McRae 1999). The area in which the Swedish language is used is becoming increasingly smaller as Finland Swedes come to constitute a smaller proportion of the total population. Furthermore, the group is strongly linked to Sweden by means of transnational cultural and linguistic bonds (Hedberg 2007; Höckerstedt 2000). Both these factors make Finland Swedes similar to other groups involved in ethnic return migration. Thus it is important to stress these features in particular to reveal the cultural dimensions of this migration process, which would otherwise remained unexplored (Danermark et al. 1997; Halfacree 2004). The absence of economic pressure to migrate from Finland to Sweden serves to distinctly illuminate the aspects of ethnic identity in this process, in contrast to other cases in this book.

The idea of analyzing Finland Swedish migration to Sweden as a process of ethnic return migration gives rise to two central questions. First, how do ethnic relations play a part in the Finland Swedish migration decision to return to Sweden in relation to both the Finnish-speaking majority in Finland and the Swedish-speaking majority in Sweden? Second, within the integration process the fact that Finland Swedes speak the same language as the Swedish majority implies certain consequences for their identity transformation. This raises the question of whether Finland Swedes continue to separate themselves in relation to Swedes or whether they assimilate in Sweden.

Language and Identity Within the Finland Swedish Migration Process
Migration Caused by the Linguistic Minority Situation

In migration theory the notion of identity is recognized as an important field of investigation (Bron 2002; Fielding 1992; Gutting 1996; McHugh 2000; Sarup 1996). Cultural causes are likely to be important explanations for migration decisions beyond economic-rational motivations (Halfacree 2004). Here, it is vital to consider the relational nature of ethnic identity, which is based on a group's relative power position in the places of origin and destination (Li et al. 1995). When migrants perceive that the position of the ethnic group will be more advantageous at the destination, this becomes a major factor influencing migration. The view of ethnicity as a cause of migration is also present in the process of ethnic return migration (Brubaker 1998; Kulu 1998; Tsuda 1999, 2000), where the initiation of the process is explained by ethnic motives in combination with surrounding economic and political conditions.

When I asked Finland Swedish migrants why they moved to Sweden, they all primarily referred to direct and instrumental reasons for their migration decision. Whereas some migrated to Sweden to work, others moved to study at a Swedish university or because they had met a Swedish partner. However, underneath the surface, and when ethnic aspects in particular are analyzed, the minority position occupied by Finland Swedes manifests itself as important in most of the migrants' narratives. The linguistic situation in Finland was mentioned by many migrants, as was the existence of a sometimes hostile atmosphere toward Finland Swedes.

The minority situation differs among the Swedish-speaking regions in Finland. In Esbo, a region in the economic and political center, Finland Swedes are an obvious minority. In a region that was almost entirely Swedish-speaking 100 years ago (Lahti 1987), the proportion of Swedish speakers had decreased to less than 10 percent by 1999 (Finnäs 2001). However, many of the Finland Swedes interviewed here had adjusted to this minority situation. They possessed good skills in Finnish, and many were bilingual. Other Esbo migrants had learned to avoid Finnish-speaking environments, both in the workplace and where they lived. A man from Esbo gave the following account:

> On the other [Finnish-speaking] side [of Esbo] it is not so nice, but there are many Finland Swedes living at the church. . . . Now [Esbo] has grown an awful lot and mostly Finnish speakers have moved in. . . . Nonetheless, it often turns out that, where there is a [Swedish] school in the vicinity and perhaps some Swedish service institutions for elderly people, that is where [Finland Swedes] are gathered.

However, other migrants who had moved to Esbo from other, more Swedish-speaking regions in Finland had opposite experiences. These migrants sometimes disliked the Finnish-speaking environment, and one migrant described how she, as a Finland Swede, had felt "like a foreign bird" in Esbo. Furthermore, almost every migrant had perceived a kind of hostility directed at Finland Swedes in the region of the city, either in the form of what might be termed distant hearsay or in the form of personal experience. Another man from Esbo gave this example:

> When you were standing in line to buy a hamburger at two o'clock at night it was like you didn't dare to speak Swedish. Many times when you spoke Swedish there was somebody who was drunk who commented on you and got very threatening. . . . It could turn into a fight relatively easily.

Although these frictions occurred most frequently among young people, often at night, and in the presence of alcohol, some Esbo migrants described them as existing among adults too, for example, in the press and in the workplace. The tensions are partly believed to derive from the myth of the Swedish speakers' historical power position in Finland, which remained fixed in the minds of many Finnish speakers. A woman from Esbo explained:

> They saw us as a little self-important, as if we were the "better people." . . . Finnish speakers were relatively intolerant of Swedish speakers with regard to the language. It was like they wanted to completely strangle "Swedishness" in Finland.

In Kimito and Jakobstad the linguistic situation was different. In both of these relatively peripheral municipalities, Finland Swedes are a regional majority, with a population of 55–65 percent Swedish speakers in 1999 (Finnäs 2001). The areas where the Swedish language is used are much more widespread in Kimito and Jakobstad than in central municipalities such as Esbo. Finnish and Swedish are often spoken on a parallel basis, so that a Finland Swede and a Finnish speaker can communicate with each other in their own mother tongues. This occurs both in workplaces and "downtown" and sometimes even within families.

Finnish and Swedish speakers in Kimito and Jakobstad live relatively segregated from one another, although contacts between the two are now increasing. Some 20 years ago, conflicts and fighting could occur between the language groups. Today, the separation is described more in terms of a social distance, which results in people preferring to socialize within their own language group. As in Esbo, an intolerant atmosphere toward Finland Swedes is present in

Kimito and Jakobstad; however, it is not experienced in the home region but at the national level. A woman from Jakobstad said:

> Every once in a while it flares up: Partly youth conflicts and sometimes I have read about it in newspapers, which were very "Finnish." . . . There are many groups that want to get rid of the Swedes altogether. . . . There have been some of these groups in the eastern parts of Finland, groups of skinheads. . . . Thus, in some towns it is dangerous to speak Swedish, you can get knocked down. But things like this have never happened in Jakobstad.

A woman from Jakobstad, who had just moved to Helsingfors, described herself as a "tourist in her own country" because she could not speak Finnish. Although Finland is a bilingual country she felt as though she had no right to use Swedish:

> I discover that I always feel that I am the one who is in the wrong; I am the bad one when I use Swedish. It always counts against me if I cannot express myself in Finnish. It doesn't feel like I should have the right to do so either. . . . I never think about the fact that the others—well shouldn't they at least be able to speak some Swedish, in any case enough to understand what you are saying?

For many Swedish speakers in Kimito and Jakobstad, it is difficult to move to Finnish-dominated areas, where most of the available jobs are to be found. The migrants from Kimito and Jakobstad often had insufficient Finnish language skills to get a job, to study at a Finnish-speaking university, or to communicate with public sector authorities. Thus it is obvious how the instrumental motivation to migrate to Sweden, to get a job, coincided with their ethnic minority position. The regional power position thus paradoxically placed them in a difficult minority position at the national level. One man from Jakobstad said:

> Since you have Finnish as a second language, you are not as good at it as you are at Swedish. And with many authorities, well, letters that you receive are written in Finnish. And of course—Finland is a bilingual country according to the law, but that doesn't work in practice. . . . I was never exposed to Finnish; I wasn't even forced to learn it, since you can manage very easily with Swedish in Jakobstad.

Many Finland Swedes from Kimito and Jakobstad therefore moved to Sweden to get a job or to study in their mother tongue. One Kimito migrant wavered between two job options, one in Stockholm and the other in Helsinki. He moved to Sweden because he wanted to speak Swedish, because he was particularly fond of Stockholm, and because he found the environment in Helsingfors hostile toward Finland Swedes.

It is thus obvious that Finland Swedish migrants experienced a minority position in Finland before migration. In line with McRae (1999), I argue that the gap between official and practical rights, the group's language instability, and their striving for "linguistic peace" make the position of Finland Swedes a complex one. In addition, the minority position occupied by Finland Swedes in Finland both forms part of their ethnolinguistic identity and constitutes a structural cause underlying their migration to Sweden within a process of ethnic return migration. Certainly other instrumental reasons for each individual to migrate to Sweden exist as well, such as studying, getting a job, or having met a partner, but they are often embedded within the minority situation.

Migration Caused by Cultural Affinity

A second cause of migration linked to the Finland Swedish identity involves the issue of the group's perceived cultural affinity with Sweden before migration. Moving to Sweden is conceived of as a short step by Finland Swedes. Many of the migrants view their migration to Sweden as a form of internal migration rather than as migration across an international border. To these migrants Sweden feels like a familiar destination and one that "was the obvious second choice to Finland." The distance to Sweden is perceived to be short compared to many alternative Finnish-speaking destinations in Finland (Hedberg 2007).

Other Finland Swedes migrated to Sweden as a middle alternative. They wanted to move abroad and do something exciting but without going too far away. They described themselves as having moved to Sweden by coincidence, but they also spoke of having close connections with the country.

The general explanation for why Sweden "happened" to be the migrants' choice of destination lay in their perception of the common Swedish language. One migrant described the low linguistic threshold as making it "almost too simple for a Finland Swede to move to Sweden." Many of the migrants enjoyed being able to express themselves in their mother tongue, as well as the fact that everything around them was in Swedish. A man from Kimito said:

> It was a very natural choice to me, . . . partly due to the language. To always be
> understood everywhere and always be able to express yourself without a feeling

of major effort—this was a relief that you looked forward to, as well as newspapers, TV: everything was in your mother tongue.

The cultural affinity with Sweden was also manifested in the various cultural, social, and economic contacts with Sweden. These were found in all regions in Swedish Finland, but they were particularly strong in Jakobstad. This town is located in Österbotten, a region known for its lasting cultural links with Sweden and a strong cross-border identity (Westerholm 2000). The cultural influence from Sweden is particularly intense in the popular culture. In Jakobstad Finland Swedes watch television programs from Sweden, read Swedish magazines, and listen to Swedish popular music. This contributes to feelings of familiarity with Sweden in Österbotten, and two of the migrants even mentioned Sweden as their "second motherland" in addition to their affinity with Finland. One of the migrants, a man from Jakobstad, said:

As a Finland Swede, as someone from Österbotten, it feels a little like the second motherland. Finland is definitely in my heart—and in ice hockey I support the Finnish team!—but if I couldn't choose Finland I think it would be Sweden. . . . You know so much about Sweden as a Finland Swede. . . . I grew up with Sweden, and I think I know more about Swedish history than I know about Finland's. . . . I watched Swedish television during the years when I was growing up, so in that way you get very used to Sweden.

During the large migration waves from Finland to Sweden after World War II, important social networks were established between Jakobstad and Kimito on the one hand and Sweden on the other, and these networks created an affinity with Sweden. This affinity has contributed to further migration, either by means of direct help from relatives and friends in getting a first job, for example, or a place to live, or simply through the awareness that other acquaintances have made the step successfully before. Previous migration served to maintain an informal flow of information between former migrants and their families and friends in Finland. The children of some of those who migrated to Sweden between the 1950s and the 1970s and who later returned to Finland with their parents have migrated back to Sweden as adults. One woman, who was born in Sweden but grew up in Jakobstad, described the situation like this:

When I was a child, I had decided that I should become a priest, and I knew that you were not allowed to be a priest as a woman in [Finland], so I would move to

Sweden. . . . Because there was something about Sweden—I don't know if it was because I was born there [but] I remember that it was a big thing for me that I had decided to move to Sweden when I grew older. At that time I was more "anti-Finland" [than now]. Perhaps also in my teenage years, I was more like "No, I'm getting out of here, to Sweden!"

These specific social networks to Sweden were not as clearly visible in Esbo. Instead, the links from Esbo to Sweden mainly took the form of economic networks, established within and between companies. Firms from Finland and Sweden have worked together for a long time, and this cooperation has increased over the last few decades. These contacts exist in part as a result of the common linguistic bonds. One Esbo man said:

> [Cooperation with companies in Sweden] is much easier [for Finland Swedes] in many ways. Like networks, which are a very personal thing, but still I think that I can call anyone in Sweden and start talking to them. . . . So definitely, it is very good to know Swedish. . . . Sweden is a large market for us.

Through these economic, social, and cultural connections to Sweden, a linguistically based affinity with Sweden has been established in a varying and changeable form within the Finland Swedish identity. The social and cultural links in the Finland Swedish case are strongly intertwined and lower the threshold to migration. Therefore Finland Swedes return-migrate, even if purely economic incentives to do so are not that strong, particularly compared to migrants moving from developing countries to developed countries.

Identity Transformation and the Swedish Language

International migrants enter a new country, and they have to reconstruct their ethnic identity in relation to new situations and groups (Hoffman 1989). This condition of "new difference" is the starting point for the process of identity transformation, in which the migrant successively negotiates his or her identity in relation to the new country and the society that has been left behind (Sarup 1996). In a dual process of integration and assimilation, migrants adjust to the new society at the same time as this society adapts to and is influenced by immigration (Alba 1999; Bauböck 1994). Assimilation is seen as a "process of becoming similar" (Brubaker 2001: 534). Within this process a parallel identification with the host society is added to the affinity with the homeland, leading to a "transnational" identity (Joppke and Morawska 2003).

Certain areas recognized as being of significance for an individual's integration are found in their social networks and cultural and media consumption (Remmenick 2003). Essential fields of integration are also the areas of legal (formal rights and citizenship) and social (social positions, employment, housing, education) integration (Bauböck 1994). Integration and assimilation are promoted to a great extent by a knowledge of the language spoken in the host country (Bauböck 1994; Diaz 1993; Portes and Schauffler 1994; Remmenick 2003). Verbal language skills are particularly important and are vital for the development of a sense of belonging in the new country and for the transformation of the migrant's identity (Remmenick 2003).

Legal and Social Integration of Finland Swedes

The legal integration of Finland Swedes in Sweden did not give rise to any major problems. As a result of a multilateral agreement among the Nordic countries—Sweden, Finland, Norway, Iceland, and Denmark—every Nordic citizen has the right to become a citizen in the other Nordic countries (Migrationsverket 2003).[4] Since 1954, free movement has been requested in a common Nordic labor market. Consequently, for Finland Swedes the issue of obtaining Swedish citizenship did not constitute a legal barrier but was rather a question of choice and of identity. For the most part, the migrants had chosen to retain their Finnish citizenship as a final bond to Finland, until they encountered some practical problem as a result of Swedish citizenship being required in a certain connection, say, getting a certain job or the requirement to do military service in Finland, which is longer and perceived as harder than it is in Sweden. In these cases the migrants were able to switch their citizenship to Sweden with ease.

In the labor and housing markets, too, the migrants experienced no problems in integrating themselves into Sweden (Hedberg 2006). They had either already signed a work contract before moving from Finland, or they had no difficulties finding a job within a short space of time following their arrival in Sweden. The migrants underlined the fact that Finland Swedes had an advantageous position in the Swedish labor market compared to other immigrant groups, thanks to the good reputation of labor from Finland established during the labor migrations of the 1960s and 1970s. They also emphasized the fact that they had never been unemployed in Sweden. In the housing market the residency patterns of migrants from Finland have tended to differ substantially from those of migrants from other countries, particularly non-European migrants (Andersson 2001). Whereas non-European migrants have generally resided in neighborhoods where Swedes are relatively sparse, migrants from Finland have lived in the same residential areas as the Swedes. In general this was also the case for the Finland Swedes interviewed.

Are They "Immigrants" in Sweden?

The situation specific to Finland Swedes in Sweden, who found it easy to integrate legally and socially, made many of the migrants hesitant as to whether they actually saw themselves as immigrants in Sweden. One migrant said that Finland Swedes in Sweden were "immigrants of luxury" because of their swift integration into many areas. This point of view was shared by other migrants, who meant that being a Finland Swedish immigrant was like being an internal migrant from another part of Sweden. A man from Jakobstad said:

> It is easy to accept [us], since the majority in Stockholm are not from [the city]. . . . To go there as a Finland Swede is no big deal; you are no more "immigrated" [than they are]. And generally, even in the labor market, the "Finns" . . . are [now] seen as rather hard working. . . . So, as a Finland Swede—as a Finlander— you are not viewed as an "immigrant."

Other migrants were more uncertain about their position as immigrants in Sweden. One woman, who wished to stress her similarity to the Swedes, admitted that her colleagues at work sometimes called her an immigrant. By contrast, another migrant from Jakobstad described himself as an immigrant but said that the Swedes had a different opinion.

> Sometimes you hear that people don't think about you as a Finland Swede, as an immigrant. Sometimes a discussion starts at work, . . . and someone might say that there are too many immigrants here. And then you are standing there: "I am an immigrant too, I have also come here." And you know that they don't mean you, . . . they don't think that it is the same thing. [And] it is of course a totally different thing—if someone comes from Iran or Finland.

Dissociation in Sweden

Finland Swedes in Sweden were well integrated in many respects, but their social positions as Finland Swedes turned out to be unclear. An important motivation for Finland Swedish migration to Sweden was related to the Swedish language and the migrants' ethnic identity. Once in Sweden, the role played by language as a separator between majority and minority groups was expected to disappear. Finland Swedes migrated to a country where their mother tongue is the majority language. With the changing status of the Swedish language, Finland Swedes would be expected either to assimilate in Sweden or to create new cultural markers to distinguish their group identity.

However, the interviews provide evidence that the migrants used their language as the most important distinction between themselves and the majority population in Sweden as well as Finland. When they first moved to Sweden, many migrants felt an obvious difference from the Swedes. Because the Swedish language demarcated the group's ethnic identity in Finland, it remained a marker of a separate identity in Sweden also. Here, the distinction in relation to the majority population took the form of a Finland Swedish variety of the Swedish language, marked by a unique intonation (Winsa 1999). Finland Swedes thus used their Swedish dialect to maintain the distance from Swedes that they perceived. One woman from Esbo explained:

> Finland-Swedishness, I guess, is southern Finland, being a minority, and the archipelago. And having one's *own* language . . . I think that Finland Swedes have the feeling of solidarity through their language *and that is a thing that you especially notice when you live here* [in Sweden]. (emphasis added)

Hence the Swedish language, which before migration had been seen as a central symbol of the migrants' ethnic identity, was transformed in the process of migration into a new linguistic boundary of Finland Swedish dialects. This finding was common to all migrants, independent of how long they had stayed in Sweden.

Thus instead of uniting them with Swedes in Sweden, the language symbolically became a divisive factor. The new position of the Swedish language sometimes caused an identity conflict in the context of the integration process. The migrants perceived themselves to have been placed in a position between Sweden and Finland, as a man from Jakobstad noted:

> When the language doesn't diverge, then you have a dialect that you are "bullied half to death" because of. You can never get away from it: In Finland, once you are there, you are called a "Swede," and in Sweden you are called a "Finn." So you are something in between, you are "neither-nor."

This feeling of being a group "in-between" was typical for Finland Swedes in Sweden, particularly at the beginning of their stay. The perceived difference from Finnish speakers in Finland was in Sweden supplemented by an additional perceived distance from Swedes, which was often described as a mental difference. In fact, once in Sweden, almost every Finland Swede labeled the Swedes "superficial" and "hard to get to know," which indicates an experience of exclusion.

The frequency of the migrants' personal social contacts with Swedes varied within the group, from none to a large number. The migrants generally spent more of their spare time within the Finland Swedish group when they were newcomers to Sweden than they did later on. They also remained separated from the Finnish-speaking migrant group in Sweden.

The difference that many migrants felt from the Swedes can be understood in terms of their altered situation, as immigrants in Sweden rather than as a Swedish-speaking minority in Finland. Through the act of migration they discovered that they occupied a more distant position in relation to Swedish society than what they had experienced in Finland, and during the initial phase of integration their ethnic affinity with Sweden diminished (see also Hedberg and Kepsu 2008). Instead, Finland Swedes experienced an increase in their levels of attachment to Finland. Their Finlandish national identity tended to become strengthened, a factor that served to challenge their ethnic identity. This was particularly evident among the migrants from Österbotten, whose identification with Sweden had been strongest before migration, as noted by the following two interviewees from Jakobstad:

> You live in Finland and you are a "Finlander," but the culture is more Swedish, like in Sweden. . . . So you can feel like you don't belong anywhere. If you are thrown out of Finland, you have nowhere to go, because Sweden doesn't want you either. . . . Then you can feel that they [the Finnish speakers] would prefer to have you out of the country and that you simultaneously don't fit in here either. . . . Sweden is not really home.

> Now you feel a little like a traitor to your country. . . . You notice somehow that you have a strong feeling for your motherland [Finland]. When you come here [to Sweden] you don't feel Swedish.

"Swedish Ignorance"

Finland Swedes' vague sense of exclusion and the maintenance of their Swedish dialect as a linguistic boundary may be due to a knowledge-related asymmetry between themselves and Swedes. Finland Swedes are not officially recognized as a minority group in Sweden, because the few minorities that are recognized as such, including the Finnish-speaking group, speak a different language (Winsa 1999). The Finland Swedes' interest group in Sweden (Finlandssvenskarnas riksförbund i Sverige, FRIS) has argued that the group is discriminated against because they speak the national language (Allardt Ljunggren 1994). The group is denied minority status in Sweden and thus does not receive the same economic funding as other minority groups.

For Finland Swedish migrants, the main concern is not the official attitude but the ignorance of the general Swedish population. Although Sweden forms an important part of the Finland Swedish ethnic identity, Swedes are often poorly informed about the Finland Swedish minority. It is common for Swedes to be unaware even of the existence of a Swedish-speaking minority in Finland. This "Swedish ignorance" means that all Finland Swedes have to explain how they are able to speak their own mother tongue. A woman from Jakobstad said:

> I get so irritated that it drives me crazy: "Oh, you speak Swedish so well!". . . .
> And, "You are speaking with a foreign Finnish accent." And that is completely
> wrong since we don't speak with a foreign accent, we have a dialect. . . . This is
> surprising—with people who are living this close to each other, on different
> sides of the sea, and still they don't know [about us].

The migrants from Kimito and Jakobstad sometimes have Finland Swedish dialects that Swedes do not recognize as originating in Finland. Instead, they are believed to be Swedes from peripheral parts of Sweden. Mostly, though, Finland Swedes are thought to be Finnish speakers who have learned to speak Swedish quickly during their time as immigrants in Sweden. One man from Esbo said:

> [In Sweden] you knew very little about Finland-Swedishness. . . . I had an ex-
> ample at the day-nursery day-care center . . . when the same woman asked, I
> think 2 or 3 times, if we didn't want [our child to be given] "mother tongue
> lessons" [in Finnish]? . . . She didn't understand that we speak Swedish at home
> . . . that on the surface there were no problems, we spoke Swedish [with each
> other]. But then again many thought that, perhaps underneath the surface, we
> spoke Finnish at home.

Many Finland Swedes experienced this lack of knowledge as strange and sometimes disappointing, in particular among highly educated people. One migrant declared the Swedes to be inflexible and to lack "imagination" and "humility" because they should understand the Finland Swedish dialect.

Nevertheless, the migrants were also proud of the difference that their Finland Swedish dialect made in Sweden. Some migrants found it "quite natural" and not in the least offensive that Swedes had no knowledge of Finland Swedes. Some of the migrants even found it positive that they could become totally incorporated into the Swedish majority and that they were thus not seen as immigrants. Others said that only a small group of Swedes were badly informed and that the majority of the Swedes had a positive attitude toward the group, as this man from Kimito noted:

> They used to say, "It sounds like you are singing!" sometimes when we speak. . . . And all Swedes say: "Keep your dialect, because that is the best thing that you have got! You express your personality; it is what gives color to your personality."

Nonetheless, although this migrant did not want to speak badly about the Swedes, he admitted that the Swedes' attitude toward Finland Swedes was sometimes bad. He had to prove to many Swedes that he was a Finland Swede rather than someone from the north of Sweden. Naturally, this distinction was important to him, because his identification with Finland was still strong.

Assimilation in Sweden
A Personal Finland Swedish Identity

Over time the migrants became increasingly integrated into Swedish society in relation to their identity. Many mentioned that their contacts with other Finland Swedes had declined significantly over the course of their stay in Sweden. Instead, their main personal social contacts were with Swedes; they were sometimes married to Swedes, and they tended to visit relatives and friends in Finland increasingly rarely. In parallel with this, their feeling of exclusion in Sweden diminished and their identity was altered once again (see also Hedberg and Kepsu 2008). They regained their affinity with Sweden, which initially had been weakened. In addition, the Finlandish national identity, which had become accentuated in the migration process, tended gradually to lose its importance. Some migrants, who had stayed in Sweden for a long time, even went so far as to refer to their identity as Swedish.

The migrants' Finland Swedish identity was transformed into a personal identity, which signified a memory of their background rather than a collective sense of belonging with other Finland Swedes. A woman from Esbo echoed this sentiment.

> In the beginning, when I first moved to Sweden, I got very annoyed with the Swedes. . . . Now I have become so Swedish that when I go to Finland I am annoyed with them. . . . I am still a [Finnish] citizen and I am definitely a Finland Swede . . . [but] I have thought about this—how you in a way lose your interest, which also depends on the fact that you live here now, in Sweden.

It might be natural to assume that as Finland Swedes lost their collective identity, the linguistic demarcation in relation to Swedes would disappear. On the contrary, though, the Finland Swedish dialect continued to function as a symbolic boundary in relation to the Swedes. Many migrants were also quite proud of their dialect, whereas a few had unsuccessfully tried to smooth it down. One woman from Jakobstad, who had already lived in Sweden for 26 years, illustrates how the dialect kept demarcating her from the Swedes, in her case involuntarily. She had no associations with Finland Swedes anymore and felt well integrated into Swedish society. Nonetheless, she emphasized that her dialect distinguished her from the majority in Sweden. She had tried to change it, but her intonation was still commented on by Swedes. Because her wish was to become similar to Swedes, the linguistic barrier continued to signify a diffuse ethnolinguistic identity conflict for this woman. For other migrants, the dialect was not problematic but was instead considered a part of their personal Finland Swedish identity.

Do Finland Swedes Assimilate in Sweden?

The final question is whether Finland Swedes assimilate in Sweden, and if so, whether they do so as first-generation immigrants. Using the definition of Brubaker (2001) that assimilation is "a process of becoming similar" without the requirement of a total extinction of cultural markers (Alba 1999), it might generally be argued that the first generation of Finland Swedes is indeed assimilating. Once their initial disappointment over the differences that the migrants perceive as distinguishing them from Swedes has passed, the migrants appear to become used to the situation in Sweden relatively quickly. In the end, it seems that the Finland Swedish dialect alone remains as a separating factor in relation to Swedes together with the immigrants' memory that they grew up in a foreign country. There are important exceptions to this general rule, however, including the migrants who continue to strengthen their Finlandish national identity in contrast to the Swedish majority. For most migrants, though, the identity conflicts that may occur in Sweden appear to be resolved through an aspiration to become like Swedes. Their Finland Swedish identities in these cases tend to turn into personal identities.

Assimilation is relatively easy for a group that is already legally and socially integrated and that speaks the national language of the new country. When Finland Swedes use their Swedish dialect to distinguish themselves from Swedes, they are using an ethnic marker that is relatively subtle. In the long run it is not distinct enough to act as a social separator. Although the migrants continue to regard it as a marker in relation to Swedes, it does not serve so much as a unifying element with the group in Finland as it does as a means of communicating with Swedes in their everyday lives. Because Finland Swedes spoke their "ethnic language" on a daily basis before migration, they were able to pass relatively unnoticed in Swedish society. They could communicate with the majority, compete in the labor market, and easily make personal acquaintances. In combination with the feelings of familiarity with Sweden that formed part of their ethnic identity from the time before migration, they started to feel ever more at home in Sweden.

Assimilation is also facilitated by the fact that the group is not recognized as a minority in Sweden, neither officially nor by Swedes in general. This contrasts with the situation of the Finnish-speaking immigrant group in Sweden, which, perhaps as a result of the difference in languages, continues to be separated from Swedes (Rodrigo Blomqvist 2002) and has caused them to redevelop a distinct ethnic identity in relation to Swedes.[5] After Finland Swedes' initial estrangement in Sweden, which was equivalent to that of other ethnic return migrants, individual Finland Swedes were able relatively easily to resocialize themselves into the Swedish majority group. As a consequence, the line between the Swedish and Finland Swedish groups in Sweden is becoming blurred.

Conclusions

In this chapter I have placed the continuous process of Finland Swedish migration to Sweden within the framework of ethnic return migration. Unlike other cases in this volume, Finland Swedes constitute a distinct example of migration mainly as a result of two principles. First, rather than migrating between remote parts of the world, Finland Swedes migrate between two neighboring countries, where tangible everyday contacts exist. Second, and related to the first principle, this migration process takes place between two economically equal countries in the developed world, so Finland Swedish migration cannot be explained primarily by economic factors. Instead, the analysis of Finland Swedish migration benefits from adding the perspective of ethnic affinity. More precisely, it has been assumed that the Swedish language, as linked to Finland Swedish ethnic identity, constitutes one of the main factors of concern in the context of this process.

On one side of the ethnic return migration process, the causes of Finland Swedish migration were found to be linked to the ethnic identity of this group, both in terms of its linguistic minority situation in Finland and by way of a perceived affinity with Sweden that existed before migration in terms of practical and attitudinal difficulties in Finland. Furthermore, as an extended Swedish-speaking area, Sweden constituted a tempting destination because it was possible to use Swedish in all domains of society and because the migrating group was familiar with Swedish culture before migration.

In general, the case of Finland Swedes strengthens the idea that the process of ethnic return migration is defined by identity issues on a deeper level. Although each migrant possesses his or her own personal motivation to migrate, including instrumental economic motives, general explanations that are linked to the Swedish language can be found for migration to Sweden on the group level. Language serves as a dividing line, which is outwardly directed toward the Finnish-speaking majority and which inwardly serves to link the group to Sweden. The causes of Finland Swedish ethnic return migration are thus tied to linguistically defined issues of ethnic identity rather than to motives underpinned by economic pressure.

On the other side of the ethnic return migration process, we find concerns relating to the various fields of integration and assimilation. For Finland Swedes the principal field of interest in this regard was that of identity construction in Sweden, because Finland Swedes were found to be well integrated in the legal and social senses. Because the group's "ethnic language" shifted its position in Sweden from being a minority to a majority language, I investigated whether Finland Swedes created new ethnic markers in Sweden or whether they assimilated in Sweden.

The study shows that Finland Swedes generally undergo a process that involves two main phases: an initial phase of dissociation from Swedes, which is then followed within a generation by a phase of assimilation, defined as "becoming similar" to Swedes (Brubaker 2001). As recent immigrants, Finland Swedes are sometimes confronted with ignorance on the part of the host society and they feel estranged in their new, unanticipated position between Swedes and Finnish speakers. Later, in the context of the process of assimilation, Finland

Swedes often lose their Finland Swedish identity as a group but retain it as a personal identity or memory.

Within this process Finland Swedes' experiences are equivalent to those found in many other examples of ethnic return migration. Their initial unexpected exclusion in Sweden and their accentuated identification with Finland after migration are similar to the experiences of Japanese Brazilians returning to Japan and of ethnic Germans returning to Germany (Münz and Ohliger 1998; Tsuda 2000). In their process of assimilation, however, Finland Swedes diverge from these other groups.

One crucial explanation for this divergence can be in Finland Swedes' knowledge of their "ethnic language," which facilitated their integration not only in relation to issues of identity but also in the legal and social fields. In addition, Finland Swedish affinity with Sweden was built on substantial transnational networks of cultural, social, and economic linkages, whereas other return migration processes were instead based on a distant myth of an ethnic home. Because Finland Swedish ethnic affinity was established on tangible contacts with Sweden, the initial differences perceived toward Swedes could be overcome relatively easily. The geographic proximity between Sweden and Finland may explain the vibrancy of the exchange between the two countries and by extension the reasons underlying the speed with which Finland Swedes were able to assimilate in Sweden.

A further conclusion is that the Swedish language has remained the main symbolic marker of Finland Swedes even in Sweden, but in the form of their distinct dialect. No other symbols were created to separate the group from Swedes, however. As they entered into the process of assimilation, the Swedish language may have been too subtle to remain as a dividing line in any sense other than symbolically. In practice, the Swedish language quite naturally does not function as a separator in Sweden but serves instead as a means of entry into the various domains of Swedish society. Thus, importantly, the assimilation process does not mean that the group's main ethnic marker, the Swedish language, disappears but rather that it declines in importance. Over the generations, Finland Swedes in Sweden might be expected to assimilate to an even greater extent and to lose the symbolic linguistic distinction in relation to Swedes. A number of personal observations also provide evidence of this trend.

In this context it should be noted that the process of assimilation does not necessarily imply a negative development, as has often been assumed in European contexts (Brubaker 2001). From an international perspective, Finland

Swedes' smooth integration into Sweden in the social and legal domains is rather unusual and is often perceived by the migrants as being positive.

In other cases of ethnic return migration, practical difficulties in speaking the ethnic language have served as a partial explanation for the dissociation that occurs when the migrants return (Clachar 1997; Tsuda 2000). The Finland Swedish example, however, underlines the fact that linguistic difficulties are not sufficient to explain the migrants' initial exclusion in Sweden. Thus the answer must be sought elsewhere rather than in the language as a simple means of communication. Migration presents a challenge to individuals even when they speak the language of the host country and even though the country and its culture may have constituted part of their ethnic identity before migration. Thus Swedish, which served as the ultimate separating factor in relation to the Finnish-speaking majority in Finland, continued to be a major symbol of partition even in Sweden. This indicates the strong symbolic value of language for ethnic identification.

In the absence of economic motivations, which serve as the main motivation in many cases of ethnic return migration, the Finland Swedish migration process thus sheds light on the cultural process of migration, which takes place beyond economic pressure. In this way, Finland Swedish migration to Sweden illustrates a migration process that is based on ethnic affinity, in this case through the linguistic relations within and between Finland and Sweden.

Notes

1. No linguistically based statistics exist before 1976, but estimations indicate that Finland Swedes migrated to Sweden 2.5 times as often as Finnish speakers (Finnäs 1986).

2. The municipalities of Finland can be either bilingual, when the proportion of minority language speakers in the municipality is 8 percent or more than 3,000 persons, or monolingually Finnish- or Swedish-speaking. In bilingual municipalities social services are provided in both Finnish and Swedish.

3. Because this chapter deals with a Swedish-speaking minority, the official Swedish names of cities and regions are used instead of the Finnish names, which are commonly used in English texts. One example is "Helsingfors" instead of "Helsinki."

4. Since 2003, Finlandish citizens also have the right to obtain dual citizenship, a right that was also granted to Swedish citizens in 2001. Thus this right was established shortly after the conduct of the interview study in 2003 and had not yet become a practical issue for the Finland Swedish migrants included in this study to consider.

5. In socioeconomic areas, however, Finnish speakers are becoming similar to Swedes (Häggström et al. 1990).

References Cited

Alba, Richard. 1999. "Immigration and the American Realities of Assimilation and Multiculturalism." *Sociological Forum* 14(1):3–25.

Allardt, Erik. 1996. "Samhällsutvecklingen i Finland och Sverige efter 1945—bakgrunden till ut- och invandringen." In *Finnarnas historia i Sverige 3: Tiden efter 1945*, Jarmo Lainio, ed. Helsinki: Finska historiska samfundet och Nordiska museet, 17–36.

Allardt, Erik, and Christian Starck. 1981. *Språkgränser och samhällsstruktur: Finlandssvenskarna i ett jämförande perspektiv.* Lund, Sweden: AWE/Gebers.

Allardt Ljunggren, Barbro. 1994. "Finlandssvenskar i Sverige: Bemötande och språklig anpassning." In *Svenskans beskrivning 20*, Anders Holmberg and Kent Larsson, eds. Lund, Sweden: Lund University Press, 82–93.

Andersson, Roger. 2001. "Skapandet av svenskglesa bostadsområden." In *Den delade staden. Segregation och etnicitet i stadsbyggen*, Lena Magnusson, ed. Umeå, Sweden: Boréa, 115–153.

Åström, Anna-Maria. 2001. "Är en dubbelidentitet möjlig?" In *Gränsfolkets barn. Finlandssvensk marginalitet och självhävdelse i kulturanalytiskt perspektiv*, Anna-Maria Åström, Bo Lönnqvist, and Yrsa Lindqvist, eds. Helsinki: Svenska litteratursällskapet i Finland, 37–49.

Bauböck, Rainer. 1994. *The Integration of Immigrants.* Strasbourg, France: Council of Europe.

Bourgeois, Etienne. 2000. "Sociocultural Mobility: Language Learning and Identity." In *Language—Mobility—Identity: Contemporary Issues for Adult Education in Europe*, Agnieszka Bron and Michael Schemmann, eds. Hamburg, Germany: Münster Lit, 163–185.

Bron, Agnieszka. 2002. "Construction and Reconstruction of Identity Through Biographical Learning: The Role of Language and Culture." Paper presented at the ESREA Biography and Life History Network seminar on European Perspectives on Life History Research: Theory and Practice of Biographical Narratives, Geneva, March 7–10.

Brubaker, Rogers. 1998. "Migrations of Ethnic Unmixing in the 'New Europe.'" *International Migration Review* 32(4):1047–1065.

———. 2001. "The Return of Assimilation? Changing Perspectives on Immigration and Its Sequels in France, Germany, and the United States." *Ethnic and Racial Studies* 24(4):531–548.

Clachar, Arlene. 1997. "Ethnolinguistic Identity and Spanish Proficiency in a Paradoxical Situation: The Case of Puerto Rican Return Migrants." *Journal of Multilingual and Multicultural Development* 18(2):107–124.

Danermark, Berth, Mats Ekström, Liselotte Jakobsen, and Jan Ch. Karlsson. 1997. *Att förklara samhället.* Lund, Sweden: Studentlitteratur.

De Geer, Eric, and Hans Wester. 1975. *Utrikes resor, arbetsvandringar och flyttningar i Fin-

land och Vasa län 1861–1890. Vasa, Finland: Skrifter utg. av Svensk-Österbottniska Samfundet.

Diaz, José A. 1993. *Choosing Integration: The Theoretical and Empirical Study of the Immigrant Integration in Sweden.* Uppsala, Sweden: Uppsala University.

Engman, Max. 1995. "Finns and Swedes in Finland." In *Ethnicity and Nation Building in the Nordic World,* Sven Tägil, ed. London: Hurst, 179–217.

Fielding, Tony. 1992. "Migration and Culture." In *Migration Processes and Patterns,* v. 1, *Research Progress and Prospects,* Tony Champion and Tony Fielding, eds. London: Belhaven Press, 201–212.

Finnäs, Fjalar. 1986. *Den finlandssvenska befolkningsutvecklingen 1950–1980: En analys av en språkgrupps demografiska utveckling och effekten av blandäktenskap.* Helsinki: Svenska litteratursällskapet i Finland.

———. 2001. *Finlandssvenskarna inför 2000-talet: En statistisk översikt.* Finlandssvensk rapport 40. Helsinki: Svenska Finlands folkting.

Giles, Howard, Richard Y. Bourhis, and Donald M. Taylor. 1977. "Towards a Theory of Language in Ethnic Groups Relations." In *Language, Ethnicity, and Intergroup Relations,* Howard Giles, ed. European Monographs in Social Psychology 13. London: Academic Press, 307–348.

Gutting, David. 1996. "Narrative Identity and Residential History." *Area* 28:482–490.

Häggström, Nils, Lars-Erik Borgegård, and Anette Rosengren. 1990. *När finländarna kom: Migrationen Finland-Sverige efter andra världskriget.* Gävle, Sweden: Statens institut för byggnadsforskning.

Halfacree, Keith. 2004. "A Utopian Imagination in Migration's *Terra Incognita*? Acknowledging the Non-Economic Worlds of Migration Decision-Making." *Population, Space, and Place* 10:239–253.

Hall, Stuart. 1996. "Introduction: Who Needs Identity?" In *Questions of Cultural Identity,* Stuart Hall and Paul Du Gay, eds. London: Sage, 1–17.

Hedberg, Charlotta. 2006. "Finlandssvenska 'ansikten': Migrationskulturer och livsbanor." In *Mellan majoriteter och minoriteter. Om migration, makt och mening,* Marianne Junila and Charles Westin, eds. Svenskt i Finland—finskt i Sverige II. Helsinki: Svenska litteratursällskapet i Finland.

———. 2007. "Direction Sweden: Migration Fields and Cognitive Distances of Finland Swedes." *Population, Space, and Place* 13(6):455–470.

Hedberg, Charlotta, and Kaisa Kepsu. 2003. "Migration as a Cultural Expression? The Case of the Finland-Swedish Minority's Migration to Sweden." *Geografiska Annaler* 85B(2):67–84.

———. 2008. "Identity in Motion: Finland-Swedish Identity Construction in the Migration Process to Sweden." *National Identities* 10(1):95–118.

Höckerstedt, Leif. 2000. *Fuskfinnar eller Östsvenskar? En debattbok om finlandssvenskhet.* Helsinki: Söderströms.

Hoffman, Eva. 1989. *Lost in Translation: A Life in a New Language.* London: Minerva.

Joppke, Christian, and Ewa Morawska. 2003. "Integrating Immigrants in Liberal Nation-States: Policies and Practices." In *Toward Assimilation and Citizenship: Immigrants in Liberal Nation-States,* Christian Joppke and Ewa Morawska, eds. New York: Palgrave Macmillan, 1–36.

Kulu, Hill. 1998. "Ethnic Return Migration: An Estonian Case." *International Migration* 36(3):313–336.

Lahti, Matti J. 1987. *Esbo: En landssocken blir storköping.* Esbo, Finland: Esbo Stad.

Li, F. L. N., A. J. Jowett, Allan M. Findlay, and Ronald Skeldon. 1995. "Discourse on Migration and Ethnic Identity: Interviews with Professionals in Hong Kong." *Transactions of the Institute of British Geographers* 20(3):342–356.

McHugh, Kevin. 2000. "Inside, Outside, Upside Down, Backward, Forward, Round and Round: A Case for Ethnographic Studies in Migration." *Progress in Human Geography* 24(1):71–89.

McRae, Kenneth D. 1999. *Conflict and Compromise in Multilingual Societies: Finland.* Helsinki: Finnish Academy of Science and Letters.

Migrationsverket (Swedish Board of Migration). 2003. "Svenskt medborgarskap." Migrationsverket Art. 200,500.

Münz, Rainer, and Rainer Ohliger. 1998. *Deutsche Minderheiten in Ostmittelund Osteuropa, Aussiedler in Deutschland: Eine Analyse ethnisch privilegierter Migration.* Demographie Aktuell 9. Berlin: Humboldtuniversität Berlin.

Portes, Alejandro, and Richard Schauffler. 1994. "Language and the Second Generation: Bilingualism Yesterday and Today." *International Migration Review* 28(4):640–661.

Remmenick, Larissa. 2003. "Language Acquisition as the Main Vehicle of Social Integration: Russian Immigrants of the 1990s in Israel." *International Journal of the Sociology of Language* 164:83–105.

Rodrigo Blomqvist, Paula. 2002. *Från assimilation till separation: Den finska invandrargruppens krav på finskspråkig skolundervisning.* Förvaltningshögskolans Rapport 47. Göteborg, Sweden: Göteborgs universitet.

Sarup, Madan. 1996. *Identity, Culture, and the Post-Modern World,* Tasneem Raja, ed. Edinburgh, Scotland: Edinburgh University Press.

Similä, Matti. 1992. "Minoritetsbegreppet och Finlands minoritetspolitiska modeller." In *Finland: Ett föredöme i minoritetspolitik? Föredrag vid Svenska kulturfondens konferens i Tammerfors den 8 november 1991,* Kjell Herberts, ed. Vasa, Finland: Institutet för finlandssvensk samhällsforskning, 41–54.

Törnblom, Lena. 1993. "Medeltiden." In *Finlands historia 1,* Märta Norrback, ed. Esbo, Finland: Schildts förlag.

Tsuda, Takeyuki. 1999. "The Motivation to Migrate: The Ethnic and Sociocultural Constitution of the Japanese-Brazilian Return Migration System." *Economic Development and Cultural Change* 48(1):1–31.

————. 2000. *Migration and Alienation: Japanese-Brazilian Return Migrants and the Search for Homeland Abroad.* Working Paper 24. San Diego: University of California, Center for Comparative Immigration Studies.

————. 2002. "From Ethnic Affinity to Alienation in the Global Ecumene: The Ethnic Encounter Between the Japanese and Japanese-Brazilian Return Migrants." *Diaspora* 10(1):53–91.

Westerholm, John. 2000. "Svenskfinland: Kustbygd i förändring." In *Öster om Östersjön,* Göran Hoppe, ed. Stockholm: Ymer Svenska sällskapet för antropologi och geografi, 63–76.

Winsa, Birger. 1999. "Language Planning in Sweden." *Journal of Multilingual and Multicultural Development* 20(4–5):376–473.

7 From National Inclusion to Economic Exclusion

Transylvanian Hungarian Ethnic Return Migration to Hungary

Jon E. Fox

HUNGARY, like many other countries examined in this volume, has long shown an interest in its co-ethnics beyond its borders. Ever since the imperial map of east-central Europe was redrawn at the end of World War I, effectively stranding millions of Hungarians in the newly created and reconfigured neighboring nation-states, Hungarian nationalists have pursued various strategies of national reunification. From a disastrous alliance with Nazi Germany in World War II, aimed at reclaiming lost territories, to Hungary's incorporation into the European Union (EU) in 2005, with its promise of the obsolescence of state boundaries, Hungary has been redefining membership in the Hungarian nation to include Hungarians in its neighboring countries. Yet unlike other national homelands discussed in this volume, Hungary seeks to accomplish its national reunification not by bringing Hungarians to Hungary but rather by bringing Hungary to them. Through the elaboration of kin-state politics over the past 15 years, Hungary has been discursively and institutionally bringing transborder Hungarians into the fold of the Hungarian nation.

At the same time, however, Hungary has struggled to reconcile this borderless vision of national unity with migration policies that recognize and reify those same state borders. The greatest challenge has come from the 1.5 million ethnic Hungarians from the Transylvanian region of Romania. Hungary would like for these Hungarians to partake in the richness of the Hungarian nation from the comfort of their own homes. But many of these Transylvanian Hungarians have instead shown a proclivity for partaking in the riches of the Hungarian labor market by working in Hungary. Transborder Hungarians' roles as both members of a culturally defined Hungarian nation and (potential) ethnic return migrant laborers have not always coexisted harmoniously.

Hungary thus has ethnic return migration without the policy framework for it. While nationalists in Hungary have been fighting over the meaning of the nation, Hungarians from Transylvania and their co-ethnics in Hungary have been fighting over access to scarce resources in Hungary's post-Communist labor market. In the process national difference has been lived, experienced, and expressed in the migrants' everyday lives much differently from how national sameness has been imagined, wished, and engineered in elite circles. Through migration, ethnic Hungarians from Romania have gradually redefined themselves as nationally distinct from their hosts in Hungary of the same name. The migrants' understandings of the nation have taken shape not in response to political imperatives but rather according to the economic contingencies of migration.

It is this mismatch between a politicized vision of national unity and the migrants' everyday construction of national disunity that is the focus of this chapter. In the first part I sketch out the view from above: the discursive and institutional elaboration of Hungarian national unity not through the promotion of ethnic return migration policies but rather through the elaboration of kin-state politics. In the second and longer portion of the chapter I turn to the view from below: the ways in which national difference is experienced, articulated, and reproduced through the ethnic return migration of Transylvanian Hungarians working undocumented in Hungary. Hungary is different from other national homelands insofar as it favors symbolic reunification over the actual return of co-ethnics. But the result is similar: The promise of national amalgamation between migrant and host is met with the construction of national difference. The discourses articulated and the policies elaborated are unable to deliver national unification in the face of the experiences of economic marginalization engendered through the course of migration.

Method

I draw on fieldwork conducted with Transylvanian Hungarian migrant workers in urban and rural settings in Transylvania and Hungary between 1995 and 2004. In the summer of 1995 I undertook participant observation research with Transylvanian Hungarian day laborers as they waited for work in Budapest. The following summer I conducted 31 interviews with migrants and would-be migrants at two sites in Romania: Oradea, a medium-size city on the border with Hungary, selected for its proximity to Hungary (and concomitant importance to migration); and a central Transylvanian Hungarian majority village (population 1,000), chosen for its typical migration links with Hungary. Between 1999 and 2004 I was part of a larger collaborative research project on nationalism and ethnicity in Cluj, Transylvania. Migration was one of three themes explored in-depth in eight 2-hour focus groups with working-class Hungarians of different ages (assembled using snowball techniques from different starting points). Migration was also a frequent topic in semistructured interviews and participant observation. All research throughout was conducted in Hungarian and Romanian. Translations are my own; names have been changed.

The View from Above

The Hungarian diaspora, unlike most other diasporas examined in this book, is not that territorially dispersed (but see Chapter 6 for the Finnish case). This is because Hungarians in the neighboring countries never left Hungary; rather, Hungary left them when the peace treaties ending World War I compelled the country to cede two-thirds of its territory to its victorious neighbors. Since then, the question of Hungarians in the dismembered territories has dominated the Hungarian nationalist agenda. Different means have been pursued to realize the unification of transborder Hungarians with the truncated homeland. In the interwar period a policy of territorial revisionism was pursued through an alliance with Nazi Germany. When war broke out, Hungary reclaimed half of Transylvania and half of Slovakia, only to relinquish them at the war's conclusion. In the postwar environment of Communist internationalism, questions of territorial revision were taboo and concerns about minority protection were muted. Officially, the international working class knew no national boundaries; unofficially, national questions found other outlets. In the 1980s a widening circle of intellectuals in Hungary began showing an interest in the fate of Hungarian minorities in the neighboring countries. With the tacit support of the Hungarian state, these intellectuals began forging cultural ties with their beleaguered brethren in Transylvania (Kürti 2001).

The Hungarian state's cautious handling of the Hungarian question ended in 1989 when the constraints of cold war politics were lifted. In this new political climate transborder Hungarians were publicly and officially embraced as an integral part of the Hungarian nation. To conform to these changing geopolitical realities, a kinder, gentler strategy for national unification was elaborated to replace the earlier discredited variants of war, population transfer, and ethnic cleansing. Kin-state politics—the institutionalization of transborder political,

cultural, and economic links between national homeland and external minorities—emerged throughout the region as the strategy of choice for (symbolically) uniting nations across state frontiers (Fowler 2004; see also Brubaker
1996; Schöpflin 2000). Hungary has led the way in extending a widening array
of quasi-citizenship rights to transborder Hungarians on the basis of their putatively shared ethnicity.[1] National unity is achieved not by changing political
boundaries but by bypassing them.

This vision of national unity has been given increasingly elaborate discursive and institutional expression over the past 15 years. Already in 1990, József
Antall, Hungary's first post-Communist prime minister, announced that "in
spirit" he was the prime minister of 15 million Hungarians—5 million more
than live in Hungary. Not to be outdone, successive governments from both
the left and the right have asserted and reasserted their obligation to transborder Hungarians. Competing visions of the Hungarian nation—and the place
of transborder Hungarians in it—have been the focus of sustained political
debate, endless newspaper commentary, and ongoing discussion among Hungarian elites in both Hungary and its neighboring countries. This is the nation
as discursive construct: It is a language of political claims making, an object of
symbolic struggle, and a means of popular legitimation (see Verdery 1991).

Hungary has thus pursued national reunification not in the first instance
through the promotion of ethnic return migration policies but rather through
the elaboration and institutionalization of a series of kin-state policies. Hungary's self-proclaimed obligation to transborder Hungarians is enshrined in Article 6 of its constitution, and it has been embraced by successive governments
as a pillar of foreign policy. It has been formulated into policy by the Office of
the Hungarian Beyond the Borders (established in 1992) and legislated into the
Status Law (passed in 2001), a package of entitlements for Hungarians in the
neighboring countries, including allowances for parents educating their children in Hungarian minority schools, benefits for health care and travel, and,
most significantly, a guest worker program. And Hungary's obligation was put
to a popular vote in a (failed) national referendum (in 2004) on the question
of extending dual citizenship to all transborder Hungarians. These various initiatives have given increasingly elaborate institutional form to the notion of
Hungarian national unity (Fowler 2004; Stewart 2003).

This deterritorialized national unity is also abetted by the eastward expansion of the European Union. Hungary and seven other east European states
(together with Cyprus and Malta) joined the EU in May 2004; Romania and

Bulgaria joined in January 2007. Officially, the EU views Hungary's kin-state politics as being at odds with its strictures against ethnic discrimination (and favoritism). At the same time, however, the EU vision of a borderless Europe has unwittingly provided nationalists in the region with a back door for realizing their ambitions of national unification (Csergő and Goldgeier 2004: 26–29; Keating 2004: 370; Kis 2001: 238–239; Weaver 2006: 177–178, 191–192; see, more generally, McGarry and Keating 2006). In his speech at the EU accession signing ceremony in Prague in 2003, Hungary's prime minister at the time, Péter Medgyessy, declared that "the Hungarians, divided into so many parts, can now grasp an opportunity to reunite across national borders" (quoted in Weaver 2006: 110). The Hungarian Democratic Forum, a consistent voice of mainstream Hungarian nationalism, campaigned for Hungary's accession to the EU with a placard depicting a topographical map of the Carpathian basin. In place of Hungary's current borders, it arranged the yellow stars of the EU around the pre–World War I borders of Greater Hungary (Weaver 2006: 110). The EU's dismantling of state boundaries has paved the way for the symbolic reunification of Hungarians in Hungary with their ethnic kin in the neighboring countries. With Romania's accession to the EU in 2007, Hungarians of all countries live in a new, common (European) home.

In the past, territorial revision was the preferred means for accomplishing national reunification. Now national homelands make house calls by bringing the nation to their external co-ethnics across increasingly porous political boundaries. Under this arrangement, transborder co-ethnics need not return home; through kin-state policies, they can enjoy quasi-citizenship rights in their countries of origin on the basis of shared ethnicity with the national homeland (Fowler 2004; Schöpflin 2000). Such policies are not precursors to territorial revision (as certain alarmist elements in the neighboring states sometimes claim); rather, they are their substitutes. Hungarians from the neighboring countries do not have to come to Hungary to enjoy membership in the Hungarian nation; rather, through kin-state policies and European unification, these Hungarians are being discursively, symbolically, and institutionally incorporated into a new twenty-first-century version of Greater Hungary.

The View from Below

But come they do. Since 1989 hundreds of thousands of ethnic Hungarians from Romania have gone to Hungary to work for higher Hungarian wages. And through this spontaneous ethnic return migration, a different understanding of national difference has been constituted. The stylized representations of national unity preferred and proffered by Hungarian nationalist elites have borne little resemblance to the experiential realities of national disunity accumulated and accomplished through the routine practices of labor migration. Here, I examine the ways in which the economic pains and uncertainties highlighted by the ethnic return labor migration of Transylvanian Hungarians have provided the context for the everyday elaboration of new modalities of Hungarian national difference.

The literature on transnationalism has drawn attention to the important role that sending countries play in establishing and nurturing transnational ties with their migrant populations abroad (see, e.g., Basch et al. 1994). These growing relations between sending and receiving countries have contributed to the emergence of new transnational forms of allegiance that challenge the continued hegemony of the nation-state paradigm. In cases of ethnic return migration, however, it is the receiving countries—not the sending countries—that sponsor the establishment and maintenance of ties with co-ethnics abroad. Migrants are traveling *to*—not from—their putative national homelands (Brubaker 1998; Joppke 2005; Skrentny et al. 2007). But the sorts of ties that Hungary favors with its co-ethnics are those enjoyed and maintained *in* the co-ethnics' countries of origin. This distinguishes Hungary from other cases of ethnic return migration, where the policy emphasis—not just the flow of migrants—is on the return of co-ethnics. Germany and Israel, the paradigmatic examples of states with the right of return, have historically granted preferential treatment to co-ethnics wishing to resettle (Levy and Weiss 2002; see also Chapters 4 and 8 for further discussion of the German and Israeli cases, respectively). In other countries, such as Japan, Korea, Italy, and Spain, ethnic affinity has been established as a principle (and rationale) for granting preferential access to local labor markets (see Chapters 5, 9, and 11). In these come-and-get-it approaches to immigration, naturalization, and labor migration, citizenship and/or labor market access is designed to be enjoyed *in* the ethnic homeland by those who return.

Hungary also offers its co-ethnics a faster track to naturalization.[2] But this is not the main thrust of Hungary's push toward national unification. Rather, the official vision of Hungarian national unity is undergirded by the principle that *all* Hungarians, irrespective of citizenship, are members of a greater cultural nation of Hungarians. Indeed, this territorially expansive version of the Hungarian nation is viable only insofar as Hungarians from the neighboring countries do not actually leave the territories where they live. Therefore, since 1990, Hungary's kin-state policies have been aimed at improving the cultural, economic, and political conditions of Hungarians *in* their countries of origin so that they can continue to thrive there as Hungarians. In Israel ethnic return migration is a key strategy for curbing the numerical decline of the country's Jewish population (see Chapter 8). In the Hungarian case, however, such demographic battles are being fought not in Hungary (where Hungarians account for more than 90 percent of the population) but in the neighboring countries where the numbers of Hungarians are in decline relative to the local majority populations (see Brubaker et al. 2006: 366–373). Thus the primary objective of legislative initiatives for the co-ethnics according to the Hungarian Standing Conference (an advisory body periodically convened between the government of Hungary and political representatives of transborder Hungarians) "is to reinforce the prospects and opportunities for [the co-ethnics to remain] in the ancestral homeland" (quoted in Kántor et al. 2004: 529).

Hungary thus encourages transborder Hungarians to stay put and wait for the ethnic homeland to come to them (Kántor 2001: 260–264). The problem, however, is that they did not stay put. Ignoring their homeland's paternal advice, these Hungarians packed their bags and left for Hungary in droves in search of work. Hungary's relative proximity and prosperity with respect to Romania made it an attractive destination for Transylvanians emerging from the detritus of Ceaușescu's harsh austerity policies. But Hungary, concerned with its own precarious economic standing, initially provided neither the legal nor the institutional framework to integrate the migrants into its labor force. Accordingly, many of the migrants have worked undocumented. As "tourists" lacking either visas or work permits, these migrants were permitted to stay (but not legally work) in Hungary for 30 days.[3] Many gave up jobs in Romania to work full-time in Hungary, leaving once a month just long enough to get their passports stamped before returning again. Over the past 15 years established networks of circular labor migration have taken shape to facilitate the continued flow of migrant workers into and out of Hungary.[4]

My focus here is on this large number of mostly undocumented Transylvanian Hungarian migrant workers. Hungary is their most favored destination. But these Hungarians did not go to Hungary in search of their ethnic homeland; they went there in search of work (Csata and Kiss 2003: 10–11). To be sure, linguistic and cultural affinities facilitated their entry into the local labor market (see Brubaker 1998: 1057–1058).[5] The limits of these affinities, however, soon became apparent. Hungary was not the benevolent mother country greeting its long-lost ethnic brethren with open national arms. Almost immediately, the symbolic myth of national inclusion was confronted with the harsh reality of economic exclusion (Fox 2003: 456–459; Pulay 2005: 148–149). This was not the ethnic homeland tacitly expected by some (see Conclusion, this volume) but a foreign country with different and at times alienating customs, habits, and institutions (on the Hungarian case, see Szakáts 1996: 115–117, 121–122; on similarities with other cases, see Chapter 9; but see Chapter 6 on the relative lack of problems experienced by Finns in Sweden). As in the other cases of ethnic return migration, nominally shared ethnicity between migrant and host did little to secure privileged access to local labor markets for the migrants. Instead, the co-ethnics were greeted with the same combination of suspicion and scorn that greets labor migrants the world over (on the Hungarian case, see Hárs 1999; see also Fábián 1998: 158–160; Fábián et al. 2001: 411; Tóth and Turai 2003: 113, 118–119).[6] Working in undesirable low-status jobs (in the construction, agricultural, and domestic sectors) for meager wages and no benefits, these undocumented migrants were socially and economically marginalized in Hungary (Szakáts 1996; see, more generally, Conclusion, this volume).[7]

"You work like crazy," one worker explained, "don't spend anything, come home, and change your money—that's the only way you can make it work." Increasingly, these differences in working and living conditions between migrant and host came to be interpreted and represented as quasi-ethnic differences (see, e.g., Bonacich 1972; Miles 1982). Migrant workers in Hungary, irrespective of their ethnicity or citizenship, were frequently referred to as Romanians (on other examples of ethnic labeling, see Conclusion, this volume). In theory, this Romanian label could function as an unmarked category referring to the migrants' country of origin. In practice, however, the label was heard by the Transylvanian Hungarian migrants as a symbolic denial of their Hungarianness. It functioned as a quasi-ethnic shorthand for migrants from the poor, backward "Balkans" whose willingness to work long hours for low wages was viewed with resentment and suspicion (Feischmidt 2004: 50–55; on the stigmatization of Brazilian Japanese migrant workers in Japan, see Chapter 9). Migration provided the context not for national reunification but rather for the experience and construction of national difference (Biró 2002: 137–139).

Research on attitudes toward foreigners in Hungary reveals that Transylvanian Hungarians are held in high regard, whereas Romanians are looked upon unfavorably (Fábián 1998: 158–160; Tóth and Turai 2003: 112, 115–116). Such findings, however, do not account for the way that category membership shifts in sending and receiving contexts. It is not enough to say that Hungarians in Hungary like Transylvanian Hungarians and dislike Romanians. Hungarians in Hungary like Transylvanian Hungarians so long as they stay in Transylvania. The moment Transylvanian Hungarians cross the border as migrant workers, they become Romanians in the eyes of their hosts (Tóth and Turai 2003: 108–110, 125). "Here [in Romania] we're Hungarians," one migrant observed. "There, we're Romanians."

For the migrants this Romanian label was heard unambiguously as an ethnic slur (Feischmidt 2004: 51–57; Pulay 2005: 149–150). Consider, for instance, the following exchange between two 20-something Hungarians from Cluj:

Zoli: Everybody thinks you're Romanian.

Éva: Romanian? *Wallachian*, excuse me, *Wallachian*.[8]

Zoli: And where did this "stinking Romanian"[9] come from? . . . That's the way they treat you a lot of the time, like you live on the street, and I don't know, you steal, and they come up with all this stuff about you. . . . It was like you were Afghan or something. . . . It didn't matter that you were Hungarian, in terms of your nationality, I'm not talking about citizenship now. . . . They don't understand what it means that . . . you're a Romanian citizen, but your nationality is Hungarian. They just don't get it.

Seemingly everyone who had been to Hungary—and many who hadn't—had stories to tell about being called Romanian (Bíró 1996; Fox 2003; Mungiu-Pippidi 1999; Pulay 2005; see also Chapter 9 for a similar phenomenon in Japan). A young Hungarian woman from Romania who had visited (but not worked) in Hungary described her experiences: "You get on the metro," she explained, and "they come and check your ticket and there's some sort of problem, you didn't validate it or something, . . . and then they check your ID and 'Phooey!—It's the Romanians again!' and so you try to prove to them that you have a completely Hungarian name, that you're Hungarian, not Romanian."

An older Hungarian from a village near Târgu-Mureş in central Transylvania said he overheard someone in Hungary referring to him and his compatriots as "Romanian thieves." Another worker from the same village was cursed by his boss as a "filthy Romanian Wallachian" for helping himself to a handful of cherries from a tree. And a teacher from Oradea, near the border with Hungary, said that her friends were greeted with "Here come the Romanians!" by their new neighbors in Hungary.

This semantic denial of Hungarian national belonging did not sit well with migrants who at least tacitly expected shared national affinities to secure them a warmer welcome. As one worker complained, "If I go over there [to Hungary], they look at me like I'm Romanian. . . . Morally speaking, . . . I should be able to consider myself Hungarian the way I really am. They shouldn't look at me like I'm Romanian, or Senegalese, or Mongolian." Hungarians in Romania, as minorities elsewhere, have a heightened awareness of themselves in ethnonational terms. Moreover, their Hungarian self-understandings were explicitly constituted in relation to lower-status Romanians (Csepeli et al. 2002: 89–90; see Tsuda 2003 for the Japanese case). To be labeled Romanian was therefore not just a challenge to the migrants' Hungarianness; it entailed a status reversal as well.

Not surprisingly, Transylvanian Hungarian migrant workers have consistently and stridently rejected the Romanian label.[10] Hearing the label as an ethnic slur has necessitated—and justified—an emotionally charged defensive embrace of the migrants' "true" Hungarianness in return. In the process migrant and host have engaged in symbolic struggles over who is really Hungarian (Csepeli et al. 2002: 83–86; see, more generally, Triandafyllidou 2001). Transylvanian Hungarians depicted themselves as carriers of the virtues of tradition, whereas they portrayed Hungarians in Hungary as exemplars of the ills of modernity. The Transylvanians symbolically denied their co-ethnics' Hungarianness by labeling them Jews, Schwabians, Gypsies, and Slovaks. According to Tamás, a craftsman from central Transylvania, Hungarians in Hungary were "nothing-people." The Transylvanians depicted themselves, in contrast, as leading a more traditional Hungarian life, speaking better Hungarian, and displaying greater pride in being Hungarian (Pulay 2005: 155–158). Like Russian Jews in Israel who implicitly claimed Russian (but not Jewish) cultural superiority in relation to their Israeli hosts (see Chapter 8), Transylvanian Hungarian claims to Hungarianness (and the higher status it entailed) was an important strategy for coping with the daily difficulties of living in a "foreign" country.

These ethnicized status distinctions also carried over into the domain of work. Transylvanian Hungarians embraced their supposedly stronger work ethic as an explicitly Transylvanian Hungarian trait. "They're always saying we take their work from them," Csaba complained to his friends (all of whom had worked in Hungary) during a focus group discussion. But for him the reasons were clear: "The best carpenters and joiners," he argued, "always come from Transylvania." His friends nodded in agreement. He added:

> It's true that [Transylvanian Hungarians] work for less than Hungarians [in Hungary]—that's why they get pissed off. But they don't even like to work. . . . I worked there a year . . . as a manual laborer. I mixed the mortar, hammered the boards, laid the bricks, whatever they needed. . . . Okay, so they worked ten hours. But the amount of time they were just screwing around was unbelievable. . . . Now the Transylvanians, *they* really work. Take my father-in-law: he works sixteen hours a day every day. Hungarians [in Hungary] are already heading home at 4:00. They make just as much as my father-in-law but they go home at 4:00. Maybe they don't need the money so badly . . . and so they don't work so hard.

Csaba and others like him rationalized the Transylvanian Hungarians' moral right to compete for jobs in Hungary by appealing to their supposedly stronger work ethic. "If you consider yourself . . . part of the Hungarian nation and feel like you can't make ends meet" in Transylvania, argued Pista, another migrant worker, "then you should have the right" to work in Hungary.

Like labor migrants everywhere, Transylvanian Hungarians went to Hungary in search of a living wage, not identity politics. But their economic woes were given an ethnic spin when their hosts called them Romanian. Competition over access to scarce resources came to be expressed in terms of competition over legitimate claims to Hungarianness. Indeed, it is not uncommon for economic inequalities to be given ethnicized or racialized expression, particularly in contexts of labor migration (Bonacich 1972: 552–554; Miles 1982: 167–175). Ethnic return migration is distinctive, however, because migrant and host nominally share the same ethnicity. The national "other," in contrast to whom the migrants understand themselves, is part of the same imaginary national "self" in the countries that the migrants call home.

These sorts of ethnicized accounts of economic hardship and indignation enjoyed widespread circulation not just among the migrants themselves but, just as important, through the networks of labor migration, back to Hungarians in Romania who had never been to Hungary. As other studies in this book similarly demonstrate, the impact of labor migration needs to be measured not only quantitatively but also qualitatively in its capacity to shape the experiences, self-understandings, and cultural repertoires of those whose lives it touches. In Transylvania the stories that circulated through networks of migration have come to form an integral part of the stock of commonsense knowledge of

Hungarians (Biró 2002: 138; Fox 2003: 460–462). A Hungarian blacksmith in a small village in Transylvania complained one day about the difficulties of making ends meet as he pounded out a horseshoe on an anvil. When asked whether he considered looking for work in Hungary, he paused and said, "I could go to Hungary, but why? There I'm just a stinking Wallachian." Another young man selling handicrafts in Cluj saw things similarly: "Half my family lives there. . . . My brother, grandparents, they told me to come, and I could go, fine, they pay well enough. But I'm not going there as a 'Romanian.'" A mother of another migrant worker gave similar reasons for why she would not be following her son to Hungary: "I'd rather be a *bozgoroică*[11] here [in Romania] than a 'Romanian' there [in Hungary]."

Neither labor market tensions nor the experiences of quasi-ethnic differences they engendered were ameliorated by Hungary's rhetoric of national unity. This vision of national unity simply did not conform to the reality of economic exclusion experienced in the day-to-day practices of labor migration (see Stewart 2003: 88). Many Transylvanians had become too jaded by years of marginalization to take Hungary's rhetoric or policy initiatives seriously. Pali, a computer salesman from Transylvania (who had never worked in Hungary), cynically regarded the package of entitlements contained in the Status Law as a cheap attempt by Hungary to curry favor with transborder Hungarians. He, for one, wasn't taken in: "It's all just stupid. . . . It's ridiculous. . . . You know what it's like? They give you a little piece of shit and you complain so you get some more—'Gimme some shit!'—But no one cares. . . . No one's even talking about . . . whether it's shit or not, or what it is they're actually getting."

His mother, a pensioner, saw things differently. Unlike Pali, Erzsi had no intention of cashing in on the law's entitlements. She was content to reap the symbolic rewards of "being Hungarian" in the comfort of her own home. As she explained to her son, "It's about the *principle* of it, it's the *principle* that Hungary finally wants to help the Hungarians in the neighboring countries in some way." Indeed, transborder Hungarians (including a disproportionate number of pensioners) did sign up for the special Hungarian identification papers that entitled them to the Status Law's benefits (Császár 2004: 321; Stewart 2003: 87). However, many did so not to take advantage of the law's material rewards but, like Erzsi, to symbolically mark their belonging in the Hungarian nation. This was an endorsement of Hungary's vision of symbolic national unity.

But others, particularly those who had experienced the hardships of economic exclusion, were less impressed by such arguments (Császár 2004: 322;

Stewart 2003: 87–88). Pali also rejected his mother's principled rationales: "You worked thirty-nine years straight." He continued, growing more agitated:

> You should get *something*, it doesn't matter *what*, but *something* at least. The Hungarians aren't giving you a *thing*, the Romanians work hard to keep you from getting anything. So many principles. Every damn thing is a principle. I'm gonna fight for something when that something is tangible, when it'll be mine, and I'm gonna know it's mine, then I'll fight. But as long as some *Hungarian* tells me 'You just keep fighting, because eventually I'll get around to giving you something,' then the Hungarians can go to hell, you understand?

This was hardly the image of Hungarian brotherly love promoted by Hungary and enshrined in the Status Law. Pali's view, however, while perhaps remarkable for its vitriol, was not atypical in its content.

Other Transylvanian Hungarians cynically predicted that the only people who would claim the law's benefits would be *non*-Hungarians. Jancsi, a stage-hand at the Hungarian opera in Cluj who had worked in Hungary on numerous occasions, predicted that the Status Law would make Hungarianness a hot commodity.

> In Romania out of twenty-three million Romanians, or rather twenty-three million *citizens*, it's going to turn out that twenty million are Hungarian [*chuckling*] and three million Bulgarians or whatever [*chuckling again*]. That's the problem with this whole thing. . . . I mean it's human fallibility, right? If I have the teeniest possibility, an ounce of a chance to get something . . .

Jancsi astutely observed how the law's entitlements encouraged the strategic manipulation of Hungarian identity to lay claim to the resources it promised. But incorporating non-Hungarians into the fold of Hungary's "unified cultural nation of Hungarians" through the law's entitlements was seen by Jancsi and other "real" (Transylvanian) Hungarians as a further degradation of the ideal of Hungarian unity. Although the law would not succeed in uniting transborder Hungarians with Hungarians in the mother country, it would succeed, according to Jancsi, in making Hungarians out of non-Hungarians.

Ultimately, few migrant workers were interested in taking advantage of the law's modest guest worker provisions (Hárs 2003: 68–69; Stewart 2003: 85–89). By the time the law passed, established networks of undocumented labor migration were funneling workers from Transylvania and elsewhere into different jobs in Hungary. The law's offer of three months of legal employment each calendar year was hardly enticing to migrants who had grown accustomed to working year-round in Hungary (Hárs and Tóth 2003: 13; Stewart 2003: 87). According to Kántor (2001: 263), these weak guest worker provisions were consistent with the "central scope of the law . . . to convince the Hungarians living in the neighboring countries to remain in their home country."[12]

The law was therefore of little practical consequence in legalizing labor migration or undoing the experiences of economic and national exclusion. Any remaining hopes that Transylvanian Hungarians may have held for securing more than symbolic benefits from their ethnic homeland were dashed by the ill-fated dual citizenship referendum held in December 2004. The controversial plans for dual citizenship went considerably beyond the Status Law by proposing to extend citizenship rights to all transborder Hungarians on the basis of putatively shared ethnicity (Kovács 2005). This was not conceived as an invitation to transborder Hungarians to return to Hungary but rather was intended to be enjoyed in their countries of origin. But the referendum's defeat (because of insufficient voter turnout) sealed the transborder Hungarians' continued exclusion. "Our Hungarian brothers screwed us over . . . with the referendum," remarked one Transylvanian Hungarian, adding sardonically, "just as I expected."

Politically privileged conceptions of the nation promulgated through official institutional and discursive practices were challenged by the everyday conceptions of national belonging grounded in the social and economic realities of labor migration (Biró 2002: 137–139). To be sure, the exclusion experienced by undocumented migrant workers was often more pronounced than that experienced by Transylvanian Hungarians who enjoyed some form of legal status in Hungary (see Gödri 2004a; Tóth 1997). But even in other cases in which the state does provide a more elaborate policy framework (if not actual incentives) for the ethnic returnees' incorporation into the host economy, legal status has provided few protections against the sorts of frustrations and anxieties that engender the experience of ethnicized difference. It is not surprising, therefore, that Transylvanian Hungarian migrant workers accepted neither the notion of Hungarian unity endorsed by the Hungarian state nor the Romanian label ascribed to them by their Hungarian hosts. Instead, the economic differences they experienced were interpreted and articulated as national differences. The official Hungarian vision of national unity was undone by their economically grounded experience of national disunity.

Conclusion

Thus, although Hungarian nationalists have been hashing out new visions of national unity, Transylvanian Hungarian migrant workers have been encountering and constituting their own versions of national disunity. Officially sponsored visions of national belonging are therefore not the best predictors of the ways that ordinary people understand themselves nationally in their daily lives. Studies that focus exclusively on the policy contexts and legal frameworks for ethnic migration can thus inadvertently overemphasize the ethnic dimensions of these migrations. Of course ethnic return migration regimes do privilege putative ethnic affinities as their foundational rationale. But shifting the view to below, onto the actual (and potential) migrants thus categorized as co-ethnics, reveals a different understanding of ethnicity. From this perspective ethnicity is less an incentive for migration than its contingent outcome. The migrant workers' quotidian experiences of economic exclusion—not the lofty ideals of nationalist discourse—provided Transylvanian Hungarian migrants with an ethnicized language for interpreting and articulating social difference. And in the process an ethnic inversion took place: Previously tacit expectations of ethnic affinity were discursively transformed into the explicit expression of ethnic difference. Shifting the analytical focus from official discourse and policy to the economic contexts of everyday life revealed the grounded ways that labor migration has provided the impetus not for national *re*unification but rather for national bifurcation.

A number of observers have argued that transnational migration processes are gradually eroding the continued salience of the nation-state paradigm (Appadurai 1996; Hannerz 1996; Hedetoft and Hjort 2002; Soysal 1994). At the same time, others have suggested that the nation-state's retreat is being hastened by European expansion and the elaboration of kin-state politics in east Europe (Fowler 2004). But these transnational processes have not necessarily engendered concomitant transnational forms of collective belonging (Waldinger and Fitzgerald 2004; Conclusion, this volume). The experiences of national difference engendered through the processes of migration continue in large part to congeal within the political boundaries supplied by the state: Hungarians from one side of the border see themselves as distinct from those on the other side; Brazilian Japanese migrant workers in Japan reappropriate the Brazilian label of their natal homeland; and Russian Jews in Israel persist in seeing themselves as Russian in Israel. These are not hybrid identities as much as more traditional state-sponsored forms of ethnonational membership adapted to and even strengthened by the experiences of migration. The state thus remains a powerfully cogent container for the organization and experience of social reality (Giddens 1987: 13; Mann 1993: 59–61; see also Torpey 2000: 11–13). This is the state not as an assemblage of powerful elites but rather as an institutional form that prescribes the culture of a territorially delineated polity. "The 'power' of the modern state," explains Mann (1993: 61), "principally concerns not 'state elites' exercising power over society but a tightening state-society relation, caging social relations over the national rather than the local-regional or transnational terrain." Elite discourse has not *trans*nationalized the migrants as much as the organizational logic of the state has *re*nationalized them.

Notes

An earlier version of this chapter was published as "From National Inclusion to Economic Exclusion: Ethnic Hungarian Labour Migration to Hungary," *Nations and Nationalism* 13(1):77–96 (2007). This revised version is reprinted with permission of Blackwell Publishing. The chapter was developed while I was a visiting scholar at the Center for Comparative Immigration Studies at the University of California, San Diego (2003–2004). I would like to thank Wayne Cornelius, Gaku Tsuda, and all the other visiting scholars for providing an ideal environment in which to conduct my research. I also benefited from the opportunity to present an earlier version of the paper at the Multiple Transnational Migrations Section on International Migration, organized by Peter Kivisto, for the Annual Meeting of the American Sociological Association in Philadelphia in 2005. I am grateful to József Böröcz, Rogers Brubaker, David Cook-Martín, Steve Fenton, David Fitzgerald, Steve Gold, István Horváth, Nadia Kim, Gregor McLennan, Endre Sik, Eszter Szilassy, Gaku Tsuda, and Eric Weaver for the comments and suggestions they have given me. Finally, I would like to thank Rogers Brubaker, Margit Feischmidt, and Liana Grancea for permission to use data from our collaborative research (*Nationalist Politics and Everyday Ethnicity in a Transylvania Town*, Princeton, NJ: Princeton University Press, 2006).

1. Poland, Romania, and Slovakia have also implemented kin-state regimes for their transborder co-ethnics in their neighboring countries; Albania, Croatia, Macedonia, Serbia, and Ukraine similarly acknowledge varying degrees of responsibility to their transborder co-ethnics (Fowler 2004).

2. Co-ethnics are required to live in Hungary for only one year (not the usual eight) before being naturalized.

3. Later this period was extended to 90 days. Hungary did not, however, lift its requirement for work permits for Romanian citizens following the accession of Romania to the EU in 2007. Instead, it initiated a plan whereby work permits would be automatically granted to Romanian nationals working in one of 245 identified professions.

4. Although the number of Transylvanian Hungarian migrant workers peaked in the mid-1990s, research conducted in 2002 showed that nearly half of employment-age Hungarians from Romania still planned short-term employment in Hungary (Sik and Simonovits 2003: 43–44; see also Bădescu 2004; Simonovits 2003). The number of work permits issued to Romanian citizens has fluctuated between 10,000 and 30,000 per year over the past 15 years (Gödri 2004b: 9–10; Juhász 1999: 9–11, 14–15). The actual number of undocumented migrants is more difficult to gauge, but estimates place it at 100,000 per year (Hárs 1999: 60; see also Juhász 1999: 21–22).

5. In this respect, Hungarians differ from other cohorts of return migrants for whom linguistic and cultural affinities are but a distant memory (if not pure fiction). The proximity of Hungarian co-ethnics to their ethnic homeland made it possible (and at times politically viable) for them to maintain ties over the past century (for similarities in the Finnish case, see Chapter 6). Hungarian national minority political activity in the neighboring countries, with support from Hungary, has helped to not only preserve but in some respects strengthen Hungarian national identification among transborder Hungarians. But these affinities cultivated by Hungarians on both sides of the border were not the migrant workers' primary objective; rather, they were a means for them to realize economic ends (see Chapter 1 on the economic determinants of ethnic return migration).

6. In Hungary, the degree of marginalization varied for differently situated migrants. Those better placed in established networks, for instance, fared better than casual laborers seeking day employment at Budapest's infamous Moscow Square human market (Sik 1999). Those with some legal documentation (usually work permits) were less stigmatized. But the legal protections afforded some migrants (including those in other settings examined in this volume) have proved to be of limited consequence in lessening the quotidian experience of social and economic alienation.

7. In contrast, the problems that Latin American workers in Spain face arise not from their economic marginalization but rather from their economic competition with middle-class Spaniards. In the Spanish case, in which host and migrant compete for the same jobs, ethnic affinity is coupled with class affinity (see Chapter 5). As Cook-Martín and Viladrich argue in Chapter 5, this is a result of Spanish policies that grant automatic citizenship to returning migrants and with it, the expectation of equal footing in the labor market with their Spanish hosts. In Hungary, though, with its weak policy framework for migrant labor, ethnic returnees are relegated to lower-status jobs in the host economy. Different policy frameworks funnel migrant workers into different forms of labor market competition and the forms of economic exclusion they sometimes entail.

8. "Wallachian" is a common slur used to refer to Romanians. Although it technically refers to Romanians from Wallachia, or the Old Kingdom, south of Transylvania, in practice it has become a synonym for Roma.

9. "Stinking Romanian" is another common slur directed at Romanians. Other favorites include "stinking Transylvanians," "Wallachian Gypsies," "Gypsies," "dirty Romanians," and "Romanian thieves." I also heard an unemployed worker from Hungary refer to the migrant workers as *bocskorosok* and *szőrös talpúak*. *Bocskor* refers to a particular type of traditional footwear still worn in some rural parts of Romania. *Szőrös talpú* means hairy-footed.

10. Ethnic return migrants in other contexts have reacted differently. Japanese Brazilian migrant workers derisively called foreigners by their hosts in Japan responded by rediscovering their Brazilianness with new intensity and resolve (see Chapter 9). Russian émigrés to Israel and *Aussiedler* in Germany reclaimed their distinctiveness by (self-)segregating into enclave communities (Levy and Weiss 2002). But the cultural affinities between Russian Jews, *Aussiedler*, and Japanese Brazilians on the one hand and their hosts on the other have been more diluted by the effects of history and geography. In contrast, Hungarians from Transylvania can—and do—claim more proximate historical and geographic ties with Hungary (for similarities on this point with the Finnish case, see Chapter 6).

11. *Bozgoroică* is a common slur used by Romanians to refer to Transylvanian Hungarians. It means without a homeland.

12. To add insult to injury, a week before the law was to go into effect, Hungary entered into a bilateral agreement with Romania (under pressure from the EU) to extend the law's guest worker provisions to all Romanian citizens, irrespective of ethnicity. What might have been viewed as a modest provision for ethnic return migration was instead stripped of its ethnic raison d'être. Although the amended law allayed EU concerns over ethnic discrimination, it did so at the cost of further offending transborder Hungarians (see Deets and Stroschein 2005).

References Cited

Appadurai, Arjun. 1996. *Modernity at Large: Cultural Dimensions of Globalization.* Minneapolis: University of Minnesota Press.

Bădescu, Gabriel. 2004. "Romanian Labor Migration and Citizenship." In *New Patterns of Labour Migration in Central and Eastern Europe*, Daniel Pop, ed. Cluj-Napoca, Romania: AMM Editura.

Basch, Linda, Nina Glick Schiller, and Cristina Szanton Blanc. 1994. *Nations Unbound: Transnational Projects, Postcolonial Predicaments, and Deterritorialized Nation-States.* New York: Gordon and Breach.

Biró, A. Zoltán. 1996. "Egyéni és kollektív identitás a kilépési gyakorlatban" [Individual and collective identity in migration practices]. In *Elvándorlók? Vendégmunka és életforma a Székelyföldön* [Emigrants? Guest workers and lifestyles in the Szekler lands], Kommunikációs Antropológiai Munkacsoport, Regionális és Antropológiai Kutatások Központja [Working Group on Communicative Anthropology, Centre for Regional and Anthropological Research], ed. Miercurea-Ciuc, Romania: Pro-Print Könyvkiadó.

————. 2002. "'Csúcsok' és hétköznapok: Szempontok a magyar-magyar reláció társadalomtudományi elemzéséhez" ["Summits" and the everyday: Perspectives on the social analysis of Hungarian-Hungarian relations]. In *Magyarország és a magyar kisebbségek: Történeti és mai tendenciák* [Hungary and the Hungarian minorities: Historical and contemporary tendencies], Glatz Ferenc, ed. Budapest: Magyar Tudományos Akadémia.

Bonacich, Edna. 1972. "A Theory of Ethnic Antagonism: The Split Labor Market." *American Sociological Review* 37(5):547–559.

Brubaker, Rogers. 1996. "National Minorities, Nationalizing States, and External National Homelands in the New Europe. In his *Nationalism Reframed: Nationhood and the National Question in the New Europe.* Cambridge, UK: Cambridge University Press.

————. 1998. "Migrations of Ethnic Unmixing in the 'New Europe.'" *International Migration Review* 32(4):1047–1065.

Brubaker, Rogers, Margit Feischmidt, Jon Fox, and Liana Grancea. 2006. *Nationalist Politics and Everyday Ethnicity in a Transylvanian Town.* Princeton, NJ: Princeton University Press.

Császár, Melinda. 2004. "A kedvezménytörvény romániai gyakorlatáról: Magyar igazolvány iránti kérelmek számának alakulása" [On the Status Law in practice in Romania: The development of requests for Hungarian identity papers]. *Demográfia* 3–4:321–334.

Csata, Zsombor, and Tamás Kiss. 2003. "Migrációs potenciál Erdélyben" [Migration potential in Transylvania]. *Erdélyi Társadalom* 1(2):7–38.

Csepeli, György, Antal Örkény, and Mária Székelyi. 2002. *Nemzetek egymás tükrében: Interetnikus viszonyok a kárpát-medencében* [Nations in each other's image: Interethnic relations in the Carpathian basin]. Budapest: Balassi Kiadó.

Csergő, Zsuzsa, and James M. Goldgeier. 2004. "Nationalist Strategies and European Integration." *Perspectives on Politics* 2(1):21–37.

Deets, Stephen, and Sherrill Stroschein. 2005. "Dilemmas of Autonomy and Liberal Pluralism: Examples Involving Hungarians in Central Europe." *Nations and Nationalism* 11(2):285–305.

Fábián, Zoltán. 1998. "Vélemények a cigányokról és az idegenellenesség Magyarországon" [Opinions about Gypsies and xenophobia in Hungary]. In *Idegenek Magyarországon* [*Foreigners in Hungary*], Endre Sik and Judit Tóth, eds. Budapest: MTA Politikai Tudományok Intézete Nemzetközi Migráció Kutatócsoport Évkönyve.

Fábián, Zoltán, Endre Sik, and Judit Tóth. 2001. "Unióra várva: Előítélet, xenofóbia és európai integráció" [Waiting for the Union: Prejudice, xenophobia, and European integration]. In *Migráció és Európai Unió* [Migration and the European Union], Éva Lukács and Miklós Király, eds. Budapest: Szociális és Családügyi Minisztérium.

Feischmidt, Margit. 2004. "A határ és a román stigma" [The border and the Romanian stigma]. In *Tér és terep: Tanulmányok az etnicitás és az identitás kérdésköréből* [Space and place: Studies on questions of ethnicization and identity], Nóra Kovács, Anna Osvát, and László Szarka, eds. Budapest: Akadémiai Kiadó.

Fowler, Brigid. 2004. "Fuzzing Citizenship, Nationalising Political Space: A Framework for Interpreting the 'Status Law' as a New Form of Kin-State Policy in Central and Eastern Europe." In *The Hungarian Status Law: Nation Building and/or Minority Protection*, Zoltán Kántor, Balázs Majtényi, Osamu Ieda, Balázs Vizi, and Iván Halász, eds. Sapporo, Japan: Slavic Research Center.

Fox, Jon E. 2003. "National Identities on the Move: Transylvanian Hungarian Labour Migrants in Hungary." *Journal of Ethnic and Migration Studies* 29(3):449–466.

Giddens, Anthony. 1987. *A Contemporary Critique of Historical Materialism: The Nation-State and Violence*, v. 2. Berkeley: University of California Press.

Gödri, Irén. 2004a. "A környező országokból érkező bevándorlók beilleszkedése Magyarországon" [The integration of migrants from the neighboring countries in Hungary]. *Demográfia* 3–4:265–299.

———. 2004b. "A Special Case of International Migration: Ethnic Hungarians Migrating from Transylvania to Hungary." *Yearbook of Population Research in Finland* 40:1–28.

Hannerz, Ulf. 1996. *Transnational Connections: Culture, People, Places*. London: Routledge.

Hárs, Ágnes. 1999. "Mi korlátozza a külföldi munkavállalók keresletét?" [What limits the demand for foreign workers?]. In *Migráció: Tanulmánygyűjtemény* [Migration: Collection of studies], v. 2, Pál Péter Tóth and Sándor Illés, eds. Budapest: KSH Népességtudományi Kutató Intézet.

———. 2003. "A kedvezménytörvény várható hatása a magyar munkaerőpiacra" [The probable effects of the Status Law on the Hungarian labor market]. In *Menni vagy maradni? Kedvezménytörvény és migrációs várakozások* [To go or stay? The Status Law and migration expectations], Antal Örkény, ed. Budapest: MTA Kisebbségkutató Intézet.

Hárs, Ágnes, and Judit Tóth. 2003. "Munkavallalás és EU csatlakozás: A személyek szabad mozgásának és a külföldiek foglalkoztatásának egyes, a munkaerőpiacra gyakorolt hatásáról" [Employment and EU unification: Some practical effects of the free movement of peoples and the employment of foreigners on the labor market]. Paper prepared for the Miniszterelnöki Hivatal Nemzeti Fejlesztési Terv és EU Támogatások Hivatala.

Hedetoft, Ulf, and Mette Hjort, eds. 2002. *The Postnational Self: Belonging and Identity*. Minneapolis: University of Minnesota Press.

Joppke, Christian. 2005. *Selecting by Origin: Ethnic Migration in the Liberal State*. Cambridge, MA: Harvard University Press.

Juhász, Judit. 1999. *Illegal Labour Migration and Employment in Hungary*. International Migration Papers 30. Geneva: International Labour Office.

Kántor, Zoltán. 2001. "Nationalizing Minorities and Homeland Politics: The Case of the Hungarians in Romania." In *Nation-Building and Contested Identities: Romanian and Hungarian Case Studies*, Balázs Trencsényi, Dragoş Petrescu, Cristina Petrescu, Constantin Iordachi, and Zoltán Kantor, eds. Budapest: Regio Books.

Kántor, Zoltán, Balázs Majtényi, Osamu Ieda, Balázs Vizi, and Iván Halász, eds. 2004. *The Hungarian Status Law: Nation Building and/or Minority Protection*. Sapporo, Japan: Slavic Research Center.

Keating, Michael. 2004. "European Integration and the Nationalities Question." *Politics and Society* 32(3):367–388.

Kis, János. 2001. "Nation-Building and Beyond." In *Can Liberal Pluralism Be Exported? Western Political Theory and Ethnic Relations in Eastern Europe*, Will Kymlicka and Magda Opalski, eds. Oxford: Oxford University Press.

Kovács, Mária M. 2005. "The Politics of Non-Resident Dual Citizenship in Hungary." *Regio* 8:50–72.

Kürti, László. 2001. *The Remote Borderland: Transylvania in the Hungarian Imagination*. Albany: State University of New York Press.

Levy, Daniel, and Yfaat Weiss, eds. 2002. *Challenging Ethnic Citizenship: German and Israeli Perspectives on Migration*. New York: Berghahn Books.

Mann, Michael. 1993. *The Sources of Social Power: The Rise of Classes and Nation-States, 1760–1914*, v. 2. New York: Cambridge University Press.

McGarry, John, and Michael Keating, eds. 2006. *European Integration and the Nationalities Question*. London: Routledge.

Miles, Robert. 1982. *Racism and Migrant Labour*. London: Routledge & Kegan Paul.

Mungiu-Pippidi, Alina. 1999. *Transilvania subjectivă* [Subjective Transylvania]. Bucharest: Humanitas.

Pulay, Gergő. 2005. "A vendégmunka mint életforma: Széki építőmunkások Budapesten" [Migrant labor as a way of life: Construction workers from Sic]. In *Erdély-(de)konstrukciók: Antropológiai kísérletek, Erdély-mítoszok és nemzeti önreprezentáció, erdélyi és magyarországi magyarok viszonyának értelmezésére* [Transylvanian (de)constructions: Anthropological essays on Transylvanian myths, national self-representations, and relations between Hungarians from Transylvania and Hungary], Margit Feischmidt, ed. Budapest: Néprajzi Múzeum, PTE Kommunikáció-és Médiatudományi Tanszék.

Schöpflin, George. 2000. *Nations, Identity, Power: The New Politics of Europe*. London: Hurst.

Sik, Endre. 1999. "'Emberpiac' a Moszkva téren" ["Human market" at Moscow Square]. *Szociológiai Szemle* 9(1):97–119.

Sik, Endre, and Bori Simonovits. 2003. "A migrációs potenciál mértéke és társadalmi bázisa a kárpát-medencei magyarok körében" [The degree and social conditions of migration among Hungarians in the Carpathian Basin]. In *Menni vagy maradni: Kedvezménytörvény és migrációs várakozások* [To go or stay? The Status Law and migration expectations], Antal Örkény, ed. Budapest: MTA Kisebbségkutató Intézet.

Simonovits, Bori. 2003. "A kárpát-medencei magyarok munkaerő migrációjának tervezett irányai" [The labor migration intentions of Hungarians in the Carpathian basin]. In *Menni vagy maradni? Kedvezménytörvény és migrációs várakozások* [To go or stay? The Status Law and migration expectations], Antal Örkény, ed. Budapest: MTA Kisebbségkutató Intézet.

Skrentny, John, Stephanie Chan, Jon Fox, and Denis Kim. 2007. "Defining Nations in Asia and Europe: A Comparative Analysis of Ethnic Return Migration Policy." *International Migration Review* 41(1):793–825.

Soysal, Yasemin Nuhoğlu. 1994. *Limits of Citizenship: Migrants and Postnational Membership in Europe*. Chicago: University of Chicago Press.

Stewart, Michael. 2003. "The Hungarian Status Law: A New European Form of Transnational Politics?" *Diaspora* 12(1):67–101.

Szakáts, Mária Erzsébet. 1996. "Az Erdélyből áttelepült magyarok otthonképe" [Transylvanian Hungarian migrants' image of home]. In *Táborlakók, diaszpórák, politikák* [Camp occupants, diasporas, policies], Endre Sik and Judit Tóth, eds. Budapest: MTA Politika Tudományok Intézete Nemzetközi Migráció Kutatócsoport Évkönyve.

Torpey, John. 2000. *The Invention of the Passport: Surveillance, Citizenship, and the State.* Cambridge, UK: Cambridge University Press.

Tóth, Pál Péter. 1997. *Haza csak egy van? Menekülők, bevándorlók, új állampolgárok Magyarországon (1988–1994)* [There's only one homeland? Refugees, immigrants, and new citizens in Hungary (1988–1994)]. Budapest: Püski Kiadó.

Tóth, Pál Péter, and Tünde Turai. 2003. "A magyar lakosság külföldiekhez való viszonyáról szóló szakirodalom összefoglalása" [A summary of scholarship on the Hungarian population's relations with foreigners]. *Szociológiai Szemle* 4:107–132.

Triandafyllidou, Anna. 2001. *Immigrants and National Identity in Europe*. London: Routledge.

Tsuda, Takeyuki. 2003. *Strangers in the Ethnic Homeland: Japanese Brazilian Return Migration in Transnational Perspective.* New York: Columbia University Press.

Verdery, Katherine. 1991. *National Ideology Under Socialism: Identity and Cultural Politics in Ceauşescu's Romania.* Berkeley: University of California Press.

Waldinger, Roger, and David Fitzgerald. 2004. "Transnationalism in Question." *American Journal of Sociology* 109(5):1177–1195.

Weaver, Eric Beckett. 2006. *National Narcissism: The Cult of Nation and Gender in Hungary.* Oxford: Peter Lang.

Former Soviet Jews in Their New/Old Homeland

Between Integration and Separatism

Larissa Remennick

I START WITH A PERSONAL NOTE. I am an immigrant myself. I moved to Israel from Moscow in 1991, the last year of the USSR's existence, as part of the mass wave of post-Communist "ethnically privileged" Jewish émigrés. For the last 15 years I have been engaged in a long-term participant observation project, trying to understand from within the social encounter between veteran Israelis and the new citizens with a Russian accent. Mine is perhaps the optimal standpoint for a migration scholar, as I have both firsthand migrant experience and cultural competence to study my fellow Russian Jews; at the same time, as a sociologist I can create enough analytical distance to reflect on this experience in more conceptual and comparative terms. Since the early 1990s I have conducted both survey research and in-depth ethnographic studies, which together create a multifaceted picture of the lived experiences of migration and adjustment among my co-ethnics. In this essay I offer a brief overview of my research on identity and acculturation, occupational integration, and gender differentials among Russian Jewish immigrants to Israel, combining macrolevel data with observations and ethnographic findings.[1] In this chapter I reflect on the expressions of integration and separatism among Russian-speaking Israelis and the causes of their relative socioeconomic marginalization. Because this volume has a comparative focus, I start by delineating some unique features of the post-1989 immigration of Russian-speaking Jews to Israel. This migration was rather distinctive on the global landscape of recent migration waves generally and ethnic return migrations specifically.

Unique Features of the Israeli Case

One has to start from the special character of Israel as an ethnic shelter country built as a result of "return migration" of Jews from multiple Diaspora countries and drawing on the jus sanguinis principle, that is, blood ties and common descent. Who counts as a Jew is defined rather broadly by the Law of Return enacted in 1950 and revised in 1970 to include grandchildren of Jews and their non-Jewish kin. The "return" in the Israeli case is purely symbolic, as one cannot return to the land that one's ancestors left 2,000 years ago; yet the myth of aliyah (literally meaning in Hebrew "ascent" or "pilgrimage") as homecoming remains one of the chief pillars of Zionism. Although the legal and moral framework of migration to Israel is similar to that in other return migration waves (e.g., of *Aussiedler* to Germany or Pontiac Greeks to Greece), the long expanse of history that has elapsed since the dispersion makes this case of ethnic return migration more virtual than a return to the homeland after several generations of exile (Joppke and Rosenhek 2002). The political rationale for receiving Jewish immigrants combines ideological, nationalist, and pragmatic goals, the main one of which is maintaining a Jewish majority in relation to the Arab population of Israel (whose fertility rates are almost twice as high), Palestinians in the occupied territories (with fertility rates two to three times higher), and the surrounding Muslim countries. A unique feature of the Israeli case of ethnic return migration is the significant contribution that this migration makes to the ongoing nation-building process in the context of insecure borders, contested territories, security threats, the demographic realities, and an unstable economy. Whereas in most European and Asian countries the nation-building process is over and the rationale for ethnic return migration is mainly ideological and humanitarian (compensation for historic grievances or asylum) or economic (labor shortages), in Israel economic grounds, while certainly present, are less salient than the nation-building cause, with the ensuing high stakes invested in the immigrants (Kimmerling 2001).

The policy of all Israeli governments to build an ethnically cohesive nation-state by means of ethnic return migration has had a dual effect on the relations between recent immigrants and the hegemonic majority. On the one hand, Jewish immigrants are entitled to citizenship and all civil and economic rights upon arrival, but on the other hand aliyah implies multiple strings attached for the *ole hadash* (new immigrant). By joining Israel, Jewish immigrants are assuming multiple responsibilities and commitments: first of all, a shared Zionist ethos, ethnic solidarity against common enemies (including mandatory military service for both men and women and annual reserve duty for men), and an expectation of expedient assimilation into the Israeli melting pot, including the severance of diasporic languages and a switch to Hebrew both in public and in private (Levy and Weiss 2002; Shuval 1998). An independent migrant to the United States, Canada, or Australia is expected to share the minimal common denominator with the native majority in the form of law abidance, basic proficiency in the host language, and economic self-reliance, but a newcomer to the Israeli ethnonational collective encounters a broader set of expectations. Most of these (except for military duty) are culture bound and implicit, but they are nevertheless potent. Immigrants who do not show a proper drive for rapid Israelization are seen as a liability and are socially excluded in many subtle ways. Given the secular background and tenuous Jewish identity of most former Soviet immigrants (Remennick 2007), Russian newcomers often have a difficult time finding common ground with the Israeli Jewish mainstream, well over 50 percent of which is religious or observant of Judaic traditions to various extents. Anthropological studies during the 1990s highlighted multiple rifts and tensions in the encounter between post-Communist Russian immigrants and all hegemonic sectors of Israeli society—Sabras (Israeli-born Jews), veteran immigrants from Europe and the Middle East, and their own co-ethnics, immigrants of the 1970s wave from the USSR. These rifts center around the issues of ideology versus pragmatism as motives for aliyah, the lack of homecoming motifs and prescribed optimism about the future, and disappointment with the real rather than the imagined Israel among newcomers (Golden 2002; Lomsky-Feder and Rapoport 2001; Markowitz 1994). The challenge of redefining their identity and showing commitment to Jewish causes has been especially prominent for non-Jewish or partly Jewish immigrants, who, because of several generations of intermarriage, made up to one-third of all arrivals in the 1990s (Tolts 2000), and many feel estranged in many social and legal settings.

Another prominent feature of the Israeli ethnic return migration is the exceptional size of this immigration wave, both in absolute terms and in relation to Israel's population of 6 million (5 million Jews and 1 million Arabs), at the time of its inception in 1989–1990. Among the 1.6 million Jewish emigrants who left the former Soviet Union after 1989, more than 950,000, or about 60 percent, resettled in Israel, forming the largest branch of the post-Communist Russian Jewish Diaspora. Including the former Soviet immigrants of the 1970s, Russian speakers now make up more than 20 percent of the Jewish population nationally, and in many areas and towns they make up between

30 percent and 40 percent (IMIA 2004; Tolts 2000). Apparently, the influx of such a critical mass of same-origin immigrants into a small country and over a short period of time made a strong impact on the host society and created conditions for the formation of a strong and self-sufficient Russian ethnic community.[2] At the same time, as in most other cases of ethnic return migration (Capo Zmegac 2005), the full measure of the economic and cultural gap between the immigrants and their hosts and the crisis of mutual unfulfilled expectations are dramatically manifested in most social domains (Feldman 2003; Fialkova and Yelenevskaya 2007; Remennick 2007).

Former Soviet Jews as a group are endowed to a high degree with what is called in current sociological vernacular human capital, mainly in terms of rates of postsecondary education and professional or white-collar background. They form the single most educated immigrant community on the global migrations map, counting in their ranks about 60 percent of university graduates (Chinese, Indians, and Koreans significantly lag behind, with 28–35 percent; Reitz 2001). On the other hand, the kind of professional skills that these migrants acquired in the former Soviet Union are not easily transferable to the skilled labor markets of the West. Living behind the iron curtain and shaped by inert Soviet organizations, former Soviet professionals, especially the older generation, often lack technical and social skills crucial for occupational relocation, such as computing, English proficiency, and the ability for self-marketing in complex and rapidly changing economies (Remennick 2003a).

Another common barrier is the need for accreditation for many registered occupations, such as medicine, law, social work, education, and civil engineering, which includes complex examinations and learning new legal frameworks for professional practice. In this respect, former Soviet professionals face a similar challenge in most host countries, with especially high formal barriers erected in Canada, Germany, and Australia (Remennick 2007; Shuval and Bernstein 1997). In Israel the legal frameworks for professional readjustment are more immigrant friendly, as the Zionist ethos implies assistance to the newcomers in their occupational and social incorporation. In line with this ideology, many state-sponsored programs offer advanced Hebrew classes and various refresher and retraining courses tailored for specific occupations and meant to aid immigrant professionals in passing licensure exams and finding relevant positions. Yet at the same time Israel's professional marketplace is small and highly saturated, creating fierce competition for the skilled jobs with local professionals and among immigrants themselves (Remennick 2003a, 2004).

Last, but not least, Soviet Jewish immigrants are highly prone to cultural retention in every destination country. At least the two most recent generations of Soviet Jews were almost completely detached from Jewish education, religion, and culture, becoming secular urban citizens and striving to downplay their Jewish origins in the anti-Semitic milieu (Remennick 2007). By way of historic irony, assimilated Jewish intellectuals played a pivotal role in the creation of modern Russian Soviet culture of the twentieth century, as a large proportion of Soviet writers, journalists, musicians, artists, theater, cinema, and TV professionals (both conformists and dissidents) were Jewish. Russian Jews are also ardent cultural consumers—prolific readers and theater and concert goers. They cherish their cultural heritage (which they associate with the high European tradition), perceive it as superior to the Middle Eastern Israeli culture, and see no reason to sever their Russianness upon migration. Living on the economic and social margins, many of them never mastered Hebrew well enough to get to know and enjoy mainstream Israeli culture. Instead, they established multiple educational and cultural institutions and have thriving mass media in the Russian language, which serves the cultural needs of this community and ensures cultural continuity for the first and maybe second generation of former Soviets (Epstein and Kheimets 2000). Yet, despite its significance for the last-wave immigrants, this thriving subculture remains largely marginal to the mainstream Hebrew-based social and cultural life. It struggles to survive by drawing on meager budgets and voluntary work, and most Israelis are oblivious to its very existence.

On Integration and Separatism

These factors set the scene for the process of social incorporation of Russian-speaking Jews into Israel. As elsewhere, this process is segmented and on the individual level highly dependent on three key assets: human capital, social networks, and social support. However, all immigrants have to define themselves in relation to their old and new identities, past and present, integration or avoidance of anything Israeli—that is, self-isolation or separatism. Here I have to make a terminological note because terms also have strings attached. From now on, I would like to set aside the key American term *assimilation*, which usually implies a total and irreversible dissolution of the minority group into the hegemonic majority (the Israeli term *absorption*, originating in chemistry, has a similar meaning). In fact, assimilation never occurs in the first generation and is seldom complete even in the second generation. The process of immigrant social insertion is segmented and nonlinear and is further challenged by the emergence of transnational ethnic networks, which are prominent in the case of Russian Jews living in Israel and in the West (Remennick 2002b, 2007).

Conversely, the word *integration* suggests that the minority group preserves its cultural core while developing additional adaptive facets of identity, skills, networks, and so on. Integration usually emerges in a form of biculturalism, including bilingualism. Integrative strategy implies double cultural competence, flexibility, and an effective situational switch between the two cultures (Berry 1990; Nauck 2001). Bilingualism and double cultural competence might also be seen as signs of acculturation. Effective integration requires diverse personal resources—languages, education, social skills, and the ability to adapt to different roles; therefore this option is not available to many immigrants who are simply not endowed with these resources. These immigrants have fewer options and often adopt separatist strategies of adjustment that they often back up with the assertion of Russian or European cultural superiority over the local Levantine mores and lifestyles (referring, for example, to flawed work ethics and sloppy child-rearing practices among many Israelis) (Fialkova and Yelenevskaya 2007). I define separatism as the ultimate expression of social and cultural retention among ethnic migrants, with the ensuing voluntary self-isolation from the receiving country's mainstream. Marginalization is their resulting socioeconomic location in Israeli Jewish society in relation to Hebrew cultural and political hegemony.

Pathways to Integration in the Context of Ethnic Return Migration

I turn now to the main paths of social integration (and its opposite—separatism) for Russian immigrants in Israel over the last 15–17 years. In the following analysis I rely on a heuristic model that draws on several measurable domains of social integration (see Remennick 2003b and 2003c for details on the methods and findings). Although developed in the Israeli context, this model should also work for other countries receiving ethnic return migrants when same-origin migrants form a sizable demographic segment endowed with cultural and economic resources. Applicability of this or a similar analytical framework of integration was demonstrated for ethnic Germans (*Aussiedler*) and other immigrant minorities in Germany (Nauck 2001), including former Soviet Jews (Remennick 2005b). Originally, this model was tested and proved meaningful in a 2001 national survey that aimed to operationalize and measure key aspects of integration among more than 800 Russian Jewish immigrants, ages 18 and older. A probability stratified sampling scheme was used to recruit respondents across Israel; the respondents were interviewed in their native language face to face, increasing the validity of the findings in the era of telephone surveys with low response rates. At the time of the survey, the respondents' mean length of stay in Israel was about eight years and their mean age was 46 years (±5.2).

I suggest five interrelated social indicators that are both determinants and expressions of social integration among first-generation migrants: employment in the mainstream economy, diversification of communication circles, cultural and media consumption, civic and political participation, and the dominant attitude of the hegemonic majority. Before describing the specific paths of integration, let me stress that proficiency in the host language (Hebrew, and also some command of English for professionals) is both a precursor and an outcome of social integration and permeates every domain of interaction between immigrants and the host society (Remennick 2003b). Because the system of Jewish education was demolished in the former Soviet Union, most Soviet Jews arrived in Israel not knowing any Hebrew; some older immigrants could retrieve basic Yiddish from their youth. Although free full-day Hebrew classes (*ulpan*) were offered to every newcomer, many immigrants dropped out early because they were compelled to make a living. Even after completing the full *ulpan* course, most immigrants (especially the older segment) obtained only basic skills in this ancient Semitic language, which is different from any other foreign language that Russian speakers had ever tried to learn. Subsequently, many newcomers could not advance in their spoken Hebrew because of minimal social contact with Israelis. In my survey about 35 percent of respondents described their command of Hebrew as good or excellent, whereas 45 percent defined it as moderate or mediocre and 20 percent had only basic Hebrew skills or none at all. Many respondents saw their limited Hebrew as a primary reason for their occupational downgrading and social estrangement. Now let us turn to the chief avenues to integration among recent migrants.

First, it is employment in the mainstream economy (for educated migrants, skilled or professional employment) rather than employment in the ethnic sector that rapidly expands in times of mass migration.[3] Successful employment results not only in the economic well-being of newcomers but also in the development of new interests and loyalties, as well as in contacts with native co-workers, which facilitates the learning of Hebrew and local cultural ways. Only a minority of former professionals were able to regain their careers in Israel, reflecting the saturated market, competition with local professionals, skill incompatibility, and other disadvantages faced by former Soviet immigrants on the Israeli market (e.g., the lack of informal social networks, ageism, and male worker preference in many occupations). In general, about one-third of academic degree holders continued to work in their original occupation or in a similar one after retraining. Women and older immigrants (often senior specialists before emigration) were less successful in career relocation than their male and younger counterparts.

The immigrant's former occupation was a salient determinant of success, reflecting culture and language dependency and market demand (Remennick 2003a). Thus physicians were rather successful; more than 50 percent of those who had applied for an Israeli medical license have completed the accreditation process and now work as doctors, albeit often in the less prestigious niches of medical care (general practice, emergency care, geriatrics). Nurses, paramedical workers, and pharmacists comprised the most demanded occupational category on the market and enjoyed simpler accreditation procedures, so that their employment rates soon reached 80–95 percent. Conversely, only about 20 percent of former teachers continued to work in Israeli schools, reflecting a broad gap in educational standards and principles between the former Soviet Union and Israel, high requirements for Hebrew proficiency, and low demand for teachers in many disciplines. Among engineers, about 25 percent work in their old engineering specialty, another 35 percent have retrained into computing and information technology, and 40 percent left engineering altogether. By and large, most Russian Jewish professionals underwent substantial occupational downgrading, which in turn reduced their motivation and ability to learn Hebrew and develop new social networks (Remennick 2007).

The second indicator of integration is diversification of communication circles, whereby immigrants' informal social networks come to include both co-ethnics and natives. Most new immigrants start building their networks from fellow immigrants (many of whom they had known back in the homeland), but as they master Hebrew and come in contact with Israeli institutions (workplaces, community organizations, schools, the military, etc.), their contacts come to include members of the host majority, that is, native Hebrew speakers. Co-ethnics often remain their primary safety net for their lifetime, but the ability to establish friendly connections with the natives is extremely important for social learning and for gaining access to invaluable social resources, such as information about work and housing, the ability to get references in Hebrew, and so on. The principal setting for meeting members of the hegemonic majority is the workplace (Remennick 2004); hence the failure of many educated immigrants to find qualified work in Israeli organizations deprived them of important opportunities to meet and befriend their native social peers. In practice, immigrants' contacts with Israelis are sporadic and limited to instrumental matters in the public domain, and their private networks remain mainly co-ethnic.

About 80 percent of respondents in my 2001 survey said that their informal contacts (people with whom they enjoy leisure, whose hands-on help they can ask for, etc.) are fellow immigrants. Only about 45 percent reported regularly meeting native Israelis at work as co-workers or clients; the majority (55 percent) either worked in the Russian ethnic sector or catered to Russian-speaking clients in the service sector (e.g., in sales, polling, and telemarketing companies) or else met Israelis as distant supervisors, which did not allow for any informal contact. Yet even respondents who were successful in their professional careers in Israel made a clear distinction between the formal domain, where they met and even befriended Israelis, and the informal circle of family and friends, all of whom spoke Russian. Co-ethnic social preferences have also been reported by young immigrants who arrived in Israel as children or teenagers (the 1.5 generation). My 2001 survey and other studies suggest that the lack of informal contact between Russian newcomers and Hebrew natives is sustained on both sides by structural barriers and social preferences, often fueled by negative stereotypes of the "other" (Fialkova and Yelenevskaya 2007). Unfortunately, Soviet immigrants of the 1970s, typically well established by the time of the last wave's arrival, played only a minor role as cultural brokers or practical aids in the adjustment of their ex-compatriots. This was due to residential and workplace separation (the old-timers live in wealthier areas and often work in tenured public sector jobs inaccessible to the newcomers) as well as ideological tension between the Zionist *olim* of the 1970s and the pragmatic *olim* of the 1990s (Golden 2002; Remennick 2004).

The third indicator of integration is the gradual shift in cultural and media consumption from one based in the language and culture of origin to mainstream cultural and media products. Apparently, this indicator of cultural transition is more salient for educated migrants, carriers of significant cultural capital from their home country, but it plays some role for all first-generation migrants (who read newspapers, watch TV, attend cultural events, etc.). A unique feature of the Israeli setting is the wide variety of venues for information and entertainment available to Russian speakers: More than 300 Russian book, video, and music stores are spread across Israel; there are several national dailies and weeklies in Russian plus popular magazines and literary almanacs; and several TV channels (one produced in Israel, others transmitted from the former Soviet Union) are received in almost every immigrant home. Russian libraries, amateur drama societies, and live tours by Russian artists and musicians in Israel complete the picture. Adult Russian immigrants show great persistence in their preference for Russian cultural products; even after 8–10 years spent in Israel, the core of their cultural and media basket remains Russian, although over time younger immigrants add some mainstream media products to this basket, for example, listening to Hebrew radio stations and buying the weekend edition of *Ma'ariv*. Younger immigrants read for pleasure almost solely in Russian, whereas their work-, study-, and information-related reading is also in Hebrew and/or English. Television-viewing patterns exhibit the greatest diversity; more than 50 percent watch Russian, Israeli, and international channels. Younger immigrants (under age 30) manifest similar patterns of cultural and media consumption, but with a larger weight of Hebrew and international media products compared to Russian ones and a greater portion of electronic media (TV, Internet) compared to print media. Israeli Russian Internet sites (offering the news, political and dating forums, e-commerce, etc.) have mushroomed over the last decade; they are frequented by computer-literate immigrants of all ages. It can be concluded that Russian-based products remain rather central on the cultural menu of the arrivals of the 1990s and will probably remain so also for their children.

The fourth indicator of social insertion has to do with civic and political participation of recent immigrants. As mentioned, all Jewish immigrants become Israeli citizens upon arrival and are therefore entitled to vote, run for political office, and participate in political life. Given the size of the immigrant population in the Jewish electorate, many Israeli politicians started courting immigrant voters, helping them to appreciate their own political potential. In the mid-1990s the Israeli political scene witnessed an upsurge of Russian ethnic politics, heralded by the great electoral success of Natan Sharansky's party Israel be-Aliya, which won 6 Knesset seats (among 120) in the 1996 election. Other Russian-origin politicians (Avigdor Lieberman on the right and Roman Bronfman on the left, to name just a few key figures) joined the race, resulting in the consolidation of a sizable Russian lobby at all levels of national and local (municipal) politics, backed up by more than 400,000 Russian votes.

The presence of *recent* immigrants in the national legislature and in several cabinet posts that they have held over the last decade is another unique feature of the Israeli political scene, unparalleled in most immigration-receiving countries. The activities of immigrant politicians and their visibility in the Israeli media peaked in the mid- to late 1990s but started to lose momentum by the early 2000s. The immigrant voters were disappointed by the lack of tangible achievements of their elected representatives on the economic front (e.g., improving terms of employment and access to public housing for immigrants) and in the contest with religious parties in matters of personal status that turn non-Jewish immigrants into second-class citizens (e.g., civil marriage, divorce, and burial of non-Jews). The *olim* voters realized that, like most other Israeli politicians, their alleged lobbyists strive mainly to keep their posts and personal benefits (Feldman 2003). Thus the outburst of Russian ethnic politics came to an end by the 2002 elections, when most Russian immigrants voted for the mainstream Israeli parties (mainly Likud, Shinui, and Ehud Leumi, representing the right wing) and Sharansky's party won only two seats. Soon after that three immigrant parties merged with regular Israeli parties as immigrant factions, and by 2006 even these had dissolved. At the time of this writing, all Russian politicians were marginal figures in the Kadima-based ruling coalition, with the exception of Lieberman, who mainstreamed his ultraright party by recruiting native Hebrew politicians and focusing mostly on the Arab-Israeli conflict.

Apart from political parties, the community life of the "Russian street" featured several voluntary associations that started from local activist groups and gradually achieved national scope. The most prominent of them is the Union of the Veterans of the Second World War—a national umbrella organization that embraces dozens of local veteran societies. The Union organized various social and cultural activities for its members, and its pivotal achievement has been the inclusion of May 9 (the official Victory Day in the USSR) in Israel's national holiday calendar. As a result of the veterans' persistent public outreach efforts, more native Israelis are aware of the Soviet Union's role in the victory over the Nazis and of Jewish soldiers' and officers' heroism during the war. Another Russian immigrant organization that gained national recognition is SOS Chernobyl, which represents 140,000 *olim* who came from regions in Ukraine, Belorussia, and Russia that were affected by the radioactive fallout from the 1986 Chernobyl nuclear disaster (Remennick 2002a). In Israel these immigrants lobbied for special benefits they had received as victims of radioactive contamination in their home countries, including tax reductions, special medical follow-up, and free medications. Recently, the map of the immigrant civic groups was further enlarged by several organizations that cater to women's and family matters (the associations of single parents and ethnically mixed families) and provide legal counseling and other forms of aid to their membership.

Thus, despite the Soviet legacy of forced collectivism and deeply entrenched mistrust of formal organizations, over the past decade former Soviet immigrants have demonstrated their ability to build alliances for the pursuit of mutual goals (Al-Haj 2002). Many of these organizations proved to be short-lived and prone to conflicts over leadership, so the bulk of community life still happens on the grapevine, that is, by means of informal personal networking (Remennick 2007: 127). However, most surveys among Russian immigrants show that, although they shy away from organized politics, they closely follow turbulent events in and around Israel and assert themselves as Israeli patriots, some as Jewish nationalists (around 15–20 percent). Most Russian immigrants are regular voters in both national and local elections (usually for right-wing candidates) and believe in their ability to influence Israeli society and its future (Al-Haj 2002; Feldman 2003).

The fifth factor shaping the pace and scope of integration is the dominant attitude of the hegemonic majority toward the immigrant community in question. A more open and inclusive attitude of the hosts is conducive to mutual tolerance, biculturalism, and greater participation of newcomers in the host social institutions. Surveys in Hebrew-speaking samples (Feldman 2003; Lewin-Epstein et al. 1997; Remennick 2003c) generally suggest that old-timer Israelis show relatively little interest in Russian immigrants and are influenced by the negative stereotypes conveyed in the mainstream media, where Russians are often portrayed as "Mafia men, prostitutes, and welfare mothers" (Lemish 2000). The segment of Israeli society more open to and inclusive of immigrants consists of younger, secular, middle-class Ashkenazi respondents, who are ready to befriend and/or date Russian partners, would like to know the Russian language, attend Russian cultural events, and so on. At the other end of the social structure—among religious, *mizrahi* (Middle Eastern origin), and less educated groups—Russian immigrants are often perceived as suspect because of their secular lifestyle, questionable Jewish affinity, and general "otherness."

Thus integration is segmented also in the sense that Ashkenazi Russian Jews have a chance to join the segment of Israeli society with a similar social profile (European origin, educated, and secular). This incorporation does happen, mainly within middle-class professional circles, but it is often limited to the institutional realm (workplace, studies). Sadly, the sociocultural gap between Russian Israelis and the Hebrew majority is maintained on both sides, drawing on mutual negative stereotypes and inertia (because bridging the gaps takes initiative and effort).

From Integration to Separatism: Continuum or Mosaic?

In a nutshell, the profile of the most integrated (i.e., bicultural) immigrants that emerged in recent social research (see Remennick 2007) includes characteristics such as immigrating before the age of 30, having a higher level of education and successful professional or white-collar employment, having been in Israel for a longer period of life, having school-age children, coming from the largest metropolitan centers of the former Soviet Union, and being born of two Jewish parents. In my estimate, about one-third of the post-1989 immigrants of working age fit this profile and thus are rather well integrated into Israel. Most adult ethnic return migrants (especially the older and retired ones) experienced significant social and economic marginalization; although most have found ways to make a living and navigate Israeli institutions, they often feel estranged from the mainstream. Overall, no significant gender differences have been found in the extent of integration, although typical venues for joining the host society are somewhat varied. Men were more integrated in the instrumental respects (professional success and income), whereas women invested more effort on the social side of integration (better Hebrew proficiency, more contacts with veteran Israelis, adoption of local everyday culture). The role of children as catalysts of parental cultural-linguistic transition reflects the faster pace of acculturation in young migrants who attend Israeli schools, learn Hebrew, and strive to join the majority culture, pushing their parents in the same direction—for example, by bringing home their Hebrew-speaking friends and watching local TV. In the context of ethnic return migration, Jewish descent is also conducive to integration, probably through stronger national identity and affiliation with Israeli values. Besides that, former Soviet Jews are typified by a more advanced educational and occupational profile compared to non-Jews (Remennick 2002b; Tolts 2000), and their greater human capital may facilitate the integration process.

On the theoretical level my findings suggest that integration and separatism are not a zero-sum phenomenon but rather a continuum including multiple transitional states and combinations. Individually, most working-age immigrants manifest some degree of integration into the institutional realm, because they must make a living and have to develop basic technical and social skills that allow them to navigate the Israeli labor market. Yet even those who are successful in their new professional lives often choose to remain ethnic separatists in the domestic and private domain, preferring to date and marry Russian partners, watching Russian TV, listening to Russian music, and so on. In most cases this separatism does not reflect political or national identification with Russia, Ukraine, or other home countries in the former Soviet Union but rather habit, convenience, and nostalgia for the "great Russian culture," especially among immigrants with limited command of Hebrew and English—a gateway to Israeli and global culture (Epstein and Kheimets 2000; Feldman 2003). Therefore I argue that the immigrant community in question—Russian Jews in Israel—is both integrated and separatist. There is no paradox in this assertion if we regard integration and acculturation as segmented experiences that together shape a complex lifestyle mosaic. By segmentation I mean the differential extent to which various domains of immigrants' lives are affected by contact with the host society. Immigrants who are seemingly well integrated at work and are fairly confident in various public contexts (shopping malls, banks, hospitals, etc.) may become Russian the moment they cross the doorstep of their home, party with their immigrant friends, or consider marital partners for their children.

A lot of what we call integration is in fact an adaptive, instrumental response aimed at survival and adjustment in the new environment. The cultural core, shaped by premigration socialization, remains largely intact, and adaptive behavioral layers (new language, social and technical skills, appearance, etc.) are glued on top of it, gradually forming a thick external shell that makes a person practically bicultural. The term *adhesive acculturation* is another good metaphor to describe this process. In general, there is usually more integration occurring in the public or formal realm than in the private or informal realm. Personal relationships, family life, and networks of friends are the least affected by the demands of integration. Similar conclusions were made by Berry (1990) for Canadian immigrant experiences and by Nauck (2001) for various immigrant minorities in Germany, including ethnic returnees (*Aussiedler*). Younger immigrants who spent similar parts of their lives in the former Soviet Union and in Israel (the 1.5 generation) are fluent in Hebrew and well integrated into Israeli social institutions (college, the military, etc.); yet in the informal domain they also show a strong tendency toward cultural retention and social preference for their co-ethnics as friends and dates (Remennick 2005a). Similar findings have been reported by Kasinitz et al. (2001), who interviewed young Russian Jews in New York, and by several scholars writing about Russian Jews in Germany (e.g., Jasper and Vogt 2000). The new transnational opportunities within the global post-Soviet diaspora further reinforce Russian cultural continuity among immigrants in various host countries, often serving as a disincentive for social integration into the country of their residence and/or citizenship. The future will show whether the second generation of Russian Jews in Israel (and elsewhere) will also cherish their cultural roots.

Notes

1. A more elaborate account of the Russian Jewish immigrant experience of the last 20 years can be found in my recent book, *Russian Jews on Three Continents* (Remennick 2007).

2. In this chapter I focus on the majority of former Soviet Jews (at least 85 percent) who are of Ashkenazi ethnic descent and who emigrated from the Slavic part of the former Soviet Union. Jews originating from the Caucasus Mountains and Central Asia (Georgian Jews, Tats, and Bukharans) represent a distinct group among former Soviet immigrants and typically form their own residential enclaves and cultural communities. Because of their ethnocultural differences from Eastern European Jews, this group is beyond the scope of this short chapter.

3. The emergence of a Russian economic sector is neither surprising nor problematic in the context of mass migration, but it rarely serves as a bridge for newcomers to enter the mainstream labor market. Russian business ventures are usually small and short-lived and cater to the consumption and service needs of the community (grocery and book stores, small real estate and legal offices, hairdressers, etc.). Small businesses were often an attempt at economic survival for educated immigrants who could not find work in the mainstream Hebrew-based labor market; once trapped in this marginal economic niche, few immigrants could later return to their original occupation (Lerner and Hendeles 1996).

References Cited

Al-Haj, Majid. 2002. "Ethnic Mobilization in an Ethno-National State: The Case of Immigrants from the Former Soviet Union in Israel." *Ethnic and Racial Studies* 25(2):238–257.

Berry, John W. 1990. "Psychology of Acculturation: Understanding Individuals Moving Between Cultures." In *Applied Cross-Cultural Psychology*, R. W. Brislin, ed. London: Sage, 232–253.

Capo Zmegac, Jasna. 2005. "Ethnically Privileged Migrants in Their New Homelands." *Journal of Refugee Studies* 18(2):199–215.

Epstein, Alek, and Nina Kheimets. 2000. "Immigrant Intelligentsia and Its Second Generation: Cultural Segregation as a Road to Social Integration?" *Journal of International Migration and Integration* 1:461–476.

Feldman, Eliezer. 2003. *"Russkii" Izrail: Mezhdu Dvuh Polusov* ["Russian" Israel: Between the Two Poles]. Moscow: Market DS.

Fialkova, Larisa, and Maria N. Yelenevskaya. 2007. *Ex-Soviets in Israel: From Personal Narratives to a Group Portrait.* Detroit, MI: Wayne State University Press.

Golden, Deborah. 2002. "Storytelling the Future: Israelis, Immigrants, and the Imagining of Community." *Anthropological Quarterly* 75(1):7–35.

IMIA (Israeli Ministry of Immigrant Absorption). 2004. *Geographic Distribution and Social Characteristics of Immigrants from the FSU.* Jerusalem: IMIA Publications (in Hebrew).

Jasper, Willi, and Bernhard Vogt. 2000. "Integration and Self-Assertion." In *Jews in Germany After 1945: Citizens or "Fellow Citizens"?* O. Romberg and S. Urban-Fahr, eds. Frankfurt: Tribune, 217–227.

Joppke, Christian, and Zeev Rosenhek. 2002. "Contesting Ethnic Immigration: Germany and Israel Compared." *Archives of European Sociology* 43:301–335.

Kasinitz, Philip, Aviva Zeltzer-Zubida, and Zoya Simakhodskaya. 2001. *The Next Generation: Russian Jewish Young Adults in Contemporary New York.* New York: Russell Sage Foundation. http://www.russellsage.org/publications/workingpapers.

Kimmerling, Baruch. 2001. *The Invention and Decline of Israeliness: State, Society, and the Military.* Berkeley: University of California Press.

Lemish, Dafna. 2000. "The Whore and the Other: Israeli Images of Female Immigrants from the Former USSR." *Gender and Society* 14(2):333–349.

Lerner, Miri, and Yitzhak Hendeles. 1996. "New Entrepreneurs and Entrepreneurial Aspirations Among Immigrants from the Former USSR in Israel." *Journal of Business Research* 36:136–151.

Levy, Daniel, and Yifat Weiss, eds. 2002. *Challenging Ethnic Citizenship: German and Israeli Perspectives on Immigration.* New York: Berghahn Books.

Lewin-Epstein, Noah, Gila Menahem, and Ruth Barham. 1997. "Yes to Immigration But What About Immigrants? Local Attitudes to Immigrant Absorption." In *Russian Jews on Three Continents: Migration and Resettlement,* N. Lewin-Epstein, Y. Ro'I, and P. Ritterband, eds. London: Frank Cass, 471–494.

Lomsky-Feder, Edna, and Tamar Rapoport. 2001. "Homecoming, Immigration, and the National Ethos: Russian-Jewish Home-Comers Reading Zionism." *Anthropological Quarterly* 74(1):1–14.

Markowitz, Fran. 1994. "Responding to Events from Afar: Soviet Jewish Refugees Reassess Their Identity." In *Reconstructing Lives, Recapturing Meaning: Refugee Identity, Gender, and Culture Change,* Linda A. Camino and Ruth M. Krulfeld, eds. London: Gordon and Breach, 57–69.

Nauck, Bernhard. 2001. "Social Capital, Intergenerational Transmission, and Intercultural Contact in Immigrant Families." *Journal of Comparative Family Studies* 32:465–488.

Reitz, Jeffrey. 2001. "Immigrant Success in the 'Knowledge Economy': Institutional Change and the Immigrant Experience in Canada, 1970–1995." *Journal of Social Issues* 57(3):579–613.

Remennick, Larissa. 2002a. "Immigrants from Chernobyl-Affected Areas in Israel: The Link Between Health and Social Adjustment." *Social Science and Medicine* 54(2):309–317.

———. 2002b. "Transnational Community in the Making: Russian Jewish Immigrants of the 1990s in Israel." *Journal of Ethnic and Migration Studies* 28(3):515–530.

———. 2003a. "Career Continuity Among Immigrant Professionals: Russian Engineers in Israel." *Journal of Ethnic and Migration Studies* 29(4):701–721.

———. 2003b. "Language Acquisition as the Main Vehicle of Social Integration: The Case of Russian Jewish Immigrants in Israel." *International Journal of the Sociology of Language* 164:83–105.

———. 2003c. "What Does Integration Mean? Social Insertion of Russian Jewish Immigrants in Israel." *Journal of International Migration and Integration* 4(1):23–48.

———. 2004. "Work Relations Between Immigrants and Old-Timers in an Israeli Organization: Social Interactions and Inter-Group Attitudes." *International Journal of Comparative Sociology* 45(1–2):43–69.

———. 2005a. "Cross-Cultural Dating Patterns on an Israeli Campus: Why Are Russian Immigrant Women More Popular than Men?" *Journal of Social and Personal Relationships* 22(4):435–454.

———. 2005b. "Idealists Headed for Israel, Pragmatics Chose Europe: Identity Dilemmas and Social Incorporation Among Former Soviet Jews Who Migrated to Germany." *Immigrants and Minorities* 23(1):30–58.

———. 2007. *Russian Jews on Three Continents: Identity, Integration, and Conflict.* New Brunswick, NJ: Transaction.

Shuval, Judith T. 1998. "Migration to Israel: The Mythology of 'Uniqueness.'" *International Migration* 36(1):1–23.

Shuval, Judith T., and Judith Bernstein, eds. 1997. *Immigrant Physicians: Former Soviet Doctors in Israel, Canada, and the United States.* Westport, CT: Praeger.

Tolts, Mark. 2000. "Russian Jewish Migration in the Post-Soviet Era." *Revue Européenne des Migrations Internationales* 16:183–199.

Ethnic Return Migration to East Asia

Global Inequities and Diasporic Return

Japanese American and Brazilian Encounters with the Ethnic Homeland

Takeyuki Tsuda

Global Hierarchies and Ethnic Return Migration

The ethnic homecomings of diasporic descendants who return to their countries of ethnic origin are fraught with difficulties. Although ethnic return migrants often feel a sense of nostalgic transnational affinity toward their ancestral homelands, their diasporic homecomings are often quite ambivalent, if not negative, experiences because they are socially marginalized as cultural foreigners and unskilled immigrant workers.

Nonetheless, ethnic homecomings vary considerably for different groups of diasporic return migrants, even those who are "returning" to the same ethnic homeland. A case in point are Japanese Brazilians and Japanese Americans who migrate to Japan. Although both groups have identical ethnic origins as descendants of Japanese who immigrated to the Americas, because of their different nationalities as Brazilians and Americans, they have quite divergent ethnic experiences in their ethnic homeland of Japan. Whereas Japanese Brazilians are subject to ethnic and socioeconomic marginalization and come to assert a defensive, nationalist Brazilian counteridentity in response to their negative experiences in Japanese society, Japanese Americans have much more positive interactions with native Japanese and develop a more accommodating transnational and cosmopolitan ethnic consciousness in response to their sojourn in Japan. I argue that such disparate ethnic homecomings among Japanese diasporic descendants from the Americas are mainly a product of the different international positions of Brazil and the United States in the global hierarchy of nations.

The relative social integration of various immigrant groups into the host society is determined by two types of factors. One type is the external sociopolitical reception of the immigrant group by the host country, which depends on its immigration and citizenship policies, domestic labor market, educational system, and level of ethnic discrimination (Portes and Rumbaut 1996: ch. 3; Reitz 2003). The social integration of a specific immigrant group tends to be better if the group is legally accepted and granted basic sociopolitical rights, has more occupational and educational opportunities in the host society, and suffers less ethnic discrimination and marginalization. The other general determinant of immigrant integration is the internal characteristics of the immigrants themselves, which includes the amount of human capital (e.g., education, skills, language ability) and social capital (ethnicity, gender, social class background) they bring with them to the host society (Borjas 1995; Portes and Rumbaut 2001; Sanders and Nee 1987; Zhou and Logan 1989).[1] The general assumption is that immigrant groups with greater human and social capital will be more economically successful and socially accepted and will have more positive immigrant experiences. Ultimately, it is a combination of external host society reception and the human and social capital that immigrants possess that determines their socioeconomic success and integration.[2]

However, one important determinant of the incorporation and acceptance of immigrants that is sometimes overlooked is the status of their sending countries in the global hierarchy of nations. The sending country's geopolitical and economic position not only affects the political and legal reception of its emigrants abroad but also influences their position in the labor market and their cultural and social acceptability. Just as global racial hierarchies (based on a continuum from white to black) affect the social reception of immigrants around the world, global national hierarchies also influence perceptions of different immigrant groups and can sometimes have a greater impact on their experiences than do other human and social capital variables, such as sociooccupational qualifications and ethnic attributes (Tsuda 2001).

Nowhere is this more apparent than in the case of Japanese Brazilian and Japanese American ethnic return migration to Japan. Their disparate ethnic homecomings in Japan cannot simply be explained by their external sociopolitical context of reception in Japan, which is quite similar. Both are legally admitted to Japan as migrants on short-term visas,[3] become part of the same Japanese socioeconomic system, and occupy the same privileged status in the Japanese ethnoracial hierarchy as *nikkeijin* (Japanese descendants born and raised abroad). They are also roughly comparable in terms of human capital (both are relatively well educated and highly skilled with similar levels of

Japanese language competence)[4] and social capital (both are Japanese-descent *nikkeijin* who share an equal racial and cultural affinity with the Japanese and have middle-class socio-occupational backgrounds).

Japanese Americans experience a more favorable ethnic homecoming than Japanese Brazilians do primarily because of the much greater international stature of the United States compared to Brazil. America's status as a rich economic superpower ensures that Japanese Americans migrate to Japan as high-status professionals and students, whereas Japanese Brazilians, despite their similar ethnic and socioeconomic background, are in Japan as unskilled factory workers in response to economic uncertainty in "third world" Brazil. As a result, not only do Japanese Americans have a much better workplace experience, they also interact with more educated and cosmopolitan middle-class Japanese who are more receptive to foreigners. In contrast, Japanese Brazilians must deal primarily with less educated working-class Japanese who have a much more parochial outlook. The much greater international prominence of the United States and its global cultural dominance also mean that the Japanese have greater cultural affinity to Japanese Americans and treat them with much more respect, compared to the ethnic prejudice and denigration that Japanese Brazilians experience.[5] Nonetheless, as Takanaka observes in Chapter 10, Japanese Brazilians still enjoy a higher ethnic status in Japan than Japanese *Peruvian* ethnic return migrants, who are supposedly from a nation that is even lower in the global order. In this manner the global hierarchy of migrant-sending countries translates directly into ethnic hierarchies among immigrant groups in the receiving country.

Thus, the national origins of immigrants should be considered an important social capital variable that will influence their eventual social incorporation or marginalization as well as their ethnic status. Even for immigrants of the same ethnic ancestry residing in the same host society, those from advanced industrialized countries will tend to have more favorable immigrant and ethnic experiences than those from developing countries. In this sense geography is destiny.

Differential Social Class Position and Divergent Ethnic Homecomings
Unskilled Immigrant Workers Versus Tourists, Students, and Professionals

The main reason for the divergent diasporic homecomings of Japanese Brazilians and Japanese Americans is their different social class status as immigrants in Japan, which is a direct product of the position of their countries of origin in the global order and not of differences in their socioeconomic background.

Although both groups of *nikkeijin* are solidly middle class and highly educated (both are overrepresented at top universities) and are predominantly white-collar professionals or business owners in their respective countries of origin, because of Brazil's much lower global position, Japanese Brazilians are employed in Japan's factories as unskilled migrant laborers, whereas their *nikkeijin* counterparts from the United States are in Japan as part of the global educational and professional elite. As a result, Japanese Brazilians have much more negative experiences in their ethnic homeland than Japanese Americans do.

The return migration of Japanese Brazilians was caused by a severe economic crisis in South America in the late 1980s and a labor shortage in the Japanese economy in the same period. Because of the significant difference in per capita income between Brazil and Japan, the Brazilian *nikkeijin* were more than eager to return-migrate and fill low-level factory jobs in their ethnic homeland, where they could earn five to ten times their middle-class Brazilian incomes. With a current immigrant population of close to 300,000, they have become the second-largest group of foreigners in Japan after the Chinese, and their numbers continue to increase at a steady pace.[6]

Many of the negative experiences that Japanese Brazilians have in Japan are conditioned by their low socioeconomic status as unskilled immigrant workers. For them, migration involves a dramatic declassing, as those who were middle-class professionals in Brazil become unskilled laborers toiling away in dirty, dangerous, and difficult factory jobs that most educated native Japanese actively shun. Although they go to Japan psychologically prepared to take on such degrading jobs because of the financial incentives, the sudden decline in social class status still comes as a shock to many of them. For instance, a second-generation Brazilian *nikkeijin* woman remarked:

> You go to Japan ready for the low level jobs you have to do in the factory. We know our social status will decline in Japan, and you accept this as a necessary consequence in order to earn money. But still, when you first put on that factory uniform and take your place on the assembly line, it really hurts. It damages your pride.

Many Japanese Brazilians also complain about the monotonous, tedious, repetitive, and physically demanding nature of factory work.

Because of their status as unskilled migrant workers, many Brazilian *nikkeijin* experience social marginalization and supposedly negative and discriminatory treatment at the hands of the Japanese. In contrast to the relatively congenial working environment they enjoyed in Brazil as white-collar professionals in air-conditioned offices, they are subjected to a noisy, alienating factory work environment where social interaction on the assembly line is minimal and often limited to Japanese supervisors barking out orders or chastising workers for mistakes. In addition, Japanese Brazilians are employed in the most peripheral sector of the Japanese labor market and are used by Japanese companies as a disposable labor force of temporary contract workers who are borrowed from outside labor broker firms and then returned when no longer needed (Tsuda 1999). As a result, they are sometimes segregated in *nikkeijin*-only work sections, eat in separate lunchrooms, are not invited to company outings and events with Japanese workers, and are excluded from Japanese social groups on the factory floor as company outsiders. They are also the first to be fired during a production downturn. Although Japanese temporary and part-time workers are treated in a similar manner, Japanese Brazilians, as an immigrant minority, are more likely to be offended by such treatment, viewing it as ethnic "discrimination." Because of such experiences of socioeconomic marginalization and discrimination, Japanese Brazilians come to perceive the Japanese as a "cold," unaffectionate, and unfriendly people who mistreat and discriminate against even Japanese descendants from abroad (Tsuda 2003: ch. 3). The comments of one Brazilian *nikkeijin* worker are illustrative of this collective experience.

> In Brazil, people always talk to each other during work, unlike the Japanese who just work and don't say anything. . . . The Japanese are cold and don't have human warmth, even among themselves. . . . The Japanese always keep us segregated from them because of the prejudices that they have. I was almost offended when I first saw this at the factory. There are some Japanese who simply don't like us. . . . So they don't try to talk with us or make friends—they don't even speak one word to us. . . . In Brazil, this type of ethnic discrimination exists only toward blacks.
>
> Yes, there is discrimination against the [Japanese] Brazilians on the job. The Japanese have the power to decide who does which task, so they always choose the easiest work for themselves and the worst jobs come to the Brazilians. . . . And when a recession comes around, we are the first to be laid off.

In contrast, Japanese Americans, living in the most prosperous country in the world, have not yet experienced an economic crisis in recent decades that would seriously threaten their middle-class socioeconomic status, nor would they earn higher wages working in Japanese factories. As a result, only a relatively small number of them migrate to Japan, and they do so as students, business personnel, highly skilled professionals, and tourists. Of my sample of twenty Japanese Americans who had been to Japan, six went for professional or work-related reasons, six as students, and eight as tourists.

Because Japanese Americans enjoy a much more privileged social status in Japan based on the higher global economic position of the United States compared to Brazil, they have considerably more positive experiences in their ethnic homeland. Not surprisingly, those who went to Japan as tourists spoke highly, if not raved, about their trips, recalling nostalgic images of cherry blossoms and festivals, shrines and gardens, art and pottery, beautiful and idyllic scenery, bullet trains, good restaurants and food, and a generally clean, orderly, and safe society.[7] Most of them had little interaction with ordinary Japanese beyond brief encounters in restaurants, hotels, and department stores, where they are in the privileged position of customers. Those Japanese Americans who went to Japan as students (usually at the college level on exchange programs with Japanese universities) reported almost equally positive experiences.[8] Most of them interacted almost exclusively with Japanese students who were quite eager to meet and talk with American students, and they experienced the fun that accompanies student life in Japan, where academic pressures are low and social and club opportunities are abundant. For example, Barbara Kitamura, a sansei (third generation) from Hawaii, recounted her experiences fondly.

> It was overall a very positive experience. There were few expectations for students. You didn't even have to go to class. The Japanese [university] students didn't study. They just wanted to go out and play. They had an international section at the university, so I joined the student clubs there. Being a student in Japan was so much fun. I mean, you just go out all the time and drink and everything was to have fun. But I know it would be very different had I gone to Japan to work.

Because of their relatively short sojourns (weeks or months compared to years, as is the case with Japanese Brazilians), Japanese American tourists and students have a rather superficial encounter with Japan through a type of external touristic gaze and fascination that does not delve sufficiently into Japanese society to discover its negative underside.

The six Japanese Americans who went to Japan for professional or work-related reasons also had generally positive experiences based on their privileged occupational status in Japan. However, because they had lived in Japan for longer periods and had more extensive experience, they tended to give more balanced and ambivalent accounts. Consider the comments of Takeyoshi, a second-generation professor who had lived in Japan as both a student and a researcher.

> Over time, I started getting disenchanted with the romantic visions I had of Japan, because you start seeing all the warts, in addition to the cherry blossoms. I had this image of [Japanese] aesthetics that I was attracted to, so I used to love going to temples and gardens. Also museums to see the artwork. I was attracted to the exotic part of Japan. But being in Japan longer, you get this critical distance—not just how beautiful the artwork is. I was struck by things that are Japanese characteristics that I didn't like, such as the overexcessive social hierarchy, and I distanced myself from that. That was what was the most disturbing. And also the racialized nationalism.

"At first, you think everything is perfect in Japan," said Yoriko, a biracial Japanese American who had gone to Japan frequently since she was 3 years old (although never to work). "Then, when I'd go to Japan later on, I started to see the negative aspects, such as the alcoholism and the strong racism there, which I sense personally, even among my family [relatives in Japan]."

Nonetheless, such ambivalent comments were rare among my Japanese American interviewees who had been to Japan. Again, this is quite a contrast to Japanese Brazilians, among whom negative comments and criticism about the Japanese and Japanese society were frequent and positive impressions were rare, demonstrating how the differential socio-occupational status of migrants in the host society, caused by the different positioning of their countries of origin in the global order, can produce divergent ethnic homecomings.

Social Class Interactions: Parochial Versus Cosmopolitan

Japanese Brazilians and Japanese Americans also interact with different groups of Japanese because of their social class position in Japan. Because of their status as unskilled immigrant workers, Japanese Brazilians primarily interact with working-class Japanese, often in smaller, industrial satellite cities and towns (sometimes in the countryside), where many Japanese Brazilians work. Not only are such blue-collar Japanese less educated, most have never lived abroad, have had little interaction in the past with foreigners, do not speak foreign languages, and are more parochial and insular in outlook as well as more prone to ethnic prejudice. In contrast, most Japanese Americans interact with better-educated middle-class Japanese living in Japan's major "global" cities, such as

Tokyo, Osaka, and Kyoto, who tend to be better informed, more globally engaged and cosmopolitan (including Japanese who have lived abroad), and less liable to have parochial, prejudicial attitudes.

It is apparent that the social marginalization that Japanese Brazilians experience in their ethnic homeland is not simply a product of their mundane and degrading immigrant jobs but also because much of their interaction with native Japanese is confined mainly to the working class. Despite a general Japanese reluctance to interact with Japanese Brazilians, who are culturally foreign and generally do not speak Japanese, the tendency certainly seemed stronger among factory workers. At the factory where I conducted participant observation (which I will call Toyama), the Brazilian *nikkeijin* wore different-colored uniforms from the Japanese because they were temporary migrant workers contracted from outside labor broker firms. As a result, they were ethnically visible and immediately subject to social exclusion on the factory floor. I was repeatedly struck by the ethnic segregation at Toyama between Japanese and *nikkeijin* workers, who rarely exchanged any words on the assembly line and remained apart during break and lunch hours, sitting in separate rooms or at different tables. Likewise, only a few Japanese Brazilians have sustained social relationships with their Japanese co-workers outside the factory or have had contact with their Japanese neighbors.

When Japanese workers were asked about their ethnic reluctance to interact with the *nikkeijin*, they often mentioned the inability to effectively communicate because of the language barrier. Others stressed the difficulty they have relating to foreigners who are culturally different. A young Japanese who worked next to me on the assembly line elaborated.

> Because we live in an ethnically homogeneous society, we are simply bad at dealing with foreigners we don't know well and can't communicate well with. We don't cope well with ethnic diversity and are not used to people who are different, like the *nikkeijin*. We have no way to react and adapt to foreigners in our midst, so we just prefer to stay away.

I was also struck by the relatively strong ethnic prejudice among Japanese workers toward Japanese Brazilians (Tsuda 2003: ch. 2), even though the ones I interviewed tended to be more open-minded individuals who sometimes even befriended the *nikkeijin*. I was told a number of times at Toyama about Japanese workers who did not interact with *nikkeijin* foreigners simply because of ethnic dislike and derogation.

Because of their globally conditioned, relatively privileged middle-class status in Japan, Japanese Americans are exposed to a better-educated and more cosmopolitan segment of Japanese society that is much more willing to socially interact with foreigners and outsiders, which results in much more engaged and positive ethnic encounters in Japan. Therefore few Japanese Americans experience the ethnic exclusion and social marginalization in Japan that Japanese Brazilians confront on a daily basis. Much of the interaction that Japanese Americans have with "mainstream" Japanese is in the service sector (restaurants, cafes, stores, hotels, banks, etc.), where politeness and courtesy backed by ritualistic use of honorific language is the norm that is impeccably maintained whether the customer is a native or a foreigner. Of course, Japanese Brazilian immigrant workers also have plenty of contact with the Japanese service sector and report generally polite and courteous service, but most of their daily work interaction is with working-class Japanese.

Japanese Americans who are in Japan as students tend to associate with Japanese students, who are educated and cosmopolitan, interested in foreign students and countries, and often speak (or want to practice) English. For example, Tom, an undergraduate at the University of California at San Diego who lived in Japan as part of a study abroad program, recounted his experiences.

> I had lots of interaction with Japanese. In fact, that was the best part. It was only at school, but there was a group of [Japanese] students that we'd always meet for lunch. We became really good friends with them. They were learning to speak English, so were interested in us. They would speak some English to us and we'd try out our Japanese, but most of the time it was English, because their English was good. They'd also come to our dorms and we'd party. They loved it, because it was different for them. They were interested in foreigners.

"The [Japanese] students were always very nice," another former exchange student in Japan remarked. "Because the university was very strong in international studies, they had an international consciousness and knew we were foreigners on exchange. So the students were always very accommodating and helpful. Some of them were curious about my ethnic background. I can't remember any bad experiences." Undoubtedly, because Japanese Americans and the Japanese in this case share the same social status as students, this facilitated interaction across cultural and linguistic barriers, as Tom noted:

> I didn't feel that much difference from the Japanese students. Yes, there are cultural differences, but both of us were students. They basically wanted to do the

same things I wanted to do. It was no big deal. I did feel the cultural gap—they knew about Japanese cultural things much better—but in everyday interaction, I didn't feel much difference.

Those Japanese Americans working in Japan as professionals may be in a less congenial and more serious and formal corporate environment, but their daily social relationships are still with relatively elite and cosmopolitan Japanese and they do not experience the overt ethnic segregation of Japanese Brazilians. One third-generation Japanese American who was in Japan as the spouse of a Japanese university professor (and was planning to work there in the future) spoke quite clearly about this.

> I don't exactly interact with ordinary Japanese because most of my associations are through the university, where I'm introduced to [my wife's] colleagues. Partly because of the language barrier, I do feel distant with them, but it's natural to their society. They don't open their arms and welcome everyone, even other Japanese, much less a foreigner like me. So I don't take it personally. It's just their culture. But I don't feel I am not socially accepted. In fact, I feel much more accepted than I thought, based on the descriptions I had heard of the Japanese. But again, these are highly educated people who know other cultures, not your ordinary Japanese.

In this manner, the global stature of the migrant-sending country can play a significant role in determining whether ethnic return migrants have positive or negative experiences in their homeland. Although there are Japanese Brazilians who are in Japan as tourists, students, and professionals and who have more positive ethnic experiences than their compatriots, because Brazil is a poorer country than the United States, their number is quite small compared to Japanese Americans. As a result, they do not sufficiently affect the generally negative ethnic homecoming of Japanese Brazilians.

Global Cultural Affinities and Ethnic Homecomings

In addition to their higher social status in Japan, Japanese Americans benefit from the international prominence of the United States in another way. Japanese feel more cultural affinity toward Americans and treat them with greater ethnic respect than they do foreigners from other countries, especially "backward" developing countries such as Brazil, which are not accorded much stature and respect in Japan.

Japanese Brazilians frequently complain about the lack of knowledge of Brazil among Japanese factory workers, who supposedly believe it is an impoverished, crime-ridden, undeveloped country with jungles, Indians, and crocodiles. "All that they show in Japan [i.e., on TV] about Brazil is the Amazon, poverty, crime, and Carnaval, and they never show the good or developed parts of the country," a Brazilian *nikkeijin* woman complained, echoing the dominant sentiments of her compatriots. "Few know about São Paulo or Avenida Paulista [the central business district in São Paulo]." Japanese Brazilians also frequently claim that they (or their acquaintances) are asked whether Brazil has electricity, cars, TVs, and telephones. Other questions include how close they live to the Amazon, whether they wear shirts and shoes in Brazil, whether they carry guns, or whether Indians walk naked in the streets.[9]

Many Japanese are also not aware that Japanese Brazilians are middle-class professionals living in developed cities in Brazil, not impoverished and desperate migrants from a developing country. A retired Japanese worker from Toyama shared this dominant perception with me:

> I hear conditions are terrible in Brazil and they can't live over there, so they come to Japan for the money and are stuffed six to a room in pig pens by labor broker companies who don't treat them as humans. Since the cost of living here is much higher, they find they can't survive in Japan and can't buy anything because it's too expensive.

Even better-informed middle-class Japanese tended to view *nikkeijin* immigrants as poor people from an underdeveloped country. Two groups of Japanese undergraduate and graduate students on assignments to interview Japanese Brazilians were surprised that they were not miserable, wretched people but individuals who lived in standard Japanese apartments (instead of in squalor) and were "properly dressed with nice shirts and socks."

Japanese Brazilians were acutely aware of such mistaken Japanese perceptions. "The Japanese think we were really poor in Brazil, living in *favelas* [shantytowns] and suffering from hunger," one of them observed. "They have no idea that we had sufficient conditions to live in Brazil, or that many of us are well-educated." Others went further. "The Japanese think we live like wild Indians in the Amazon without toilets and that we bathe in the river nearby," one *nikkeijin* woman claimed. "I get this impression from the questions that they ask about Brazil." A common story told by Japanese Brazilians is about how they (or an acquaintance) showed photographs of their houses and possessions in Brazil to Japanese workers, who were surprised and amazed at their relatively high middle-class living standards back home and wondered why they had come to Japan as lowly migrant workers if they had lived so well.

Many Brazilian *nikkeijin* in Japan are offended by the stereotypes about Brazil as a backward and primitive country with poor people and feel ethnically stigmatized by such Japanese attitudes. Few of them encounter Japanese who have respect for (or even know anything about) Brazil, Brazilian culture, or their ethnic background (although in actuality, there are a few). Some of them were even concerned that *nikkeijin* who acted too "Brazilian" in Japan (or even flaunted their Brazilianness) by talking loudly in Portuguese, engaging in publicly overt displays of affection, wearing loud "Brazilian" clothes, and disturbing Japanese neighbors by making noise in their apartments were worsening the already negative Japanese image of Brazilians in Japan (Tsuda 2003: ch. 6).

In vivid contrast, the economic, cultural, and political status of the United States as a global leader has been admired and emulated by Japan for more than a century, beginning with its efforts to modernize and catch up to the West during the Meiji Period and continuing with its post–World War II recovery with American assistance and military protection and its subsequent development of close diplomatic, economic, and cultural ties with the United States. As a result, Japanese know a lot about the United States, study English, and embrace American popular culture and media, and a good number have traveled to or have lived in the United States as tourists, businessmen, and students. Therefore a number of Japanese I interviewed noted that they felt a much greater cultural affinity and familiarity toward Japanese Americans and could at least culturally relate to them and attempt to communicate in English, whereas Japanese Brazilians were much more culturally alien and spoke a language with which the Japanese had no familiarity. In fact, at the Toyama factory, some Japanese supervisors would try to communicate with their Japanese Brazilian workers using what little English they could speak, usually to no avail.

Therefore, although Japanese Brazilians in Brazil have actually retained the Japanese language and culture more than their *nikkeijin* counterparts in the United States, because they are "newer" immigrant minorities (second and third generation, vs. Japanese Americans, who are mainly third and fourth generation) who have faced less historical and current pressure to assimilate to mainstream society, such cultural affinities seem to be negated by the greater familiarity that Japanese have with Americans. In addition, Japanese tend to regard Japanese Americans with greater respect as well-educated middle-class professionals from a rich country, not poor people from a backward country.

Such benefits of being American in Japan were especially felt by Japanese Americans who lived in Japan for extended periods of time and had sustained contact with native Japanese. For them, their Americanness was more of an ethnic asset and a source of interest than a disadvantage because of the cultural affinity and favorable perceptions Japanese have toward the United States. This was quite apparent from the comments of the following two Japanese Americans:

I think Japanese attitudes toward Japanese Americans are positive. A lot of [Japanese] people wish they could go to the U.S. There's even a sense of awe. Japanese like to come here and go to Vegas. They like American popular culture, American movies, and American franchises are everywhere, so they are pretty aware of Americans. So having an American background is quite positive.

I didn't feel any prejudice being a foreigner in Japan, except the language thing. The Japanese friends I chose were really interested in America and American pop culture. I was their informant about America, and they seemed to like me for that. My Americanness was therefore more of an asset than anything else.

Indeed, there are even Japanese Americans who feel a sense of superiority in Japan, such as John, who was a fully bicultural second-generation nisei with extensive experience living in Japan. "In Japan, my ethnicity isn't really an issue because in the end, I'm like, 'Sorry, America is above you, Japan,'" he said. "You don't tell me what to do, I tell you what to do. I'm arrogant and egotistical. I feel this superiority in Japan as an American. In fact, I make a point that I'm American."

Even those who briefly visited Japan experienced the cultural affinity and positive perceptions that Japanese have of Americans. According to one Japanese American woman who had been in Japan as a tourist:

One time, we were stuck in a remote area at night without a train ticket with two other Caucasians, and this Japanese man picked us up with his car and drove us back home. He had lived in the U.S., spoke some English, and was really kind and nice. He probably saw my Caucasian friends and assumed we were American and therefore decided to be really nice.

Unlike Japanese Brazilians, none of my informants reported being ethnically stigmatized or denigrated in Japan. In fact, only two of my informants reported any possible negative perceptions of Japanese Americans in Japan.[10]

The global prominence of the United States has also created another, less apparent transnational cultural affinity between Japan and the United States: a small but younger generation of truly bicultural cosmopolitan Japanese Americans able to be socially accepted in both societies. As Japan became economically prosperous after World War II, large-scale Japanese labor migration to the Americas ceased. However, because of its international stature, a small number of Japanese continued to migrate to the United States for educational, professional, or business reasons, and a number of them settled permanently. This produced a new, postwar second generation of Japanese American children, a number of whom attended Japanese Saturday schools for the children of Japanese businessmen temporarily residing in the United States. In addition, because their Japanese parents were from a higher and more elite segment of Japanese society (in contrast to earlier Japanese immigrants, who were predominantly from poor rural areas), they tended to maintain strong ties to Japan and often traveled back with their children, enabling them to experience both countries. Unlike the older, pre–World War II nisei, who suffered from discrimination, were interned in concentration camps, and felt the need to assimilate and demonstrate their loyalty as Americans, these new second-generation nisei grew up in an American society that has come to accept multiculturalism; in addition, Japan's postwar rise to global prominence has made it acceptable, if not advantageous, to identify with Japan and to maintain transnational cultural and social connections to their ethnic homeland in a globalized era where such cross-border affiliations have become quite common.

Three Japanese Americans from my sample were fully bilingual and bicultural nisei who had traveled often to Japan since childhood and had attended Japanese Saturday schools in the United States with Japanese children. For such cosmopolitan individuals,[11] Japan was never truly a foreign country, and they are able to sufficiently speak and "act Japanese" to the point where they have no trouble being socially accepted in Japan and feel quite comfortable living there. Consider the experiences of Mark, a bicultural nisei who had worked in Japan.

> My experiences in Japan are quite positive. I can easily switch to a Japanese identity. Otherwise, if you stick out, you make things difficult for yourself there. I know how to be Japanese because growing up, my mom taught me Japanese manners, customs, and spoke both languages to me. I had plenty of Japanese friends growing up and related well to my teachers and peers at Japanese school, so knew what Japanese culture was like. Interacting with Japanese in general

is pretty natural for me. So in terms of living in Japan, it was very easy and comfortable for me. . . . It was sort of a reproduction of my Japanese school experiences in the U.S.

In fact, such Japanese Americans have the ability to assert whichever ethnic identity makes their adaptation to Japan easier. "I can be totally accepted as Japanese in Japan if I want," remarked John, another bicultural nisei. "I used to be really sensitive about acting Japanese in Japan. It used to bother me when the Japanese saw me as different. So I felt I had to be more Japanese than other Japanese people. But now I make it clear that I'm different, that I'm American. That's fine in Japan because so many Japanese come to the states, so they are familiar with the U.S. It makes it easier that way because I don't have to be Japanese and can act whatever way I want."

"I make a conscious effort to blend in in Japan and speak mostly Japanese," said Kiyoshi. "When I talk loudly with my sister in English in the subway, people start looking at you. But there are certain times when I identify as American because I don't care, and speak English with my sister."

Because of Brazil's lower socioeconomic status, Brazil did not attract Japanese middle-class and business elites after World War II, nor did it create transnational economic, cultural, or political ties with Japan that would help foster such transnational biculturalism among Japanese Brazilians. This is not to say that there are no bilingual second-generation Japanese Brazilians. As noted, Brazilian *nikkeijin* have done a better job of maintaining the Japanese language than Japanese Americans for various reasons. However, most Brazilian nisei did not have opportunities to travel to Japan (until they began doing so as immigrant workers in the late 1980s) or to attend special schools with Japanese children from Japan. In some cases, fully bicultural Brazilian nisei in Japan felt almost as alienated as their more Brazilianized compatriots, as their socioeconomic marginalization seemed to override their Japanese cultural competence.

Diasporic Homecomings and Ethnic Identity: Nationalist Versus Transnational

Because Japanese Brazilians and Japanese Americans feel a certain nostalgic, emotional attachment to their ancestral homeland as ethnic return migrants, their disparate diasporic homecomings have some important long-term implications for their ethnic identities. This contrasts with other types of immigrants who move to completely foreign countries with which they feel little affiliation and ethnocultural commonality. Although Japanese Brazilians in Brazil had developed a stronger transnational attachment to Japan than Japanese Americans had before return migration, when faced with socioeconomic and ethnic marginalization in their ancestral homeland, they distanced themselves from the Japanese and reinforced their Brazilian nationalist sentiments, which often became a defensive ethnic counteridentity asserted against Japanese society (see Capuano de Oliveira 1999: 292–301; Koga 1995; Linger 2001: ch. 6; Sasaki 1999: 268–269; Tsuda 2003: ch. 3; Watanabe 1995: 99). Ironically, Japanese Americans, who are more assimilated in the United States and feel less attachment to their ethnic homeland, developed a greater appreciation of their ethnic roots in Japan as well as a more accommodating transnational and cosmopolitan identity in response to their much more positive ethnic homecoming.

Japanese Brazilians: Deterritorialized Migrant Nationalism and the Search for Homeland Abroad

Before return-migrating to Japan, Japanese Brazilians felt a stronger affiliation with their ethnic homeland, not only because they were more recent immigrant minorities than Japanese Americans but also because of the relative global positioning of Brazil and Japan. Japanese Brazilians are generally well regarded by mainstream Brazilians for their educational and socioeconomic achievements in Brazil and for their affiliation with the highly respected "first world" country of Japan and the positive cultural stereotypes about the Japanese that accompany it. In turn, Brazilian *nikkeijin* take pride in their Japanese descent and cultural heritage and identify rather strongly with positive images of Japan and Japanese culture. While acknowledging their status as Brazilian nationals, they maintain a transnational ethnic identification as "Japanese" in Brazil and believe that they have retained many positive aspects of their ethnic heritage (Tsuda 2003: ch. 1).

As a result, when Brazilian *nikkeijin* return-migrate, they are quite disconcerted because their Japaneseness is apparently denied in their ethnic homeland, causing them to strengthen their nationalist sentiments as Brazilians. Although they have been officially welcomed by the Japanese government as co-ethnic Japanese descendants, they are ethnically excluded in Japan because of a restrictive Japanese identity in which Japaneseness is defined not only by racial descent but also by complete linguistic and cultural proficiency. As a result, despite their Japanese descent, Japanese Brazilians are treated as foreigners in Japan because of their Brazilian cultural differences. When talking about their migrant experiences, they frequently say, "We were considered Japanese in Brazil, but are seen as Brazilian foreigners here in Japan." Their previous assumptions of cultural commonality with the Japanese are seriously questioned as they realize that their supposedly "Japanese" cultural attributes, which were sufficient to be considered "Japanese" in Brazil, are woefully insufficient to qualify as Japanese in Japan, or even to be socially accepted. The remarks of one second-generation *nikkeijin* man were representative of this type of experience.

> We think we are Japanese in Brazil, but in Japan, we find out that we were wrong. If you act differently and don't speak Japanese fluently, the Japanese say you are a Brazilian. To be considered Japanese, it is not sufficient to have a Japanese face and eat with chopsticks. You must think, act, and speak just like the Japanese.

Many Japanese Brazilians therefore realize in Japan that they are culturally much more Brazilian than they ever were "Japanese," leading to a nationalization of their ethnic identity. For instance, although they had frequently noted their more quiet and restrained, if not shy, "Japanese" demeanor in Brazil, they discover in Japan that their manner of walking, dressing, and gesturing is strikingly different from the Japanese. It was quite remarkable that virtually all my informants claimed that it is extremely easy to tell Japanese Brazilians apart from the Japanese on the streets because of such differences. For instance, consider the following statement by Tadashi, a good friend of mine at Toyama:

> I can see a [Japanese] Brazilian coming from a mile away with about 90 percent certainty. . . . The Brazilians walk casually with a more carefree gait and glance around at their surroundings and they are dressed casually in T-shirts and jeans. The Japanese are more formally dressed and walk in a more rushed manner. The Brazilians also gesture much more than Japanese and walk around in groups, whereas the Japanese are usually alone.

The shift in ethnic identity among the *nikkeijin* from an initially stronger Japanese consciousness in Brazil to an increased nationalist awareness of their Brazilianness is also a response to their experiences of social alienation in Japan. Because of their strong personal affiliation with their ethnic homeland, many expect to be socially accepted by the Japanese in a manner consistent with an ethnic "homecoming" of Japanese descendants. As a result, when such expectations are sorely disappointed by their ethnic rejection as culturally alien foreigners and socioeconomic marginalization as low-status unskilled migrant workers in Japan, the Brazilian *nikkeijin* feel quite alienated, as shown by their numerous reactions of disillusionment and even dismay.

A good number of my Japanese Brazilian informants were surprised, if not "shocked," by their ethnic and social marginalization in Japan. My roommate, Rodney, was certainly one of them.

> In Brazil, we were always proud of our Japanese ancestry and our ties to Japan and thought of the Japanese people in positive ways. Although I don't speak Japanese that well, I thought the Japanese would accept us because we are Japanese descendants. Coming to Japan and being treated as a foreigner despite my Japanese face was a big shock for me, a shock I'll never forget. I think it's unfair that we are not socially accepted here simply because we've become culturally different.

I was also struck by the number of times the Brazilian *nikkeijin* referred to their social segregation in Japan as "discrimination" or even used the more ethnically charged term of "racism." For example, consider the comments of an older *nikkeijin* man.

> The Japanese always keep us separated from them because of the prejudices that they have. I was offended when I first saw the social separation at [Toyama]. There are some Japanese who simply don't like us and don't trust us because we are Brazilian. If you don't understand Japanese culture and act just like the Japanese, they discriminate against you and you can't enter their group. The Japanese are racists, so even the [Japanese] Brazilians experience discrimination here.

The social alienation that Japanese Brazilian ethnic return migrants experience in Japan therefore completely undermines their previously favorable images of and nostalgic attachment to their ethnic homeland of Japan. As Japan comes to take on a quite negative meaning for them, many of them emotionally distance themselves from the country and no longer experience it as an ethnic homeland. Homeland is not simply a place of origin—it must be imbued with positive emotional affect as a place of desire and longing to which the individual feels a strong sense of attachment and identification (cf. Al-Ali and Koser 2002: 7). Therefore, even though Japan technically remains the country of ethnic and ancestral origin for Japanese Brazilians in an objective sense, it is no longer associated with the feelings of affiliation and fondness that make homelands subjectively meaningful.

Because Japanese Brazilians are alienated from their *ethnic* homeland of Japan, they strengthen their nationalist attachment to Brazil as the *natal* homeland where they truly belong and originated. In this manner their country of birth is reconceptualized in nationalist terms as the true homeland in contrast to their country of ethnic origin. Milton, one of my good friends at Toyama, expressed this common sentiment:

> We come to Japan and realize Japan is not our country. It is the country of our parents and grandparents. Although we are Japanese descendants, we don't belong here. We can't enter Japanese society because the Japanese don't accept us. Instead, our country is Brazil. It is where we were born and where we grew up.

However, Brazil does not become the true homeland for the Brazilian *nikkeijin* simply because they have been denied their ethnic homeland in Japan. In order for a country of origin to become subjectively meaningful and significant as a real homeland and therefore as a source of nationalist identity, it must be viewed in a positive and desirable manner. For Japanese Brazilians, Brazil emerges as the true homeland through the migration process because it is imbued with positive meaning and affect when contrasted with the negative social experiences Japanese Brazilians have in Japan (cf. Linger 2001: 266–267). When they return-migrate and are confronted with the exclusionary nature of Japanese society that marginalizes even Japanese descendants, they begin to value and appreciate the ethnically receptive and inclusive nature of multiethnic Brazil to a much greater extent than before. The supposedly cold and impersonal nature of Japanese social relationships causes many of them to reminisce (almost nostalgically) about the emotionally warm and affectionate social relationships they had in Brazil. Others (especially *nikkeijin* women) also note the gender inequality prevalent in Japan, both at the workplace and in spousal relationships, in contrast to which they portray Brazil as a society of more equality and mutual respect among the sexes. Other aspects of the Japanese that are frequently brought up for specific criticism are their excessive dedication to work and company at the expense of fulfilling family or social lives, their group conformity and obedience, and the overly restrictive and structured nature of their lives, which many *nikkeijin* again contrast with their more favorable social experiences with Brazilians and their ability to enjoy life.[12] In this manner, as they discover many of the negative aspects of Japan and distance themselves from their previous ethnic identification as "Japanese," Japanese Brazilians simultaneously rediscover and reaffirm the positive aspects of Brazil that they had previously taken for granted, which produces a renewed appreciation of their status as Brazilian nationals.

Because Brazil is favorably reconstituted in this manner by Japanese Brazilians abroad, it no longer remains simply an affectively neutral place of birth but suddenly becomes an emotionally charged, almost idealized object of desire, worthy of a true homeland. As a result, many Japanese Brazilians ironically feel a greater sense of nationalist loyalty and identification with Brazil in Japan than they ever did in Brazil. Some of my informants (especially those who had been living in Japan for several years) recalled their natal homeland with rather fond memories. Although Japanese Brazilians were frequently critical of many aspects of Brazilian society back home, I observed a notable tendency among them to praise Brazil in Japan, even to an exaggerated extent. Brazil is still characterized as a country with serious political, economic, and social problems, but other aspects of Brazil are spoken of highly and are contrasted favorably with Japan, such as its people, culture, material living conditions, natural resources and agriculture, sports heroes, and food. One of my informants spoke about this positive reassessment of Brazil in the clearest terms.

> Brazilians always think other countries are much better. The Japanese Brazilians saw Japan in this way too. But now, I realize we were wrong. We didn't know what we had in Brazil. There is no better place than Brazil to live, especially because we were born there and have no cultural problems. The people are better there and so are the conditions of living. I value Brazil much more now.

Some Brazilian *nikkeijin* in Japan even used affect-laden terms such as *nationalism, patriotism,* and *love* to express their renewed emotional affiliation to their natal homeland. "In Brazil, I never gave too much value to the country, but now I do," a sansei woman said. "I feel more patriotism toward Brazil." Another declared: "My sentiments for my homeland of Brazil and my love for the country will never leave me no matter how long I stay in Japan." Others expressed similar feelings.

A number of Japanese Brazilians also assert their Brazilian nationalist identities in their daily behavior as an ethnic minority counteridentity in opposition to a negatively perceived Japanese society. This ranges from constantly identifying themselves as Brazilian foreigners to avoid being mistaken as Japanese to more overt, if not defiant, demonstrations of their cultural Brazilianness by wearing "Brazilian" clothes, speaking Portuguese loudly in public, dancing samba in the streets, and "acting Brazilian" in other ways (Tsuda 2003: ch. 5). This greater sense of Brazilian national allegiance and pride among the *nikkeijin* in Japan is also symbolized by the prominent display of the Brazilian flag in their ethnic stores and restaurants, although the flag is hardly ever displayed in Brazil.[13] During the 2002 World Cup (held in Japan and Korea), thousands of Japanese Brazilians waving the Brazilian flag and dressed in national colors showed up in stadiums all over Japan to cheer on their national team, causing the American TV broadcasters to wonder why so many "Japanese" were so fervently rooting for the Brazilian team![14]

In this manner the dislocations of migration can produce a form of de-territorialized nationalism in which national loyalties to natal homelands are articulated outside the territorial boundaries of the nation-state. In fact, countries of birth are often discovered and articulated as homelands in the process of migration and travel (cf. Clifford 1997) because it is frequently physical absence from a place of origin that allows it to be conceptualized as a homeland. Migrants' encounters with foreign societies frequently disrupt the taken-for-granted nature of their own country, causing them to reevaluate it in a much more favorable light compared to the negative experiences of social rejection and alienation abroad. This produces a greater sense of national allegiance and identification toward the country of origin as the true homeland.

Japanese Americans: A Broadening of Ethnic Consciousness

Because Japanese Americans have a much more favorable ethnic homecoming, they do not react ethnically against Japanese society through an assertion of their nationalist sentiments. Instead, their positive experiences as ethnic return migrants increase their identification with their ethnic homeland of Japan and produce a more ethnically inclusive transnational consciousness as members of a diasporic community of Japanese descendants.

Although Japanese Americans are also treated as foreigners in Japan, such ethnic perceptions do not bother them as much, partly because most of them did not identify with their ethnic homeland as strongly as Japanese Brazilians did to begin with. A case in point is Jamie, a fourth-generation Japanese American who lived in Japan as a student.

> I had no consciousness of being culturally Japanese before going to Japan. I see myself as a foreigner in Japan. Of course, I do feel some kind of affinity to Japan, but I'm still a foreigner. So it was no shock to me that I was seen as American in Japan. Even among my non-Japanese [American] Asian friends [in the United States], I felt very American. They'd call my dad at home and say he sounds white. So it's pretty obvious that the Japanese are going to treat me as a foreigner.

However, the main reason that Japanese Americans do not react negatively is because they are American, not Brazilian, foreigners in Japan. In contrast to Japanese Brazilians, none of the Japanese Americans I interviewed felt socially alienated or ethnically excluded in Japan because of their foreigner status. Although the Japanese were sometimes initially confused or surprised when they met Japanese-looking people who could not speak the language and may have initially seen them as handicapped, strange, or uneducated, Japanese Americans report that they were treated quite nicely and courteously once it became apparent that they were Americans. Again, the Japanese American experience in this regard is quite different from that of Japanese Brazilians, who are sometimes bothered by the glances and stares as well as the aloof treatment they receive from the Japanese when they speak Portuguese despite having a Japanese face. According to Catherine, a third-generation Japanese American who had been to Japan many times:

> I think the Japanese handle people like us very well. Actually, much better than how Americans treat foreigners who don't speak English or people of color. They never stared at us, were always courteous, and very patient with us. And it helped that we could say a few words in Japanese. I didn't feel the Japanese treated me differently.

"It was much better than when I went to Spain," another Japanese American observed. "There, people were kind of impatient and rude because I stuck out a lot. The locals also had a negative way of interacting with tourists that I didn't like. In Japan, everyone treated us well. I felt I blended in better because everyone looked like me and I didn't stick out as much as a foreigner. It was much better than the rumors I heard about the Japanese."

Rather than being ethnically stigmatized, as Japanese Brazilians were, a couple of informants noted that it was actually an advantage when it was discovered that they were Americans, not Japanese. Takeyoshi, who had lived in Japan for many years, mentioned how his cultural difficulties as an American foreigner in Japan would even elicit a positive, friendly reception from the Japanese. He recounted his experiences as follows:

> When I first lived in Japan, I couldn't read signs very well and had trouble even ordering food at restaurants. I was embarrassed I didn't know such simple things because I look Japanese . . . but some people were actually excited by my cultural incompetence. They were curious; they wanted to be my friend.

I remember I went to a clothing store and the salesman was shocked an adult person didn't know his clothing size. So I explained to him that I'm American. So then, the guy was really interested in me and became my friend and even gave me clothes for free!

A number of my interviewees claimed that the Japanese could tell they were Americans by the English they spoke, their demeanor and dress, and the people they were with (which sometimes included white Americans, especially for those who were students or tourists) and that therefore there was not much ethnic confusion.

Like Japanese Brazilians, some Japanese Americans who had lived in Japan for longer periods mentioned that they would always introduce themselves as Americans to avoid the initial confusion and disorientation among Japanese who encountered Japanese-looking people who had trouble speaking the language. Yet, unlike Japanese Brazilians, who spoke of the social exclusion that resulted once it was discovered that they were foreigners, none of the Japanese Americans had such experiences. "Whenever I speak to Japanese at stores or wherever, I preface everything by saying I'm a student from America and my Japanese is not very good," Jamie explained. "That seemed to facilitate things. They [the Japanese] seemed fine with that, and I can't remember an instance when people distanced themselves from me because of it." Even Japanese Americans like Takeyoshi, who lived in Japan for years and became fluent in the language, would always introduce themselves as Americans.

> For short conversations, it's not noticeable that I'm a foreigner. So if I go into a store, I just act like a Japanese. But if I get into a longer conversation, I like to tell people I'm American. It makes things so much easier that way because otherwise, you become an idiot if you don't know something all Japanese are supposed to know or make a mistake speaking the language. It's a defensive mechanism and there's no stigma about being American in Japan. In fact, people become interested and want to be my friend, not in an exploitative way, but a friendly way.

In fact, only one of my informants mentioned that she received the aloof silent treatment when it was discovered she was American. "Then they would basically be like, OK, just go away. Pay your 100 yen and just go away," she recounted.

Because of their relatively positive socio-occupational and ethnic reception in Japan, none of my Japanese American informants developed negative sentiments toward Japanese society or felt alienated from their ethnic home-land. As a result, they did not experience a resurgence of an oppositional na-tionalist identity in Japan as their Brazilian counterparts did. Some of them did mention that they felt more American in Japan, but it was more of a recogni-tion of their cultural differences with the Japanese than a negative defensive reaction against them. Kiyoshi, a bicultural nisei, was one of them.

> In Japan, I probably feel my Americanness more because I notice more differ-ences than similarities, even though I can do a decent job of getting by. I have a Japanese side I can activate, and a lot of times, I do, for courtesy's sake. I don't need to advertise that I'm from the U.S. But I definitely feel my Americanness. I don't think I could go back to school there, or be a regular Japanese company employee.

Another informant mentioned that he feels his Americanness in Japan be-cause of his greater exposure to and familiarity with various ethnic groups in the United States, especially in California, compared to the Japanese, who are used to living in an ethnically homogeneous society. A mixed-descent second-generation Japanese American shared similar feelings, which were based on a consciousness of not only cultural but also racial difference.

> Going to Japan makes me feel more American. I feel kind of awkward in Japan, like I don't really fit in. I'm not pure Japanese [descent] and I know that's not a good thing in Japan. I get this feeling from my [Japanese] relatives. Their at-titude is like, "Why did my father marry a white woman in America?" The way you interact with family in Japan is much more formal, not casual like it is here. I come home [to the United States] and realize I like where I am. I love to travel and see things, but because it helps me to define myself better. I'm half Japanese, but I realize it's a very small half, in terms of what it actually means to me. I'm really much more American than Japanese.

At times, this heightened sense of Americanness in Japan was a reaction to aspects of Japan that my informants did not like, which did lead to some ambivalence, but nowhere as strong as what their *nikkeijin* counterparts from Brazil experienced. For instance, Takeyoshi mentioned that he distanced himself from aspects of Japanese culture, such as excessive hierarchy, that he did not like and was thus conflicted as he vacillated between his Japanese and American sides. "It was a sense that I could never completely fit in there, would never be like them. It was a combination of distance and intimacy."

Consider the similar comments of Mark, a bicultural nisei who had worked in Japan.

> When I was younger, [my trips to Japan] probably reinforced my Americanness. I could relate to the culture and it was not hard for me to fit in, but I didn't like it. I preferred American culture—it's more free and not as strict. But as I got older and mature, I realized that's just how it is. It's not necessarily bad, just different.

An equal, if not greater, number of Japanese Americans actually spoke about how their sojourn in Japan made them feel more connected to their Japanese ethnic roots and strengthened their sense of affiliation to their ethnic homeland. "I feel somewhat of a stronger affinity with Japan now," Jamie, who had studied in Japan, noted. "It's because I know more about Japanese culture and how it works. Now, I want to learn more, so that Japan becomes more natural for me, so when I go back, I can fit in more." For Tom, another fourth-generation exchange student, his greater affinity with his ethnic homeland was even a matter of ethnic pride.

> Going to Japan and seeing everything there makes you proud that I'm Japanese [descent], that this is where I'm from. People respect Japan. I'm now prouder to be of Japanese ancestry. I felt this is where I should be, because people looked like me, even if they don't dress like me, and people there were really nice.

Even Yoriko, who was only half-Japanese, said she felt more "tied to Japan," especially going to the town and temple where her father was raised and becoming close to her Japanese family.

I was also struck by the number of Japanese Americans for whom their Japanese sojourn produced a more expansive transnational and even cosmopolitan consciousness that was not based on a restrictive nationalist loyalty to one country at the expense of the other. This was especially true among the ethnically bicultural nisei, who felt transnationally connected to both countries. For Mark, this was a gradual maturational process. Although he initially reinforced his American identity as a partial reaction to those aspects of Japan he did not like when he was younger, he eventually came to adopt a more accommodating transnational ethnic consciousness.

> I went [to Japan] the past summer, and the year before, and came to reinforce my sense of relating to my Japanese side, because by that time, I had grown and can appreciate Japan. I don't act defensively anymore and say I'm American. I

just totally fit in and embrace Japan. I feel cosmopolitan, especially when I feel my Japaneseness and feel connected to Japan while feeling American at the same time. When I'm in Japan, I feel great, like I could live there for a long time. But when I get back to the U.S., I feel great being back home. I can operate fine in both cultures.

For another bicultural nisei, John, who felt he "can be Japanese and American at the same time," this type of transnational ethnic identity was more a product of being caught between two different cultures and countries.

Ultimately, I feel more shin-nisei [postwar second-generation Japanese American] than either American or Japanese. I'm in a bind because I'm not Japanese, but I'm more Japanese than most Japanese Americans since I have these Japanese cultural tendencies inside me that I keep fighting. I can easily be Japanese and go to Japan and get a job and seriously be Japanese. But then, I'm here and I want to be here and stay here and want my children to stay here, so I have to be Japanese American.

At the same time, John seemed to privilege his American side, not in a restrictive nationalist sense but because of its more cosmopolitan global nature compared to an insular Japanese national identity. "I get mad at myself that I have these Japanese tendencies, which don't help me," John remarked. "We live in a global community, and if you want to step out and compete with the Western world, you need to be more Western. I try to break stereotypes. In Japan, I don't have to be Japanese, even if I can. It's a global community, so I'm going to act as whatever. It's easier to do this in Japan because many Japanese have come to and are familiar with the U.S." The ultimate cosmopolitan statement came from Jamie, who was not fully bicultural and did not necessarily think of herself in national terms as Japanese or American.

I don't necessarily feel a greater need to maintain my Japanese heritage after studying in Japan. My personal consciousness is to be able to adapt to any situation. To be able to act naturally in any country, whether it's Japan, France, or Australia. I want to know how to make the least amount of friction when I'm there. My stay in Japan increased my desire to become more cosmopolitan and operate in different cultures and languages.

Again, the contrast with the ethnic identity of Japanese Brazilians in Japan is quite stark. Only one of my 45 Japanese Brazilian interviewees expressed any type of cosmopolitan ethnic consciousness after living in Japan. Most of them developed a much more restrictive, deterritorialized Brazilian migrant nationalism in Japan that excluded the Japanese.

Conclusion: Same Homeland, Different Homecomings

When I was conducting participant observation among Japanese Brazilian workers at Toyama factory in Japan, I was wearing the same uniform, doing the same type of work, speaking to them in Portuguese, and living with them in the same company apartments. As a Japanese American anthropologist, I was a consummate insider. Nonetheless, my Japanese Brazilian co-workers and roommates would sometimes say, "Your life in Japan must be easier than ours because you are an American [or a student or a researcher]." Of course, I was a student researcher in Japan, not a real migrant factory worker, *because* I was American. If I had been Brazilian, I might very well have been working at Toyama factory for the money, not for research, and for years, not for months. We were of the same Japanese ethnic origin, but because we were born in different countries, we had been consigned to different fates as ethnic return migrants in Japan. Again, in this case, geography is destiny. This was a fact not lost on one of my Japanese Brazilian interviewees.

> I think it's absolutely absurd that the Japanese Brazilians have to come to Japan to do this kind of work. It just shows how incompetent the Brazilian government is when even well-educated and middle-class Brazilians have trouble surviving economically. If we were Japanese American, we would never have had to do this.

In this manner, even among immigrants of the same ethnic origin with similar educational and socioeconomic backgrounds living in the same host country, their social status, ethnic experiences, and identity consequences can be widely divergent depending on the global positioning of their home countries. Immigrants from countries with greater international stature enjoy a higher social status in the host society as well as more cultural and ethnic respect. Migration studies scholars need to pay closer attention to the national origins of immigrants as a form of social capital, because national origin can have a more significant impact on their political, socioeconomic, and cultural reception than other human and social capital variables, such as educational level, occupational and linguistic skills, length of stay in the host country, or ethnic and social class background.

The case of Japanese Brazilians and Japanese Americans in Japan illustrates how two *nikkeijin* ethnic return migrant groups can experience quite divergent homecomings in their ethnic homeland by virtue of their different status as Brazilian and American nationals. Although Japanese Brazilians are of Japanese descent, have developed a considerable cultural affinity with their ethnic homeland, and are highly skilled middle-class professionals, such ethnic and socioeconomic advantages seem to be canceled out by the relatively low position of Brazil in the global order, causing Japanese Brazilians to toil as low-status unskilled migrant laborers on the margins of Japanese society. Despite its financial rewards, transnational mobility for Japanese Brazilians has not led to an expansive cosmopolitan ethnic consciousness but rather to defensive nationalist identities in response to social degradation and discrimination in their ethnic homeland. Meanwhile, their *nikkeijin* counterparts from the United States benefit from their country's international prestige as they migrate to their ethnic homeland as part of the global tourist, educational, or professional elite, and they are accorded the appropriate social status and respect of nationals at the top of the global order. They have emerged from their migratory experiences with a stronger transnational connection to their ethnic homeland and with a greater cosmopolitan confidence to engage in a global world. Likewise, as Takenaka demonstrates in Chapter 10, the differential ethnic positioning of Japanese Brazilians versus Japanese *Peruvians* in Japan, based on the higher status of Brazil over Peru in the global order, causes these two groups to construct quite different ethnic identities as well.

Interestingly, the fateful decision by the Japanese ancestors of the *nikkeijin* to emigrate from Japan to either the United States or Brazil (or Peru, for that matter) was itself determined by the differential global position of these countries in the world order. Many Japanese emigrated to Brazil because of the discriminatory closing of the United States to further Japanese immigration in response to domestic anti-Japanese sentiment, starting with the Gentlemen's Agreement in 1907 and culminating in the Oriental Exclusion Act of 1924. Although Brazil experienced a similar anti-Japanese backlash, its government decided not to ban Japanese immigration. Because of its lower international economic and political position, Brazil could not attract sufficient labor migration from Europe, nor did it have the diplomatic stature to risk offending the government of a rising Japanese nation (Lesser 1999: ch. 4; Tsuda 2001).

In this manner, the historical global inequalities that caused and structured the migration of Japanese to different countries in the Americas have persisted and continue to determine the migratory opportunities and outcomes of their *nikkeijin* descendants. The *nikkeijin* in Brazil (and Peru) have been victimized by economic uncertainty in South America and, like their Japanese ancestors before them, have again joined the subordinate class of unskilled labor migrants seeking better economic fortunes at the margins of the global economy. Meanwhile, the *nikkeijin* in the United States have enjoyed the economic security of the developed world and benefit from America's global stature when they migrate abroad as highly skilled students and professionals. Although the scholarly literature often celebrates the transnational hybridity, flexible citizenship, and cosmopolitan identities that are supposedly emerging in an era of globalization (see, e.g., Appadurai 1996; Basch et al. 1994; Kearney 1991; Ong 1999), it seems that only a privileged class of global elites, mainly from wealthy developed nations, are able to fully partake in the opportunities of globalization by developing transnational attachments to various countries, multicultural skills, and an ethnically inclusive cosmopolitanism. Undoubtedly, countries positioned lower in the global order have also participated in the increasingly global movement of populations, but they do so as subordinate and marginalized peoples who reproduce restrictive, local, parochial attachments in response to their ethnosocial exclusion in the global ecumene. In this sense national origin can trump cultural affinity and socioeconomic background in determining the access that migrant groups have to global opportunities. Indeed, it seems that ascribed social characteristics, such as race, gender, and national origin, more than personal achievements and skills, determine whether global mobility becomes truly liberating or simply perpetuates and exacerbates preexisting systems of subordination by reproducing them in multiple localities.

Notes

1. Human capital is based on individual-level skills and attributes, and social capital is the resources available to individuals because of their membership in a social group (Portes and Rumbaut 2001: 353; Portes and Sensenbrenner 1993).

2. Immigrants with greater human and social capital will improve their host society reception, and different host society receptions can make certain human and social capital variables more important than others (Tsuda et al. 2003; cf. Portes and Rumbaut 2001: 46–48).

3. In fact, Japanese Brazilians are more legally privileged than Japanese Americans because they are admitted on preferential visas with no activity restrictions and these visas can be indefinitely renewed so long as their documents are in order. In contrast, most Japanese Americans go to Japan on short-term work or student visas

with activity restrictions and time limits, although they are technically entitled to the same visas as Japanese Brazilians.

4. Although neither speak much Japanese, Japanese Brazilians again have a slight edge because they have done a better job of maintaining the language than their counterparts from the United States.

5. After nine months of fieldwork in two cities with Japanese Brazilian communities in Brazil (1993–1994), I conducted one year of fieldwork in two cities in Japan (1994–1995) with relatively large Japanese Brazilian immigrant communities. I worked for four intensive months as a participant observer in a large electrical appliance factory in Japan with Japanese Brazilian immigrant workers and conducted close to 100 in-depth interviews with Japanese Brazilians and Japanese workers, residents, and employers as well as with local and national government officials. My fieldwork with Japanese Americans consists of 45 extensive interviews and participant observation among Japanese American ethnic organizations and community events in San Diego and Phoenix.

6. This number excludes the approximately 650,000 Korean Japanese who are still registered in Japan as foreigners. Although 80 percent were born in Japan, they are not granted Japanese citizenship and many have not naturalized.

7. Unlike China and Korea (Kibria 2002: 298; Louie 2001, 2002), the Japanese government does not sponsor ethnic heritage tours for *nikkeijin*. Because tourists are brief visitors and therefore different from other types of migrants and immigrants, I do not deal much with them in this chapter.

8. Even ethnic return migrants from developing countries who are students tend to have more positive experiences than other types of immigrants (see Choi 2006; Yang 2006).

9. My interviews with Japanese workers indicate that they are not quite as ignorant as the *nikkeijin* make them out to be. They also sometimes had cheerful, brighter images of Brazil, such as samba, Carnaval, soccer, beaches, and Rio de Janeiro.

10. One informant mentioned that Japanese emigrants were seen as "screwups" who could not make it economically in Japan. However, she was not sure whether this image came from older Japanese in Hawaii (where she was born and raised) or from her stay in Japan. She also felt it was a Japanese perception of issei (first-generation Japanese immigrants) and was never applied to her specifically as a fourth-generation Japanese American. Another informant mentioned that the Japanese disdain Japanese Americans a bit because they are seen as completely American with no understanding of their Japanese heritage. However, he noted that he never experienced such perceptions personally because he is completely bilingual and fits in well in Japan.

11. According to Hannerz (1996: ch. 9), cosmopolitans are people who have cultural competence in foreign societies.

12. It is quite evident that the negative perceptions that the Brazilian *nikkeijin* develop of Japan are being structured by some common stereotypes of the Japanese and Brazilians.

13. The only exception is during the World Cup, when the Brazilian flag is sold by the thousands and is plastered on every store, office, home, car, and T-shirt.

14. The explanation they finally came up with is that because of the number of Brazilians playing on Japanese teams, Brazilian soccer has quite a following in Japan.

References Cited

Al-Ali, Nadje, and Khalid Koser. 2002. "Transnationalism, International Migration, and Home." In *New Approaches to Migration? Transnational Communities and the Transformation of Home*, Nadje Al-Ali and Khalid Koser, eds. London: Routledge, 1–14.

Appadurai, Arjun. 1996. *Modernity at Large: Cultural Dimensions of Globalization*. Minneapolis: University of Minnesota Press.

Basch, Linda, Nina Glick Schiller, and Cristina Szanton Blanc. 1994. *Nations Unbound: Transnational Projects, Postcolonial Predicaments, and Deterritorialized Nation-States*. Amsterdam: Gordon and Breach.

Borjas, George J. 1995. "Assimilation and Changes in Cohort Quality Revisited: What Happened to Immigrant Earnings in the 1980s?" *Journal of Labor Economics* 13(2):201–245.

Capuano de Oliveira, Adriana. 1999. "Repensando a Identidade Dentro da Emigração *Dekassegui*" [Rethinking identity in the context of *dekasegi* emigration]. In *Cenas do Brasil Migrante* [Scenes of migrant Brazil], Rossana Rocha Reis and Teresa Sales, eds. São Paulo, Brazil: Boitempo Editorial, 275–307.

Choi, Woogill. 2006. "Ethnic Koreans from China: Korean Dreams, Adaptation, and New Identities." Paper presented at a conference on Korean ethnic return migration, University of Auckland, New Zealand, November 27–28.

Clifford, James. 1997. *Routes: Travel and Translation in the Late Twentieth Century*. Cambridge, MA: Harvard University Press.

Hannerz, Ulf. 1996. *Transnational Connections: Culture, People, Places*. London: Routledge.

Kearney, Michael. 1991. "Borders and Boundaries of State and Self at the End of Empire." *Journal of Historical Sociology* 4(1):52–74.

Kibria, Nazli. 2002. "Of Blood, Belonging, and Homeland Trips: Transnationalism and Identity Among Second-Generation Chinese and Korean Americans." In *The Changing Face of Home: The Transnational Lives of the Second Generation*, Peggy Levitt and Mary C. Waters, eds. New York: Russell Sage, 295–311.

Koga, Eunice Ishikawa. 1995. "Kyojyu no Chokika to Aidenteitei no Naiyo: Nikkei Burajirujin no Baai" [Long-term residence and the content of identity: The case of the Brazilian *nikkeijin*]. In *Chiiki Shakai ni Okeru Gaikokujin Rodosha: Nichi/O ni Okeru Ukeire no Genjyo to Kadai* [The foreign labor problem in local societies: Issues and realities of acceptance in Japan and European countries], Takashi Miyajima, ed. Tokyo: Ochanomizu University, 43–52.

Lesser, Jeffrey. 1999. *Negotiating National Identity: Immigrants, Minorities, and the Struggle for Ethnicity in Brazil.* Durham, NC: Duke University Press.

Linger, Daniel T. 2001. *No One Home: Brazilian Selves Remade in Japan.* Stanford, CA: Stanford University Press.

Louie, Andrea. 2001. "Crafting Places Through Mobility: Chinese American 'Roots-Searching' in China." *Identities* 8(3):343–379.

———. 2002. "Creating Histories for the Present: Second-Generation (Re)definitions of Chinese American Culture." In *The Changing Face of Home: The Transnational Lives of the Second Generation,* Peggy Levitt and Mary C. Waters, eds. New York: Russell Sage, 312–340.

Ong, Aihwa. 1999. *Flexible Citizenship: The Cultural Logics of Transnationality.* Durham, NC: Duke University Press.

Portes, Alejandro, and Rubén G. Rumbaut. 1996. *Immigrant America: A Portrait.* Berkeley: University of California Press.

———. 2001. *Legacies: The Story of the Immigrant Second Generation.* Berkeley: University of California Press.

Portes, Alejandro, and Julia Sensenbrenner. 1993. "Embeddedness and Immigration: Notes on the Social Determinants of Economic Action." *American Journal of Sociology* 93:1320–1350.

Reitz, Jeffrey G. 2003. "Host Societies and the Reception of Immigrants: Research Themes, Emerging Theories, and Methodological Issues." In *Host Societies and the Reception of Immigrants,* Jeffrey Reitz, ed. Center for Comparative Immigration Studies Anthology. La Jolla: University of California at San Diego, 1–18.

Sanders, Jimy M., and Victor Nee. 1987. "Limits of Ethnic Solidarity in the Enclave Economy." *American Sociological Review* 52:745–773.

Sasaki, Elisa Massae. 1999. "Movimento *Dekassegui*: A Experiência Migratória e Identitária dos Brasileiros Descendentes de Japoneses no Japão" [The movement of *dekasegi*: Migration experiences and identity of Japanese-descent Brazilians in Japan]. In *Cenas do Brasil Migrante* [Scenes of migrant Brazil], Rossana Rocha Reis and Teresa Sales, eds. São Paulo, Brazil: Boitempo Editorial, 243–274.

Tsuda, Takeyuki. 1999. "The Permanence of 'Temporary' Migration: The 'Structural Embeddedness' of Japanese-Brazilian Migrant Workers in Japan." *Journal of Asian Studies* 58(3):687–722.

———. 2001. "When Identities Become Modern: Japanese Immigrants in Brazil and the Global Contextualization of Identity." *Ethnic and Racial Studies* 24(3):412–432.

———. 2003. *Strangers in the Ethnic Homeland: Japanese Brazilian Return Migration in Transnational Perspective.* New York: Columbia University Press.

Tsuda, Takeyuki, Zulema Valdez, and Wayne A. Cornelius. 2003. "Human Capital Versus

Social Capital: Immigrant Wages and Labor Market Incorporation in Japan and the United States." *Migraciones Internacionales* 2(1):5–35.

Watanabe, Masako. 1995. "Nikkei Burujirujin kara Mita Nihonjin no Amoru" [The love of the Japanese, as seen by the *nikkei* Brazilians]. *Socially* 3:99–100.

Yang, Young-Kyun. 2006. "The Return Migration of Korean Chinese (*Joseonjok*) from a Comparative Perspective." Paper presented at a conference on Korean ethnic return migration, University of Auckland, New Zealand, November 27–28.

Zhou, Min, and John R. Logan. 1989. "Returns on Human Capital in Ethnic Enclaves: New York City's Chinatown." *American Sociological Review* 54:809–820.

Ethnic Hierarchy and Its Impact on Ethnic Identities

A Comparative Analysis of Peruvian and Brazilian Return Migrants in Japan

Ayumi Takenaka

AS NUMEROUS STUDIES have indicated, ethnic return migrants, although officially incorporated as co-ethnics, are often treated as foreigners in their ethnic homelands. Whether this is due to the migrants' alien cultures (e.g., Kawamura 2000) or their status as newcomers (e.g., Capo Zmegac 2005), "ethnic ties" do not necessarily facilitate migrants' assimilation into or acceptance in their ethnic homelands. In return-migrating, migrants typically experience rejection and subsequently face the need to reevaluate their ethnic identities. Some strengthen a sense of attachment to their countries of birth (e.g., Chinese Americans in China may realize how American they are). Some embrace their multicultural backgrounds (asserting that they have the best of both worlds). And some transform or reinterpret their previous identities (Transylvanian Hungarians in Hungary regard themselves as the bearers of "authentic" Hungarian traditions as opposed to more modernized Hungarians in Hungary [Capo Zmegac 2005; Fox 2003]). Ethnic return migration thus ironically enhances awareness of ethnic difference rather than of similarity among co-ethnics dispersed across countries. Migrations driven by alleged ethnic affinity may, in practice, generate new forms of ethnic heterogeneity in the receiving context (Brubaker 1998).

Latin Americans of Japanese descent also go through similar experiences in Japan. Having been admitted as Japanese (more precisely, as families of Japanese), those return migrants, mostly from Brazil and Peru, have nonetheless found themselves treated as Brazilians or Peruvians in Japan. Japanese Brazilians and Japanese Peruvians[1] began to migrate to Japan in the late 1980s in response to Japan's ethnicity-based immigration policy, mostly for economic reasons because of severe recessions in South America. Ever since then, Brazilian and Peruvian migrants have grown in number, surpassing 316,000 and 59,000, respectively, in 2007.[2] Although most of them are Japanese descendants, they have become Japan's new ethnic minorities.

In response to this ethnic rejection, Japanese Brazilians and Japanese Peruvians, who had previously held identities as Japanese in Brazil and Peru, have engaged in the construction of difference in relation to the Japanese in Japan (Capo Zmegac 2005). Their reactions, however, have not been uniform. Japanese Brazilians typically asserted a Brazilian national identity in contrast to the Japanese by strengthening their sense of pride and awareness as Brazilians (see, e.g., Chapter 9; Mori 2000). They commonly expressed "patriotic sentiments" (Capuano de Oliveira 1998) in Japan, displaying the Brazilian flag in ethnic stores, dancing the samba in public sites, and wearing buttons and clothes with Brazilian flags, even though they did none of these things in Brazil (see Chapter 9).

Peruvians of Japanese descent, in contrast, were less inclined to display Peruvian national symbols in Japan. Compared to their "more nationalistic" Brazilian counterparts, many Japanese Peruvians told me that they were often more ambivalent about their identities. The Peruvian flag was seldom displayed, and Peruvian cultural activities were less common in public sites. Instead of developing a greater sense of allegiance to Peru, Japanese Peruvians generally strengthened their identity as *nikkei* (Japanese descendants), which they described as neither completely Peruvian nor completely Japanese but a unique blend of the two. Echoing the sentiments of many Japanese Peruvians in Japan, one return migrant said, "We are not completely Peruvian, and here in Japan, we are *gaijin* [foreigner]. So, we don't have a *patria*," referring to a homeland as Tsuda (Conclusion, this volume) defines the term—where one feels emotionally attached and one truly belongs. "So, we need to create our own *patria*. Let's call it *Nikkeilandia*." Polls do indicate a stronger tendency to identify first as *nikkei* among Japanese Peruvians (65 percent) than among Japanese Brazilians (44 percent); only 12 percent of Japanese Peruvians surveyed responded that they identified first as Peruvians, whereas 26 percent of their Brazilian counterparts said they were Brazilian first (JICA 1992). As a primary basis for one's identity, the idiom of the nation-state is often evoked in the process of identity negotiations among ethnic return migrants (e.g., Fox 2003; Louie 2004). Yet return migrants do not always resort to the nation as a strategy for coping with the status loss and humiliations they often experience in their ancestral homelands. As Tsuda (Chapter 9, this volume) points out, ethnic return migrants undergo different experiences even in the same host country.

What explains the variation in migrants' ethnic responses to ethnic return migration? When do ethnic return migrants reframe their identities in terms of country of citizenship? When do other factors, such as race, ethnicity, culture, or class, become salient in reevaluating their identities? And to what extent are the processes of identity transformation accounted for by return migration policies or premigration legacies?

In this chapter I examine various ethnic responses to, or ethnic consequences of, ethnic return migration by comparing the experiences of Japanese Peruvians and Japanese Brazilians in Japan. I argue that two consequences of return migration play a significant role in shaping return migrants' ethnic responses. One is the way in which migrants are incorporated into a hierarchy in the host society—an ethnic hierarchy created and reinforced in the process of return migration. The other is within-group variation (along lines of race, class, and legal status) that is enhanced as a result of the ethnic hierarchy.

In a nutshell, Brazilians are ranked higher than Peruvians in the ethnic hierarchy in Japan for a number of reasons. First, Brazil is considered to have a higher status than Peru in the global hierarchy of nations because of its higher GDP, larger population, and greater political influence. As Tsuda argues in Chapter 9, the status of migrants' sending countries in the global hierarchy plays an important role in shaping how migrants are treated in the host society. Japanese Peruvians face more problems in using the idiom of the nation in contrast to Brazilian return migrants, who often resort to Brazil to restore their self-esteem in response to the ethnic rejection they experience in Japan. Second, Japanese Brazilian return migrants, in general, retained more Japanese cultural and phenotypic features akin to the host population than Japanese Peruvian return migrants. They were more likely than Japanese Peruvians to speak Japanese and less likely to be racially mixed. Similarly, among return migrants from Brazil, there were fewer Brazilians of non-Japanese descent; returnees from Peru, on the other hand, included many more non-Japanese descendants who were generally of poorer origins and entered Japan by using fraudulent documents. Consequently, unlike Japanese Brazilians who asserted their Brazilianness, Japanese Peruvians, particularly those of racially unmixed and middle-class backgrounds, tried to distance themselves from "pure Peruvians," or non-Japanese Peruvians, emphasizing instead their status as *nikkei* Japanese descendants. In doing so, the distance between Japanese Peruvians and other Peruvians increased in the context of return migration. While return-migrating to their same ancestral country under the same conditions, therefore, Japanese Brazilians and Japanese Peruvians underwent different processes of identity transformation. Consequently, not only did they develop different kinds of identities in relation to the local population, but the two groups also had relatively little interaction between them.

Ethnic return migration in itself generates ethnic consequences by effectively creating ethnicities and a hierarchy in which ethnic groups are differentially positioned (Brubaker 1998; Joppke and Rosenhek 2002). That is because ethnic return migration necessarily distinguishes between privileged migrants and others on the basis of ethnicity (Münz and Ohlinger 1998), setting criteria for defining ethnicity and drawing ethnic boundaries—who is a co-ethnic and who is not, or who is eligible and who is ineligible to return migrate—even though such boundaries are often blurred in the sending country as a result of acculturation and intermarriage. Moreover, ethnic return migration fosters a hierarchy by increasing a pool of potential co-ethnic migrants; it provides an incentive to identify as co-ethnics (Brubaker 1998; Joppke and Rosenhek 2002), intensifying, as a result, competition for ethnic authenticities (who is a real ethnic and who is less so). Thus ethnic return migration is not simply a passive product of ties presumed to exist for the sake of shared ancestry; it actively produces ties by defining and discriminating co-ethnics. These consequences, as seen in the case of Japanese Brazilians and Japanese Peruvians, shape the experiences of return migrants. Having been incorporated differently into the ethnic hierarchy, Brazilian and Peruvian return migrants in Japan came up with different strategies to cope with the reality they confronted. The difference in their ethnicity evaluation processes—or ethnic responses, as I call them—is a manifestation of this.

The findings reported in this chapter are drawn from my fieldwork conducted in Japan in 1996–1997 and 2003–2004. My work primarily consisted of interviews with return migrants from Peru, but I also interacted with a number of Brazilians, mostly business owners, community leaders, and workers at the factory where I conducted participant observation in 1997. The more than 100 Peruvians interviewed were both of Japanese and non-Japanese descent. In addition, I conducted a survey in 2003–2004 among 40 Peruvian households, yielding life histories of 128 individuals (household members).[3] The personal names used in this chapter are all pseudonyms.

New Ethnic Hierarchy in Japan

The ethnicity-based immigration policy of Japan created a hierarchy by stipulating one's ethnic background as a decisive factor in determining who could be admitted to Japan. The new immigration policy, implemented in 1990 to control growing inflows of illegal migration, strictly banned any type of unskilled migration with the exception of those with "special ethnic ties." Under this policy, Japanese descendants, or *nikkeijin*, were automatically granted a special visa, making them de facto the only group of foreigners allowed to engage in any type of work, including unskilled labor. As co-ethnics, *nikkeijin* were also provided with a number of public services, such as subsidized Japanese-language lessons and employment assistance and counseling. Although citizenship was not granted automatically, *nikkeijin* were still able to obtain citizenship and permanent residency more easily than others because of the descent-based immigration and naturalization policies in Japan.

The revised immigration law thus effectively created divisions among foreign workers based on the criterion of "Japanese blood" (Yamanaka 2004: 78). As an extension, foreign workers were further divided hierarchically by race or nationality instead of by skills or qualifications (Shipper 2002). At the top of the hierarchy, according to Shipper (2002), were South Americans with "Japanese blood" along with long-term well-acculturated Korean residents, and at the bottom were illegal and "darker-skinned" South Asians with casual jobs, poorer pay, and worse working conditions. ("Fairer-skinned" migrants from Europe and North America, who tended to engage in skilled jobs, were missing from Shipper's analysis.) In short, there was a close correlation between nationality (or race), the type of job or occupation, and legal status (Takenoshita 2006). Compared to other, often illegal, unskilled laborers, *nikkeijin* were indeed privileged; they engaged in more stable work and earned more, and they were often preferred by employers because of their legal status (Tsuda et al. 2003). According to Shipper (2002), the hierarchy, backed up by government officials and employers, reflects and reinforces the underlying notion of the Japanese public that matches certain ethnicities and nationalities with certain kinds of occupations and legal rights.

The privileged status of *nikkeijin* over other foreigners (at least unskilled foreign laborers) was justified on the basis of their "special ties" to the Japanese. A Ministry of Justice officer explained, "For the sake of being Japanese descendants, those people have special ties to Japan. They have relatives here. So, it is natural that they have a desire to visit their families and learn about Japan. And we have the duty to accommodate their desires" (Ministry of Justice 1990: 12). Furthermore, *nikkeijin*, as family visitors, were allowed to engage in unskilled labor, because "it costs money to visit families"; according to another officer: "*Nikkeijin* should be allowed to work in order not to be permanent burdens on their families" (Ministry of Justice 1990: 12). Even though most *nikkeijin* had little contact with, or even remembrance of, their Japanese relatives in reality, they were admitted under the premise of familial ties to the Japanese. The ethnic immigration policy, as always, was justified as family migration instead of labor migration.

Specifically, "family visitors" were defined as those who could claim Japanese ancestry within three generations (i.e., those having one Japanese grandparent) and their spouses. In other words, they had to be second- or third-generation descendants of at least one Japanese immigrant (or they had to be children or grandchildren of a Japanese citizen). Second-generation Japanese descendants (nisei) were eligible for a three-year-long renewable visa, and third-generation descendants (sansei) were entitled to a one-year-long renewable visa. Later-generation Japanese descendants (fourth generation and thereafter) did not qualify to enter Japan under this policy. Second-generation descendants were also able to obtain Japanese permanent residency and citizenship more easily than third-generation descendants (the residency requirement for nisei was typically 5 years as opposed to 10 years for sansei). Furthermore, second-generation descendants were exempt from presenting a record of criminal history, which became mandatory in 2005 for third-generation *nikkei* visa applicants.

Generation mattered, fundamentally because it was a measure of social distance from the Japanese. Each generation removed from Japan was considered to have fewer ties. Second-generation children of Japanese nationals were thought to have closer ties to Japan than third-generation grandchildren. Fourth- and later-generation descendants of Japanese immigrants, according to one policymaker interviewed, had "practically nothing Japanese"; with the passage of generations, he asserted, intermarriage became more common and a knowledge of Japanese culture diminished. In this way, race and culture were together considered important symbols of ties to Japan. Racially and culturally unrecognizable as Japanese, later-generation Japanese descendants were simply assumed to have few ties to Japan, whereas descendants up to the third generation were thought to maintain some Japanese phenotypic features and culture and would accordingly integrate into Japanese society more easily than other foreigners.

To be admitted as *nikkeijin*, therefore, applicants had to demonstrate generational proximity, or child-parent relations, to Japanese citizens by way of *koseki* (Japanese family registry), together with birth, death, and marriage certificates of each relevant family member and a family genealogical tree. Also required were ties to guardians who would guarantee one's financial well-being while in Japan. Applicants needed to submit letters from an employer or a family member, in addition to a guarantor, who were all expected to be Japanese nationals or residents.

Although familial and social ties to Japanese citizens were important, cultural competency was not. There was no language requirement, and knowledge of Japanese culture was not tested. Possibly, policymakers assumed that Japanese descendants had some cultural familiarity; as Joppke and Rosenhek (2002) point out, "true co-ethnics" should not have any cultural integration problems. Although they might have been true co-ethnics, South Americans of Japanese descent were not granted the same rights as citizens—such as citizenship—and the process of naturalization did require basic Japanese-language competency. Alternatively, then, cultural competency did not really matter, because *nikkeijin* were to engage in temporary manual labor in any case. In this way, even though policymakers regarded Japanese-language proficiency as an important requisite for foreigners' successful integration into Japanese society, most *nikkeijin* were admitted to Japan with neither sufficient command of Japanese nor actual ties to their (distant) Japanese relatives. Still, they were granted relatively privileged positions over other foreigners on the premise and expectation that they shared something fundamental with the Japanese.

Brazilians and Peruvians in the Ethnic Hierarchy

Nikkeijin were not homogeneous, however. Nor were they treated uniformly in Japan. The most noticeable difference among them was coded in terms of nationality. Brazilians maintained, and were considered to maintain, more Japanese cultural and ethnic features than Peruvians on average and were subsequently ranked higher than Peruvians in the ethnic hierarchy in Japan. And this was reinforced by the higher status of Brazil in the global hierarchy of nations compared to Peru.

Language

Above all, Brazilians tended to speak better Japanese than Peruvians. According to a study on *nikkeijin* in Japan (JICA 1992), 30.4 percent of Japanese Brazilians surveyed responded that they spoke Japanese well or fluently, whereas only

5 percent of Japanese Peruvians did. Moreover, more than half of Brazilian respondents (53.4 percent) reported that they grew up speaking Japanese at home in Brazil, compared to only 11 percent of Peruvians. More than a decade later, the level of Japanese proficiency among Japanese Peruvian migrants remained noticeably low. A study conducted by the *International Press* ("Encuesta a la comunidad," 2005) showed that only 10 percent of Peruvian respondents "understood and spoke Japanese well enough" and 40 percent "did not understand or speak it." In comparison, 45 percent of Brazilians surveyed by Kajita (1998) responded that they spoke Japanese "fluently" or "well." Another study showed that 64 percent of Brazilian respondents reported that they could understand or speak Japanese well, in addition to 17 percent more who said they were also able to write and read without any difficulty (Koyo Sokushin Jigyodan 1997).[4]

One explanation for the difference lies in the timing of Japanese immigration. Japanese immigration to Brazil began later (1908) than Japanese immigration to Peru (1899) and continued for longer, until the 1970s. During the post–World War II period, Brazil was the major destination and one of five designated destinations, along with Paraguay, Bolivia, Argentina, and the Dominican Republic, to which the Japanese state sent emigrants as part of its postwar emigration policy. In contrast, Japanese immigration to Peru effectively ended in the 1930s when Peru broke diplomatic relations with Japan as a wartime enemy (and an ally of the United States) and banned Japanese immigration altogether. As a result, Japanese immigrants in Brazil were more recent arrivals; likewise, more Brazilian return migrants surveyed in Japan were first and second generation—5.5 percent and 41.2 percent, respectively—compared to 0.6 percent and 26.3 percent for Peruvian migrants (JICA 1992). Japanese Brazilians, therefore, were more likely than their Japanese Peruvian counterparts to maintain closer contact with the immigrant (and presumably Japanese-speaking) generation.

Another reason can be found in settlement patterns. A relatively large proportion of Japanese immigrants in Brazil settled and remained in rural agricultural enclaves where they were able to maintain the Japanese language more easily in more or less isolated communities. The fact that many of them arrived as whole families (Adachi 2004) also facilitated the maintenance of the Japanese language. In the 1930s and 1940s most Japanese immigrants in Brazil owned land and continued to engage in agriculture (Adachi 2004); on the contrary, in Peru most Japanese immigrants were not able to own land and had to leave farmlands for urban centers. This explains Japanese Brazilians' relative geographic dispersion today in comparison to more urban-centered Japanese Peruvians; whereas 74 percent of Japanese immigrants and their descendants in Peru were concentrated in Lima, the capital, only 26 percent of the Japanese Brazilian population were in the city of São Paulo, their largest concentration, according to estimates of the Centro de Estudos Nipo-Brasileiros (2002). Similarly, 90 percent of return migrants from Peru, in comparison to 30 percent of Brazilian migrants surveyed in Japan by JICA (1992), were from Lima and São Paulo, respectively.

Arguably, the wartime experience had a decisive impact on the ability to retain the Japanese language in both countries. During and immediately before World War II, Japanese immigrants and their descendants in Brazil and Peru faced a series of discriminatory measures. Use of the Japanese language was banned, as were the Japanese ethnic press, schools, and assembly. Yet nowhere in South America did Japanese experience such measures more directly and severely than in Peru (e.g., Konno and Fujisaki 1984), where Japanese immigrants and their descendants became the direct target of the country's worst racially motivated riot (1940) and where 1,800 community leaders and businessmen were forcibly sent to U.S. detention camps. Although such measures often aimed to debilitate the Japanese community in Peru, in Brazil they were generally carried out in the context of the country's nationalization (or Brazilianization) project to assimilate its immigrant population (some of the measures, however, were implicitly directed at the Japanese [Lesser 1999]).

Finally, the geographic origins of their ancestors may explain migrants' differential levels of Japanese proficiency. The majority (60–70 percent) of Japanese immigrants in Peru (compared to roughly 10 percent in Brazil) hailed from Okinawa, where Okinawan, a language distinct from standard Japanese, was spoken. Several Japanese Peruvians pointed out to me that because they spoke and heard Okinawan at home, they were at a disadvantage in "maintaining" the Japanese language in the first place.

Race

In addition to their generally superior command of Japanese, Brazilian return migrants, on average, maintained more phenotypic features akin to Japanese natives than Peruvians did. According to the same survey by JICA (1992), only 10 percent of Japanese Brazilians identified themselves as "racially mixed," in comparison to 30 percent of Japanese Peruvians. A widespread perception among scholars, the public, and policymakers also suggests that Japanese Peruvians were more racially mixed than their Brazilian counterparts, because they were more readily assimilated in Peru (or Peruvianized) (e.g., Ninomiya 1995; Watanabe 1996). Yet the racial difference, in reality, was more a result of who ended up migrating to Japan than of the degree of assimilation and inter-marriage in Peru. The endogamy rate among Japanese descendants in Peru, estimated to be about 60 percent, was probably as high as or even higher than that in Brazil (see Morimoto 1991). In short, racially mixed Japanese Peruvians were overrepresented among Peruvian migrants to Japan; likewise, racially unmixed Japanese descendants (particularly from rural areas) were probably overrepresented among Brazilian return migrants, especially in the early 1990s (T. Tsuda, personal communication, 2006). In addition, there were more non-Japanese descendants among Peruvian return migrants. In 2004, 7,300 Peruvians in Japan were estimated to be illegal (i.e., of non-Japanese descent), compared to just 4,700 for Brazilians (Ministry of Justice 2005). The Peruvian consulate in Tokyo estimates that the figure is roughly double the Japanese official figure (K. Paerregaard, personal communication, 2005). According to some remittance companies, close to half of all Peruvians residing in Japan trace no Japanese heritage at all (see also Masuda and Yanagida 1999).[5]

There were several explanations for why more non-Japanese descendants migrated from Peru than from Brazil. One was the visa exemption policy that Japan had with Peru until 1994. Taking advantage of this policy, many Peruvians of non-Japanese descent entered Japan as tourists and overstayed their visas. No exemption policy existed for Brazilians in the 1990s.

Another factor was the lax system of keeping old population records in Peru. This resulted in the prevalent abuse of family registry documents, sold and bought most commonly in remote rural areas. Along with the sale of documents, facial (eye) operations were performed in these areas (no such reports surfaced in Brazil or elsewhere). The abuse of documents spread further because of the difficulties in obtaining proper documents in Peru. Having fallen victim to document abuse, some "real" descendants had to resort to clandestine means to "fix" their documents. (One Japanese Peruvian return migrant told me that he confronted a problem in applying for a visa upon discovering that he had 38 "brothers" who had apparently migrated to Japan using his surname.) Some Okinawan descendants had difficulty securing old papers from Okinawa, where much was destroyed in the ground battle there during World War II. The Peruvian custom of using multiple names in one's documents (instead of using one surname and one given name, as in Brazil and elsewhere) also complicated the process, as did the common practice of changing names in the process of immigration, because every name had to match all the documents. All these practices added to the process of and demand for falsifying documents, which, in turn, encouraged clandestine migration.

In addition to non-Japanese descendants, relatively large numbers of racially mixed Japanese descendants return-migrated from Peru. That was because poorer Japanese descendants, who were more likely to return-migrate, tended to be racially mixed. It was particularly the case in (poorer) rural areas where Japanese immigrants, although small in number, frequently intermarried with the native population. The relationship between race and class was not as noticeable in Brazil, where many Japanese immigrants and their descendants remained in rural, as well as urban, areas and represented all class strata in Brazil (Mori 2000; Koga 1995, cited in Noiri 2005). Lima's Japanese community, originally established by wealthier immigrants, was more uniform, cohesive, and geographically concentrated (Takenaka 2003). Its membership was primarily limited to middle to upper middle-class Japanese descendants, and core members, who tended to maintain more Japanese cultural and phenotypic features than others, were less likely to return-migrate to Japan.

Even though the mixed-race background of many Peruvian migrants was a result of migrant selectivity, this nonetheless shaped the stereotype of Japanese Peruvians in Japan. Mari Shimabuku, a Japanese Peruvian return migrant of racially unmixed background, lamented that she was always mistaken for a Brazilian or Argentinean in Japan because of her "Japanese face." "Most Peruvians [in Japan] are racially mixed or are not *nikkei* at all," she said. "So people automatically assume that I am not Peruvian." This perception that Japanese Peruvians were "less Japanese" than Japanese Brazilians justified the ethnic hierarchy propagated by the return migration policy. The hierarchy was then reinforced by the clandestine entry of many Peruvians, fueled further by widely publicized crimes committed by some Peruvians (most recently, the murder of a 7-year-old Japanese girl by a racially mixed Japanese Peruvian) and occasional negative media reports from Peru (e.g., on the hostage crisis in 1997). In proportion to their population, Peruvian migrants have indeed committed more crimes than Brazilians (in 2005, 778 Peruvians and 137 Brazilians were indicted for crimes [National Police Agency 2006]). Although crimes involving Brazilians have been on the increase and although the number of non-Japanese Brazilians has grown (Yamaguchi 2003), the relatively negative image of Peruvians had already taken root in Japan, shaping public perceptions as well as employers' preferences.

Consequences for the Ethnic Hierarchy

Reflecting the hierarchy, Brazilians generally assumed better-paying jobs than Peruvians. Brazilians, along with Argentineans, who tended to speak relatively good Japanese, were also more likely than Peruvians to assume higher posts (such as group leaders in factories) and to serve as interpreters and labor brokers. According to several Peruvian and Brazilian observers, Peruvians were generally the first to be fired in times of recession. In the midst of Japan's recession in 2000, the unemployment rate among Peruvians was higher, 4.3 percent, than that among Brazilians, 2.6 percent (the national average was 2.9 percent) (Statistics Bureau 2005). Brazilian migrants were also more successful in establishing businesses in Japan, particularly large companies, such as the International Press, a media conglomerate, and Brastel, a telecommunication company, both founded by first-generation Japanese Brazilians. There were no comparable Peruvian-owned companies in Japan as of 2006. Also, on average, Brazilians earned more—17,000 yen more per month than Peruvians, according to a 1991 survey by Koyo Kaihatsu Center.

Return migrants were keenly aware of this ethnic hierarchy. Peruvians commonly acknowledged that Brazilians spoke better Japanese and exhibited more Japanese facial features than they did. In the eyes of many Peruvians, Brazilians also acted more like Japanese. As a result, "they feel they have more right to be in Japan," according to Nori Oshiro, a return migrant from Lima, Peru, and they "always look down on us." Japanese Brazilians, meanwhile, spoke badly of some "low-level" Peruvians who committed crimes and caused problems.

Communications between Brazilians and Peruvians were almost always in Portuguese. Brazilians never bothered to learn Spanish, according to the Peruvians I interviewed, and Peruvians always learned to speak Portuguese in Japan. This was partly a reflection of numbers, as there were more Brazilians than Peruvians. (In the United States, where there are more Spanish speakers, Margolis [1993] reports that Brazilian immigrants usually learn to speak Spanish, often better than English.) Yet Peruvians also seemed to adopt an Argentinean accent when speaking to Argentineans, even though there were fewer Argentineans in Japan. One Japanese Peruvian explained that because of their poorer command of the Japanese language, they have to turn to Brazilians (or Argentineans) to ask what Japanese leaders are saying. "When we want to speak to the Japanese, we ask Brazilians for help." Also, they simply found Portuguese much more accessible in Japan. Because there were more Brazilians in Japan, more information and resources were available in Portuguese than in Spanish. (For

Peruvians, Portuguese was certainly easier to learn than Japanese.) There usually were more jobs advertised in the Portuguese version of the weekly *International Press*, so some Peruvians told me that they resorted to the Portuguese version, rather than the Spanish one, in looking for jobs.

Japanese Peruvians made sense of the hierarchy not only because Brazilians spoke better Japanese and looked more Japanese than they did but also because, in their view, there were no *chicas* (false *nikkei*) among Brazilians. "Compared to us, 90 percent of Brazilians are Japanese descendants," said one Japanese Peruvian when asked about the major difference between Brazilians and Peruvians in Japan. The presence of *chicas*, they believed, damaged the image of the entire Peruvian population and posed obstacles to gaining acceptance in Japan. "Because of them," said a Japanese Peruvian of racially unmixed background, "the Japanese think that Japanese descendants in Peru don't look at all like Japanese." "Because of them," complained another, it has become difficult for all Peruvians to obtain and renew Japanese visas: "Whenever Japanese officials see Peruvian documents, they scrutinize them extra carefully. We have to wait longer than Brazilians to get our visas renewed." All the interviewed Japanese officers denied this, but many Japanese Peruvians insisted that it took them six months to renew a visa, whereas it took Brazilians only three months.

The problem, as Japanese Peruvians saw it, lay in other Peruvians—a problem they believed was not shared by their Brazilian counterparts. More precisely, even though they were brought in as descendants, they were lumped together with other Peruvians as unhyphenated Peruvians. This was problematic for real Japanese descendants, not only because they, as privileged migrants, were more highly placed in the ethnic hierarchy in the context of return migration but also because they generally came from relatively well-to-do backgrounds in the Peruvian context. (According to the survey I conducted among Peruvian migrants in Japan in 2003–2004, 55 percent of Japanese descendants previously held white-collar occupations in Peru, whereas only 25 percent of non-Japanese Peruvians did.) A Japanese descendant, Jorge Watanabe, said, "You never know about Peruvians here in Japan, because some of them come from really low-class backgrounds and they commit crimes." Consequently, Japanese Peruvians, particularly middle-class ones of unmixed racial backgrounds, consciously tried to distinguish themselves from other Peruvians by asserting their ethnic difference. Within-group difference—along lines of race, legal status, and socioeconomic status—thus was a critical factor shaping ethnic return migrants' responses to ethnic return migration.

Dealing with Internal Differences

Pointing out a growing influx of non-Japanese descendants from Brazil in recent years, Yamaguchi (2003) argues for the importance of looking at groups' internal differences. Conflict is frequently generated by internal difference, in terms of descent and social origins in Brazil, and this in turn projects negative images onto outsiders (i.e., the Japanese) (Yamaguchi 2003). Still, for Japanese Brazilians the major "other" remained the Japanese of Japan, and subsequently asserting a Brazilian national identity was the most effective strategy to distinguish themselves from the Japanese. This was particularly so because the status of Brazilians was relatively high in Japan compared to other South Americans, such as Peruvians. Moreover, because racially Japanese Brazilians were the majority of Brazilian migrants in Japan, they had relatively more freedom to express (their version of) Brazilianness; anything different from the Japanese could be interpreted as Brazilian, unlike Japanese Peruvians who struggled to present "authentic" Peruvian culture in the presence of numerous "other Peruvians." Thus, even though many Japanese Brazilians did not know how to dance samba "properly" (Tsuda 2003), their samba was still Brazilian enough in the eyes of the average Japanese. And so anything that stuck out as different in Japan, from clothing to mannerisms, was indeed interpreted and expressed as distinctly Brazilian by Japanese Brazilians in Japan (Capuano de Oliveira 1998). Positive "Brazilian characteristics," such as "human warmth," were emphasized in contrast to the "cold-hearted Japanese," and values associated with Japanese in Brazil, such as "hard work," became Brazilian in a land where most Brazilian workers put in long hours of work (Capuano de Oliveira 1998). A Japanese Brazilian return migrant I interviewed expressed his identity transformation succinctly: "In Brazil, I was a third-generation Japanese. But here in Japan, I am a first-generation Brazilian," he said, emphasizing the word "Brazilian." In asserting their Brazilianness, not only did they differentiate themselves from the Japanese but they also chose not to forge alliances with their fellow South Americans or emphasize their *nikkei*-ness (or commonality with Japanese Peruvians).

Japanese Peruvians, on the other hand, had trouble claiming a Peruvian national identity to the same extent that Japanese Brazilians did. In contrast to "nationalistic Brazilians" who always bragged about Brazil being "the biggest country in the world," said a second-generation Japanese Peruvian, Nobu Arakaki, their identities were "more problematic." Ricardo Oshiro explained that Peruvians did not like to publicize the Peruvian flag as much, because "first of all, the Japanese wouldn't recognize the Peruvian flag. They will confuse it with the Canadian flag, and if they realize it's Peruvian, they might burn it," he giggled. This type of negative comment was particularly common at the time of the Peruvian hostage crisis in 1997, when Japanese diplomats and businessmen were taken hostage by the Peruvian terrorist group MRTA. At the factory where I worked around the same time, it was quite a contrast to see many Japanese Brazilians place stickers of the Brazilian flag on their lockers, whereas there was not a single Peruvian flag in sight.

Japanese Peruvians often felt ashamed to be Peruvian. Their Brazilian counterparts had some positive Brazilian images they could resort to, such as famous soccer players recognized and praised by the Japanese, but as Fernando Guibu lamented, there was "absolutely nothing positive" about Peru. All about Peru, he said, was poverty, crime, and terrorism. And this image, they felt, was tainted further by "those Peruvians" (of non-Japanese descent) who "sneaked into" Japan illegally and committed crimes. Thus, unlike their Brazilian counterparts, Japanese Peruvians faced another "other" (other Peruvians) in addition to the Japanese, in negotiating their ethnic identity in Japan.

The separation between the two groups originated in Peru, yet it further increased in Japan as a consequence of return migration. That was fundamentally because Japan's ethnic return migration policy resulted in redefining the term *nikkei* and redrawing the boundary between *nikkei* and non-*nikkei*. In Peru, *nikkei* was a racial term, referring mostly to Japanese descendants with Japanese phenotypic features, and the term was most commonly used within Lima's tight-knit Japanese community circles. In Japan, however, it became a status symbol with legal privilege. Because the Japanese government automatically granted privileged legal status to all Japanese descendants (up to the third generation), the definition was broadened. Although *nikkei* mainly referred to racially "pure" and middle-class Japanese Peruvians in Peru, in Japan it legally encompassed all Peruvians who had at least one Japanese grandparent. In Japan *nikkei* also became synonymous with *legal* Peruvians (whereas non-*nikkei* were labeled illegal). A third-generation Peruvian with one Japanese grandfather expressed it well: "I don't look Japanese and I am not familiar with any Japanese customs. I had never heard of the term *nikkei* and never considered myself *nikkei* in Peru. I learned only in Japan that I am *nikkei* because I have a Japanese grandfather. Yes, I am *nikkei* because to me it's a matter of blood." He then added that when he goes back to Peru, however, he would cease to be *nikkei*. Likewise, racially mixed and poorer Japanese Peruvians, who had previously been excluded from Lima's *nikkei* community associations, discovered in Japan that they too were *nikkei* because of their Japanese "blood."

With the legal privilege conferred on Japanese "blood," *nikkei* became a status symbol in Japan. It meant the right to be in Japan, or greater right than that of non-Japanese Peruvians to stay and work in Japan. Because the surname served as the primary symbol of *nikkei*-ness, its value rose. Thus Japanese Peruvians of mixed descent almost always used their Japanese surnames in Japan as a way of asserting their *nikkei*-ness, even if it was their maternal name, rarely used in Peru. A quarter-Japanese Peruvian, Carlos Kori, went by Kori (a simplified and changed spelling of his maternal Japanese name Kuwaori), although in Peru he always went by his paternal name: "That way, people recognize that I'm a descendant [and thus legal]. Then people treat you better if you have something Japanese." Simultaneously, Carlos added, their employers (factories) often encouraged Peruvians to use a Japanese surname "to make things look better on paper" because of the legal status automatically associated with Japanese descendants. *Nikkei*-ness, symbolized by a Japanese surname, meant legal privilege and thus increased status and employability.

In response to the amplified notion of *nikkei*-ness, a stricter definition of group membership emerged; racially Japanese and middle-class Japanese Peruvians who had cultivated a sense of Japaneseness in Peru through Lima's Japanese community activities were now called true *nikkei*, legitimate *nikkei*, or *nikkei nikkei* in contrast to racially mixed (and poorer) *nikkei* in Japan. Although the *nikkei nikkei* used these terms to distinguish themselves from "suspicious" *nikkei* and to protect their increasingly prestigious *nikkei* status, other Peruvians used the terms to refer to the group that is racially distinct (with "slanted eyes") and socially "closed" and "racist." Thus the ethnic boundaries between real *nikkei* and racially mixed *nikkei* have hardened in Japan in response to the ethnic hierarchy created as a result of return migration.

Unlike Brazilian return migrants who established communities as Brazilian in Japan, the emerging community among Peruvians was consciously defined as *nikkei* (or more precisely *nikkei nikkei*) rather than Peruvian. Although some large-scale events were held together, such as the Dekasegui Soccer League (1997), newly created associations were mostly for *nikkei*, with membership and leadership limited primarily to *nikkei* Peruvians.

For Japanese Peruvians who experienced downward mobility in Japan, claiming a true *nikkei* identity was a way to restore their honor, especially in a context where *nikkei*-ness, in contrast to Peruvianness, was associated with more status and privilege. This was quite in contrast to Japanese Brazilians. Being ranked higher in the ethnic hierarchy as Brazilians in Japan, Japanese Brazilians had little interest in associating with lower-ranked Peruvians as "*nikkei* South Americans" or "Latinos." Unlike their Peruvian counterparts, who were troubled by the large presence of non-Japanese descendants, Japanese Brazilians were able to claim Brazilian identities more freely while simultaneously retaining prestige associated with *nikkei* status. In short, Brazilianness was more readily available for them to use to make sense of the ethnic rejection they experienced and the difference enhanced in return-migrating to Japan.

Conclusion

As this case attests, ethnic return migration heightens ethnic divisions more often than it forges ethnic solidarity. In their ethnic homeland, return migrants are typically treated as foreigners and are marginalized. Migrants, in response, develop a discourse of difference in relation to the local population; even where cultural or racial differences are minor, as in the case of Hungarian Croatians in Hungary, reported by Capo Zmegac (2005), minute differences are emphasized or created (Capo Zmegac 2005). Simultaneously, divisions among ethnic return migrants also increase because ethnic return migration creates an ethnically defined hierarchy and stipulates who has the right, or more right, to enter and stay in the host land based on the degree of ethnic proximity.

Ethnic return migration to Japan also increased ethnic divisions not only between the Japanese and the migrants but also among the migrants themselves. Brazilian return migrants who were racially and culturally "more Japanese" than Peruvians were ranked higher in the ethnic hierarchy, and this made it easier for them to maintain distance from their fellow South Americans. Japanese Peruvians, on the other hand, engaged in the construction of difference from the Japanese *and* from other Peruvians of non-Japanese descent. As the definition of *nikkei* became amplified as a result of return migration, the boundaries between pure Japanese-descent Japanese Peruvians, mixed-descent Japanese Peruvians, and other Peruvians were hardened with stricter group memberships. For Japanese descendants this hardening was a strategy for gaining recognition as "authentic descendants," who were granted higher status within the Japanese ethnic hierarchy. In this way, transnational migration does not always lead to the construction of more inclusive, expansive, diasporic, and multiple ethnic identities among migrants but can result in the narrowing of previous ethnic identities (Tsuda 2003).

The different processes of ethnic identity transformation between Japanese Brazilians and Japanese Peruvians reflected their strategies and positions in the new ethnic hierarchy in Japan. The hierarchy created divisions among return migrants, and the strategies used by return migrants in response further enhanced their internal differentiations. Just as the government used the notion of ethnic ties to justify their needs (to incorporate cheap labor), ethnic return migrants used the newly defined notion of ethnicity to enhance their own status given their positions in the new society. Ethnic responses of return migrants, therefore, were highly localized; the identities that Japanese Brazilian and Japanese Peruvian return migrants constructed as Brazilians and *nikkei* were not transnational identities; they were constructed in contrast to the Japanese of Japan and non-*nikkei* Peruvians in the Japanese context.

Ethnic return migration does have important consequences for shaping ethnic identities of both migrants and the host population. Promoted in the name of inherent ethnic ties, ethnic return migration uses ethnicity as a tool to induce migration. Likewise, return migrants use ethnicity as a device for making sense of their newly found realities. Far from inherent, ethnic ties are constantly generated. And ethnic return migration plays an active role in the process of generating them.

Notes

1. Not all Brazilian and Peruvian migrants were of Japanese descent. More non-Japanese Peruvians were estimated to have entered Japan than non-Japanese Brazilians.

2. These figures include those who are officially registered in Japan and exclude undocumented migrants and first-generation Japanese immigrants and their descendants holding Japanese or dual nationalities. Foreign nationals who reside in Japan for more than three months are required to register in local municipalities.

3. The survey was conducted in collaboration with the Latin American Migration Project and Alvaro del Castillo.

4. These studies primarily targeted Brazilian migrants in Japan, but small proportions of their samples (2–6 percent) were Peruvians. These studies did not make a distinction between different nationalities.

5. All illegal migrants are by definition non-*nikkei*, yet not all non-Japanese descendants are necessarily illegal.

References Cited

Adachi, Nobuko. 2004. "*Japonês*: A Marker of Social Class or a Key Term in the Discourse of Race?" *Latin American Perspectives* 31(3):48–76.

Brubaker, Rogers. 1998. "Migrations of Ethnic Unmixing in the 'New Europe.'" *International Migration Review* 32(4):1047–1065.

Capo Zmegac, Jasna. 2005. "Ethnically Privileged Migrants in Their New Homeland." *Journal of Refugee Studies* 18(2):199–215.

Capuano de Oliveira, Adriana. 1998. "Japanese in Brazil or Brazilians in Japan? The Identity Issue Inside of a Migratory Context." Paper presented at the conference "Cultural Encounters Between Latin America and the Pacific Rim," Center for Iberian and Latin American Studies, University of California, San Diego, March 6–7.

Centro de Estudos Nipo-Brasileiros. 2002. *Nikkei Shakai Jittai Chosa Hokokusho* [Report on the survey on *nikkei* society]. São Paulo: Centro de Estudos Nipo-Brasileiros, University of São Paulo.

"Encuesta a la comunidad" [Community survey]. 2005. *International Press*, January 1. Tokyo: International Press.

Fox, Jon. 2003. "National Identities on the Move: Transylvanian Hungarian Labour Migrants in Hungary." *Journal of Ethnic and Migration Studies* 29(3):449–466.

JICA (Japan International Cooperation Agency). 1992. *Nikkeijin Hompo Shiro Jittai Chosa Hokokusho* [Report on *nikkeijin* laborers in Japan]. Tokyo: JICA.

Joppke, Christian, and Zeev Rosenhek. 2002. "Contesting Ethnic Immigration: Germany and Israel Compared." *Archives Européennes de Sociologie* 43(3):301–335.

Kajita, Takamichi.1998. "Dekasegui 10-nen go no Nikkei Burazirujin" [*Nikkei* Brazilians 10 years after their *dekasegui* migration began]. *Kokusai Kankeigaku Kenkyu* [Journal of International Relations] 25:1–22.

Kawamura, Lili. 2000. *Nihon Shakai to Burajiru-jin Imin* [Japanese society and Brazilian migrants]. Tokyo: Akashi Shoten.

Konno, Toshihiko, and Yasuo Fujisaki, eds. 1984. *Iminshi* [History of Japanese emigration]. Tokyo: Shinsensha.

Koyo Kaihatsu Center. 1991. *Gaikokujin Rodosha Mondai Shiryoshu* [On foreign migrant workers]. Tokyo: Koyo Kaihatsu Center.

Koyo Sokushin Jigyodan. 1997. *Nikkeijin Rodosha no Koyo kanri to Chiiki Sangyo kan Ido* [Labor control and job mobility among nikkeijin workers]. Tokyo: Koyo Sokushin Jigyodan.

Lesser, Jeffrey. 1999. *Negotiating National Identity: Immigrants, Minorities, and the Struggle for Ethnicity in Brazil*. Durham, NC: Duke University Press.

Louie, Andrea. 2004. *Chineseness Across Borders: Renegotiating Chinese Identities in China and the United States*. Durham, NC: Duke University Press.

Margolis, Maxine L. 1993. *Little Brazil*. Princeton, NJ: Princeton University Press.

Masuda, Yoshio, and Toshio Yanagida. 1999. *Peru: Taiheiyo to Andesu no Kuni* [Peru: A Pacific and Andean country]. Tokyo: Chuo Koron Shinsha.

Ministry of Justice. 1990. *Nikkeijin no U-turn gensho wo ou* [Researching the U-turn migration of *nikkeijin*]. Kokusai Jinryu [International Human Mobility] 7. Tokyo: Ministry of Justice.

———. 2005. "Shutsunyukoku Kanri" [Immigration control]. http://www.moj.go.jp/. Accessed December 26, 2005.

Mori, Koichi. 2000. "Burajiru kara no Nikkeijin Dekasegi no 15-nen Kanryu-gata Iju" [Circular migration of Japanese Brazilians over the past 15 years]. *Raten Amerika Repoto* [Latin America Report] 16(2):2–13.

Morimoto, Amelia. 1991. *Población de Origen Japonés en el Peru: Perfil Actual* [People of Japanese origin in Peru: Present profile.] Lima: Comisión Conmemorativa del 90 Aniversario de la Inmigración Japonesa del Peru, Centro Cultural Peruano-Japonés.

Münz, Rainer, and Rainer Ohliger, eds. 2003. *Diasporas and Ethnic Migrants: Germany, Israel, and Post-Soviet Successor States in Comparative Perspective*. London: Frank Cass.

National Police Agency. 2006. *Keisatsu Hakusho* [White Paper on policing]. Tokyo: National Police Agency.

Ninomiya, Masato, ed. 1995. *Nikkei Community no Shorai* [The future of *nikkei* communities]. Tokyo: Burajiru Nihon Bunka Kyokai.

Noiri, Naomi. 2005. "Okinawa ni okeru nikkeijin teiju gaikokujin no kokkyo wo koeru ido to ethnic network: Amerikajin Taiwanjin Nikkei Perujin Nikkei Burajirujin no ishiki chosa kara" [Overseas migration and ethnic social networks in Okinawa: A case study of American, Taiwanese, *nikkei* Peruvian and *nikkei* Brazilian]. *Ningen Kagaku: Ryukyu Daigaku Hobun Gakubu Ningen Kagakuka Kiyo* [Human Sciences, a journal published by the Faculty of Human Sciences, Ryukyu University] 15(15):91–113.

Shipper, Apichai W. 2002. "The Political Construction of Foreign Workers in Japan." *Critical Asian Studies* 34(1):41–68.

Statistics Bureau. 2005. *Kokusei Chosa Hokoku* [Report on population census]. Tokyo: Statistics Bureau, Management and Coordination Agency.

Takenaka, Ayumi. 2003. "Paradoxes of Ethnicity-Based Immigration: Peruvian and Japanese-Peruvian Migrants in Japan." In *Global Japan: The Experience of Japan's New Immigrants and Overseas Communities*, Roger Goodman, Ceri Peach, Ayumi Takenaka, and Paul White, eds. London: Routledge Curzon, 222–236.

Takenoshita, Hirohisa. 2006. "The Differential Incorporation into Japanese Labor Market: A Comparative Study of Japanese Brazilians and Professional Chinese Migrants." *Japanese Journal of Population* 4(1):56–77.

Tsuda, Takeyuki. 2003. *Strangers in the Ethnic Homeland: Japanese Brazilian Return Migration in Transnational Perspective*. New York: Columbia University Press.

Tsuda, Takeyuki, Zulema Valdez, and Wayne A. Cornelius. 2003. "Human Versus Social Capital: Immigrant Wages and Labor Market Incorporation in Japan and the United States." In *Host Societies and the Reception of Immigrants*, Jeffrey Reitz, ed. La Jolla, CA: Center for Comparative Immigration Studies, 215–252.

Watanabe, Masako, ed. 1996. *Dekasegui Nikkei Brazirujin* [*Dekasegi nikkei* Brazilians]. Tokyo: Akashi Shoten.

Yamaguchi, Ana Elisa. 2003. "Nihon ni okeru gaikokujin kyojusha to chiiki jumin no shomondai no saikento: Nikkei burajirujin jumin no shiten kara" [Reconsidering the conflicts between foreign migrants and local residents in Japan: The case of Japanese Brazilians]. *Ratin Amerika Karibu Kenkkyu* [Latin American and Caribbean Studies] 10:21–31.

Yamanaka, Keiko. 2004. "Citizenship and Differential Exclusion of Immigrants in Japan." In *State/Nation/Transnation: Perspectives on Transnationalism in the Asia Pacific*, Brenda Yeoh and Katie Wills, eds. New York: Routledge, 67–92.

Brothers Only in Name

The Alienation and Identity Transformation of Korean Chinese Return Migrants in South Korea

Changzoo Song

THE 2 MILLION ethnic Koreans in China are descendants of those Koreans who migrated to Manchuria (the three northeastern provinces of China today) between the second half of the nineteenth century and the first half of the twentieth century. Because of the policy of the Manchus, who prohibited any Han Chinese or Koreans from migrating into their ancestral lands, not many people were living in Manchuria before the mid-nineteenth century. The policy eased later, and to defend Manchuria from the encroaching Russians, the Manchus allowed Han Chinese and Koreans to migrate to Manchuria in 1885.[1] Koreans migrated to Manchuria at different times from different parts of Korea. Earlier migrants were impoverished peasants from the northernmost part of the Korean peninsula, and they settled in Kando (Jiandao) in southern Manchuria across the River Tuman from Korea.

A larger number of Koreans migrated to Manchuria and to the Russian Far East in the early twentieth century, when Korea was occupied by Japan. During the Japanese occupation impoverished and politically motivated Koreans who tried to escape Japan's rule continued to migrate to Manchuria and the Russian Far East. Especially after Japan's invasion of China and the consequent establishment of Manchukuo in 1932, Korean peasants from southern parts of the Korean peninsula were semiforced by the Japanese government, which wanted to develop the lands and the abundant resources, to migrate to northern Manchuria.

Political developments in northeast Asia during and after World War II brought many changes to the lives of ethnic Koreans in Manchuria. Soon after the collapse of the Japanese empire and the liberation of Korea in August 1945, about 700,000 Koreans returned to Korea from Manchuria.[2] The civil war and political upheavals in China in the 1940s, the occupation of Korea by the USSR and the United States, and the Korean War (1950–1953) added complexities to the lives of ethnic Koreans in Manchuria. When the People's Republic of China was established in 1949, Koreans in Manchuria were recognized as legitimate citizens thanks to their anti-Japanese struggles and support of the Chinese Communist Party during the Civil War. Ethnic Koreans enjoyed equal rights with the dominant Han Chinese, and in 1952 the Yanbian Korean Autonomous Prefecture was established.[3]

During the cold war China recognized North Korea as the only legitimate Korean state and considered South Korea an illegitimate political entity. For this reason ethnic Koreans in China could maintain contact only with North Koreans, and they were totally disconnected from South Koreans. This situation changed in the 1980s, when the cold war eased and China adopted its reform policy. By the mid-1980s, as China opened itself to the outside world, Korean Chinese learned about South Korea, particularly its economic prosperity in contrast to the poverty and ideological rigidity of North Korea. This changed perceptions of Korean Chinese toward South Korea, and soon Korean Chinese developed transnational ethnic affinity with South Koreans. Therefore in the mid-1980s "blood is thicker than water" became a popular saying among Korean Chinese when they thought of South Korea, their long-lost ancestral homeland (see Hŏ 2001b: 456–457). They began to visit South Korea in the late 1980s, and by the end of the 1980s several thousand Korean Chinese were already staying in South Korea. The number of ethnic Korean returnees from China grew drastically after the establishment of formal diplomatic relations between South Korea and China in 1992. Each year tens of thousands of Korean Chinese visitors arrived in South Korea, and many of them chose to work there. Currently, more than 370,000 Korean Chinese are in South Korea, of which approximately 10 percent are undocumented migrant workers. Familiar with both Chinese and Korean culture, Korean Chinese easily fit into South Korea and lead a transnational lifestyle between China and South Korea.

This ethnic return migration of Korean Chinese to South Korea was facilitated by the macroeconomic and sociopolitical conditions in China and South Korea in the last two decades: China's opening and incorporation into the global economy and South Korea's transition from a labor-exporting country to a labor-importing country. Although the economic conditions of coastal regions of China improved rapidly after the reform policy, peripheral northeast China, where ethnic Koreans are concentrated, has been left far behind in terms of economic development.

This made Korean Chinese turn to the employment opportunities in urban areas and overseas, particularly South Korea. Meanwhile, the South Korean economy demanded cheap labor, and South Koreans, out of nostalgia for their co-ethnics in China, whom they had not met for several decades, viewed this positively.

These expectations and nostalgic feelings of Korean Chinese and South Koreans, however, were betrayed when Korean Chinese migrated to South Korea in great numbers throughout the 1990s. Korean Chinese were disappointed by the discriminatory treatment they received from their South Korean co-ethnics and the harsh realities of life as foreign workers of the 3D (dirty, dangerous, and difficult) jobs sector that locals disdain. Meanwhile, South Koreans grew disillusioned with their rather "Sinicized" brethren from China. Alienated and marginalized in their ethnic homeland, Korean Chinese came to recognize their being Chinese rather than Korean, which is similar to the case of Japanese Brazilian return migrants whose Brazilian identity was reinforced through their experiences of return migration to Japan (Tsuda 2000, 2001, 2003; Chapter 9).

This changed perception of Korean Chinese imposes a challenge to Korean nationalism and national identity, which are based on primordial notions of Korean "blood" and ethnic homogeneity.[4] Considering the importance of this implication, in this chapter I investigate the process in which the two groups—South Koreans and Korean Chinese—changed their initially positive views toward each other to negative feelings after the substantial ethnic return migration of Korean Chinese to South Korea. In particular, I look at the changes in Korean Chinese notions of ethnic homeland in regard to their ethnic return migration experiences in South Korea and how these experiences of alienation in their ethnic homeland changed their notion of national identity.

To understand the identity changes of Korean Chinese in South Korea, I conducted in-depth interviews with 12 Korean Chinese returnees in late 2004 and early 2005 in Korea. These interviews are supplemented with Korean Chinese literary works and Korean Chinese intellectual discussions regarding their relations with their ethnic homeland. For South Korean perceptions of Korean Chinese, I looked at how Korean Chinese are represented in South Korean popular discourse, such as films, TV dramas, and media reports.

Nostalgia for the Ethnic Homeland and the Korean Dream

Before the mid-1980s, Korean Chinese did not know much about South Korea and its society. If they knew anything at all, their knowledge was influenced by cold war propaganda of China and North Korea. It was after the 1986 Asian

Games and the 1988 Summer Olympics—both held in South Korea—that Korean Chinese came to have a more realistic view of South Korea. Through these events they were positively impressed by the economic prosperity of their ethnic homeland, and many of them were eager to visit their relatives in South Korea (Chŏng 2000; Im 2003). However, not many of them could visit South Korea because traveling overseas was not easy in China at that time. In addition, to obtain permission to enter South Korea, Korean Chinese were required to submit invitations from their South Korean relatives, which was not easy because they had been disconnected from their relatives for many decades. It was not until the establishment of formal diplomatic relations between South Korea and China in 1992 that a large number of Korean Chinese were able to visit South Korea. Since then tens of thousands of Korean Chinese have arrived in South Korea each year. They came as trainees, migrant workers, students, tourists, and brides of South Koreans. Once in South Korea, most of them tried to find work regardless of their visa status, because they could earn as much as 20 times more than they could in China. Korean Chinese quickly became the largest group among all foreign workers in South Korea, exceeding 100,000 by the mid-1990s, which is more than 5 percent of the entire Korean Chinese population in China or more than 10 percent of their labor force (Kwŏn and Pak 2005: 147).[5]

Behind such a large-scale ethnic return migration of Korean Chinese to South Korea are economic, social, and cultural factors. First, the employment opportunities and the wage differentials between China and South Korea are most important. Migration was also facilitated by the migrants' ability to speak the Korean language. Korea was their ancestral homeland, and the two countries are geographically close. Another crucial and more fundamental factor was the relative decline of the socioeconomic status of Korean Chinese compared to their Han Chinese neighbors. These multiple factors provoked Korean Chinese nostalgia for their ancestral homeland.

The Decline in the Socioeconomic Status
of Ethnic Koreans in Postreform China

Korean Chinese scholars recognized that the economic status of ethnic Koreans in China had been degenerating in postreform China (Chŏng 2000: 93). Many of my Korean Chinese informants told me that they felt that their socioeconomic status had been declining in the last two decades compared to their Han Chinese neighbors.[6] This decline in economic status was accompanied by gradual political alienation of Korean Chinese within the Yanbian Korean Autonomous Prefecture and in many other Korean villages in rural areas, where ethnic Koreans lost their majority status because of increasing numbers of Han Chinese migrants to the region. This was felt rather painfully by Korean Chinese, who used to be proud of their economic prosperity and high educational level within China.

From the early days of migration to Manchuria, Korean and Chinese settlers formed separate communities because of their different agricultural backgrounds. Being used to wet rice cultivation, Korean migrants settled mostly in lowlands, along rivers (Chŏn 1991: 80). Han Chinese settlers, meanwhile, most of whom came from the impoverished Shandong Province, chose higher lands, as they were used to dry-land crops. Forming their own ethnic communities, Korean settlers maintained the same lifestyle as they had in Korea.[7] They also kept close contact with their motherland and were fed by the continuous flow of migrants from Korea until the mid-1940s. After the establishment of the People's Republic of China in 1949, ethnic Koreans received the same citizenship rights and lands as did Han Chinese. More than 80 percent of ethnic Koreans in Manchuria were farmers, and most of them were engaged in growing rice before the 1980s (Hŏ 2001a: 265). Because rice is a higher-value crop than dry-land crops in northeast China, Koreans enjoyed a better life than their Chinese neighbors in rural northeast China (Chŏng 2000; Kim 2003: 110; To 1992: 169). They also maintained the highest educational rate among all ethnic groups in China and were considered the most successful minority in China (Chŏng 2000; Hoffmann 1986; Lee 1986).

By the late 1980s, however, Korean Chinese began to feel that their socioeconomic status was declining compared to that of the Han Chinese in the region. In large part this was because of the unbalanced development between urban and rural areas in postreform China. Although the urban economy developed rapidly, the rural economy did not develop much, and this gap has been growing in the last two decades. The speed of economic development in Yanbian was slower than in other regions of China. Between 1949 and 1989 the annual average growth of industrial production in Yanbian was 9 percent, whereas it was 13.9 percent for the whole country and 12.2 percent for Jilin Province (K. Kim 1998: 10–11). In addition, the economic status of ethnic Koreans declined relative to that of Han Chinese in rural northeast China. This was due to Koreans' sticking to rice growing while their Chinese neighbors diversified their economic activities by running small businesses (Chŏng 2000: 93). A Korean

Chinese researcher describes how the living standard of Han Chinese exceeded that of ethnic Koreans in northeast China in the 1990s.

> Except for the cases of ethnic Koreans who worked overseas, the living standard of ethnic Chinese is higher than that of ethnic Koreans in general. . . . The Korean "field economy" is slower in development than the "hill economy" of Han Chinese in Yanbian region. (Ryang 2001: 155)

In addition, ethnic Koreans also felt that their political status within their own communities had weakened in relation to Han Chinese. Although Korean Chinese generally admit that they have enjoyed equal rights with the dominant Han Chinese, they are well aware that politically they are totally dominated by Han Chinese.[8] This was particularly true during the late 1950s and the 1960s, when ethnic minorities suffered greatly under the ultra-leftist movements, such as the Great Leap Forward Movement and the Cultural Revolution.[9] My informants told me that, although the Chinese government is relatively generous to ethnic minorities, any political movements of ethnic Koreans are always closely scrutinized by the government and ethnic Koreans are not given real power, even within their autonomous local governments.[10] One of them stated, "We, Koreans, are the secondary people even in the Yanbian Korean Autonomous Prefecture. Koreans are given nominal positions, but it's the Han Chinese that possess real power." This was accompanied by a low fertility rate among Korean Chinese—the lowest among all ethnic groups in China—and rising Han Chinese nationalism. Therefore ethnic Koreans in China today believe that they are "relatively low in economic status and are outside of mainstream Chinese society, which is dominated by people of the Han nationality" (Kim 2003: 110–111). This perceived fear of Han Chinese domination and their own political weakness have reinforced Korean Chinese nostalgia for their ancestral homeland.

According to Gurr (1970), frustration is not necessarily felt by a minority group only when severe poverty or oppression is the norm in a given society. Rather, frustration ensues when a minority group feels a "relative sense of deprivation," even when things are improving (Gurr 1970). This was the case with ethnic Koreans in northeast China throughout the 1980s and 1990s. When they felt frustrated about not having any political channels to express themselves, Korean Chinese looked outside the border to their motherland. As a matter of fact, as an ethnic minority whose motherland is right across the border, historically Korean Chinese have been transnational. As a Korean Chinese scholar points out, ethnic Koreans in China have kept the characteristics of "border people" (Kim 2001a: 25), and they tend to look for opportunities across the border, especially in times of difficulty. During the political upheavals in China in the 1960s and 1970s, a few thousand Korean Chinese escaped to North Korea (Hŏ 2001a: 259). Since the late 1980s tens of thousands of Korean Chinese have gone to Russia as street peddlers, and currently there are more than 30,000 of them there (see Kim 2004).

In any regard, nostalgia tends to intensify, especially when one is experiencing hardship outside one's homeland yet knows of the existence of a well-to-do motherland. By the late 1980s Korean Chinese were prepared to pursue employment opportunities in South Korea, even by illegal means. The many success stories of Korean Chinese who returned home with large sums of money provoked the Korean Dream—getting rich quickly by working in Korea—among other Korean Chinese.

The Korean Dream

If the push factor behind the ethnic return migration of Korean Chinese to South Korea at the end of the 1980s was nostalgia for their ethnic homeland, aggravated by the relative decline of their socioeconomic and political status in China, the pull factor was employment opportunities and higher wages. Until recently South Korea was a typical sending country so far as international migration was concerned. Throughout the 1970s and 1980s, each year tens of thousands of South Koreans migrated to wealthy regions, such as the United States, Japan, and Western Europe. In 1990, however, South Korea passed the turning point, and the number of Koreans leaving the country exceeded the number of foreign workers entering it (Park 1994). This was due to continuous economic growth combined with social and demographic changes in South Korea. The labor disputes of the 1980s and 1990s, which frequently developed into violent demonstrations and strikes, resulted in rising labor costs. At the same time, following the pattern of Western economies, South Korea's industries shifted in the 1980s from the Fordist production and accumulation system to more flexible forms of production and accumulation (see Harvey 1989: 145). At this time South Korean employers moved their manufacturing facilities overseas and began to import low-cost and flexible foreign workers from less developed Asian countries. This shift in South Korean industries and its labor market at the end of the 1980s coincided with the visits of Korean Chinese to South Korea.

In the late 1980s, when Korean Chinese began to visit their South Korean relatives, they brought Chinese herbal medicines as gifts for their South Korean relatives. Some sold these herbal medicines on the street, and curious or sympathetic South Koreans bought them. Soon selling herbal medicine became a popular business for Korean Chinese visitors. The stories of success spread into China's ethnic Korean community, and more Korean Chinese came to South Korea. Many of them found employment in South Korea because they could earn at least 10 to 20 times more than they could in China (Im 2003: 293). After working for a few years in South Korea, they would return to China as "rich" men and buy land, houses, and businesses. A typical success story of the Korean Dream in the early 1990s was as follows:

> Mr. Kim (38 years old) lives in Yanji City of the Yanbian Korean Autonomous Prefecture.... He came to Korea in 1991 with an invitation from his relatives in Korea. When his visit was confirmed, Mr. Kim created a big fund by selling his house and borrowing money from his relatives. Then he bought a big amount of Chinese herbal medicine and came to Korea to start his "Korean Dream." He successfully sold his herbal medicines at busy subway stations in Seoul and in less than a year he earned quite big money. Then he returned to Yanji, where he bought an apartment at the city center and opened a blanket factory and two restaurants. (*Chosun Daily*, January 21, 2000)

Because many South Korean manufacturers relocated their factories to China in the 1990s for cheap labor and a bigger market, they also provided employment opportunities for Korean Chinese. These factories were mostly concentrated in the coastal cities of Qingdao, Tianjin, and Dalian, and they employed Korean Chinese, who knew both Korean and Chinese. For Korean Chinese this was a good opportunity because these South Korean companies normally paid much higher wages than Chinese companies in the region. This experience further motivated them to go to South Korea in search of better opportunities. In South Korea employers preferred Korean Chinese workers over other foreigners because Korean Chinese spoke the Korean language. Korean Chinese workers are concentrated in such industries as construction and domestic services, where communication skills are demanded, whereas non-Korean workers—from China, Bangladesh, the Philippines, and Uzbekistan—are predominantly employed in the manufacturing sector. Although many of these Korean Chinese failed in achieving their dream, those who succeeded passed on new hopes to others. Showing off their wealth by frequenting expensive restaurants, bars, and hiring taxis, those who returned home would further provoke the Korean Dream in others.

South Korean Perceptions of Korean Chinese Returnees: Before and After

As Korean Chinese developed a nostalgic affiliation with their ancestral homeland before their return migration to South Korea, South Koreans also cultivated nostalgic feelings toward their co-ethnics in China. First, the nationalist historiography of South Korea recognizes Korean Chinese for their anti-Japanese struggles during the colonial period. South Koreans also positively evaluated the fact that Korean Chinese kept alive many old Korean traditions that South Koreans themselves had lost in the process of industrialization. South Koreans also developed a romantic idea that Korean Chinese would play an important role in the unification of the nation. The positive views, however, were seriously challenged when South Koreans encountered large-scale Korean Chinese return migration to South Korea in the 1990s. In addition, Korean Chinese were not free from the negative images of their adopted homeland (China) in the minds of South Koreans.[11]

Before the Return Migration

Just as their co-ethnics in China did not know much about South Korea until the mid-1980s, South Koreans did not pay much attention to ethnic Koreans in China (and in the Soviet Union). After the mid-1980s, however, the South Korean media began to report about them frequently. This change came with the easing of the cold war, but it was also a result of South Korea's growing economic and political engagements with its Communist neighbors in the 1980s. The South Korean economy had shown rapid growth for more than three decades by then, and it reached the stage where diversification of trading partners and development of new markets became essential. For this reason, South Korean business leaders were keen to expand their businesses into the newly emerging markets of China and the Soviet Union, and they realized that ethnic Koreans in these countries could be beneficial to their business projects. Meanwhile, the South Korean government was also seeking the political support of China and the Soviet Union (later Russia) with regard to its North Korean policy. It was in this context that more and more South Korean business leaders and politicians started to emphasize the importance of ethnic Koreans in these two countries.[12] The following statement by a researcher for a South

Korean think tank, who eloquently asserts the value of overseas Koreans for South Korea's global economic policy, exemplifies the trend:

> There live two million Koreans in China, eight hundred thousand in Japan, and one million two hundred thousand in the U.S., and half a million in the former Soviet Union. The size of the overseas Korean population is almost five million. . . . We, together with these overseas brothers, must form a "Pan-Korean Economic and Cultural Community," and let these overseas Koreans act as intermediaries between us and their host countries to enhance the bilateral relationships. (Ku 1995: 177–178)

Chŏng Chu-yŏng, the late chairman of Hyundai, also stressed the importance of the ethnic Koreans of China and Russia in his company's project to develop the natural resources of Siberia. He insisted on this in terms of Korea's competition with Japan.

> Although Japan began developing the Siberian resources much earlier than we did . . . we can outdo the Japanese because there are many ethnic Koreans on Sakhalin and in Siberia. We can also utilize Korean Chinese labour for our resources development projects in Siberia. . . . Working with the people who share the same culture and language with us is much easier than working with foreigners. (Chŏng 1997: 141–142)

In a similar vein many South Koreans underlined the possible role of Korean Chinese in the unification of the two Koreas. Emphasizing Korean Chinese experiences of Communism in China and their familiarity with North Koreans, South Korean nationalists regarded Korean Chinese as "missionaries of unification" (see Yi 1994). Korean Chinese intellectuals also share a similar belief that Korean Chinese can contribute to the unification of their divided homeland (Chŏng 1996; Kim 2001b). Such an expectation was reinforced by South Korean historiography, which acclaims the anti-Japanese struggles of Koreans in China during the colonial period. Many South Korean historians also stress that ethnic Koreans in China today are descendants of the Korean victims who had been forced to migrate to Manchuria by the Japanese colonialists for Japan's imperialist ambitions (see Pak 1990; Yi 1994). Such historiography and the efforts of political and business leaders to expand their political and economic influence among the ethnic Koreans of China and the former Soviet Union constitute an exemplary case of deterritorialized nationalism, in which nation-states attempt to retain some control over their overseas nationals and to secure their loyalty beyond their borders (see Glick Schiller 1997: 160–161; Guarnizo 1997: 305, 309; Tsuda 2003: 256–257).

South Koreans also praised their co-ethnics in China for their preservation of many old Korean traditions, despite the fact that they are surrounded by Chinese cultural influence. For this reason South Koreans often admired Korean Chinese for being culturally "pure," implying some lamentation that they themselves had lost much of their old Korean traditions in the process of modernization and industrialization. The popular cultural representations of Korean Chinese in South Korea in the last decade also show relatively positive perceptions of Korean Chinese by South Koreans. For example, South Korean films and TV dramas feature Korean Chinese women in a positive, if somewhat condescending, manner, by usually depicting them as pure and innocent.[13] The numerous photo exhibitions of Korean Chinese in South Korea in the last decade, including the most recent Pinguori exhibition in 2004, are good examples of such a view.[14] Many of the photos exhibited there were of Korean Chinese from rural areas, who were still using traditional farming tools that had long since disappeared in South Korea. These exhibitions not only showed Korean Chinese as people who kept old Korean traditions alive but also hinted at the primitiveness of the lives of Korean Chinese and of China as being a less developed country. Therefore these exhibitions inspired South Korean nostalgia for the old days and sympathy for their co-ethnics in China.[15]

As such, South Koreans imagined Korean Chinese as pure, traditional, patriotic, and beneficial to the future of the Korean nation. Nonetheless, such a hopeful and positive view of Korean nationalists was not necessarily shared by ordinary South Koreans—which is similar to the case of the views of Hungarian nationalists toward Hungarian ethnic returnees from neighboring Romania (see Chapter 7).

After the Return Migration

After the initial expectations, curiosity, and sympathy from their brethren from China, South Koreans developed an ambivalent attitude toward them when a large number of Korean Chinese return-migrated to South Korea. Negative reports on Korean Chinese in the South Korean media increased gradually throughout the early 1990s. Some of the common criticisms on *Chosŏnjok*—a popular name for Korean Chinese among South Koreans, which became somewhat derogatory later—were in regard to their weak work ethic, opportunistic attitudes, untrustworthiness, and lack of loyalty to South Korea. These negative qualities were considered to be associated with Korean Chinese being overly Sinicized in their attitudes and behavior.

The herbal medicine trade in the early 1990s, mentioned earlier, was the first major event in which Korean Chinese were perceived negatively by South Koreans. As the number of Korean Chinese peddlers grew, consumer complaints about the quality of the herbal medicine also rose. These complaints were widely reported in South Korea in 1990 and 1991, which persuaded South Koreans that the Chinese herbal medicines brought by Korean Chinese were of low quality and did not have much medicinal effect. Eventually, in November 1991 the South Korean authority declared that it would prohibit the selling of Chinese herbal medicines on the streets. Soon, other reports of violations of visa regulations and crimes by Korean Chinese followed. One of the most prominent cases was the murder of eleven South Korean and Indonesian crewmen by six Korean Chinese on a South Korean fishing boat in the South Pacific in August 1996 (*Chosun Daily*, August 26, 1996). Although it was reported later that the murder was related to the abuse of Korean Chinese crewmen by their South Korean superiors, this was shocking news for most South Koreans. Many South Koreans were sympathetic to Korean Chinese, but these incidents aggravated the increasingly ambivalent notions of South Koreans toward Korean Chinese, and South Koreans became concerned about the increasing number of undocumented Korean Chinese migrant workers.[16]

South Korean employers were also increasingly complaining about the character of Korean Chinese employees. General remarks were that Korean Chinese, coming from a socialist regime, were not able to meet the high demands of labor production in a capitalist society. Korean Chinese workers were said to have a "weak work ethic," to "only care about money," and to be "not trustworthy" (U and Han 2002; Yu 2002). A popular newspaper in South Korea reported such negative characteristics of Korean Chinese by quoting a construction company owner who used to hire Korean Chinese workers.

> Korean Chinese workers are very opportunistic and cunning. They are very well organized these days. About ten people would form a team, led by a foreman, who are well connected to each other with mobile phones. When a foreman hears from another that wages are higher in one place, then he and the entire team would move to that site at night without telling anything to their employer. Many construction companies lost money because there is no way for them to find workers to replace the Korean Chinese who left. (*Donga Daily*, August 17, 2002)

Such criticism of the "untrustworthy" behavior of Korean Chinese is shared by South Korean employers in China who had employed Korean Chinese. This is well described in a 2001 report by two South Korean journalists, who interviewed more than 100 South Korean businesspeople in China. According to the report, 90 percent of South Korean employers had experienced cheating by their Korean Chinese employees (U and Han 2002). In the early days of their ventures in China, they used to hire Korean Chinese because they themselves did not speak Chinese. Later, however, they preferred hiring Han Chinese and avoided Korean Chinese (U and Han 2002: 148). Similar episodes were reported in Korean Chinese newspapers in China, and one of them quotes a South Korean businessman who says that Korean Chinese workers are "lazy, and demand high wages from the beginning" (Hŏ 2001b: 463).

Reflecting South Koreans' generally negative views of Korean Chinese, South Korean popular culture also represents Korean Chinese in a similarly critical manner. In particular, Korean Chinese tend to be portrayed as money-hungry and fraudulent figures. For example, the 1998 film *Namnam Pungnyo* (Southern Man and Northern Woman) features a Korean Chinese man in Yanji, the capital of the Yanbian Korean Autonomous Prefecture, as streetsmart, money grabbing, and shameless; he cheats an innocent South Korean boy. Such an image of Korean Chinese in South Korea reflects the fact that more and more South Koreans view them as people who are not free from all the negative tenets of China as a less developed and less civilized country. In a sense, South Koreans distinguish Korean Chinese from other "overseas brothers," particularly ones from wealthy areas such as the United States, Japan, and Western Europe. Although these people are considered civilized (see Chapter 12), Korean Chinese are viewed mostly as poor brethren who are willing to take 3D jobs in South Korea.

South Koreans also perceive that Korean Chinese are overly Sinicized not only in their attitude but also in their identity. Koreans assume that Koreanness is not only racial but also cultural (see Lie 1998; Shin 2006), and they strongly assume that "Koreans" should speak the Korean language and have a clear identity as Koreans. Therefore South Koreans tend to be deeply annoyed when Korean Chinese identify themselves as Chinese citizens. Born and having lived in China for more than several decades, Korean Chinese usually consider China their fatherland and Korea their motherland (Choi 2005: 67). In addition, as one of the 56 ethnic groups of China, they naturally regard themselves as Koreans (*Chosŏnjok*) in ethnic terms but Chinese in political terms. In fact, being well aware of the negative perceptions of South Koreans, Korean Chinese tend to conceal their identity whenever possible,[17] but when they have to say who they are, they often say they are Chinese. This seemingly unpretentious statement tends to offend South Koreans, who have an essentialist attitude toward national and cultural identity.

If South Koreans cannot imagine Korean Chinese as being the same Koreans as themselves, what could Korean Chinese be other than Chinese? Facing such exclusion and negative attitudes on the part of South Koreans, many Korean Chinese have come to question their being Korean in their ethnic homeland.

Alienation in the Ethnic Homeland and Reflections on Identity

Because the initially romantic expectations of South Koreans about Korean Chinese were seriously undermined when they encountered Korean Chinese return migrants, most Korean Chinese also found their nostalgic affiliation with their ethnic homeland severely challenged when they came to South Korea. First, as cheap foreign workers, they encountered difficult working conditions in South Korea and experienced status degradation. They were also discriminated against compared to other overseas Koreans from wealthy countries such as the United States and Japan, which led them to feel alienated in their ethnic homeland.

Alienation in the Ethnic Homeland

The Korean Dream of Korean Chinese was not an easy dream from the beginning, as obtaining a South Korean entry visa was difficult. The South Korean government tightly controlled entry visas for foreign workers, including Korean Chinese. First it had the Industrial Trainees Scheme, under which a limited number of unskilled foreign workers were imported for the manufacturing sector. This scheme, however, did not work well and it was criticized for its exploitative character. In 2004 the new Employment Permit System was launched, and it allowed foreign workers more freedom and equal rights. It was under this scheme that ethnic Koreans from China and the CIS were given some priority, even though the quota set aside for them was always much lower than the actual number of applicants, which produced a large number of illegal migrants.[18] Under these circumstances, until recently, it was not unusual for Korean Chinese to pay large sums of money to visa brokers to obtain South Korean visas. Most of them paid anywhere between US$7,000 and US$12,000 to brokers (Kwŏn and Pak 2005: 167), and cases of fraud regarding visa brokerage were frequently reported in the media. Because almost all of them had borrowed money from their relatives and friends to come to South Korea, this kind of fraud resulted in tragic disputes, and often families were destroyed when they were unable to repay their debts (Chŏng 2000: 172; Im 2003: 335). This again aggravated Korean Chinese grievances toward the South Korean government for its tight visa regulations.

Having arrived in South Korea, Korean Chinese experience adaptation problems. Many experience status degradation. As mentioned, ethnic Koreans in China are generally used to being better off than other ethnic groups, and they tend to have high self-esteem in China. In addition, many of the migrant workers had been managers and professionals in China. In South Korea, however, they have to engage in manual labor, such as construction or household chores, which are normally shunned by locals. Although wages in South Korea are much higher than in China, Korean Chinese find themselves economically marginalized in South Korea, and their general living conditions in South Korea are dismal. Most of them work almost 10 hours a day to make about 1–1.5 million Korean won (US$1,000–$1,500) per month, which they save while leading an extremely simple life. Such harsh conditions make them feel that they were leading a much more humane life in China, even though wages were lower there. Most of my informants said that they wanted to stay in South Korea only temporarily and that they wished to return to China after making enough money. This is because they can lead a better life in China with the money they earned in South Korea, whereas they will lead a marginalized life if they stay in South Korea.[19]

The more difficult challenges that Korean Chinese encounter in South Korea are the prejudice and discrimination they experience from their South Korean co-ethnics. As stated, South Koreans consider Korean Chinese untrustworthy and inferior and not free from the negative qualities of China. Thus South Koreans are seen as cold and arrogant toward Korean Chinese. Like Japanese Brazilians, who are not accepted as Japanese in Japan despite being of Japanese descent but are ethnically marginalized as foreigners because of their Brazilian cultural differences (Tsuda 2003; Chapter 9), Korean Chinese are similarly marginalized and alienated in South Korea. Most Korean Chinese think that South Koreans are egotistical, arrogant, and "not humane" (*injŏng i memarŭn*) (Im 2003: 349).[20]

Korean Chinese feel particularly frustrated because the South Korean government discriminated against them compared to other overseas Koreans, such as the ones from wealthy countries like the United States and Japan. Korean

Chinese believe that South Korean discrimination against Korean Chinese was clearly manifested in the 1999 Law on the Entry/Exit and Status of Overseas Koreans, which excluded ethnic Koreans from China (and the former Soviet Union) from the status of "overseas brothers" (*chaeoe tongp'o*). Designed to attract investments from wealthy overseas Koreans in the United States, Japan, and other Western countries after the 1997 financial crisis, the law allowed overseas Koreans to visit and conduct business in South Korea freely. In the early stages of preparing the law, an "overseas Korean" was defined broadly as anyone who is ethnically Korean and residing overseas with or without foreign citizenship. Later, however, the definition was modified to pertain only to those who had left Korea after 1948 (the year the South Korean government was established) and their direct descendants. This change was introduced to prevent Korean Chinese and Soviet Koreans from flooding the South Korean labor market[21] and to stave off protests from the Chinese government.[22]

Because Korean Chinese consider themselves Koreans or overseas Koreans, they tend to feel deeply frustrated and alienated when they are treated by South Koreans as merely unskilled foreign workers. Korean Chinese intellectuals point out that Korean Chinese migrant workers feel worse in South Korea than they do in Japan, even though they are treated similarly in both countries. This is because Korean Chinese feel bitter when they are maltreated by ethnic Koreans (South Koreans) as opposed to foreigners (Japanese) (Kim 2001b: 426–427). This is similar to the case of Japanese Brazilians in Japan. Because Japanese Brazilians have ethnic ties with the Japanese, the degree of alienation they feel is much greater than what non-Japanese workers experience (Tsuda 2000).

In addition to their marginalized status in South Korea, Korean Chinese felt that this discriminatory measure aggravated their sense of alienation in absolute terms. In her novel about Korean Chinese return migrants to South Korea (*Flower of Wind*, 1996), Korean Chinese novelist Hŏ Ryŏnsun describes the frustrations of the Korean Chinese through her main protagonist, Jiha. Jiha cries out to a South Korean journalist who asks him why Korean Chinese are so critical of South Korea.

> What would it be other than the discriminatory policy of the South Korean government toward us, Koreans from China? Why does South Korea restrict entry visas of Korean Chinese while it allows free entries to Korean Americans and Korean Japanese? Isn't it because they are rich and we are poor? Right? (Hŏ 1996: 157)[23]

Because of the negative experiences they had in South Korea, Korean Chinese developed critical feelings toward South Korea. These negative feelings were widespread in the Korean Chinese community in China by the mid-1990s, and Korean Chinese reflected on their identity and relationship with their ethnic homeland.

Korean Chinese Reflections on Homeland and Identity

The experiences of discrimination, alienation, and many shattered Korean Dreams in South Korea not only made Korean Chinese return migrants critical of South Korea but also provided them with opportunities to reflect on the meaning of homeland and their being Korean. Such reflections on ethnic homeland and identity were intense in the mid-1990s, when several books and articles on the subject were published in the Korean Chinese community in China and in South Korea. In most of the discussions about their homeland, Korean Chinese distinguished the ethnic homeland, where their ethnic group originated, and the adopted homeland of China, where they were raised or "parented." Between these two homelands, Korean Chinese preferred the Chinese parenting or adopted homeland after their disappointing experience in South Korea.[24]

Chae-guk Kim (1998) uses the metaphor of the biological mother (Korea, to which Korean Chinese owe the "love of giving birth" [naajun chŏng]) and the parenting mother (China, to which they owe the "love of parenting" [kiwŏjun chŏng]). Claiming that the love of parenting is greater than the love of giving birth, Kim (1998: 203) suggests that China is the country that Korean Chinese should eventually rely on, whereas South Korea is only a place where they can be guests. Such rhetoric of China as the parenting mother for Korean Chinese is not uncommon in Korean Chinese discourse. A Korean Chinese newspaper, Hŭngnyonggang Daily, stated in an editorial (September 12, 1995) that Korean Chinese should not betray the love of parenting they received from China.

In a similar vein, Chŏng (1996) stresses the importance of the adopted homeland (China) over the native homeland (Korea) by using the figure of a married daughter, in which Korean Chinese are likened to a Korean daughter who marries a Chinese man. According to Chŏng, such a daughter should first serve her husband and his parents and learn the ways of her husband's family. Reminded of the Korean tradition, he advises that the Korean daughter should keep a certain distance from her own Korean family. He even warns Korean Chinese that as an immigrant minority in China, they should not threaten China by establishing strong ties with their ethnic homeland (Chŏng 1996:

271–272). This figure of the married daughter reveals the dormant fear on the part of Korean Chinese of the counteraction from the dominant Han Chinese should they try to deepen their ties with their ethnic homeland.

In criticizing the assimilationist stance of Chŏng, Kim (2001a: 4–6) asserts that Korean Chinese should be proud of their transnational character and should take advantage of their being both Korean and Chinese while not forgetting that they are citizens of China. Meanwhile, Hŏ points out that the discriminatory treatment Korean Chinese experience in South Korea forces them to strengthen their identity as Chinese (Hŏ 2001b: 466). In the novel *Flower of Wind*, another Korean Chinese returnee, In-gyu, utters his final words to his good friend Jiha, urging him to leave South Korea and return to their homeland.

> I sincerely beg you to return quickly to our homeland, which raised us! Homeland is like your clothes that protect you from cold wind and rain. I will put my head toward my homeland when I die. (Hŏ 1996: 270)

In these discussions of Korean Chinese intellectuals, it is clear that Korean Chinese realized that their natal homeland (China) is more important than their ancestral homeland (Korea). This also defines their identity more as Chinese than Korean. Eight of my informants told me that they realized that they were more Chinese than Korean after their return migration. The other four said that they feel both Chinese and Korean, implying a hybrid identity.

Conclusion

The last 15 years of ethnic reunion between Korean Chinese and South Koreans shows that both groups experienced changes in their views of each other. South Koreans, on the basis of the notion of ethnic nationalism, had initially developed a romantic perspective regarding their brethren from China, idealizing the Korean Chinese' Koreanness as well as considering them a great resource for the nation's future. However, after the large-scale ethnic return migration of Korean Chinese to South Korea, South Koreans concluded that their co-ethnics from China were backward, untrustworthy, and most of all, of dubious identity.

Similarly, before their ethnic return migration to South Korea, Korean Chinese developed a positive view toward South Korea as their long-lost ancestral homeland. This positive view was strengthened by the relative decline of their socioeconomic status in postreform China as well as the employment opportunities in South Korea. Through their experiences of the harsh realities of migrant workers in South Korea, however, they were deeply disappointed by the discriminatory treatment on the part of the South Korean government and of their South Korean brethren, whom they saw as contemptuous and lacking in brotherly love. Through such experiences, much like Japanese Brazilians in Japan (see Tsuda 2003; Chapter 9), Korean Chinese discovered that they could not be accepted as Korean in their ethnic homeland (South Korea) and that their future lies more in their natal homeland (China). Thus Korean Chinese learned that they are more Chinese than Korean.

The case of Korean Chinese ethnic return migrants in South Korea shows that identities of ethnic return migrants can be changed depending on their experiences in their ethnic homelands even when their identities are based on primordial notions. Therefore this case of Korean Chinese identity changes in their ethnic homeland challenges the conventional notion of the ethnonationalism of Korea (which is based on the belief in Korean "blood"). Similar to the cases of many other ethnic return migrants to their ancestral homelands, such as Japanese Brazilians (Tsuda 2003; Chapter 9), Germans, Israelis, and Russians (see Chapters 4 and 8; Münz and Ohliger 2003), Korean Chinese also experienced discrimination and alienation in their ethnic homeland, which led to the transformation of identity.

Notes

I am grateful to Takeyuki (Gaku) Tsuda for his valuable comments on this chapter.

1. The migrations of Chinese and Koreans to Manchuria and of Russians to Siberia are important parts of global migration in the second half of the nineteenth and early twentieth centuries. However, they have been somewhat neglected by migration historians. See McKeown (2004).

2. Among the 700,000 return migrants, about 400,000 returned to the southern part of Korea and the other 300,000 returned to the northern part of Korea. After this return migration there were about 1 million Koreans left in Manchuria in 1946 (Kwŏn 2005: 17–18).

3. Yanbian was the center of early Korean migrants near the Korean border, where Koreans were the majority.

4. For the basis of Korean ethnic nationalism, see Shin (2006).

5. In 2003 the total number of foreign workers in South Korea reached about 570,000, including 244,000 undocumented migrant workers. It was estimated that there were 150,000 Korean Chinese at the end of 2003 (Kwŏn and Pak 2005: 38). In 2008 the number of Korean Chinese in South Korea reached 375,000 (Ministry of Justice).

6. I interviewed 12 Korean Chinese ethnic return migrants in Ansan, south of Seoul, in November 2004. Then, in June 2005 I also visited Yanji, the capital of the Yanbian Korean Autonomous Prefecture in Jilin Province, China, where I conducted interviews with 15 Korean Chinese who had stayed more than two years in South Korea before returning to their home in Yanji.

7. In this regard, the Korean Chinese were different from their co-ethnics who went to Hawaii in the early twentieth century. Whereas the Koreans who migrated to Hawaii as plantation workers lost their traditional lifestyle, Koreans in Manchuria kept the traditional Korean peasant culture.

8. China allegedly has a generous policy toward its national minorities, but in reality minority nationalities in China are economically marginalized and they have been politically and culturally suppressed. For China's national minority questions, refer to Rossabi (2004) and Gladney (2004).

9. However, Hoffmann reports that Koreans were relatively fortunate in terms of ethnic oppression because they could maintain their ethnic dress, ethnic newspapers and magazines, and ethnic schools, including Yanbian University, even though they had to adapt to socialist and Han Chinese ways (Hoffmann 1986: 17).

10. Interviews with Korean Chinese return workers from Heilongjiang and Jilin Provinces of China.

11. Ethnic return migrants tend to be treated differently and thus experience different identity transformations depending on the global political and economic positions of their countries of origin, as Tsuda (Chapter 9) and Takenaka (Chapter 10) suggest.

12. It was only in the late 1980s that the South Korean news media began to include the 2 million ethnic Koreans of China and the 500,000 Soviet Koreans as "overseas brothers" (*Haeoe Tongp'o*). The Ministry of Foreign Affairs and Trade has included Korean Chinese and Soviet Koreans in their official reports since 2003.

13. Korean Chinese women are generally represented as innocent figures, who keep traditional feminine values. This is well exemplified in films (e.g., *Innocent Steps*, 2005) and TV dramas (e.g., *The Pure-Hearted Nineteen-Year-Old*, 2006). Regarding South Korean popular cultural representations of ethnic Korean women from China and Uzbekistan, refer to Song (2006).

14. *Pinguori* is the name of the fruit, a cross between an apple and a pear, that Korean Chinese are famous for in the Yanbian region. Organized by a newspaper company in Seoul in 2004, the photo exhibition was one of the most popular.

15. It also gave a sense of superiority to South Korean viewers. Grinker observes a similar case in an exhibition of everyday goods from North Korea in Seoul in 1993. According to Grinker, through such photos South Koreans view North Koreans as the "other" through whom they reaffirm their superior position in the global economic hierarchy (Grinker 1998: 49–72).

16. Although major newspapers reported the incident with a sympathetic understanding of the abusive treatment of Korean Chinese by South Korean supervisors, South Koreans' shock and anger against Korean Chinese regarding the incident were well reflected in the "readers' opinion" sections of the newspapers at that time.

17. Almost all my Korean Chinese informants in South Korea said that they did not want South Koreans to know about their being Korean Chinese.

18. In 2006 there were more than 220,000 illegal migrant workers in South Korea, and among them more than 37,000 were Korean Chinese (Ministry of Justice).

19. Still, many Korean Chinese want to stay in South Korea, and the great majority of them are usually former farmers who do not have pensions in China. Others have family members in South Korea, for example, elderly parents whose daughter lives in South Korea after marrying a South Korean. Other than these, most Korean Chinese workers want to go back to China, where they can lead a relatively good life with the money they have made in South Korea.

20. Tsuda also reports that Japanese Brazilian ethnic return migrants make similar remarks about their host society: "coldness" (Tsuda 2001: 70).

21. Three years later, the law was declared unconstitutional by the court. When the law was revised in 2003, Korean Chinese and Soviet Koreans were still excluded from preferential treatment.

22. The Chinese government expressed serious concerns about Korean Chinese ties with their ancestral homeland, and it warned the South Korean government when the Law on the Entry/Exit and Status of Overseas Koreans was enacted and revised.

23. Similarly, a Korean Chinese (undocumented) worker in South Korea says, "We would not be treated this way if China were a wealthier country than South Korea" (*Chosun Daily*, December 24, 2001).

24. Nadia Kim (Chapter 12) states that Korean American ethnic return migrants in South Korea also realize that it is cultural familiarity and understanding, not shared identity, that makes them feel that a place is home.

References Cited

Choi, Woogil. 2005. *Chungguk Chosŏnjok Yŏn'gu* [A study of Korean Chinese]. Asan, Korea: Sunmoon University Press.

Chŏn, Song-rim. 1991. *Yŏnbyŏn Kyŏngje Chiri* [Economic geography of Yanbian]. Yanji, China: Yŏnbyŏn Inmin Ch'ulp'ansa.

Chŏng, Chu-yŏng. 1997. *Saeroun sijakeŭi yŏlmang* [The desire for a new start]. Ulsan, Korea: Ulsan National University Press.

Chŏng, P'an-ryong. 1996. *Segyesogŭi uri minjok* [Our nation in the world]. Shenyang, China: Ryonyŏng Minjok Ch'ulp'ansa.

Chŏng, Sin-ch'ŏl. 2000. *Chungguk Chosŏnjok: Kŭdŭrŭi mirae nŭn* [Ethnic Koreans in China: Their future]. Seoul: Sin In'gansa.

Gladney, Dru C. 2004. *Dislocating China: Reflections on Muslims, Minorities, and Other Subaltern Subjects*. Chicago: University of Chicago Press.

Glick Schiller, Nina. 1997. "The Situation of Transnational Studies." *Identities: Global Studies in Culture and Power* 4(2):155–166.

Grinker, Roy Richard. 1998. *Korea and Its Futures: Unification and the Unfinished War*. New York: St. Martin's Press.

Guarnizo, Luis Eduardo. 1997. "The Emergence of a Transnational Social Formation and the Mirage of Return Migration Among Dominican Transmigrants." *Identities: Global Studies in Culture and Power* 4(2):281–322.

Gurr, R. T. 1970. *Why Men Rebel*. Princeton, NJ: Princeton University Press.

Harvey, D. 1989. *The Condition of Post-Modernity: An Inquiry into the Origins of Culture Change*. New York: Blackwell.

Hŏ, Myŏng-ch'ŏl. 2001a. "Chungguk Chosŏnjok chŏngch'esŏngyujie kwanhan sago" [Reflections on the maintenance of the identity of Chinese Koreans]. In *Chungguk Chosŏnjok*, Kim and Hŏ, eds., 246–283.

————. 2001b. "Chungguk Chosŏnjok sahoewa Hanguk sahoeganŭi munhwagyoryu hyŏnhwangmit kŭ taean" [The current status and alternative of the exchange relationship between Chinese Korean community and South Korean society]. In *Chungguk Chosŏnjok*, Kim and Hŏ, eds., 451–481.

Hŏ, Ryŏnsun. 1996. *Paramkkot* [Flower of wind]. Seoul: Pŏmusa.

Hoffmann, Frank. 1986. "The Korean Minority in China: Education and Publishing." *Korea Journal* 26(4):13–26.

Im, Kye-sun. 2003. *Uriege tagaon Chosŏnjogŭn nuguin'ga* [Who are the Chinese Koreans who came to us]. Seoul: Hyŏnamsa.

Kim, Chae-guk. 1998 [1996]. *Hangugŭn ŏpta* [No more South Korea]. Mudanjiang, China: Hŭngryonggang Chosŏn Minjok Ch'ulp'ansa.

Kim, In-sŏn. 2004. *Rossiya changsagil* [My experience of peddling in Russia]. Yanji, China: Yŏnbyŏn Inmin Ch'ulp'ansa.

Kim, Kang-il. 2001a. "Chungguk Chosŏnjok sahoe chiwiron" [A thesis on the status of ethnic Koreans in China]. In *Chungguk Chosŏnjok*, Kim and Hŏ, eds., 3–44.

————. 2001b. "Nambuk t'ongire issŏsŏ Chungguk Chosŏnjok ŭi yŏkhal" [The role of Korean Chinese in the unification of the two Koreas]. In *Chungguk Chosŏnjok*, Kim and Hŏ, eds., 414–450.

Kim, Kang-il, and Myŏng-ch'ŏl Hŏ, eds. 2001. *Chungguk Chosŏnjok: Sahoeŭi munhwa usewa palchŏn chŏllyak* [Korean Chinese: Their cultural power and development strategies]. Yanji, China: Yŏnbyŏn Inmin Ch'ulp'ansa.

Kim, Kyu-bang. 1998. *Yŏnbyŏn Kyŏngje Palchŏn Chŏllyak* [Economic development strategy for Yanbian]. Yanji, China: Yŏnbyŏn Inmin Ch'ulp'ansa.

Kim, Si Joong. 2003. "The Economic Status of and Role of Ethnic Koreans in China." In *The Korean Diaspora in the World Economy*, C. Fred Bergsten and Inbom Choi, eds.

Institute for International Economics Special Report 15. Washington, DC: Institute for International Economics, 101–127.

Ku, Chong-sŏ. 1995. "Pŏmhan minjokchu'ŭiga 21-segi Hankug'ŭi sŏnt'aek" [Pan-Korean nationalism is the choice of Korea in the 21st century]. *Win*, August, 176–179.

Kwŏn, Taihan. 2005. "Chosŏnjok ingu'ŭi ch'use" [Population trends of ethnic Koreans in China]. In *Chungguk Chosŏnjok Sahoeŭi Pyŏnhwa: 1990-nyŏn ihurŭl chungsimŭro* [The changes of China's ethnic Korean society: Post-1990s], Taihan Kwŏn and Kwang-sŏng Pak, eds. Seoul: Seoul National University Press, 15–34.

Kwŏn, Taihan, and Kwang-sŏng Pak. 2005. "Hanguk Chosŏnjok nodongja chiptanŭi hyŏngsŏng" [The formation of the Chinese Korean labor group in South Korea]. In *Chungguk Chosŏnjok Sahoeŭi Pyŏnhwa: 1990-nyŏn ihurŭl chungsimŭro* [The changes of China's ethnic Korean society: Post-1990s], Taihan Kwŏn and Kwang-sŏng Pak, eds. Seoul: Seoul National University Press, 147–175.

Lee, Chae-jin. 1986. *China's Korean Minority: The Politics of Ethnic Education.* Boulder, CO: Westview Press.

Lie, John. 1998. *Han Unbound: The Political Economy of South Korea.* Stanford, CA: Stanford University Press.

McKeown, A. 2004. "Global Migration, 1846–1940." *Journal of World History* 15(2):155–189.

Münz, R., and R. Ohliger, eds. 2003. *Diasporas and Ethnic Migrants: Germany, Israel, and Post-Soviet Successor States in Comparative Perspective.* London: Frank Cass.

Pak, Kŏyng-ri. 1990. *Malli changsŏngŭi nara: Pak Kyŏng-ri Chungguk kihaeng* [Visiting the Great Wall country: Pak's records of trip to China]. Seoul: Tonggwang Ch'ulp'ansa.

Park, Yong-bum. 1994. "The Turning Point in International Migration and Economic Development in Korea." *Asian and Pacific Migration Journal* 3(1):149–174.

Rossabi, Morris, ed. 2004. *Governing China's Multiethnic Frontiers.* Seattle: University of Washington Press.

Ryang, Ok-kŭm. 2001. "Chungguk Yŏnbyŏn Chosŏnjok Chach'iju minjok kwangyeŭi hyŏngsŏngkwa palchŏn" [The formation and development of ethnic relations of the Yanbian Chinese Korean Autonomous Region]. In *Chungguk Chosŏnjok*, Kim and Hŏ, eds., 138–165.

Shin, Gi-Wook. 2006. *Ethnic Nationalism in Korea.* Stanford, CA: Stanford University Press.

Song, Changzoo. 2006. "Nostalgia for Women of Purity, Honesty, and Strength: Images of Diasporic Women in Korean Film." Paper presented at the 2006 Association for Asian Studies Meeting, San Francisco, April 6–9.

To, Hŭng-ryŏl. 1992. "Chungguk Sosuminjok Munje wa Chosŏnjok Sahoe" [China's Minority Question and Ethnic Koreans in China]. In *Chungguk Chosŏnjok Sahoe Yŏn'gu* [A study on the society of ethnic Koreans in China], Yŏng-mo Kim, ed. Seoul: Korea Welfare Policy Institute, 165–191.

Tsuda, Takeyuki. 2000. "Acting Brazilian in Japan: Ethnic Resistance Among Return Migrants." *Ethnology* 39(1):55–71.

———. 2001. "From Ethnic Affinity to Alienation in the Global Ecumene: The Encounter Between the Japanese and Japanese-Brazilian Return Migrants." *Diaspora* 10(1):53–91.

———. 2003. *Strangers in the Ethnic Homeland: Japanese Brazilian Return Migration in Transnational Perspective.* New York: Columbia University Press.

U, Kil, and Myŏng-hŭi Han. 2002. *Chungguk esŏ chari chabŭn Han'gugindŭl* [South Koreans established in China]. Seoul: Kumto.

Yi, Kwang-gyu. 1994. "Hanguk chŏngbunŭn haeoe Hanin chŏngch'aegŭl pakkwŏya handa" [The Korean government should change its overseas Koreans policy]. *Sahoe Pyŏngnonŭi kil* 15(2):23–29.

Yu, Myounggi. 2002. "Dilemma of Joseon People: Ethnicity vs. Nationality." *Korea Focus* 10(6):100–115.

Finding Our Way Home

Korean Americans, "Homeland" Trips,
and Cultural Foreignness

Nadia Y. Kim

NUMEROUS SCHOLARS have ably documented how younger generations of Asian Americans are racialized as foreigners despite their U.S. citizenship, their residence in the United States, and their so-called model minority achievements (for an overview see Kim 1999). In contrast, most scholars have not studied how later-generation Asian Americans often become *cultural* foreigners when they visit their ethnic homelands. As Mia Tuan (1999: 106) contends, these Asian Americans face an "authenticity dilemma" in the United States as neither real "Americans" nor real Asians. In this chapter I analyze this authenticity dilemma in a transnational context by examining how young Korean Americans make sense of their tourist visits to their home country (see Kibria 2002a). In fact, because Korean Americans are racially marginalized as foreigners in the United States (Tuan 1998) and are exposed to their parents' exhortation that Korea is their "roots," they construct a romanticized view of South Korea as the country where they *racially* belong, akin to the manner of the Korean Chinese (see Chapter 11). Yet, like the so-called *joseonjok*, these Korean Americans find that racial similarity to South Koreans means little in light of the ethnic homeland's restrictive definitions of cultural "Koreanness." Given the importance of phenotypic appearance for the United States' racial categorization system, Korean Americans' inability to gain acceptance from people who look just like them proves strikingly disappointing. Whereas in the United States they are racialized as Asian even if they do not act "authentically" Asian or Korean, in South Korea they are not seen as authentic unless they are both racially *and* culturally Korean.

As racial foreigners in the United States, where they are treated as Asian, not American, and as cultural foreigners in South Korea, where they are seen as too

American, not Korean, the younger generations must persistently wrestle with some form of foreignness and "homelessness," in the words of Espiritu (2003). Korean Americans' tourist trips to the ethnic homeland thereby bring their struggles with race/ethnicity, nationality, and culture into bold relief. Specifically, they come to define home as the place of cultural familiarity, that is, the United States. Like the Korean Chinese, they also come to define the homeland as the place of their ethnic roots and ancestors but not necessarily where they feel at home. Although most young Korean Americans become more convinced that the United States is where they belong, they cannot deny the way in which their treatment as nonwhite guests in the American house renders the United States a place where they feel only partly at home.

Theory and Background

Although mainstream America has positively racialized Asian Americans as model minorities, often for hegemonic political purposes (Kim 1999),[1] many scholars have documented how Asian Americans have been negatively racialized as foreigners and "inauthentic Americans" (Tuan 1998, 1999; see Ancheta 1998; Espiritu 1992, 2003; Jiobu 1988; Kibria 2002a; Kim 1999; Lowe 1996; Min 1995; Palumbo-Liu 1999; Takaki 1987, 1998; Wei 1993). As both model minorities and forever foreigners, Asian Americans experience dual and seemingly opposed racialization processes. Yet at the same time Asian Americans' status as foreigners, despite being model minorities, reveals how Asians' subordination hinges on cultural notions of who is an insider and who truly belongs. In other words, anti-Asian bias hinges on cultural notions of citizenship (Ancheta 1998). The subordination of Asian Americans stands somewhat in contrast, then, to the traditional notion of racial subordination, which hinges on color (mostly with regard to African Americans). Rather, Asian Americans' foreignness is defined in relation to the authentic and deserving Americans, a status held by whites (Lipsitz 1998). In her empirical study Tuan (1998) found that even third- to fifth-generation Asian Americans who were successfully middle class and far removed from ethnic culture endured the foreigner bias. Kibria (2002a) found that second-generation Korean and Chinese Americans—most of whom had little practical ethnic engagement—were similarly marginalized.

Although the racialized foreignness of Asian Americans has been well established by scholars, less has been said about their status as what I call cultural foreigners in their ethnic homelands. At its simplest, the concept of a cultural foreigner in the ethnic homeland differs from that of a racial foreigner in

U.S. society insofar as culture, not racial phenotype, is the key marker of social difference. More specifically, young Korean Americans are rendered culturally foreign for having a "Korean face" but lacking facility in the Korean language and history, Confucian norms, and styles of dress and comportment. They are especially foreign in a nationalistic society that conflates race and culture (e.g., Korean blood explains our diligence; Koreans *naturally* love kimchi). In this way children of immigrants completely disrupt South Koreans' sense of identity. The United States, however, as a historically diverse immigrant nation, does not define itself by way of *one* culture. Rather, it prides itself on incorporating many cultures, as multiculturalist ideology bears out. Furthermore, the United States has not had to trumpet ethnic or cultural nationalism because it has been a superpower largely since independence and has not had to overthrow more racially powerful oppressors. To be sure, U.S. society tends to rely more on phenotype than on culture to categorize peoples, as American panethnic categories of race lump and homogenize many different ethnic and national groups. Yet foreigner stereotypes of Asian Americans have also led white Americans to expect "Asian" cultural behaviors to match an Asian racial phenotype (Tuan 1999). As an example, Tuan (1999) found that Americans expressed surprise when the Asian Americans she interviewed did not act ethnic enough ("You don't know *your* language, *your* country?").

Because American sociologists tend to focus their studies on U.S. society and have only recently turned their attention to the younger generations' transnational links to the home country (Levitt and Waters 2002b), they have underappreciated young Asian Americans' struggles with cultural foreignness in their ethnic homelands. For instance, although tourist visits make apparent their cultural foreignness, Asian Americans in particular are constantly told by the older generations and by white Americans alike that "where they're really from" is a foreign land, not the United States (see Tuan 1999). The parents, for instance, draw on their own nationalist sentiments, notions of identity as phenotype and blood, and efforts to resist racism in the United States to urge their children to maintain their Koreanness and be proud of it. But owing to their busy work lives, the parents often cannot transmit "explicit ethnic markers or behaviors" (e.g., language, customs) to their children (Kibria 2002a: 302). In addition, given that the youth grow up and are educated in the United States, they are culturally more mainstream American than South Korean.

In light of anti-Asian racism and U.S. society's racial homogenization of Asian ethnics in general, the younger generations often look to their ethnic identity as an important resource to resist racism and racial homogenization (Fernandez-Kelly and Schauffler 1994; Glick-Schiller 1999; Kibria 2002a, 2002b; Waters 1999). In particular, the youth sometimes draw themselves closer to their ethnicity by also conceptualizing the home country as a place where they truly belong. Because they do not feel like authentic Americans and insiders in the United States, as evidenced by whites' association of their group with Asia, they long for a place where they *are* racial insiders. They romanticize the ethnic homeland as such a place (Kondo 1990; Louie 2002; Tsuda 2003; Chapter 9). These longings are part of their *symbolic* transnational ties to their ethnic homeland, which scholars contend are just as important as *literal* transnational ties, that is, immigrants shuttling back and forth for work or political involvement or sending remittances (Espiritu and Tran 2002). Indeed, symbolic transnationalism influences the way the younger generations "imagine themselves, their social membership, and future plans" (Espiritu and Tran 2002: 370) and how they view and act on familial and other emotional ties (Wolf 2002).

Despite largely symbolic ties among Korean Americans (Kibria 2002a) and other second-generation groups (Espiritu and Tran 2002; Louie 2002; Wolf 2002), studies have shown that these ethnics find not a warm welcome but "othering" and rejection when they visit their ethnic homeland (Chapters 7, 9, and 11; Kibria 2002a; Kondo 1990; Tsuda 2003). Part of the rejection stems from the nationalistic home country's derision of those who went to the United States as traitors who left when times were bad. When the children of these immigrants visit South Korea and have weak Korean proficiency or know little about their ethnic homeland, their ignorance adds insult to injury. The younger generations must therefore wrestle with the contradiction of ethnic homeland residents' essentialization of them as "one of us" (Louie 2002) but "othering" of the youth as linked to the "traitors." Because the younger generations have already had to wrestle with contradictions in the United States, such as the country's promise of equality for all yet unequal treatment of nonwhites, South Korea becomes another site of unsettling contradictions. Young Korean Americans therefore experience a rude awakening that precludes them from romanticizing their authentic belonging in the ethnic homeland.

Methods

For this study I conducted in-depth open-ended interviews with 22 younger-generation Korean Americans from Los Angeles County, California, in 2001. All but two interviewees in the sample are second generation, those who were born and raised in the United States or who immigrated by age 11. The remaining two informants are part of the 1.5 generation and came to the United States at the ages of 12 and 14 (they will be specified in this chapter). All the informants were asked to comment on experiences and meanings of race, ethnicity, nationality, and culture in their everyday American lives, with respect to their various transnational ties and, most important, with respect to their tourist visits to South Korea. I recruited the overall sample by means of snowball sampling (using as many diverse starting points as possible); through churches and schools; and through a few social, community service, and political groups.

In line with demographic trends, most of the interviewees came from families who fell somewhere in the middle class, from small business to professional classes (most of the first generation hail from a middle-class background and have regained some semblance of that position in the United States)[2] (Ong and Azores 1994). A few had working-class parents who over the years had achieved middle-class status. With regard to education, all were college graduates (eight were currently in graduate school), except for two college-bound high school seniors and one college student. Those who were old enough to have their own careers had also attained middle-class status (throughout, social class status was determined by parents' and informants' education, occupations, and incomes and by self-description). The full-time workers included attorneys, physicians, teachers and others in educational arenas, nonprofit administrators (community workers), and a few others in journalism, design, business, and the ministry. Specifically, the sample included 12 men and 10 women who ranged in age from 17 to 42, with only three interviewees in the 17–18 year range and only one in his 40s (average age is 25). Each interviewee is identified in the text by a pseudonym.

All the Korean Americans went to their ethnic home country as tourists, often to visit their families and relatives. One informant had temporarily worked in South Korea at a Christian camp. Some had gone to South Korea every summer or every few summers in their youth for a series of years. One young woman went every one or two years to visit her parents. Most, however, had gone once or twice for stays that ranged from two weeks to three months. As part of these tourist visits, some of the informants had gone for summer language and cultural study programs, and three had traveled as part of a summer activist program to learn about, and make links with, South Korean social justice activists. Because most of the informants were visiting similarly middle-class family members and friends or were attending summer university programs, their interactions were mostly with members of the same social class.

Overall, the interviews I conducted ranged from one and a half to six hours (depending on how much the interviewees shared and how busy they were); the interviews were transcribed and coded for spoken and unspoken themes using Atlas.ti software.

Being Racialized Foreigners in the United States

Like most Koreans in general, the Korean American informants conformed to the hegemonic U.S. identity of American as white. Since the founding of the nation, the United States has racialized itself as white and has defined Americanness as white, unless otherwise qualified (Lipsitz 1998). In line with U.S. ideology, the Korean word for a person of European descent in the United States is *miguk saram*, literally, "American person." Virtually all the young Korean American informants attached the term *American* when talking about themselves and other nonwhite Americans (e.g., Asian American, Mexican American). They did not do so for whites. Their language supported their own accounts that they were treated like foreigners while whites were the authentic Americans (some even specified "blond people"), and that African Americans were next in line in terms of belonging (see Kim 2008). Given whites' entitlement to authentic Americanness (Tuan 1998), most of the respondents agreed that even if Korean Americans reached the exact same level as whites in all facets of society, whites would still not treat them like fellow whites. In essence, Koreans and other Asians would always be outsiders in some way. Jenny, a 28-year-old graduate student, replied in this manner to the question "Would whites treat us like one of them if we reached all the exact same levels as them in U.S. society?"

> Jenny: No. . . . I think that [way] because we're always going to be different.
> Nadia: You mean, in the way we look?
> Jenny: Yeah! The way we look . . . I think like with other immigrants, Caucasian immigrants from Europe or whatever, it's easier for them to blend in. And you can't really tell so you talk to somebody [who says], "Oh my parents are actually from Italy" or whatever. . . . But with Asians or Koreans I think it's very obvious. . . . I think it's always a sense like, "Oh, they're the outsiders."

In response to the same question, 42-year-old Joe, a nonprofit administrator, paused briefly, then replied emphatically:

> Joe: No.
> Nadia: Why do you not think that?

Joe: Um, 'cause whites think Asians are foreigners.

Nadia: . . . even if we were just like them in all levels of society?

Joe: No.

Even others who proffered a more sanguine view were still not optimistic about equal treatment. Lance, a 24-year-old financial analyst, replied that there would "be a lot less" prejudice but still concluded that prejudice against Koreans or Asians would always exist.

These notions of forever foreignness among Korean Americans tend to foster their romantic construction of South Korea as a place where they would not be seen as the "other," as a racialized minority. For instance, Todd's beleaguered outlook on the United States given his bouts with racial bias, especially at the mostly white law firm where he worked, led to his idealized lens on South Korea. He starts his narrative with a view he has shared with his cousins in Seoul.

> [I told them] "In Korea you have the advantage [because] race is not a filter through which you have to view life." And that is actually incredibly, like a stress-reducing thing to have, and so they're very fortunate in that way. . . . I'm very tied to my ethnic identity. . . . I think for some Koreans, yeah, that's what you turn into. That's what you turn to when you become disappointed with certain aspects of life in the U.S.

Todd's narrative reveals his direct connection between the racism he experiences in the United States and his "love" for South Korea. Similarly, a 27-year-old teacher named Poppy linked her resistance to the racism that she experienced in the United States to her strong sense of attachment to South Korea. She expressed that her attachment was fostered by her immigrant mother, with whom she was close.

> Poppy: I was always very strong, strong about my identity. . . . And part of it is [because the] one person that I talked to most growing up was my mother, and she couldn't speak English.
>
> Nadia: [referring to Poppy's earlier comments] Oh, I see, so do you think partly your ties to Korea being strong had to do with, you know, you feeling like a minority here, feeling like some things about Korea were better than [the United States]?
>
> Poppy: Oh, yeah!

In short, most of the Korean Americans linked a sense of racialized foreignness in the United States to their transnational romanticization of South Korea.

Culturally Foreign South Korea

Koreans celebrate their country as ethnically homogeneous and as boasting pure Korean blood (despite increased inflows of labor migrants; Lie 1998) (see Chapter 11). This bloodline courses through the veins of all Koreans and explains the group's common cultural attributes as a people (smart, hardworking, resilient). In other words, a Korean racial phenotype gets conflated with Korean cultural tendencies. As noted earlier, this expectation serves as one major point of contention between South Koreans and the children of Korean immigrants in the diaspora.

Another point of contention between these two groups points to nationalist ideology. The mainstream Korean conception of nations generally attributes the strength or weakness of a nation to the strength or weakness of its people (see Balibar 1991; Stoler 1995). As noted earlier, Korean nationalism and collective memory have prompted those who stayed behind to malign those who left for America as national traitors. South Koreans often trace the mass out-migrations to the wealthy Koreans of the 1970s who were enamored with "America" and left without helping rebuild their country or elevating its status (after Japanese rule and after the Korean War). Moreover, those Koreans who left went to the imperialist power, the United States, which has occupied South Korea since the 1940s and has long been the target of nationalist movements. Had these Korean immigrants not left, perhaps South Korea (or Korea writ large) would be a much more powerful nation today. Locals also dislike the boastful and ostentatious swagger of some Korean immigrants who visit from the United States. Although South Koreans recognize that the offspring of these immigrants are not as culpable as their parents, they often assume that the children have been indoctrinated with pro-American ideology just the same.

In addition, once young generations of Korean Americans themselves visit the ethnic homeland, their romanticized outlook is often disrupted by what they consider the stark cultural differences of South Korean society. Not only do the local residents see Korean Americans as culturally foreign, then, but Korean Americans see the ethnic homeland as culturally foreign as well.[3] For instance, some expressed disdain for Korean cultural norms such as "impolite" and "aggressive" people who do not conform to queues or respect personal space (it is normative in Seoul for people to forcefully bump each other). Others cited the incredibly long work hours and the overcrowded, polluted, fast-paced character of Seoul as intolerable. Owing to their culture shock, Korean Americans did not desire to live in South Korea.

For example, although Samuel, a 29-year-old area development manager for learning centers, really enjoyed his ethnic homeland the first time he visited, especially because he was not a minority for once in his life, he was not so laudatory of his second visit about four years later. He explained:

> Samuel: They were very, . . . like, their impatience, they're—I mean, I'm not patient either—but they are very impolite and very, uh yeah, *yeah, I didn't feel at home.*
>
> Nadia: Oh, you didn't? . . . So when you were living in Korea until the age of eleven, do you remember if Koreans were like that then too?
>
> Samuel: Yeah, but . . . I noticed that they were a lot more materialistic. [emphasis added]

It is noteworthy that Samuel links his sense of not feeling at home in Seoul, Korea, to the ethnic homeland's cultural norms of impatience and materialism (elsewhere in the interview he derides the intense working culture of twelve-hour days and six-day weeks). His statement also reveals his expectation that South Korea *should* feel like home, especially because he felt so the first time he visited. His narrative suggests that home is a place where people treat members of their same group well and value human relations over material gain.

Sarah, part of the 1.5 generation, concluded that despite her fluency in Korean and familiarity with Seoul, she no longer belonged there after visiting. After she cited "too many differences" as the reason, I asked her, "When you went back to Korea, what were some of the differences you noticed between you and the rest of Koreans in society?"

> Sarah: Ah, thinking. [Our] minds are just, just *absolutely* different.
>
> Nadia: Like, for example . . . ?
>
> Sarah: They're not honest, they always have to hide [their problems or low status]! So even though I saw my old friend [from] when I was young, they don't tell the truth. . . . I changed when I got here, 'cause I look at things differently, honestly! You don't have to be a showoff, just be a truth person.

Following this statement, I asked her if she desired to visit Korea more often or perhaps desired to live there in the future. She replied:

> Sarah: Ah . . . I would like to visit, but I've, I've *never* dreamt about it.
>
> Nadia: Of living there?
>
> Sarah: Of living there or just visiting.

> Nadia: Why do you think that is?
> Sarah: I . . . don't think I belong there anymore!

In addition, several of the women cited more restrictive gender norms as the reason for their reluctance, or opposition, to living in the ethnic home country. For instance, a 30-year-old attorney named Audrey condemned the South Korean norm of middle-class women "not working" and just "worrying about shopping and the next handbag they'll get." She was critical despite her strong literal transnational ties; that is, she corresponded with her family and visited often, desired to live there with her husband and child, and believed that all Korean Americans should know their roots. Other women were deeply disturbed by South Korea's more "traditional" gender norm (a concern that the men rarely aired). Whether female or male, however, the visitors were often shocked and disturbed by the cultural differences in South Korea from etiquette to pollution to gender. As a result, they began to realize that *cultural familiarity was what made a place feel like home.* Despite their romanticized hopes, then, South Korea did not match the criterion.

Being Culturally Foreign in South Korea

As noted, South Koreans often celebrate a unified and unproblematic notion of Koreanness until they meet immigrants from the United States or elsewhere. Young Korean Americans who return to the home country to visit or live are especially treated as cultural foreigners despite their status as racial insiders. Typically, the biggest difference is young Korean Americans' inability to speak Korean or their American-accented Korean. In addition, South Koreans expressed contempt for the youths' lack of literacy in Korean culture, which ran the gamut from Confucian norms to styles of dress. Also, cultural norms of frankness prompted local residents to be quite vocal when they noticed their American brethren's differences. The youths' encounters with these marginalizing experiences were usually highly traumatic given their romanticized expectations and their disempowered status in South Korea. Although many informants considered the noted lifestyle differences in South Korea disconcerting, most of them were much more affected by the "othering" and rejection they experienced in the home country. For example, Carol, a 23-year-old part-time graduate student and teacher, was born and raised in Spain (and did not move to the United States until she was 11), but she had visited South Korea as a little girl nearly every summer with her parents. She had thus maintained a relatively high level of Korean language proficiency and practiced Korean cultural norms. As she grew older and visited Seoul as a college student, however, she felt "less like a Korean."

> Carol: One time we went into the city and we met up with some of our roommate's friends. . . . We went to this café, and we were just talking and stuff and then out of nowhere this guy, he was like, "You know, aren't you embarrassed that you can't speak Korean?" . . . And my friend got really upset and she was like, "What!?" right? He's like, "You're Korean and you should be able to speak Korean between you. . . . You're not Korean, you're just American." . . . When they see me they don't even see a Korean.
> Nadia: Do . . . they think you act like a white American?
> Carol: Yeah.

Carol's bouts with exclusion and foreignness led to identity conflict, distress, and a lack of desire to live in her ethnic homeland. Following her statement about the encounter in the café, she rhetorically asked, "I mean, how do they know that I'm not from Korea?" She noted how many of the residents' cultural antennae picked up on her different clothes, yet she surmised that it had to be more than that, because she would intentionally wear clothes from local stores and would still be singled out. Other informants remarked how South Koreans noticed differences in body shape by pointing to Korean Americans' sometimes heavier and stockier frames than typically wiry, thin South Koreans (largely because of diet).

David, a 26-year-old graduate student, felt similarly distressed by his cultural foreigner status. David was part of an activist group that organized a yearly summer program in which Korean American and South Korean activists met to build transnational bridges (I use the pseudonym KAN for this group). As someone who was excited about learning more about the ethnic homeland and finding his roots there, especially given his bouts with American racism, the alienation he suffered in Seoul was painful.

> David: I so wanted to identify as Korean, 'cause, you know.
> Nadia: Why?
> David: Just because, like, you're going back to your roots, you've, like, found your homeland, you want to be, like, "Yeah, I'm there, I'm with the people." Yeah, so that [rejection] was real eye-opening. In fact, I was real bitter about it and decided to write a piece about how . . . I felt like a Korean

>*American* when I was in Korea. . . . One of the most extreme positions I
>heard was on KAN where we visited one group of [activist] men and one
>of the guys was, like, kind of yelling . . . about us . . . : "Why are these people
>here visiting us? If there's a Korean War they're not going to be here! . . . So
>what if they're Korean? They're not really Korean, they don't live here, they
>don't know our pain." . . . [So] they've put me in their box already.

Like many others, David had romanticized his trip to the homeland, not least
because he was there as an activist concerned about the Koreas and desiring
to be part of transnational social justice movements. His rude awakening had
embittered him so much that he wrote a critical article about it. The fact that
David, a progressive activist who understood South Koreans' anti-American
politics, felt so bitter indeed speaks volumes about the younger generations'
need to belong. His long-standing woes over his exclusion and foreignness in
both the United States *and* South Korea were a persistent theme throughout
his interview.

Other informants noted their confusion over the ways that phenotype
mattered more in the U.S. racial categorization system than it did in South
Korea's. Sunhi, a 31-year-old marketing manager for a large pharmaceutical
company, noted her perplexity as part of the reason that she did not want to
live in South Korea.

>Sunhi: I think I'd be actually a little bit more uncomfortable. . . . I remember
>feeling . . . , actually I was pretty sad coming back from my trip. That was
>the first time I think that I was old enough to realize that I wasn't all full
>Korean either.
>Nadia: Like the Koreans in Korea?
>Sunhi: Right, right, and . . . they definitely noticed that there was something
>different about me as well. I remember thinking how weird, we don't really
>belong. We belong out here more so than there; *but in terms of physical ap-*
>*pearance, we don't look like a lot of Caucasians here; whereas you go to Korea*
>*and you may blend in in terms of your looks but when you open your mouth*
>*they realize right away that you're someone different.* [emphasis added]

For Sunhi, not only does this cultural exclusion foster her reluctance to live in
her ethnic home country, but also its paradoxical nature saddened her. That
Sunhi's Korean phenotype and background meant little in her ethnic homeland struck her as odd, given that race was precisely the major division between

her and "Americans" in the United States. This also struck Carol (from an earlier example) as odd.

> [In Korea] they look at me and they don't think I'm Korean and it'd be really strange. Here at least [*pause*], it's weird but it's kind of normal, . . . *you don't look American so they don't really treat you like that* [a white American], *it just kind of feels natural. . . . But in Korea it's like really strange when you go; you kind of blend in* [racially], *but then they always point you out, you know?* [emphasis added]

As the historical whitening of Southern and Eastern immigrants bore out, a European phenotype in the United States is racially categorized as white regardless of a cultural enactment of whiteness. Such a consolidation of whiteness came about through Europeans' desire to dissociate from blackness (Ignatiev 1995). As such, cultural behaviors are less central in the United States. In fact, American racial categorization has hinged on homogenizing and lumping together ethnic groups that are culturally distinct and often at odds with each other. Korean Americans find out that having a shared racial phenotype in the ethnic homeland does not automatically make them Korean. Rather, their phenotype and their cultural behaviors must match. Such a conflation of race and culture is not surprising in light of South Korea's national identity as homogeneously Korean (despite increasing ethnic diversification) and its emphasis on collectivism and conformity. Moreover, Korean nationalism is less forgiving toward Koreans from *America*. That is, South Koreans' animosity toward so-called national traitors and attempts to quash any sense of superiority on the part of U.S. immigrants have intensified the demands that "the kids from America" act culturally Korean.

Such a demand ultimately prompted the young adults to decide that home was where they felt culturally at home. They became more cognizant that America was where their cultural ideas, acts, and lifestyles were more normative. Liza, a seminary student, recounted how she was culturally considered the "other" in Seoul, despite her proficiency, when she visited as a teenager. A taxicab driver reprimanded her for supposedly speaking the language poorly, and this experience fostered her identity as both Korean and American.

> In one taxicab ride . . . the taxicab driver started yelling at my mother how she [had] poorly raised me, thinking, like just because we went to America we weren't Korean anymore. . . . And so my mom got so mad and she yelled at him and said, "Drop us off right here!" She totally defended me. . . . I felt so

bad for my mother and then *so angry* at this guy. I just picked up on things in the Korean culture that I realized I really don't like! . . . And then I realized, you know, that I don't think I'm totally Korean. . . . That's when I realized maybe I'm Korean American. I have to accept both sides.

Liza's narrative reveals how South Koreans' cultural denigration of her (yelling at her for not speaking perfect Korean) also feeds her cultural "othering" of South Korea ("I just picked up on things in the Korean culture that . . . I really don't like!"). More important, her struggles with cultural foreignness in the ethnic homeland caused her to temper the proud Korean identity and strong identification with South Korea that she had honed in response to white American dominance. Rather, she realized that she needed to accept the culturally American side of her and accept America as more her home than she had previously wanted to acknowledge. Similarly, another informant, Poppy (see earlier example), strongly identified as Korean, articulated a strong transnational connection, and was angered by U.S. nativistic racism, yet her visits to the ethnic homeland confirmed to her that she felt fewer constraints of class and gender in the United States. When I asked her if she desired to live in South Korea in the future, she replied:

Poppy: No.

Nadia: Why is that?

Poppy: Because even though I consider myself very strongly attached to my mother country, I think that I'm very American. I'm more American than Korean. . . . Another reason why I don't want to live in Korea is that they're very status-conscious. . . . And I think there is much more to status, much more to life than status, and so I feel like I have to be someone that I'm not or, you know, also as a woman, I have to follow some kind of standard; over here too [I have to follow the standard], but it's not as, it's not as constraining.

Although Poppy realized that she was more "American than Korean," whereas Liza came to identify herself as equally both, they similarly understood their tourist trips as signaling their cultural Americanness. Not surprisingly, neither of them wanted to live in South Korea in the future.

Even the two 1.5-generation Korean Americans, who spoke more fluent Korean and more accented English and were more comfortable in first-generation Korean circles, described their realization that the United States was their home. As noted, however, such sentiments do not mean that Korean Americans feel completely at home in the United States either. Rather, they resign themselves to feeling in-between. They grow resigned to the fact that they will continue to be treated and feel like guests in what I call America's racial house. Although the many earlier narratives on perpetual foreignness in the United States already conveyed Korean Americans' guest status, perhaps Sarah provides the most apt summary.

Nadia: This is where you belong?
Sarah: Yeah, hmm, but I, I don't think 100%. I'm not satisfied . . . both here [or] there. I would say in America about 75% and in Korea [*pause*], I only belong there like 25%!

Sarah's statement supports many Korean Americans' belief that they cannot escape being seen as the "other" in either societal context. At the same time, they realize that the country that is culturally familiar is the place that feels like home, although the conclusion feels bittersweet. The Korean Americans thus no longer associate South Korea with the *feeling* of home, as they had transnationally imagined before their visits. After the visits they supplant their wishful and emotive view with the more factual view that Korea is where they or their parents were born.

Conclusion

As is true of Korean Chinese with respect to their two countries, the later-generation Korean Americans in this study clearly had to navigate the authenticity dilemma (Tuan 1999), that is, being inauthentic both in the United States and in South Korea. As Kibria (2002a: 307) found in her study of Korean and Chinese Americans, people in the United States homed in on the younger generations' Asian *racial* identity, whereas those in the ethnic homeland homed in on their American *cultural* identity. The fact that South Korean society treats co-ethnics from both China and the United States in this manner betrays the country's ambivalence about its brethren abroad. South Korea's own insecurity about its position in the racialized global economic hierarchy also sheds light on why state immigration policy prefers Korean Americans (and Korean Japanese) above the so-called *joseonjok* (see Chapters 2 and 11).

In light of young Korean Americans' racial foreignness in the United States and their romanticized view of the ethnic homeland, these children of immigrants wished for a seamless connection to South Korea. They believed that such a connection meant that they would have racial insider status and that, accordingly, they would *feel* at home in a way that they could not in white-dominated

America. They were rudely awakened, however, by their cultural foreigner status in the home country. South Koreans' cultural discrimination against them despite racial similarity was bewildering and spurred emotions of sadness, disappointment, and anger. These strong emotions are paralleled by Espiritu and Tran's (2002: 392) work on Vietnamese Americans, in which the parents' charges against their children as not Vietnamese enough deeply hurt them. Indeed, such accusations "essentially strip[ped] the young Vietnamese Americans of all meaningful identity," given their exclusion also from an American identity (Espiritu and Tran 2002: 392). Adding to the Korean Americans' dismay was their view of South Korea as more culturally divergent from the United States than they had expected. Although some simply criticized South Korea's demographic environment, public norms, and gender arrangements, others' critiques came on the heels of harsh rejections by South Koreans.

Beyond having their romanticized hopes crushed, the Korean American informants struggled with South Koreans' distinct construction of race relative to that in the United States. Whereas U.S. society categorizes ethnic groups primarily based on racial phenotype or lineage, South Koreans categorized race/ethnicity based on the uniformity between race and cultural behaviors. Moreover, South Koreans likely felt that they had cause to be more critical of Korean Americans owing to the latter's residence in the most dominant nation and sporadic arrogance. To be certain, a primordial essentialist notion of ethnic identity did not just haunt Korean Americans in the home country; it haunted them in the United States as well. Although white Americans' expectations were considerably milder and more varied given the United States' superpower status and lesser need for ethnic or cultural nationalism, they still invoked "forever foreigner" stereotypes of Asian Americans (Tuan 1998). That is, they expected Korean Americans to be more culturally Korean than was usually possible. Moreover, these expectations by mainstream Americans and South Koreans seemed at times to attribute Korean Americans' lack of cultural awareness to individual failings rather than to constraining structural and contextual factors. Such factors include U.S. society's English-language focus and assimilation pressures as well as the immigrant parents' busy lives. These expectations also revealed contradictions. For instance, although mainstream American ideology stresses minority groups' assimilation into whiteness as a key to making it, the public often expects Korean Americans to be versed in Korean language and culture and are sometimes surprised when they are not (see Tuan 1999). Similarly, South Korean ideology stresses making connections with Koreans in the diaspora for political, economic, and cultural reasons (see Louie 2002). Yet, when these children come, the South Korean public typically derides their cultural difference rather than seeing the children's visit as an expression of Korean ethnicity. As a result, South Koreans help to sever rather than nurture ties with young Koreans in the United States and elsewhere.

Perhaps some would argue that the young Korean Americans should have been prepared for their treatment in Seoul, given the many first-generation Asian immigrants in the United States who also chastise them for not being ethnic enough (Pyke and Dang 2003; Tuan 1999). But the fact that the youth were surprised once they got to South Korea suggests their romanticized hopes. In the end, the Korean Americans respond to their otherness in both contexts by differentiating between Korea the *homeland* and America the *home*, a differentiation that Song and Tsuda (Chapters 9 and 11) find true of Korean Chinese and Japanese Brazilians. The Korean Americans here come to define home as a place of cultural familiarity and belonging where they can speak the language, interact with others, and navigate information and social structures in a familiar social context. Their homeland trip affirms to them that the United States feels more like this home. They come to define the homeland, then, as the place of their ethnic roots and ancestors but not necessarily as a place of cultural familiarity and belonging. Although some of the later-generation Korean Americans continued to participate in a transnational social field (see Glick-Schiller 1999), for which they frequently traveled to see family and forged other key relationships in South Korea, most maintained a more symbolic version of such ties. That is, they identified with the country as a place of ancestors, parents, and origins. In realizing that the United States was their home, they simultaneously expressed a heightened sense of in-betweenness and hybridity. Indeed, some became resigned to seeing themselves as culturally both Korean *and* (white) American but not fully either. Such a realization was often bittersweet, because it meant that race still mattered in America. That is, the Korean American informants still had to resign themselves to making the most of an American home in which they are treated as guests, or, as Sarah believes, where they are "75 percent" at home.

Notes

I thank Takeyuki (Gaku) Tsuda for his critical and incisive comments on this chapter.

1. Scholars have problematized the model minority notion as a myth that depends on essentializing the culture of Asian Americans (all are exceptionally hard-working, thrifty, politically passive, and so forth) (Kim 1999). This essentialization

is further supported by its marking of Asian Americans as "minorities" and cultural "others" rather than as those deemed more "one of us," "us" being white America. Finally, the stereotype also erases the many social disparities *among* Asian Americans (see Takaki 1998).

2. Yoon (1997) claims that more working-class Koreans have emigrated in recent years.

3. I am indebted to Takeyuki (Gaku) Tsuda for this point.

References Cited

Ancheta, Angelo. 1998. *Race, Rights, and the Asian American Experience.* New Brunswick, NJ: Rutgers University Press.

Balibar, Etienne. 1991. "The Nation Form: History and Ideology." In *Race, Nation, and Class: Ambiguous Identities,* Etienne Balibar and Immanuel Wallerstein, eds. New York: Verso, 86–106.

Espiritu, Yen. 1992. *Asian American Panethnicity.* Philadelphia: Temple University Press.

———. 2003. *Homebound: Filipino American Lives Across Cultures, Communities, and Countries.* Berkeley: University of California Press.

Espiritu, Yen, and Thom Tran. 2002. "Viet Nam, nuoc toi" [Vietnam, my country: Vietnamese Americans and transnationalism]. In *The Changing Face of Home,* Levitt and Waters, eds., 367–398.

Fernandez-Kelly, Patricia, and Richard Schauffler. 1994. "Divided Fates: Immigrant Children in a Restructured U.S. Economy." *International Migration Review* 28(4):662–689.

Glick-Schiller, Nina. 1999. "Transmigrants and Nation-States: Something Old and Something New in the U.S. Immigrant Experience." In *Handbook of International Migration: The American Experience,* Charles Hirschman, Philip Kasinitz, and Josh DeWind, eds. New York: Russell Sage Foundation, 94–119.

Ignatiev, Noel. 1995. *How the Irish Became White.* New York: Routledge.

Jiobu, Robert. 1988. *Ethnicity and Assimilation: Blacks, Chinese, Filipinos, Japanese, Koreans, Mexicans, Vietnamese, and Whites.* Albany: State University of New York Press.

Kibria, Nazli. 2002a. *Becoming Asian American: Second-Generation Chinese and Korean American Identities.* Baltimore: Johns Hopkins University Press.

———. 2002b. "Of Blood, Belonging, and Homeland Trips: Transnationalism and Identity Among Second-Generation Chinese and Korean Americans." In *The Changing Face of Home,* Levitt and Waters, eds., 295–311.

Kim, Claire. 1999. "The Racial Triangulation of Asian Americans." *Politics and Society* 27(1):105–138.

Kim, Nadia. 2008. *Imperial Citizens: Koreans and Race from Seoul to LA.* Stanford, CA: Stanford University Press.

Kondo, Dorinne. 1990. *Crafting Selves: Power, Gender, and Discourses of Identity in a Japanese Workplace.* Chicago: University of Chicago Press.

Levitt, Peggy, and Mary C. Waters, eds. 2002a. *The Changing Face of Home: The Transnational Lives of the Second Generation*. New York: Russell Sage Foundation.

———. 2002b. "Introduction." In *The Changing Face of Home*, Levitt and Waters, eds., 1–30.

Lie, John. 1998. *Han Unbound: The Political Economy of South Korea*. Stanford, CA: Stanford University Press.

Lipsitz, George. 1998. *The Possessive Investment in Whiteness: How White People Profit from Identity Politics*. Philadelphia: Temple University Press.

Louie, Andrea. 2002. "Creating Histories for the Present: Second-Generation (Re)definitions of Chinese American Culture." In *The Changing Face of Home*, Levitt and Waters, eds., 312–340.

Lowe, Lisa. 1996. *Immigrant Acts: On Asian American Cultural Politics*. Durham, NC: Duke University Press.

Min, Pyong Gap. 1995. "Major Issues Relating to Asian American Experiences." In *Asian Americans: Contemporary Trends and Issues*, Pyong Gap Min, ed. Thousand Oaks, CA: Sage, 38–57.

Ong, Paul, and Tania Azores. 1994. "Asian Immigrants in Los Angeles: Diversity and Divisions." In *The New Asian Immigration in Los Angeles and Global Restructuring*, Paul Ong, Edna Bonacich, and Lucie Cheng, eds. Philadelphia: Temple University Press, 100–129.

Palumbo-Liu, David. 1999. *Asian/American: Historical Crossings of a Racial Frontier*. Stanford, CA: Stanford University Press.

Pyke, Karen, and Tran Dang. 2003. "'FOB and 'Whitewashed': Identity and Internalized Racism Among Second Generation Asian Americans." *Qualitative Sociology* 26(2):147–172.

Stoler, Ann Laura. 1995. *Race and the Education of Desire: Foucault's History of Sexuality and the Colonial Order of Things*. Durham, NC: Duke University Press.

Takaki, Ronald. 1987. *From Different Shores*. New York: Oxford University Press.

———. 1998. *Strangers from a Different Shore: A History of Asian Americans*, 2nd ed. New York: Penguin Books.

Tsuda, Takeyuki. 2003. *Strangers in the Ethnic Homeland: Japanese Brazilian Return Migration in Transnational Perspective*. New York: Columbia University Press.

Tuan, Mia. 1998. *Forever Foreigners or Honorary Whites? The Asian Ethnic Experience Today*. New Brunswick, NJ: Rutgers University Press.

———. 1999. "Neither *Real* Americans nor *Real* Asians? Multigeneration Asian Ethnics Navigating the Terrain of Authenticity." *Qualitative Sociology* 22(2):105–125.

Waters, Mary. 1999. *Black Identities: West Indian Immigrant Dreams and American Realities*. Cambridge, MA: Harvard University Press.

Wei, William. 1993. *The Asian American Movement: A Social History*. Philadelphia: Temple University Press.

Wolf, Diane L. 2002. "There's No Place Like 'Home': Emotional Transnationalism and the Struggles of Second-Generation Filipinos." In *The Changing Face of Home*, Levitt and Waters, eds., 255–298.

Yoon, In-Jin. 1997. *On My Own: Korean Businesses and Race Relations in America.* Chicago: University of Chicago Press.

Conclusion

Diasporic Homecomings and Ambivalent Encounters
with the Ethnic Homeland

Takeyuki Tsuda

THE CHAPTERS IN THIS BOOK have demonstrated how ethnic return migration is a distinctive type of population movement worthy of its own study. Although ethnic return migration certainly resembles other types of labor migration, when migrants and their hosts are related through common descent, ethnicity becomes increasingly salient as a factor that both motivates migration and constitutes the experience of the migrants. This introduces new complexities and unexpected paradoxes to the usual dislocations of migration.

Like other types of labor migration, ethnic return migration is initiated by economic pressures, yet transnational ethnic affinities, not preexisting social networks, direct the migrant flow to the ancestral homeland. Perhaps the most unexpected outcome, however, is that the privileged status of ethnic return migrants as co-ethnics does not lead to the expected social payoff. The bloodline and ancestry that they share with the host population does not prevent them from becoming ethnically and socioeconomically marginalized as minorities in the ethnic homeland. Despite their presumed ethnic similarity, they often share the same problems as other immigrants in the host society.

Of course, this does not mean that ethnicity does not matter for ethnic return migrants. On the contrary, it matters a great deal. Not only is their ethnicity the reason that they return to the ancestral homeland, but it is also ironically the basis for their social exclusion as immigrants. Although ethnic similarity between migrants and their hosts is what brings them together, ethnic difference is what pulls them apart. This is not as contradictory as it sounds, because different aspects of ethnicity are involved in each case. The mutual transnational ethnic affinity that causes diasporic descendants to return-migrate to their ethnic homelands is primarily based on commonalities in *racial* descent and bloodline. However, such essentialized ethnic assumptions are quickly challenged as both migrants and hosts discover a multitude of prominent *cultural* differences between them, a product of generations of living apart. These cultural differences cause ethnic return migrants to be excluded as minorities in their ancestral homelands despite their shared descent. In other words, during the migratory process, the emphasis shifts from race to culture as the main determinant of ethnic inclusion or exclusion. In most cases, therefore, ethnicity for diasporic return migrants comes to be based not on ancestral racial origins (where they are originally from) but on their cultural backgrounds and upbringing outside the ethnic homeland (where they were born). In this manner diasporic return also has a more significant impact on the ethnic identities of migrants (as well as their hosts) compared to other cases of labor migration. In general, interaction with peoples who are ethnically similar (but who remain different) often has a greater impact on ethnic consciousness than interaction with those who are completely different and have little ethnic relevance.

As a concluding summary, I analyze the ambivalent nature of diasporic homecomings in this chapter by focusing on their ethnic consequences for both migrants and their hosts. After examining the marginalization of ethnic return migrants in the ancestral homeland, I look at how this marginalization forces them to reconsider their ethnonational identities and loyalties as well as their conceptions of home and homeland. In addition, their poor social integration has also exposed the limits of homeland governments' racialized conceptions of ethnic citizenship and national belonging that encouraged diasporic descendants to return from abroad. As a result, homeland countries are increasingly adopting more restrictive ethnic return migration policies based on exclusionary cultural definitions of who belongs to the nation.

Ambivalent Homecomings: Ethnic and Socioeconomic Marginalization in the Ancestral Homeland

As the book's contributors make clear, the presumed racialized similarity between diasporic descendants and the homeland populace has a profound impact on the actual ethnic encounter between migrants and their hosts, leading to unintended outcomes. In contrast to ordinary labor migrants, who view the receiving society as mainly a place of economic opportunity, ethnic return migrants often expect an ethnic homecoming of sorts. Indeed, they are admitted as ethnic compatriots and brethren by the homeland government, often with full citizenship and an array of social integration and welfare benefits. Yet despite this official welcome, few ethnic return migrants experience the warm ethnic reception they anticipated in their ancestral homelands; most of them are treated as culturally alien foreigners who are socioeconomically marginalized as unskilled immigrant workers from poorer countries (Capo Zmegac 2005: 199; Remennick 2007: 2). Such a negative ethnic reception is disappointing, if not dismaying, for many of them and shatters their previously favorable romantic images of their ethnic homeland (Stefansson 2004: 9).[1] The host populace can also be quite disillusioned, because the presumed co-ethnics end up being alienated immigrant minorities who do not integrate into mainstream society as anticipated. As a result, the initial ethnic welcome is often replaced by practices of social exclusion and discrimination. As shown by the contributors to this volume, such experiences are especially prevalent among Russian Jews in Israel, ethnic German *Aussiedler*, Hungarian Romanians in Hungary, Japanese-descent Latin Americans in Japan (see Tsuda 2003b), and Korean Chinese in South Korea, as well as others (for the case of repatriated ethnic Russian descendants, see de Tinguy 2003; Pilkington 1998).

Ethnic Exclusion: Diasporic Returnees as Cultural Foreigners

What explains the often sharp discrepancy between the government's official welcome toward their diasporic returnees and the social alienation that awaits them in their homelands? Most of the diasporic return migrants considered in the case study chapters simply lack the linguistic and cultural competence necessary for acceptance as co-ethnics in their ancestral homelands. Because they have been born and raised in foreign countries, they have generally lost their ancestral language and customs, especially if they are diasporic peoples who have lived outside their ancestral countries for many generations. A number of them have also been subject to past nationalist assimilation projects or ethnic discrimination in their countries of birth that suppressed minority cultures and diasporic allegiances to their ancestral homelands, especially in former Communist regimes. This includes the Russification, secularization, and stigmatization of Soviet Jews (Remennick 1998), the ethnocultural discrimination against ethnic German descendants in Eastern Europe, and the prohibition of Korean Chinese minority culture during the Chinese Cultural Revolution (Chapter 11; Yang 2006). Japanese-descent ethnic minorities in South America (especially in Brazil) and Spanish- and Italian-descent Argentines have also been historically influenced by nationalization projects, often under dictatorships (Cook-Martín 2005; Tsuda 2001).[2] Even with greater current tolerance of multiculturalism, the ethnic cultures of these minority groups are mainly limited to symbolic practices and invented traditions. Although James Clifford (1994: 307) claims that diasporas resist nationalist projects of assimilation because of their important allegiances to their homelands, this is certainly not the case with later-generation diasporic peoples.

Therefore, when diasporic descendants return to their ethnic homelands, they are ethnically excluded as culturally different foreigners and strangers (cf. Capo Zmegac 2005: 206–207). Despite their shared bloodline, their ethnic heritage is seemingly denied on cultural grounds by their ancestral compatriots when they are identified as foreign nationals. For instance, Jews in Israel are called "Russians," ethnic Germans are labeled "Russians" or "Poles" in Germany, ethnic Hungarian descendants become "Romanians" in Hungary, Korean-descent *chosŏnjok* become "Chinese" in South Korea, and Japanese-descent *nikkeijin* from South America are seen as "Brazilians," "Peruvians," or simply *gaijin* (foreigners) in Japan. In this manner, co-ethnic descendants from abroad who were once seen as integral members of a deterritorialized and racialized ethnic nation based on shared bloodline are now excluded from the ethnonational community on the basis of cultural difference.

The cultural marginalization and social exclusion that return migrants experience is especially acute in more ethnically homogeneous East Asian societies such as Japan and South Korea, which have restrictive ethnonational identities that demand not only shared racial descent but also complete linguistic and cultural proficiency for national inclusion and even social acceptance. In both countries, essentialized racial ideologies are particularly strong, and those of common descent are naturally expected to be culturally similar even if they were born and raised abroad.[3] Thus ethnic descendants who look racially identical but are culturally foreign and cannot speak the language are sometimes stigmatized as ethnically inadequate and strange or are even reprimanded in ways that other immigrants are not (see Chapters 11 and 12; Kweon 2006; Tsuda 2003b: ch. 2). Even in countries where ethnonational ideologies are not quite as restrictive, ethnic return migrants are held to higher cultural standards than other immigrants. For instance, Remennick argues (Chapter 8) that because Jewish diasporic returnees in Israel are seen as critical for nation building and are granted full citizenship, they are expected to assimilate quickly and demonstrate national loyalty or else face social exclusion as liabilities.

Often, the alien cultural characteristics of ethnic return migrants are seen in a pejorative manner by the host society, especially if the migrants come from countries that are less developed and lower in the global hierarchy of nations. In such cases the national labels that the host populace uses to refer to them ("Russians," "Romanians," "Chinese," "Brazilians," etc.) are based on negative stereotypes and prejudices toward these countries as economically backward and culturally inferior and can even be used as ethnic slurs. For instance, Israeli attitudes toward Russian Jews are influenced by negative stereotyping of Russians in the mass media as "mafia men, prostitutes, and welfare mothers," and there is considerable suspicion about their secular lifestyle, lack of Jewishness, and foreignness (Remennick 2003, 2007: 154). Hungarians view their co-ethnics from Romania scornfully with suspicion and disdain as poor people from an inferior country who may even take jobs away from Hungarians (Fox 2003: 456–457). In South Korea negative reports have proliferated about ethnic Korean *chosŏnjok*, emphasizing their insufficient work ethic, untrustworthiness, over-Sinicized behavior and attitudes, and lack of Korean national loyalty (see Chapter 11). Japanese Brazilians are often viewed by mainstream Japanese as poor, lazy, easygoing, culturally inferior, overly individualistic, and noisy (Tsuda 2003b: ch. 2). Even the Argentines of Spanish descent analyzed by Cook-Martín and Viladrich (Chapter 5) are seen as unreliable workers with a questionable work ethic. In some countries with newer diasporic populations, for example, Russia, Japan, and South Korea, ethnic return migrants can be seen as descendants of traitors who left and betrayed the ethnic homeland or as descendants of poor, uneducated emigrants who could not survive economically and had to abandon their home country (Park 2006; Pilkington 1998: 168–171; Tsuda 2003b: ch. 2).

Because diasporic return migrants have prior expectations of ethnic belonging in their country of ancestral origin, most of them are surprised, if not shocked, by their ethnic rejection and social exclusion. Because their previous idealized and nostalgic images of their ancestral country are seriously disrupted, they become culturally alienated immigrant minorities who are strangers in their ethnic homeland. Although they were often minorities in their countries of birth because of their foreign racial descent, they again become ethnic minorities when they return to their country of ancestral origin, this time because of their cultural foreignness. Diasporic return is therefore not a type of ethnic consolidation or regrouping. Instead it is producing new ethnic minorities through an increased consciousness of cultural heterogeneity among peoples of shared descent.

The level of ethnic marginalization that diasporic return migrants experience varies, depending on the cultural and linguistic distance between them and the homeland populace. This is partly a function of the length of time that they have lived outside their homelands and partly a function of their level of assimilation and loss of ethnic heritage in their countries of birth. The extent of ethnic marginalization also depends on whether the homeland and its diasporic peoples are located in different cultural regions of the world. For instance, ethnic Korean *chosŏnjok* from China returning to South Korea remain within the East Asian cultural region, whereas Latin American *nikkeijin* returning to Japan are crossing a greater cultural divide. Ethnic return migrants moving from former Communist countries to advanced capitalist countries also encounter significant cultural barriers associated with two very different socioeconomic systems.

In contrast, when Argentines of Spanish descent migrate across a vast geographic distance to Spain, they are in an ethnic homeland that shares a broader Hispanic culture and language because of Spain's historical colonial ties to Argentina and because of Argentina's strong affinity to Europe. Therefore Spanish Argentines seem to enjoy greater ethnic acceptance in their homeland (see also Viladrich 2005), and the problems they encounter seem mainly to be related to their low-level immigrant jobs and socioeconomic marginalization, as described in Chapter 5. In contrast, Argentines of Italian descent who return-migrate to Italy feel greater cultural and linguistic differences with the local populace, and their social integration is more difficult (Grossutti 2005).

In general, diasporic descendants whose ethnic homelands are in neighboring countries tend to encounter fewer cultural difficulties upon return migrating, because they tend to have much greater contact with the homeland, allowing them to maintain their cultural heritage. This is especially the case with Finland Swedes, whose linguistic and cultural affinity with neighboring Sweden enables them to ethnically integrate successfully in their ancestral homeland. Another example is ethnic Russians who relocated during Soviet expansion to nearby Communist countries, which were under Russian political and cultural influence for decades. As a result, ethnic Russian repatriates encounter fewer problems than other ethnic return migrants because they share a common Russian language and culture with the host populace (de Tinguy 2003: 125; Ohliger and Münz 2003: 6–7; Pilkington 1998: 173–175). The cultural affinities between ethnic Hungarians in Romania and in Hungary are less strong because they have been living in separate countries since World War I with different social norms and institutions. However, Hungarian Romanians have retained their native language in their ethnic communities, and although they experience ethnic prejudice as foreigners in their homeland, most of their negative experiences seem to be related to their degrading immigrant jobs (Fox 2003: 452–453; Chapter 7).

Socioeconomic Marginalization:
Dealing with Degrading Immigrant Jobs

As indicated by a number of the book's contributors, diasporic returnees are also socioeconomically marginalized because they are frequently offered only low-status unskilled immigrant jobs that are shunned by the majority populace. Because most of them are from relatively well-educated middle-class backgrounds, ethnic return migration therefore involves considerable declassing and downward mobility. Although they are granted favorable legal and citizenship status because of their *racial* ties to the host society as diasporic descendants, this does not give them privileged access to the labor market because of the linguistic and *cultural* barriers they face. In addition, their educational credentials and skills from developing countries are often not recognized or not transferable in advanced capitalist countries.[4] Others are recruited specifically to fill unskilled labor shortages in their ethnic homelands and do not have the social network contacts needed to access higher-level jobs.

Not only are ethnic return migrants generally confined to the lowest sector of the labor market, some of them, such as ethnic Germans, Russian Jews, and ethnic Russians, have unemployment rates that are sometimes higher than the national average (see also Berthomière 2003; Pilkington 1998: 141–150). The problem seems especially acute for those working in weaker Eastern European economies (de Tinguy 2003: 122–123; Flynn 2003: 181–182) and for those who are in their homelands illegally, namely, Hungarian Romanians and Korean Chinese, who must accept the most exploitative jobs with low wages and no benefits (see also Choi 2006; Fox 2003).

Many of the negative experiences that ethnic return migrants have in their homelands are therefore the result of their socioeconomic marginalization, which is often just as severe as for other immigrant workers. Not only must they toil as unskilled manual laborers in difficult, stigmatized jobs, they must also cope with a serious decline in social status from their former respected middle-class occupations to degrading working-class jobs, which can have negative effects on their self-worth and self-esteem and can become a source of social class

prejudice in the majority society. Even ethnic return migrants who have maintained their ancestral heritage and are less culturally alienated in their ethnic
homelands often still have negative diasporic homecomings because of the degrading and low-status jobs they must endure. According to Cook-Martín and
Viladrich (Chapter 5), occupation downgrading has been especially difficult
for Spanish Argentines, who expect jobs and wages commensurate with other
Spanish nationals because of their cultural similarities and equal citizenship
status. As a result, their disillusionment with their downward mobility and social degradation seems to be a greater issue for them than any possible ethnic
exclusion based on cultural difference (see Viladrich 2005). Hungarian Romanians in Hungary seem to have analogous experiences.

Because of their marginalization as immigrant minorities, many ethnic return migrants remain socially unintegrated in their homelands. In some cases
they are segregated in immigrant ethnic communities and interact primarily
among themselves in their own languages. Some of these communities, such as
those of ethnic German *Aussiedler*, Russian Jews in Israel, and Japanese-descent
nikkeijin in Japan, have become quite cohesive and extensive with an array of
ethnic businesses and services and an active ethnic mass media, which enables
many of them to conduct their daily lives without much contact with the local
populace (see also de Tinguy 2003: 124; Remennick 2003: 378–379).[5] In response to their social exclusion in their homelands, ethnic return migrants have
withdrawn into their enclaved communities and subcultures, often resisting attempts by mainstream society to culturally assimilate and socially incorporate
them (Remennick 2003: 382, 378–379; Tsuda 2003b: ch. 5).

Therefore, despite their racialized ethnic affinity with their ancestral homeland, the homecomings of ethnic return migrants are ambivalent, if not negative, experiences, because the migrants become culturally foreign immigrant
minorities confined to low-status jobs and subject to social segregation. In
fact, they often experience levels of ethnic and socioeconomic marginalization
equivalent to ordinary labor migrants (cf. Ohliger and Münz 2003: 15). However, diasporic returnees often feel much more socially alienated than other
immigrants because their stronger prior ethnic affiliation and identification
with the homeland causes them to expect an ethnic homecoming befitting
diasporic descendants returning to their land of ancestral origin. When it does
not materialize and they are confronted with social exclusion instead, they feel
more estranged and disillusioned than other immigrants who do not arrive
with such ethnic expectations. Ironically, therefore, the immigrant group that is

most ethnically related to the host society can often experience the most social alienation. This is again the "problem with similarity" (Chapter 5).

Ethnic Return Migration from the Developed World: A More Positive Homecoming?

As shown by the contributors in Part 3, the ethnic reception of diasporic returnees from developed countries seems to be somewhat better for a number of reasons. Although they are just as culturally alien as their counterparts from developing countries and can be subject to some ethnic prejudice, they are generally more respected because of their origins in the developed world. Most important, they are not socioeconomically marginalized in stigmatized working-class jobs because most of them return-migrate with relative high status as professionals, investors, or students, leading to a more positive reception and social experiences.[6]

Ethnic return migrants from developed countries definitely benefit from the higher stature of their countries of birth and are not subject to the negative stereotypes attached to developing countries. For instance, Korean Americans in South Korea can be perceived as role models and valuable assets because they represent the English-speaking internationally successful global Korean. Such images are derived from past respect for the United States, as a source of prosperity, cultural capital, and popular culture in a globalized world, as well as from mass media portrayals of Korean Americans as model minorities in the United States (Park 2006). Nonetheless, they are still subject to negative attitudes about the United States and are also singled out for their lack of cultural competence as people who have become too Americanized (Chapter 12; Kibria 2002; Park 2006). As a result, they do not feel ethnically accepted as culturally different foreigners, although their social alienation and disappointment in their ethnic homeland are considerably less than among their counterparts from China.[7] In Chapter 9, I examined similar trends among Japanese Americans in Japan, whose ethnic experiences seem more positive than those of Korean Americans, partly because the Japanese generally have a more favorable attitude toward the United States than Koreans do.[8]

Finland Swedes seem to have the best of both worlds. As ethnic return migrants from Finland, they are socioeconomically well integrated into Sweden as middle-class professionals and students, and as diasporic descendants from a neighboring country, they are culturally similar to majority Swedes. As Hedberg demonstrates in Chapter 6, Finland Swedes enjoy an advantageous position on the Swedish job market, live in mainstream neighborhoods, and eventually assimilate into mainstream society. Asians and Jewish Americans who return to their ancestral homelands on ethnic heritage tours seem to generally have positive experiences as well and develop a stronger appreciation of their ancestral roots, although they simultaneously recognize their status as ethnic outsiders in their ancestral countries. Unlike ethnic return migrants, they are tourists whose visits are organized and choreographed to create favorable impressions, and their interactions with locals are brief, highly structured, and welcoming.

Diasporic Return and Ethnic Identity

The negative ethnic reception and ambivalent homecoming that many diasporic return migrants from the developing world experience in their countries of ethnic origin has a significant impact on their ethnonational identities. This is another unintended consequence of their migration. Because most of them return-migrate for economic (and not ethnic) purposes, few expect to have their ethnic identities transformed in the process as well. When confronted with social alienation as immigrant minorities, most of the ethnic return migrant groups considered in this book experience a decline in their transnational diasporic attachments to their ethnic homelands and a strengthening of nationalist identifications in response to their sociocultural differences with the homeland populace (cf. Capo Zmegac 2005: 208–210). Others seek out alternative forms of ethnonational belonging as they reconsider their position in the diaspora. For most ethnic return migrants, therefore, a previously stronger diasporic consciousness based on their ancestral racial origins is replaced by more parochial ethnic identifications based on their separate cultural backgrounds. In this manner diasporic return demonstrates how transnational mobility across national borders does not always produce hybrid transnational identifications with multiple countries of origin or more expansive diasporic identities but can intensify mutually exclusive and restrictive ethnic and nationalist sentiments.

From Transnational Affinity to Deterritorialized Nationalism

In most cases, ethnic return migrants strengthen their nationalist attachments to their countries of birth in response to their ethnic and socioeconomic marginalization in their ancestral homelands. This type of nationalization of ethnic identity among diasporic return migrants is most evident in the chapters dealing with Russian Jews, ethnic German *Aussiedler*, Spanish-descent Argentines,

Japanese Brazilians, and Korean Chinese. Not only do they realize that they are cultural foreigners who do not belong in their country of ethnic origin, but they also often develop negative perceptions of the host country because of the discrimination they face as ethnic minorities and their degrading work experiences. This causes them to distance themselves from their ancestral homeland by affirming their status as foreign nationals, which can become a defensive counteridentity asserted in opposition to the host society. Some of them also develop a renewed nationalist appreciation of their country of birth in response to their negative experiences in their country of ethnic origin. In this manner the dislocations of migration can produce a form of deterritorialized migrant nationalism in which national loyalties are articulated outside the territorial boundaries of the nation-state.

This deterritorialized nationalism among ethnic return migrants is ironic because most of them were ethnic minorities in their countries of birth who had never adopted strong nationalist identities. For instance, Japanese Brazilians were seen (and saw themselves) as a "Japanese" minority in Brazil and did not strongly identify with majority Brazilians. However, they suddenly embrace their "Brazilianness" in Japan to an extent they never had in Brazil (see also Tsuda 2003b: ch. 4). Likewise, *Aussiedler* were regarded as "Germans" in Russia but are seen as "Russians" after return migration to Germany (Chapter 4). Korean Chinese were an ethnic "Korean" minority in China but see themselves as "Chinese" in South Korea (see also Choi 2006; Yang 2006). This resurgence of nationalist identification with the country of birth among ethnic return migrants is often accompanied by active engagement in its national cultural activities. Thus we find Japanese Brazilians dancing samba (often for the first time) in their ethnic homeland of Japan and German *Aussiedler* singing Russian songs in Germany.[9]

The strength of deterritorialized nationalism among diasporic return migrants depends on the level of ethnic alienation they experience in their ancestral homelands. For instance, although Argentines of Spanish descent in Spain become more aware of their Argentine backgrounds and culture when faced with an ambivalent ethnic homecoming, because they are more culturally similar to their Spanish hosts their assertion of nationalist difference seems to be less strong than that of other diasporic returnees (see also Viladrich 2005). In contrast, Italo-Argentine return migrants, who do not feel as much linguistic and cultural commonality with their Italian homeland, seem to develop a stronger nationalist attachment to Argentina (Grossutti 2005).

For other groups of ethnic return migrants the assertion of nationalist dif-ference in response to their negative diasporic homecoming is not based on an increased cultural attachment to their countries of birth but on a reaffir-mation of their ancestral nationalities by claiming that they have maintained ethnic cultural traditions abroad better than their co-ethnics living in the homeland. As Fox makes clear in Chapter 7, this is the case with ethnic Hun-garian descendants from Romania who return-migrate to Hungary. When they are socially excluded and labeled "Romanians" by mainstream Hungar-ians, Hungarian Romanians refuse to accept this ethnic categorization and instead claim a purer Hungarian identity (as the "real Hungarians"), which becomes a form of nationalist differentiation from their Hungarian hosts, who have supposedly been contaminated by modernity and are no longer truly Hungarian (Fox 2003: 458–459). Unlike other diasporic descendants, ethnic Hungarians in Romania never emigrated abroad to settle in and assimilate to a foreign country but were simply cut off from their ethnic homeland by shifting borders and have thus maintained their Hungarian heritage. In addi-tion, ethnic Hungarian descendants enjoyed a higher status as minorities in Romania and even felt culturally superior to Romanians, making it difficult for them to identify nationally as Romanians when denied their Hungarian-ness in Hungary (Fox 2003: 459). Ethnic Russians who repatriate to Russia,[10] ethnic Greeks in Asia Minor, and ethnic Croats in the former Yugoslavia who return-migrate to their homelands seem to have analogous experiences (Capo Zmegac 2005: 212).

In this manner, the ethnic encounter between diasporic descendants and their ancestral compatriots often leads to exclusionary nationalist identities based on cultural difference rather than transnational identifications based on shared ethnic commonalities among peoples from different countries. Be-cause most ethnic return migrants feel that their ancestral heritage is denied by their negative reception in their homelands, few develop multiple trans-national attachments to both their country of birth and their country of eth-nic origin. Instead, they come to identify more exclusively as nationals from a foreign country or claim a more authentic ethnonational identity that excludes their co-ethnics in the homeland. The sense of shared descent and bloodline that initially created transnational ethnic attachments across borders between diasporic descendants and their homeland populaces is overridden by the stark national cultural differences that emerge when these co-ethnics actually meet in the ancestral homeland. This is another example of how transnational mobility ironically creates a renewal of nationalist attachments instead of producing transnational hybrid identifications across national borders.

Nonnationalist Diasporic Identities

Although most ethnic return migrants redefine their identities in nationalist ways, some groups seem to adopt a nonnationalist ethnic identity as diasporic people whose sense of belonging cannot be defined in nationalist terms. This occurs among diasporic returnees who distance themselves from the host society in response to their negative ethnic homecoming but remain reluctant to embrace a nationalist identification with their country of birth for various reasons. For instance, when Japanese Peruvian returnees in Japan are denied their previous "Japanese" ethnic identities, they do not strengthen their nationalist identities as "Peruvians" because Peruvianness is not well regarded in Japan and the immigrant community contains illegal non-Japanese-descent Peruvian nationals. Instead, according to Takenaka in Chapter 10, Japanese Peruvians adopt a diasporic ethnic identity as *nikkei* (people of Japanese descent born and raised abroad), which serves as a means of cultural differentiation from the Japanese while also distancing themselves from illegal non-*nikkei* Peruvians.

It is also possible that ethnic return migrants who suffer considerable exclusion and discrimination in *both* their countries of birth and their ethnic homelands may adopt nonnationalist, diasporic ethnic identities that are not based on loyalty to either nation-state. This process of double marginalization seems to be the case with Korean Americans in South Korea, who do not feel completely at home in either the United States, where they are racialized minorities, or in South Korea, where they are cultural minorities. Thus diasporic return produces a heightened sense of hybridity and in-betweenness for them as people who are both American and Korean but not fully either (see Chapter 12), causing some of them to use the diasporic term *chaemi kyopo* (ethnic Korean descendants from America) to refer to themselves (Park 2006). Like the *nikkei* consciousness of Japanese Peruvians, these Korean Americans are also adopting an identity as diasporic descendants abroad who do not belong to either their country of birth or their country of ethnic origin.[11]

Transnational Identifications

Only a few ethnic return migrants from developed countries who enjoy a certain degree of social acceptance in their homelands seem to develop a transnational identification in which their allegiance to their country of birth is accompanied by a strengthened attachment to their ethnic homeland. For instance, although Korean Americans and Japanese Americans do experience some ethnic marginalization in their homelands (which can lead to a heightened sense of Americanness), their more positive reception and socioeconomic position leaves them with a greater appreciation and pride in their ethnic heritage and an awareness of the possible financial and professional rewards of engagement in their ethnic homeland (Kibria 2002). Therefore some Korean Americans in Korea (especially those who have achieved economic success) seem to appropriate a more cosmopolitan transnational identity as "globalized Koreans" (Park 2006). As shown in Chapter 9, a number of Japanese Americans in Japan also emerge from their sojourn with a transnational appreciation of their ethnic heritage as well as a greater cosmopolitan consciousness.[12] This may also be the case with Finland Swedes (Chapter 6), whose sociocultural integration into and assimilation to Swedish society over time is quite successful (see also Hedberg and Kepsu 2008). Because they eventually adopt a majority Swedish identity while retaining their Finland Swede identities in private, they may be developing multiple, transnational affiliations to both Sweden and Finland.

The Limits of Jus Sanguinis Citizenship and Immigration Policy

The social marginalization and identity alienation of most diasporic return migrants in their ethnic homelands demonstrates the serious limits of citizenship, immigration, and social integration policies based on the principle of shared descent and race (jus sanguinis). In most Western European countries (as well as Israel and some Eastern European countries), ethnic return migrants are granted full citizenship status. In Germany, Israel, Russia, and Greece they also have access to extensive social integration and welfare benefits, which can include housing programs, language courses, job training, educational assistance, health insurance, unemployment benefits, and pensions.[13] In East Asia, ethnic return migrants are granted legal status and rights superior to all other immigrant groups (with the exception of South Korea) and benefit from some government assistance programs.

Nonetheless, such generous jus sanguinis immigration policies and programs have not guaranteed the social incorporation of ethnic return migrants in their ancestral homeland because of the cultural differences that have emerged between migrants and their hosts (cf. Capo Zmegac 2005: 200, 205). As mentioned earlier, they are often just as ethnically and socioeconomically segregated and marginalized as other immigrant groups who do not receive these legal and social benefits. This demonstrates that even if ethnic return migrants are granted formal (juridical) citizenship by the nation-state because of their shared racial descent, they lack the cultural citizenship[14] necessary for national belonging and socioeconomic incorporation, which prevents them from actually exercising their equal rights (substantive citizenship).

As a result, homeland governments are increasingly moving away from immigration and citizenship policies based on racialized notions of national membership because they have realized that the shared descent and blood ties of ethnic return migrants do not always produce the cultural commonalities necessary for national inclusion. Because their previously open admission of diasporic descendants has produced large numbers of culturally alienated immigrant minorities, a number of homeland governments have introduced restrictions on their ethnic preference policies. As Skrentny and colleagues demonstrate in Chapter 2, this is especially the case in Europe, where the return of diasporic descendants from abroad was justified on the basis of their ethnocultural affinity as members of a broader deterritorialized nation of co-ethnics. The difficulty of socially incorporating them into the national fabric, despite expensive social integration programs, has therefore partly undermined the rationale of these ethnic preference policies.[15]

Perhaps the most serious attempt to restrict ethnic return migration is in Germany. The government has taken such action partly because the original intent of its ethnic German *Aussiedler* policy (to protect them from ethnic persecution) could no longer be justified after the end of the cold war. However, as the writers of Chapters 3 and 4 indicate, it is also a response to a dramatic rise in *Aussiedler* who lack German linguistic and cultural competence and are poorly integrated into German society. This has led to an increasing realization that *Aussiedler* are not that different from other immigrants, despite their German descent, and to a public backlash against the generous and costly benefits that they receive from the German government (see also Joppke 2005: 190). As a result, the German government in the 1990s started to restrict *Aussiedler* entry and has cut back on its social integration programs for them. In addition, to increase their cultural acceptability, the government now requires *Aussiedler* to pass a German language and culture test and plans to phase out their immigration over the long run by denying entry to those born after 1993. Italy also seems to have cracked down on ethnic return migration since 2002 in response to the sudden influx of Italian Argentines during the economic crises in Argentina in the late 1980s and late 1990s (Grossutti 2005; Joppke 2005: 247). In Spain active recruitment of ethnic return migrants seems to have subsided. Similar trends can also be observed in other European countries, such as Russia.[16]

Some scholars argue that ethnic preference policies will remain resilient in countries where diasporic returnees serve an important economic, demographic, or national security function (such as in Israel or East Asia) (de Tinguy 2003: 126). This certainly seems to be the case in Israel, which has recently faced challenges to its law of ethnic return similar to those in Germany (most Jews are no longer actively persecuted and recent diasporic returnees from Russia have been culturally foreign and remain socially unintegrated). However, as Joppke and Rosenhek argue in Chapter 3, Israel's ethnic return policy remains resilient because of its continued importance to nation building and security (through population expansion) in light of the ongoing political conflict with the Palestinians (who have a higher birth rate).[17]

In contrast, ethnic return policies have become increasingly controversial in East Asian countries despite their important economic function of providing much-needed immigrant labor. Because co-ethnic returnees have been considerably more socially and culturally disruptive than initially anticipated, these governments have also started to restrict their entry. In Japan, immigration policymakers did not anticipate that such a large number of Japanese-descent Latin American *nikkeijin* would return-migrate and settle in the country, and policymakers have been disappointed that they were not as culturally Japanese as initially expected. Despite their ethnic affinity with the Japanese, they have proven to be just as ethnically controversial and socioeconomically marginalized as other foreign workers in Japan. As a result, the government has attempted to reduce the level of *nikkeijin* return migration through more stringent enforcement of visa requirements and renewals. In addition, a 2006 Ministry of Justice panel interim report on future immigration policies[18] recommended that the government no longer grant preferential admission to *nikkeijin* on the basis of blood ties and that it require that they have a certain level of Japanese language proficiency or face the same immigration restrictions as other migrant workers seeking admission to Japan.[19]

Likewise, although the South Korean government initially encouraged the return migration of Korean Chinese, it has continued to limit their legal immigration because of fears of being inundated by *chosŏnjok* from nearby poorer China. In 1999 it passed a law that encourages primarily Korean Americans and Canadians to visit and invest in South Korea. However, the law excludes Korean Chinese and ethnic Koreans from the former Soviet Union (Lim 2006:

264).[20] In 2005, the abusive trainee program, which had been the primary legal means for ethnic Koreans to return-migrate, was abolished. Although Korean Chinese and Soviet Koreans are now offered five-year visas under the new Visit and Work program, the number of visas is limited and applicants must pass a Korean language test. As a result, many of them will probably continue to migrate to Korea illegally. In recent years the government has more aggressively apprehended and deported illegal immigrants, 40–50 percent of whom are estimated to be Korean Chinese (Changzoo Song, personal communication, 2008). Despite their blood ties, the *chosŏnjok* today are not seen as appreciably different from other immigrants (Lim 2006: 241; Chapter 11).

Such restrictive changes in ethnic return migration policy by homeland governments is nothing short of a reconsideration of their ethnonational ideologies. In both European and Asian countries, ethnic descendants from abroad were initially welcomed because they fit racialized conceptions of national identity and belonging based on the presumption that those of shared racial descent were part of a broader cultural community.[21] However, because they have been much more culturally foreign than expected, they have disrupted national ideologies based on this assumed correspondence between race and culture. Homeland states seem to have implicitly realized that the racial ties of diasporic descendants do not ensure cultural similarities sufficient for national inclusion and that they are, in many ways, just as foreign as other economic labor migrants.[22] Therefore admitting them solely on the basis of shared bloodline has become problematic and has led to an apparent decline of ethnic preferences in immigration policy and to an attempt to admit only those with the requisite cultural competence necessary for national membership, as determined through language and culture tests.[23] As a result, in the future, ethnic return migrants are increasingly likely to be treated like ordinary immigrants and to face the same restrictions. Diasporic return has therefore caused homeland governments to move away from previously broader notions of ethnonational membership based on common racial descent and to adopt more restrictive and exclusionary cultural definitions of who belongs to the nation.

Ethnic Return Migration, Immigrant Settlement, and the Changing Meanings of Home and Homeland

Not only have ethnic return migrants distanced themselves from their homelands in response to their cultural alienation, host societies have questioned their initially racialized ethnic affinity with their diasporic descendants and are adopting more restrictive policies toward them as cultural foreigners. As ethnicity is increasingly defined not by racial commonalities but by cultural differences, a process of mutual ethnic alienation has occurred between migrants and their hosts. Ethnic return migrants not only do not feel at home but are also increasingly unwelcome in their homeland.

Therefore diasporic return does not simply transform migrants' ethnic identities; it causes them to reconsider the meaning of homeland. Ethnic return migrants technically have two homelands: the ethnic homeland, where their ethnic group originated, and the natal homeland, where they were born and raised. Unlike other types of immigrants, who are often part of the majority society in their natal homeland, most ethnic return migrants were ethnic minorities in their country of birth because of their foreign descent. However, when they return-migrate to their ethnic homeland, they become minorities all over again because of their foreign cultural upbringing, and this causes some of them to feel that they are a people without a homeland.

Quite often, the negative diasporic homecomings and sociocultural alienation that most ethnic return migrants experience challenge their previously idealized and nostalgic affinity for their ethnic homeland. As a result, their country of ethnic origin comes to no longer feel like a homeland (Capo Zmegac 2005: 205; Christou 2006b: 1048; Fox 2003: 457) because it has lost the positive emotional affect as a place of desire and longing that makes homelands meaningful.[24] However, as shown in Chapters 9 and 11 on Japanese Brazilians and Korean Chinese, when diasporic returnees are alienated from their ethnic homeland, they may redefine their natal homeland as the true homeland (for ethnic Russians and other groups, see Capo Zmegac 2005: 206; Pilkington 1998: 194). Although they did not initially regard their country of birth as a homeland per se, when they were separated from it through migration and were confronted with a negative ethnic reception abroad, they became homesick and developed positive nostalgic sentiments for their natal country as the place where they truly belonged. In this manner, homelands are often discovered through migration and physical absence, causing ethnic return migrants to prioritize their natal homeland over their ethnic homeland.

At the same time we must be careful to distinguish the concept of homeland from the concept of home. Although the two words are often conflated and used interchangeably in the literature (based on the assumption that home is located in the homeland) (e.g., see Al-Ali and Koser 2002b; Buff 2001; Espiritu 2003: 2, 11; Glick Schiller and Fouron 2001: 6; Parreñas 2001: 55–56), the two places do not always correspond for migrants. *Homeland* is a place of origin to which one feels emotionally attached, whereas *home* is a stable place of residence that feels secure, comfortable, and familiar (cf. Castles and Davidson 2000: 130–131; Constable 1999: 206–207; Markowitz 2004: 24; Stefansson 2004: 174). Although it is often the case that homeland is a place where individuals feel at home (e.g., Frykman 2002: 132–134), home and homeland are not always the same place.

In fact, diasporic return can create a disconnect between home and homeland. This seems to be especially true for Korean Americans in South Korea. Although they do not feel as alienated from their country of ancestral origin as their counterparts from the developing world, they certainly do not feel at home in their ethnic homeland. As a result, according to Kim (Chapter 12), they eventually differentiate between South Korea as their homeland of racial origin and the United States as their home, where they feel more culturally familiar and comfortable (see also Park 2006). In this case, it is the concept of home (not homeland) that shifts, from the place of racial belonging (South Korea) to the place of cultural belonging (United States).

Even if ethnic return migrants do not initially feel at home in their ethnic homeland, this has not prevented them from settling in the host society and eventually making it into a new home. Despite their ethnic and social alienation in their ancestral country, most of them are not returning to their countries of birth because of the greater economic opportunities and security they enjoy in the host society.[25] Just as instrumental economic pressures (not ethnic affinity per se) initiated their return migration, it seems that such practical economic considerations and incentives again influence their decision to settle long term, if not permanently, in the ancestral country, even if it remains an ethnically inhospitable place where they are not socially well-integrated. Undoubtedly, economic factors are the fundamental determinants of migration and settlement patterns.

Because ethnic return migrants in Western Europe (especially Germany) and Israel have been invited back by homeland governments in historical recognition of their right of return, they are automatically granted citizenship and immigrate with the intention of settling permanently. Even ethnic return migrants in Spain and Italy, who apparently resemble target earners responding to temporary economic crises in Argentina, seem to be settling long term or permanently (Chapter 5; Grossutti 2005). Although ethnic return migrants in East Asia are temporarily admitted for economic needs, a good number have prolonged their stays in an attempt to achieve their financial goals, have called over their family members, and are becoming immigrant settlers (see Tsuda 1999).[26]

The settlement of ethnic return migrants is causing another disjuncture between home and homeland. Although the ethnic homeland does not feel like a homeland to many of them, it has definitely become a home over time, as many have decided to settle long term with their families and have grown accustomed to life in these countries. As mentioned earlier, large return migrant groups, such as Russian Jews, ethnic German *Aussiedler*, ethnic Russian repatriates, and Japanese-descent *nikkeijin*, have created cohesive immigrant ethnic communities with a wide range of ethnic businesses, various services, organizations, and churches and an active ethnic media, all supported by extensive transnational economic, political, and social connections with their sending countries (see de Tinguy 2003: 124; Flynn 2003: 180–181; Remennick 2003; Tsuda 2003b). Although they remain socially alienated in the host society, they feel well situated and comfortable living in these self-contained immigrant communities, where they can conduct their daily lives among family and compatriots in culturally familiar settings without much contact with mainstream society while remaining actively in touch with their countries of birth. As a result, they have created a home away from the natal homeland. Undoubtedly, the immigrant host society does not have to be experienced as a homeland for it to be considered a home. In fact, immigrants around the world have shown a remarkable ability to create homes in alienating, foreign places (cf. Castles and Davidson 2000: 131–132; Constable 1999: 208; Markowitz 2004: 25), and ethnic return migrants are no exception, enabling them to resist the negative effects of their social alienation and homesickness abroad (Tsuda 2003a). In this sense the diaspora *has* truly come home.

Notes

1. Even first-generation return migrants rarely receive the homecoming they expect. In fact, they often have difficulties readapting, reintegrating, and being socially accepted in their homelands as well (see Long and Oxfeld 2004).

2. Past discrimination and the questioning of the national loyalty of Japanese Americans (and to a lesser extent, Chinese Americans) have also promoted their assimilation and allegiance to the United States.

3. In both Japan and South Korea, there seems to even be a perception that their ethnic descendants abroad have maintained cultural traditions better than those in the modernized and Westernized homeland (Chapter 11; Tsuda 2003b: ch. 2).

4. Ethnic return migrants from former Communist countries, such as Russian

Jews, often find that their occupational skills are outdated and not applicable to advanced capitalist economies (see Chapter 8; Berthomière 2003; Remennick 2003: 277).

5. In a few cases, such as the *Aussiedler* in Germany, they live in immigrant ghettos with higher rates of crime, mental illness, and alcoholism and lower levels of education than the general populace (see also von Koppenfels 2003: 308).

6. In fact, certain homeland governments, such as South Korea, attempt to attract wealthy descendants from developed countries while discriminating against supposedly poor ethnic Koreans from developing countries.

7. Korean Japanese who return-migrate to South Korea from Japan experience similar perceptions and cultural pressures. In addition, their Japanese cultural differences are stigmatized because of historical animosity toward Japan as a former colonizer. Nonetheless, their adaptation in Japan is relatively successful (Kweon 2006).

8. For American ethnic return migrants, the level of anti-American sentiment in their ethnic homelands has a significant impact on their host society reception (cf. Christou 2006a: 836–837).

9. In other cases, diasporic descendants did not strongly identify with their ethnic homeland before return migration and therefore simply retain (or reinforce) their national identification with their country of birth upon diasporic return. For instance, although Russian Jews were assimilated to majority Russian society and did not feel much attachment to Israel or Jewish culture, when they return-migrate, their Jewish identification does not increase because of their ethnic marginalization in Israel and therefore they retain their Russian national identities and cultural activities (see also Remennick 1998, 2003).

10. Like the ethnic Hungarians, they are return-migrating from nearby Soviet successor states and maintained strong linguistic and cultural ties to Russia during the cold war. Because they considered themselves part of the Russian elite who were sent abroad during Soviet expansion, they assert their cultural superiority as the true, traditional Soviet Russians in contrast to the lazy, poor, and less cultured Russians they supposedly encounter in their ethnic homeland (de Tinguy 2003: 125; Pilkington 1998: 168–171).

11. An analogous process occurs among Korean *Japanese* ethnic return migrants in Japan (Kweon 2006). Some ethnic Germans also seem to adopt a nonnationalist diasporic identity as *Aussiedler*, who are neither Russian nor German (see Chapter 4).

12. This also seems to be the case with Chinese Americans on ethnic heritage tours in China (Louie 2001, 2002).

13. These social integration programs are most extensive in Germany and Israel and less so in other countries (de Tinguy 2003: 121; Ohliger and Münz 2003: 14). Russia has a number of assistance programs for ethnic returnees but few resources to properly implement them (Pilkington 1998: 154–156). Even in Germany and Israel, these programs have been overwhelmed by the sheer number of diasporic returnees.

14. Cultural citizenship refers to the cultural attributes necessary to be considered members of the national community (see Ong 1996; Turner 1994: 159). It is also used to refer to the right granted to ethnic minorities to maintain their different minority culture (Castles and Davidson 2000: 124–126).

15. These policies have also been challenged by the European Union, which has put pressure on member states to adopt universalistic nonethnically discriminatory norms (e.g., Joppke 2005: 250).

16. Russia seems to have stopped actively encouraging ethnic Russians from nearby Soviet successor states to return because of the high cost of socially integrating and accommodating them.

17. Also, because all Jews in the Diaspora are granted the right of return by virtue of their ethnic ancestry (even if they have not been persecuted), the decline of anti-Semitism has not undermined the rationale of the policy (Chapter 3).

18. Ministry of Justice, "Recommendations on the Future Admission of Foreigners" (in Japanese), http://www.moj.go.jp/index.html.

19. For those *nikkeijin* already working in the country, the report recommends providing them with Japanese-language education and requiring a certain level of language proficiency as a condition for remaining in Japan.

20. Because this law was declared unconstitutional by the Korean Constitutional Court, it was revised in 2003 to include Korean Chinese as well as Soviet Koreans. However, because the law prohibits Korean ethnic return migrants from performing unskilled labor, they continue to be excluded de facto.

21. This assumption seems to be particularly strong in East Asia (especially Japan and South Korea) and less so in Europe. Most countries that were not built by immigrants and whose populations were based on one ethnic group seem to have this perception to a considerable extent toward their diasporic descendants.

22. Indeed, a number of governments (especially Germany, Israel, and Japan) have now given up their previous claim that ethnic return migrants are not immigrants but co-ethnic repatriates in the homeland (cf. Joppke 2005: 171).

23. Some other countries, such as Greece and Poland (Iglicka 1998: 1008), also seem to have cultural and language proficiency requirements for ethnic return migrants.

24. This is true even for some first-generation return migrants (Constable 1999; Riccio 2002).

25. There are, however, reports of ethnic Germans returning to Russia because of their poor socioeconomic situation in Germany (Chapter 4).

26. Perhaps the only exceptions to this pattern of long-term settlement are in Hungary, where most ethnic returnees are illegal and can easily go back and forth across the Hungarian-Romanian border, and in South Korea, where the mainly illegal Korean Chinese lack a long-term legal basis to remain and permanent settle-

ment seems less prevalent (Yang 2006). Diasporic return migrants from the developed world also tend to be temporary sojourners seeking short-term professional and educational opportunities, because they have less economic incentive to stay in the host society compared to their poorer counterparts from the developing world.

References Cited

Al-Ali, Nadje, and Khalid Koser, eds. 2002a. *New Approaches to Migration? Transnational Communities and the Transformation of Home.* London: Routledge.

———. 2002b. "Transnationalism, International Migration, and Home." In *New Approaches to Migration?* Al-Ali and Koser, eds., 1–14.

Berthomière, William. 2003. "Integration and the Social Dynamic of Ethnic Migration: The Jews from the Former Soviet Union in Israel." In *Diasporas and Ethnic Migrants,* Münz and Ohliger, eds., 338–354.

Buff, Rachel. 2001. *Immigration and the Political Economy of Home: West Indian Brooklyn and American Indian Minneapolis, 1945–1992.* Berkeley: University of California Press.

Capo Zmegac, Jasna. 2005. "Ethnically Privileged Migrants in Their New Homeland." *Journal of Refugee Studies* 18(2):199–215.

Castles, Stephen, and Alastair Davidson. 2000. *Citizenship and Migration: Globalization and the Politics of Belonging.* New York: Routledge.

Choi, Woogill. 2006. "Ethnic Koreans from China: Korean Dreams, Adaptation, and New Identities." Paper presented at a conference on Korean ethnic return migration, University of Auckland, New Zealand, November 27–28.

Christou, Anastasia. 2006a. "American Dreams and European Nightmares: Experiences and Polemics of Second-Generation Greek-American Returning Migrants." *Journal of Ethnic and Migration Studies* 32(5):831–845.

———. 2006b. "Deciphering Diaspora—Translating Transnationalism: Family Dynamics, Identity Constructions, and the Legacy of 'Home' in Second-Generation Greek-American Return Migration." *Ethnic and Racial Studies* 29(6):1040–1056.

Clifford, James. 1994. "Diasporas." *Cultural Anthropology* 9(3):302–338.

Constable, Nicole. 1999. "At Home but Not at Home: Filipina Narratives of Ambivalent Returns." *Cultural Anthropology* 14(2):203–228.

Cook-Martín, David. 2005. "The Long Way Home or Back Door to the EU? Argentine Claims of Ancestral Nationalities." Paper presented at the conference "Diasporic Homecomings: Ethnic Return Migrants in Comparative Perspective," Center for Comparative Immigration Studies, University of California at San Diego, May 20–21.

de Tinguy, Anne. 2003. "Ethnic Migrations of the 1990s from and to the Successor States of the Former Soviet Union: 'Repatriation' or Privileged Migration'?" In *Diasporas and Ethnic Migrants,* Münz and Ohliger, eds., 112–127.

Espiritu, Yen Le. 2003. *Home Bound: Filipino American Lives Across Cultures, Communities, and Countries.* Berkeley: University of California Press.

Flynn, Moya. 2003. "Returning Home? Approaches to Repatriation and Migrant Resettlement in Post-Soviet Russia." In *Diasporas and Ethnic Migrants,* Münz and Ohliger, eds., 173–187.

Fox, Jon E. 2003. "National Identities on the Move: Transylvanian Hungarian Labor Migrants in Hungary." *Journal of Ethnic and Migration Studies* 29(3):449–466.

Frykman, Maja Povrzanovic. 2002. "Homeland Lost and Gained: Croatian Diaspora and Refugees in Sweden." In *New Approaches to Migration?* Al-Ali and Koser, eds., 118–137.

Glick Schiller, Nina, and Georges Eugene Fouron. 2001. *Georges Woke Up Laughing: Long-Distance Nationalism and the Search for Home.* Durham, NC: Duke University Press.

Grossutti, Javier. 2005. "De Argentina al Friuli, Italia (1989–1994): Un caso de migración de retorno?" [From Argentina to Friuli, Italy (1989–1994): A case of return migration?]. *Estudios Migratorios Latinoamericanos* 19(56):97–122.

Hedberg, Charlotta, and Kaisa Kepsu. 2008. "Identity in Motion: The Process of Finland-Swedish Migration to Sweden." *National Identities* 10(1):95–118.

Iglicka, Krystyna. 1998. "Are They Fellow Countrymen or Not? The Migration of Ethnic Poles from Kazakhstan to Poland." *International Migration Review* 32(4):995–1014.

Joppke, Christian. 2005. *Selecting by Origin: Ethnic Migration in the Liberal State.* Cambridge, MA: Harvard University Press.

Kibria, Nazli. 2002. "Of Blood, Belonging, and Homeland Trips: Transnationalism and Identity Among Second-Generation Chinese and Korean Americans." In *The Changing Face of Home: The Transnational Lives of the Second Generation,* Peggy Levitt and Mary C. Waters, eds. New York: Russell Sage, 295–311.

Kweon, Sug-In. 2006. "Returning Ethnic Koreans from Japan in Korea: Experiences and Identities." Paper presented at a conference on Korean ethnic return migration, University of Auckland, New Zealand, November 27–28.

Lim, Timothy. 2006. "NGOs, Transnational Migrants, and the Promotion of Rights in South Korea." In *Local Citizenship in Recent Countries of Immigration: Japan in Comparative Perspective,* Takeyuki Tsuda, ed. Lanham, MD: Lexington Books, 235–269.

Long, Lynellyn D., and Ellen Oxfeld, eds. 2004. *Coming Home? Refugees, Migrants, and Those Who Stayed Behind.* Philadelphia: University of Pennsylvania Press.

Louie, Andrea. 2001. "Crafting Places Through Mobility: Chinese American 'Roots-Searching' in China." *Identities* 8(3):343–379.

———. 2002. "Creating Histories for the Present: Second-Generation (Re)definitions of Chinese American Culture." In *The Changing Face of Home: The Transnational Lives of the Second Generation,* Peggy Levitt and Mary C. Waters, eds. New York: Russell Sage, 312–340.

Markowitz, Fran. 2004. "The Home(s) of Homecomings." In *Homecomings: Unsettling Paths of Return*, Fran Markowitz and Anders Stefansson, eds. Lanham, MD: Lexington Books, 21–33.

Münz, Rainer, and Rainer Ohliger, eds. 2003. *Diasporas and Ethnic Migrants: Germany, Israel, and Post-Soviet Successor States in Comparative Perspective.* London: Frank Cass.

Ohliger, Rainer, and Rainer Münz. 2003. "Diasporas and Ethnic Migrants in Twentieth-Century Europe: A Comparative Perspective." In *Diasporas and Ethnic Migrants*, Münz and Ohliger, eds., 3–17.

Ong, Aihwa. 1996. "Cultural Citizenship as Subject-Making: Immigrants Negotiate Racial and Cultural Boundaries in the United States." *Current Anthropology* 37(5):737–762.

Park, Christian J. 2006. "Korean Americans in South Korea." Paper presented at a conference on Korean ethnic return migration, University of Auckland, New Zealand, November 27–28.

Parreñas, Rhacel Salazar. 2001. *Servants of Globalization: Women, Migration, and Domestic Work.* Stanford, CA: Stanford University Press.

Pilkington, Hilary. 1998. *Migration, Displacement, and Identity in Post-Soviet Russia.* London: Routledge.

Remennick, Larissa I. 1998. "Identity Quest Among Russian Jews of the 1990s: Before and After Emigration." In *Jewish Survival: The Identity Problem at the Close of the Twentieth Century*, Ernest Krausz and Gitta Tulea, eds. New Brunswick, NJ: Transaction, 241–258.

———. 2003. "A Case Study in Transnationalism: Russian Jewish Immigrants in Israel of the 1990s." In *Diasporas and Ethnic Migrants*, Münz and Ohliger, eds., 370–384.

———. 2007. *Russian Jews on Three Continents: Identity, Integration, and Conflict.* New Brunswick, NJ: Transaction.

Riccio, Bruno. 2002. "Senegal Is Our Home: The Anchored Nature of Senegalese Transnational Networks." In *New Approaches to Migration?* Al-Ali and Koser, eds., 68–83.

Stefansson, Anders H. 2004. "Refugee Returns to Sarajevo and Their Challenge to Contemporary Narratives of Mobility." In *Coming Home? Refugees, Migrants, and Those Who Stayed Behind*, Lynellyn D. Long and Ellen Oxfeld, eds. Philadelphia: University of Pennsylvania Press, 170–186.

Tsuda, Takeyuki. 1999. "The Permanence of 'Temporary' Migration: The 'Structural Embeddedness' of Japanese Brazilian Migrant Workers in Japan." *Journal of Asian Studies* 58(3):687–722.

———. 2001. "When Identities Become Modern: Japanese Immigrants in Brazil and the Global Contextualization of Identity." *Ethnic and Racial Studies* 24(3):412–432.

———. 2003a. "Homeland-less Abroad: Transnational Liminality, Social Alienation, and Personal Malaise." In *Searching for Home Abroad: Japanese Brazilians and Transnationalism*, Jeffrey Lesser, ed. Durham, NC: Duke University Press, 121–161.

————. 2003b. *Strangers in the Ethnic Homeland: Japanese Brazilian Return Migration in Transnational Perspective*. New York: Columbia University Press.

Turner, Bryan S. 1994. "Postmodern Culture/Modern Citizens." In *The Condition of Citizenship*, Bart van Stennbergen, ed. London: Sage.

Viladrich, Anahí. 2005. "Going Back Home? Argentine Return Migrants in Transnational Perspective." Paper presented at the conference "Diasporic Homecomings: Ethnic Return Migrants in Comparative Perspective," Center for Comparative Immigration Studies, University of California at San Diego, May 20–21.

von Koppenfels, Amanda Klekowski. 2003. "Who Organizes? The Political Opportunity Structure of Co-Ethnic Migrant Mobilization." In *Diasporas and Ethnic Migrants*, Münz and Ohliger, eds., 305–323.

Yang, Young-Kyun. 2006. "The Return Migration of Korean Chinese (*Joseonjok*) from a Comparative Perspective." Paper presented at a conference on Korean ethnic return migration, University of Auckland, New Zealand, November 27–28.

Contributors

STEPHANIE CHAN is a Ph.D. candidate in the Department of Sociology at the University of California at San Diego. Her dissertation is about how culture influences American opinion makers' assessments of foreign problems, particularly related to China. She has recently published an article, "Cross-Cultural Civility in Global Civil Society: Transnational Cooperation in Chinese NGOs," in *Global Networks.*

DAVID COOK-MARTÍN is an Assistant Professor in the Department of Sociology at Grinnell College. He is a political sociologist whose work on migration and nationality policies in Latin America and Europe has been published in the *Journal of Historical Sociology,* the *Journal of Ethnic and Migration Studies,* and *Citizenship Studies.* He is currently completing a book on citizenship and state policy in Argentina, Italy, and Spain. In addition, he is studying immigration policies at the subnational level and working on a collaborative project examining the links between political liberalism and racialized preferences in the immigration and nationality laws of 22 countries in the Americas since 1850.

JON E. FOX is a Lecturer (Assistant Professor) in the Department of Sociology at the University of Bristol. His research focuses on ethnicity, nationalism, and international migration. He is particularly interested in the ways that ethnicity and nationhood are reproduced by ordinary people in the routine contexts of their everyday lives. His relevant publications include "Everyday Nationhood" in *Ethnicities* (2008) (co-authored with Cynthia Miller-Idriss) and *Nationalist Politics and Everyday Ethnicity in a Transylvanian Town* (Princeton University Press, 2006) (co-authored with Rogers Brubaker, Margit Feischmidt, and Liana Grancea).

CHARLOTTA HEDBERG is a Researcher in the Department of Human Geography at Stockholm University. Her research interests include transnational migration processes, immigrant labor market integration and participation and intra-urban variations, and entrepreneurship of migrant women. Her main publications are "Identity in Motion: The Process of Finland-Swedish Migration to Sweden" in *National Identities* (2008) (co-authored with Kaisa Kepsu), "Direction Sweden: Migration Fields and Cognitive Distances of Finland Swedes" in *Population, Space, and Place* (2007), and "Migration as a Cultural Expression? The Case of the Finland-Swedish Minority's Migration to Sweden" in *Geografiska Annaler* (2003) (co-authored with Kaisa Kepsu).

CHRISTIAN JOPPKE is a Professor of Political Science in the Graduate School of Government at the American University of Paris. He has published widely on immigration, citizenship, social movements, and the state. His most recent book is *Veil: Mirror of Identity* (Polity Press, 2009). He has just completed a book on immigration and citizenship, to be published by Polity Press in 2010.

DENIS WOO-SEON KIM is an Assistant Professor at Sogang University in South Korea. His research interests include transnational migration and its impact on religion and civil society. He has published several articles and is currently working on a book titled *Church and Civil Society in South Korea After Democratization: NGOs' Activism for Transnational Migrants*.

NADIA Y. KIM is an Assistant Professor in the Department of Sociology at Loyola Marymount University. She is the author of *Imperial Citizens: Koreans and Race from Seoul to L.A.* (Stanford University Press, 2008) and "Patriarchy Is So Third World," published in *Social Problems*. Her other work on migration has appeared in *Critical Sociology* and the *Du Bois Review*. She is currently working on a project about immigrant participation in the environmental justice and health movements.

LARISSA REMENNICK is a Professor and Chair of the Department of Sociology and Anthropology at Bar-Ilan University in Israel. She immigrated to Israel in 1991 from Moscow, Russia, and lives in Tel Aviv. Her research interests include immigration, migrant integration, ethnic diasporas and transnationalism, and Soviet Jews. Her most recent book is *Russian Jews on Three Continents: Identity, Integration, and Conflict* (Transaction, 2007).

ZEEV ROSENHEK is a Senior Lecturer in the Department of Sociology, Political Science, and Communication at the Open University of Israel. His fields of research include state-society relations, labor migration, ethnic hierarchies, and the political economy of the welfare state. He has published articles in journals such as *Acta Sociologica, Archives Européennes de Sociologie, Ethnic and Racial Studies, International Sociology, Journal of Ethnic and Migration Studies, Review of International Political Economy,* and *Social Problems.*

JOHN D. SKRENTNY is a Professor in the Department of Sociology at the University of California at San Diego. His research focuses broadly on law and inequality. He is the author of two books on civil rights politics and law in the United States: *The Minority Rights Revolution* (Harvard University Press, 2002) and *The Ironies of Affirmative Action* (University of Chicago Press, 1996). His more recent research compares immigration policy in East Asia and Europe and has appeared in the journals *International Migration Review* and *Ethnicities.*

CHANGZOO SONG is a Lecturer in the School of Asian Studies at the University of Auckland in New Zealand. He received his Ph.D. in political science from the University of Hawai'i at Manoa, and his research interests include ethnic nationalism and nation building of Korea and Korea's policy toward the Korean diaspora in China and the Commonwealth of Independent States (CIS). Currently he is conducting research on the ethnic return migration of Korean Chinese. He has published several articles, including "Korea and China over Korean Minority in China: Deterritorialised Nationalism vs. *Zhonghua* Nationalism" in *International Review of Korean Studies* (2007) and "Business Elite and the Construction of National Identity in Korea" in *Acta Koreana* (2003).

AYUMI TAKENAKA is an Assistant Professor in the Department of Sociology at Bryn Mawr College. She has conducted research primarily in the areas of immigration and ethnicity. She has written about Japanese Peruvians in Japan, Peru, and the United States and is currently working on immigrants' social mobility across countries, including Japan, the United States, and the United Kingdom. Her recent publications include *Global Philadelphia: Immigrant Communities, Old and New* (Temple University Press, 2009) (co-edited by Mary Osirim) and "How Diasporic Ties Emerge: Pan-American *Nikkei* and the Japanese State" in *Ethnic and Racial Studies* (2008).

TAKEYUKI (GAKU) TSUDA is an Associate Professor of Anthropology in the School of Human Evolution and Social Change at Arizona State University. His primary academic interests include international migration, diasporas, ethnic minorities, ethnic and national identity, transnationalism and globalization, ethnic return migrants, the Japanese diaspora in the Americas, and contemporary Japanese society. His publications include numerous articles in anthropological and interdisciplinary journals as well as the book *Strangers in the Ethnic Homeland: Japanese Brazilian Return Migration in Transnational Perspective* (Columbia University Press, 2003). He is also the editor of *Local Citizenship in Recent Countries of Immigration: Japan in Comparative Perspective* (Lexington Books, 2006) and co-editor of *Controlling Immigration: A Global Perspective* (2nd ed., Stanford University Press, 2004) and *Ethnic Identity: Problems and Prospects for the Twenty-first Century* (AltaMira Press, 2006).

ANAHÍ VILADRICH, a medical anthropologist and sociologist of Argentine origin, is currently an Associate Professor in the Urban Public Health Program at Hunter College and a faculty member of the Doctoral Program in Public Health at the Graduate Center, City University of New York, and at the Department of Sociomedical Sciences, Columbia University. She received a Ph.D. in 2003 and an M.Phil. in Sociomedical Sciences (anthropology) from Columbia University in 2000. She has published widely on gender, immigration, and health in Argentina and in the United States in various journals, including the *Journal of Ethnic and Migration Studies*; *Culture, Medicine and Psychiatry*; the *Journal of Contemporary Ethnography*; *Human Organization*; *Ethnicity and Disease*; the *Journal of Popular Culture*; and the *Journal of Immigrant and Minority Health*.

AMANDA KLEKOWSKI VON KOPPENFELS is a Lecturer (Assistant Professor) of Migration Studies in the School of Sociology, Social Policy and Social Research and the Director of the master's degree program for the Migration Studies Programme at the University of Kent at Brussels. She received her Ph.D. in 1999 from Georgetown University and has published on human trafficking, regional consultative processes, and ethnic German migration and citizenship. Her publications include "Second-Class Citizens? Restricted Freedom of Movement for *Spätaussiedler* Is Constitutional" in the *German Law Journal* (2004) (http://www.germanlawjournal.com), "The Political Opportunity Structure of Co-Ethnic Migrant Mobilization: Post Cold War Co-Ethnic Migrants to Israel and Germany" in *Diasporas and Ethnic Migrants: Germany, Israel, and Russia in Comparative Perspective* (Frank Cass, 2003), and "Informal but Effective: Regional Consultative Processes as a Tool in Managing Migration" in *International Migration* (2001).

Index

The authorized representative in the EU for product safety and compliance is:
Mare Nostrum Group
B.V Doelen 72
4831 GR Breda
The Netherlands